Office 2003 Programming:
Real World Applications

TY ANDERSON

Apress®

Office 2003 Programming: Real World Applications

Copyright © 2005 by Ty Anderson

ISBN (pbk): 1-59059-139-9

Printed and bound in the United States of America 9 8 7 6 5 4 3 2 1

Lead Editors: Tony Davis, John Franklin

Technical Reviewers: John Paul Mueller, Bob Phillips

Editorial Board: Steve Anglin, Dan Appleman, Ewan Buckingham, Gary Cornell, Tony Davis, Jason Gilmore, Chris Mills, Dominic Shakeshaft, Jim Sumser

Project Manager: Kylie Johnston

Copy Edit Manager: Nicole LeClerc

Copy Editor: Andy Carroll

Production Manager: Kari Brooks-Copony

Production Editor: Ellie Fountain

Compositor: Molly Sharp

Proofreader: Katie Stence

Indexer: Valerie Robbins

Artist: April Milne

Cover Designer: Kurt Krames

Manufacturing Manager: Tom Debolski

Distributed to the book trade in the United States by Springer-Verlag New York, Inc., 233 Spring Street, 6th Floor, New York, NY 10013, and outside the United States by Springer-Verlag GmbH & Co. KG, Tiergarten-str. 17, 69112 Heidelberg, Germany.

In the United States: phone 1-800-SPRINGER, fax 201-348-4505, e-mail orders@springer-ny.com, or visit http://www.springer-ny.com. Outside the United States: fax +49 6221 345229, e-mail orders@springer.de, or visit http://www.springer.de.

For information on translations, please contact Apress directly at 2560 Ninth Street, Suite 219, Berkeley, CA 94710. Phone 510-549-5930, fax 510-549-5939, e-mail info@apress.com, or visit http://www.apress.com.

The source code for this book is available to readers at http://www.apress.com in the Downloads section.

To Amy, Lilly, and Hayden

Contents at a Glance

Contents

About the Author

TY ANDERSON has been developing Office-based solutions for over 10 years and continues to believe Office is where a business's real development efforts begin.

Ty is a founding partner of Credera, a Richardson, Texas, based business management and IT consulting firm. He currently leads Credera's Microsoft-based application development services.

Ty lives in Dallas, Texas, with his wife and two children. He likes to spend his time hanging around the house with his family, just being a daddy and a husband. Ty is a baseball fanatic and mourns openly when the Oakland Athletics disappoint (which is almost every year). He also loves music and carries his iPod wherever he goes. A good day for Ty starts with a Venti Americano, it includes a productive day building software and helping his clients, a bike ride fit in anywhere time allows, a grueling wrestling match with his hyperactive black lab, and it ends with an evening loving on his family.

Acknowledgments

Writing this book has been a great experience and one that would not have been possible without the help and support of others. I would like to specifically thank the following people:

Gary Cornell helped shape my original idea for a book and then showed enough confidence in my writing skills to give me a book contract.

John Franklin reviewed the early chapters and offered valuable advice for the chapters that remained.

John Mueller did a great job with technical edits. Thanks for muddling through my code and helping prepare it for publication.

Andy Carroll had the arduous task, as copy editor, of ensuring everything I said made sense and was interesting. Thanks for hanging in through the end!

Ellie Fountain put all the pieces together to create the book you are now holding in your hands. Thanks Ellie—there are no more changes!

Tony Davis guided the technical and copyedit processes and made sure the final product was solid. Thanks for the incredible effort you put into the project and into me as a writer.

Kylie Johnston kept me on task, helped manage priorities and kept my spirits high during some rather tight deadlines and difficult client work. Thanks Kylie for making it all work!

I know there are many others at Apress who touched this book that I don't know about—you folks deserve my gratitude as well.

My partners at Credera, who were incredibly flexible in helping me juggle the demands of our client work with the deadlines of this book. Thanks to each of you.

Damon Armstrong served as a valuable sounding board for several ideas and helped out by writing sample code for two chapters. Thanks for taking the ideas for those chapters and turning them into useful applications.

To MOTO. Ahhhh maaaaannnnnn! What are we gonna do now? Maybe we can take the big guy out to the range and shoot a couple of them sporting clays…or maybe we can go jump in Taca's pool and wake up the neighbors, or some silly things like that. You just keep doing your thing big guy!

To my wife Amy. This book is as much yours as it is mine. Thanks for laboring through the whole process with me. You gave up a lot of evenings and kept everything else going while I worked in the "shade" office cranking out this book. You definitely kick it!

Introduction
The Office Platform
and Its Possibilities

Microsoft has invested heavily in building development tools for the Office platform. Historically, Microsoft has provided a built-in macro language that has allowed developers (and more adventurous users) to automate these applications.

Each successive version of Office has seen improvement in the development tools and languages. With the release of Office 97, a single language, Visual Basic for Applications (VBA), was integrated into each Office application (though to varying degrees). In Office 2000 and Office XP, COM add-ins provided the ability to build extensions to Office using Visual Basic 6.

With the release of Office 2003, Microsoft has further enhanced Office and the ability of Visual Basic developers to build applications. VBA continues to be the native development language within Office, but it has not been upgraded significantly since Office 2000. VBA will continue to exist in Office for many more versions (and may never truly leave us) but Microsoft is clearly emphasizing the .NET platform with new development tools like Visual Studio Tools for Office and the Information Bridge Framework that utilize .NET but are targeted at the Office platform.

The new feature receiving the most attention in this regard is Office 2003's deep support for XML, which provides powerful opportunities to the Office developer. For example, it greatly enhances the ability of Office to interact with web services. By using web services and custom XML schemas, a business can now use Office applications as the front end to its main applications that contain critical business data (such as customer records, company financial records, employee records, and the like).

XML becomes even more significant when you consider that it is one of the key components of solutions built with Microsoft Visual Studio Tools for the Microsoft Office System (VSTO). Using VSTO, developers can create a custom XML schema file to define data in a targeted Word, Excel, or InfoPath file. VSTO is the bridge Microsoft is building to move Office developers from the land of VB 6/VBA to the managed code world of .NET, and all Microsoft Office applications will eventually have their own version of VSTO—or so it appears now. For the time being, however, VBA continues to be the language integrated into the suite, along with its antiquated Visual Basic Editor tool. Good or bad, that's the situation. As a result, VBA will continue to be a factor in any Office platform development.

About the Book

This book is intended to provide experienced Visual Basic developers with relevant examples of the application development possibilities that exist when using the Office System platform.

Each chapter shows you how to build a real business application using Office 2003 and Visual Basic. Through these examples, you will find out how to utilize the new Office development capabilities provided by Visual Studio .NET and the .NET Framework, and you will learn how to take advantage of these features to build custom department- or enterprise-wide applications. Along the way, you will encounter numerous examples of effective methods for building practical Office solutions.

At the end, you will have a set of real applications that can be used as-is or that can be customized and extended to meet your specific requirements.

Many (though not all) of the core Office applications will be discussed, and I will show you how they can be utilized as development components (almost as if they were a third-party ActiveX component).

How This Book Is Organized

Each chapter in this book presents a case study that demonstrates effective techniques and strategies for building a specialized business application using the Office suite of applications and Visual Basic. Each chapter first presents the application from a general utility perspective, outlining

- The architecture of the application

- The workflow from both a user and developer perspective

- The specific technologies and tools used

- The key coding techniques and strategies that underpin the application

- The business case for developing the application, in the context of a fictional company

Each chapter then shows how to actually build the application.

Chapter 1: Building Office Applications with VB .NET

This chapter illustrates the basic three-tier architecture used by every application in the book (data tier, business tier, and client tier), giving general examples of which technologies and techniques will be used and how.

This chapter also introduces Bravo Corp, a (fictional) professional services company that specializes managing large-scale events. It explains the company's business and development strategies and illustrates how a business such as this could benefit from the applications built in this book.

Chapter 2: The Presentation Generator

How to Auto-Generate PowerPoint Presentations Using PowerPoint, SQL Server, and a COM Add-In

Chapter 2 explains how to build a tool that streamlines the process of creating presentations in PowerPoint. This is done by building a managed COM add-in using Visual Basic .NET and hooking it into Microsoft PowerPoint. The code customizes the PowerPoint menu to include additional buttons for the add-in, uses XML to save application settings to the user's system, and connects to a SQL Server database to download presentation template file. You will also learn how to build a wizard inside a single PowerPoint file that walks the user through the process of creating a new presentation. The wizard is built with tried-and-true VBA and Office UserForms. The chapter also explains how to use VB .NET to invoke a VBA method in the presentation file.

Chapter 3: Document Generator

Automating Document Creation Using Word, Outlook, and a COM Add-In

Chapter 3 discusses how to build a COM add-in within Microsoft Outlook that streamlines the process of creating and populating Word documents. You will learn how to automate Word in VB .NET and how to insert values from an Outlook contact record into the Word document using Word bookmarks. You will also learn how to dynamically populate a Windows form based on the bookmarks discovered in the Word document. Additional techniques covered in this chapter include accessing folders in the Outlook hierarchy and building a managed COM add-in targeted for Outlook.

Chapter 4: Email Template Engine

Combining Outlook and Regular Expressions in a COM Add-In to Automate Frequently Used Content

Chapter 4 builds one last COM add-in that is also targeted at Microsoft Outlook. We will use regular expressions and VB .NET to build an engine that uses email templates as the basis for new email messages. We will look at how to create custom InfoTags to define data types inside an email template that will eventually be replaced with data from an Outlook contact record through the use of regular expressions. You will also learn how to take Office CommandBars to a new level by building code that continually monitors the data in the email templates folder and builds (and rebuilds) the add-in's custom Outlook menu to include buttons for each available email template. Finally, you will learn how to treat these menu buttons like a Visual Basic 6 control array by hooking each dynamically created menu button to a single Click event method.

Chapter 5: Service-Failure Reporting Application

Creating a Custom Workflow Using InfoPath, Web Services, and Microsoft Access

Chapter 5 moves beyond building COM add-ins and into the realm of connecting Office applications to external applications, such as web services. Here you will learn how to use VB .NET to build a web service that contains a rudimentary workflow engine for notifying individuals of task assignments. We will also look at how to build InfoPath forms that reference a web service and submit data to it—data that ultimately is inserted into an Access database. Other topics covered in this chapter include building database access code that inserts and updates database records, building classes that encapsulate functionality for specific object types, and building an ASP .NET web page to track the status of the issues represented by the InfoPath forms.

Chapter 6: The Budget Consolidator

Creating, Distributing, and Summarizing Budgets Using Excel Workbooks, an Excel Add-In, and VBA

Chapter 6 shows how to use VBA and Excel to automate the process of creating consolidated budgets. You will learn how to build an Excel template worksheet that guides the user through completing a budget that conforms to a preestablished format. In addition, you will learn how to build another Excel workbook that consolidates completed budget templates into a single, summary Excel workbook. The code written in this chapter works as an Excel-specific add-in and is incorporated into Excel add-in files (which have an .xla extension). Key concepts covered in this discussion include how to customize Excel's menu using VBA, how to create Excel lists and load list data into a UserForm, how to protect an Excel document, and how to enforce a standard, consistent worksheet architecture. The chapter also demonstrates how to distribute template budget files to individuals via email.

Chapter 7: Timesheet System Using Excel

Using Visual Studio Tools for Office to Create a System for Assigning Time to Tasks

Chapter 7 presents a Timesheet System built with VSTO. We will look at how to create a managed code assembly with VB .NET that hooks into an Excel workbook and provides the custom logic behind the Excel file. You will also learn how to build an additional Excel workbook to be used as a time-reporting tool. Each of the workbooks use a web service that provides access to the solution's database. Additional concepts include how to build a login form and how to create a custom save dialog box implementing a custom save scenario. This save dialog box trumps the default save dialog box provided by Excel.

Chapter 8: The Account Details Smart Tag

Putting Backend Customer Data at the User's Fingertips with Smart Tags and the Microsoft Information Bridge Framework

Chapter 8 introduces the Microsoft Office Information Bridge Framework (IBF) and shows how to create a smart tag to interface with a preexisting IBF solution using VB .NET. We will look at how to build an Office 2003 smart tag, how to recognize terms in a document using XML data, and how to invoke a method provided by an IBF system.

Chapter 9: The Event-Site Order System

Automating the Order-Entry Process Using Word, Smart Documents, and a Web Service

Chapter 9 discusses how to build an ordering system within Microsoft Word, using VB .NET and smart documents. You will learn how to leverage the new smart document technology included in Office 2003 to include tools that help a user create an order document in Word. Key concepts discussed in this chapter include smart documents, the Word task pane, XML, and web services.

Appendix: How to Deploy a Managed Add-In

Utilizing a Shim to Bridge the Gap Between the COM and Managed Code

The appendix discusses how to deploy a managed COM add-in built with VB .NET. Managed COM add-ins fall under the .NET Framework's security policies and thus involve some deployment steps not typically required with Office-related development. Key concepts include .NET security, how managed code relates to Office, and how to create a shim that helps connect the two security models provided separately by Office and the .NET Framework.

Who Should Read This Book?

If you are a Visual Basic developer interested in building business applications featuring Microsoft Office, this book is for you. In addition, this book was written to teach experienced Microsoft Office developers how to take advantage of the extended development scenarios available with Visual Basic (6.0 and .NET).

What You Need to Know

The primary audience for this book is the experienced developer who builds business applications for a living. The book will be of most immediate benefit to a developer who has had some prior exposure to the following technologies:

- Visual Basic (6.0 and .NET)

- The .NET Framework

- Relational databases

- XML

- ActiveX/COM

- The Office application suite (at a "user" level)

However, the detailed descriptive text and code explanations should also allow less experienced readers to gain invaluable insight into how such applications are built and how they work.

How to Use This Book

One of my goals in writing this book was to present each case study as an encapsulated unit. This makes it possible for you to go through the material in any order you like. None of the chapters depend on features from the others. In addition, the subjects of the different chapters do not particularly build upon each other. In cases where the subject presented is specifically enhanced by information included in other chapters, cross references are provided.

To receive the most benefit from the information provided in these pages, you should read through each case study in detail and build the application as you go.

Downloading the Source Code

For your convenience, the full source code for the projects in this book is available on the Apress web site at `http://www.apress.com`. Click the Downloads link on the home page and follow the directions to download the code.

■ ■ ■

CHAPTER 1

Building Office Applications with VB .NET

This book is about building reusable business applications using Visual Basic and Microsoft Office applications. Each chapter explains how to build a fully functioning business application. Together, this series of applications will:

1. Illustrate how to create useful Office applications that extend beyond the desktop.

2. Provide examples of how to utilize the new Office development capabilities provided by Visual Studio .NET and the .NET Framework.

3. Provide examples of methods for building "real-world" Office solutions (not always pretty under the hood, but definitely working and useful).

4. Serve as a reference and springboard for your own Office-related development projects.

Each application will teach you some core VB .NET and Office programming skills and can be easily extended to meet your specific requirements.

■**Note** In order to keep the focus on building business-related functionality, the majority of the code in this book lacks the error-handling logic required by production-ready applications.

Application Architecture

To provide optimal performance across the enterprise, both for internal and external users, the applications in this book employ an n-tier architecture (see Figure 1-1). For the most part, the traditional presentation, business, and data tiers are used. This architectural approach provides the required amount of flexibility, because application logic is kept separate from the overall design and business rules of the application.

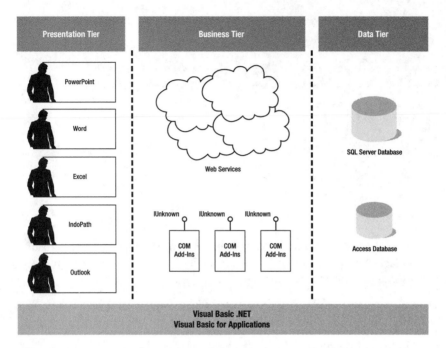

Figure 1-1. *The basic architecture of the applications*

The Data Tier

Relatively little emphasis is placed on the data tier in this book. It is typically a SQL Server (or Access) database that acts as a central repository for application resources (for example, approved PowerPoint presentation templates in Chapter 2).

The Business Tier

From a development perspective, this is where the majority of the work goes on. It is here that we implement the business logic to extend our Office applications. We will use a variety of techniques, from the traditional (such as the use of VBA and COM add-ins to automate the creation of Word documents in Chapter 3) to the cutting edge (such as building an XML web service that contains a rudimentary workflow engine in Chapter 5).

Let's take a brief tour of some of the technologies involved, how we'll use them, and the key programming skills and techniques that they demonstrate.

Customizing Office Applications Using VB .NET

The Office suite of applications has more functionality than a single person could ever use, and yet it still falls short of meeting every business requirement. That's okay, because extending Office to meet the specific needs of a business is as simple as writing a VB .NET program. In this book, we'll use VB .NET extensively to create custom Office solutions. For example, we'll use it

- To build managed COM add-ins (such as the PowerPoint Generator in Chapter 2)

- In conjunction with Visual Studio Tools for Office to attach code to an Excel workbook (such as the Timesheet System in Chapter 7)

- To build smart tags (such as the Account Details Smart Tag in Chapter 8) and create smart documents (such as the Event-Site Order System in Chapter 9)

- In conjunction with VBA to automate common Office tasks, such as creating Word or Excel templates (as in Chapters 2 and 6).

XML and Web Services

Business transactions deal with information. Proposals, marketing brochures, orders, invoices, purchase orders, and emails are just a few of the many types of information produced and consumed each day.

With the increasing popularity of Extensible Markup Language (XML) and its incorporation into leading applications like Office and SQL Server, information is more mobile than ever. This is because an XML document contains not only data, but also the data schema. This means that no matter where an XML document travels, an application will be able to interpret the meaning of the information.

■**Note** This book does not cover the ins and outs of XML. It is assumed you are comfortable with and have a working knowledge of XML and its related components. To learn more, pick up a copy of *XML Programming: Web Applications and Web Services with JSP and ASP* by Tom Myers and Alexander Nakhimovsky (from Apress) or visit `http://www.xml.org`.

From a business perspective, the key point is that the applications that create the data are less critical than the data itself. The focus is on the data and how to consume it. By implementing XML, disparate data sources can be connected without much effort. XML enables an enterprising corporation to quickly change its data requirements as the needs of its clients evolve. For example, new applications can be built to address a specific client's need without too much concern for the nature of their backoffice systems. Using XML, the data from the application can be transformed into the format required by the backend architecture. XML and web services will be covered further in Chapters 5, 8, and 9.

■**Note** Throughout several chapters in the book, custom XML schemas are implemented as part of the chapter's solution. None of Microsoft's proprietary schemas, like WordML, are utilized.

Web services are used in three of the sample applications. Web services are methods that are made available over a network for other applications to use. In this book, they are used to provide additional logic for desktop solutions built using the Office applications. Web services are built using XML and the HTTP protocol, which makes them useful for centralizing business logic that can be utilized across several applications. A good example of this concept in action is the Timesheet System discussed in Chapter 7. This system includes two separate Excel workbooks that access user-authentication logic.

Using web services, we will create methods that provide data to applications (such as retrieving a list of users from a database) and then access them in Office applications like InfoPath (Chapter 5). In addition, we will also see how to submit XML data to web service methods that parse the data and then insert it into a database (Chapters 5, 7, and 9). We will also look at how a web service can be made compliant with the new Microsoft Office Information Bridge Framework (Chapter 8).

Other Coding Techniques

In addition to the technologies already mentioned, we will also look at the following key coding concepts:

- Using regular expressions to create your own InfoTags to describe insertion locations in an email template, and then to replace the tags with the appropriate data (Chapter 4).

- Manipulating the Office command bars (menus) to provide users with quick access to key features of the custom application (Chapters 2, 3, 4, and 6). In addition, we will dynamically create button controls on a command bar reflecting the types of items found in an Outlook folder (Chapter 4).

- Building a wizard form that walks a user through a custom process for creating a presentation (Chapter 2).

- Deploying a managed COM add-in so that is fully trusted by Office 2003 (Appendix).

The Presentation Tier: Microsoft Office

In the dot-com era, the trend was to create web versions of existing business-critical applications. As a result, developers turned to the Internet and built browser-based applications that mirrored the functions and features found in their desktop-based applications. Although this strategy achieved the goal of "always-available" information, a significant cost was incurred to the overall user experience. Many of the gains in desktop application productivity were lost, and users were forced to deal with less-than-satisfactory experiences. This is in addition to the increase in developer time required to create the web applications and add client-side scripts to enhance the browser-based programs.

With the release of the .NET Framework in 2001 and the growing acceptance of web services, a new trend has emerged to web-enable the fat-client applications of the desktop. This is in large part due to the portability of information via XML and web services.

The great thing about the applications in this book is that, from a user perspective, they largely present the "normal" Office interface that everyone is familiar with. Microsoft Office is the most successful set of desktop applications in the history of computing. With a market share exceeding 90 percent, it is now the de facto standard of desktop productivity.

As well as working with basic PowerPoint templates, Excel spreadsheets, and Word documents, the applications in this book also employ some of the new technologies introduced in Office 2003.

XML and Office 2003

XML is perhaps one of the most significant new features in Office 2003, as it enables developers to incorporate data from disparate systems within Office applications like Excel, InfoPath, Word, and Access. By using XML, it is possible to repurpose business data across applications.

In fact, it is conceivable that by using XML, Office applications could be used as smart clients to enterprise backend systems. In such a scenario, Word could be used to create an order document that conforms to an XML schema. Once the order is completed, the XML data could be submitted to a company's accounting system. Chapter 9 covers a simplified version of an order entry system built with a Word-based smart document.

Smart Documents

Smart documents use .NET code to update the Office task pane so that it includes controls and information relevant to the current document context. They rely on an XML schema attached to the Word or Excel document to inform the .NET assembly of the current document context.

Smart documents provide a developer with a powerful framework for creating documents that contain a certain amount of intelligence. From the user's perspective, smart documents are souped-up Excel, Word, and InfoPath documents that know what data should be entered into the document and that provide tools (in the form of boilerplate text, information pulled from external systems, and the like) to enable a quicker and cleaner document authoring process.

InfoPath Forms

InfoPath is a new application available with Office 2003 Professional. It is targeted at forms-based solutions where the input data should ultimately end up in a database or, potentially, a backend accounting, CRM, or sales system. InfoPath is completely XML-based, and it is intended to create structured XML data that is then submitted to a web service, database, SharePoint, or any other application that can receive XML data. The best feature of InfoPath is that no code is required to interface with web services, databases, or SharePoint. These connections are all handled through InfoPath's dialog boxes, which makes submitting XML documents created with InfoPath to web services a snap (see Chapter 5).

Example Scenario: Bravo Corp

The applications in this book are of general utility, and I specifically demonstrate their utility and flexibility in helping a fictional company, Bravo Corp, streamline its business activities and increase the productivity and effectiveness of its employees.

Bravo Corp specializes in delivering products and services related to trade show and event management. Most of the company's revenue is generated by managing these events for its clients (typically trade associations and Fortune 500 companies) and by providing ancillary services to event exhibitors. Typically, an organization hires Bravo Corp to run the event because they do not have the talent or resources to tackle such an endeavor. Bravo Corp manages all aspects of an event, including event logistics, freight, show setup and tear down, and exhibit construction. This list is by no means exhaustive, but it does shed some light on the dynamic nature of Bravo Corp's business.

Over the last ten years, Bravo Corp has experienced a significant increase in business, which has caused a need for desktop tools that better enable its staff to communicate with clients and perform the activities required by their job functions. This book covers a series of application solutions built using Microsoft Office applications that address the needs of Bravo Corp's growing business.

Bravo Corp's Business Strategy

The executives of Bravo Corp created an internal Productivity Improvement and Efficiency (PIE) team. The PIE team was kept small in order to avoid decision by committee, and it included staff from all departments and all levels within the company. The PIE team was responsible for creating a strategy and developing the tools necessary to meet the most important requirements of each department. These needs were driven first and foremost by a focus on increasing business value (that is, return on investment).

In the spirit of the new project, PIE adopted an approach for developing the business strategy that would emphasize the needs of business users throughout the enterprise. The basic philosophy was that business users drive IT requirements, so instead of allowing the IT department to run with the project, it was decided that the managers and service personnel would be allowed to decide requirements and shape the new strategy. The goal was to create a feature-set that ultimately met the clients' expectations. The best method to accomplish this goal was to let those who best understood Bravo Corp's business strategy make all the decisions. The IT department played a role and handled many of the sessions to help prioritize the requirements, but their main role was to execute and deliver the required features.

The PIE team included a single, high-level IT manager to advise the team members and educate them about the current system architecture within Bravo Corp. This reduced the tendency of the IT department to shoot down good ideas before they were fully understood.

Bravo Corp Development Strategy

As noted, Bravo Corp already extensively utilizes Office and installs every application included with the Office Professional Edition 2003 onto each user's laptop (Outlook, Excel, Word, Access, InfoPath, etc.).

The team decided to utilize Office as the user interface, or presentation tier. Users were already trained and proficient with the Office suite. In fact, a sense of community had developed throughout the organization as project team members shared their tips and tricks with one another on a daily basis. Therefore, PIE focused its technical designs on utilizing the Office applications as much as possible. Taken with the extensive XML support, as well as the ability to connect to disparate data systems either directly or through web services (among other methods), the PIE team felt that Office would provide a rich set of features to the users and offer flexibility as needs change.

Thus, through Bravo Corp, we will demonstrate, in a highly practical fashion, how to implement the technologies, techniques, and architecture discussed previously to solve real business problems.

Business Benefits

As with any growing company, Bravo Corp's client portfolio has become increasingly diversified. For years, Bravo Corp focused its attention on working for larger clients that hosted large trade show events. Today's opportunities include smaller clients who simply want to set up a booth at these events to market their company. This diversity has exposed the need for a set of tools that improve the way Bravo Corp fulfills the needs of their clients. Table 1-1 lists the problems faced by Bravo Corp along with the applications built in this book to solve them.

Table 1-1. *Bravo Corp Problems and Application Solutions*

Problem	Problem Description	Solution Overview	Tools Utilized	Chapter
Lack of consistent sale presentations	The sales and marketing team constantly reinvent the wheel when creating new PowerPoint presentations that communicate their overall value proposition.	The Presentation Generator was built to take advantage of approved, standard presentations and to automate the presentation-creation process through the implementation of an easy-to-use wizard.	PowerPoint, managed code COM add-in, VBA-based PowerPoint template, SQL Server	Chapter 2
Too much time taken to create frequently used documents	Account management staff was spending an inordinate amount of time creating client-related documents (contracts, proposals, etc.) and not enough time in front of the clients. In addition, the documents were prone to data-entry errors.	The Document Generator was built to automate key legal documents by automatically inserting client information into available standard documents.	Word, Outlook, managed COM add-in, SQL Server	Chapter 3
Slow response time to client information requests	Many questions raised by clients fall into the category of "frequently asked questions." In the past, Bravo Corp staff crafted a new email response to provide answers to questions.	The Email Template Engine provides an Outlook-based tool allowing Bravo Corp staff to create email templates with pre-authored content. These templates are then used to quickly create a new email automatically filled with a template's content.	Outlook, regular expressions, managed COM add-in	Chapter 4
Poor service-failure resolution methods	Customer service failures are a fact of life for any business. Bravo Corp lacked a tool for coordinating efforts among its staff to improve the service-failure resolution process.	A tool was put in place to better track all activities related to identifying and resolving a service failure.	InfoPath, web services, Access	Chapter 5

continues

Table 1-1. *continued*

Problem	Problem Description	Solution Overview	Tools Utilized	Chapter
Lack of standardized budgets	The budgeting process across departments was inconsistent and created additional problems when attempting to create a company-wide, consolidated budget.	The Budget Consolidator application is a tool for creating consistent budgets across all departments. In addition, the tool allows a manager to create a consolidated budget that contains rolled-up numbers from each departmental budget.	Excel, VBA	Chapter 6
Lack of labor-related data	Bravo Corp did not have any tools for tracking the effort required for each task performed while managing an event. As a result, it was unable to effectively manage its labor costs.	The Timesheet System provides an easy-to-use interface allowing Bravo Corp's labor force to quickly and easily input the time it spends completing assigned tasks.	Excel, Visual Studio Tools for Office, web services, Access	Chapter 7
Inability to access client information contained in backend systems	Bravo Corp has several enterprise systems (ERP, CRM, etc.) that contain client information. This data is not always easily accessible, and users must open additional applications to access it.	The Account Details Smart Tag is a tool that retrieves client information from these backend systems and makes it available within Word (allowing the user to access the data while authoring a document).	Smart tags, Word, Information Bridge Framework	Chapter 8
Lack of efficient event-site order-entry tools	Bravo Corp offers a wide range of products at an event site, from desks, chairs, and lamps to carpet, network cabling, and computers. Bravo Corp had a paper-based form clients used to select their desired products, but because of the range of products and their related options, clients frequently made mistakes in their orders.	The Event-Site Order System was created to improve and automate the order process.	Smart documents, Word, XML, web services, SQL Server	Chapter 9

Summary

Office 2003 is more than a suite of applications sitting on a user's desktop. In fact, for years developers have been building applications on the Office platform that enhance a user's productivity by streamlining business processes, providing data from external data systems, and more. With the 2003 version, the Office platform, along with its new developer features and related technologies, is more than capable of handling the custom office application needs of any business.

In the chapters that follow, you will learn how Bravo Corp implemented their strategy by building each of the project applications yourself. Each of the following chapters is a separate case study explaining the applications in detail—from design to deployment.

CHAPTER 2

The Presentation Generator

How to Auto-Generate PowerPoint Presentations Using PowerPoint, SQL Server, and a COM Add-In

This chapter shows you how to build the Presentation Generator, which automates the creation of custom presentations by allowing reuse of standard "published" presentation templates. For example, say your company stores a set of published PowerPoint presentations, of proven effectiveness, in a central repository (say a SQL Server database). The application that we'll develop in this chapter will allow users to download these template presentations to their desktop and use them as a basis to develop new presentations, targeted for a specific audience, easily and effectively. For example, a CEO who needs to prepare for a board meeting could use the add-in to create a presentation that includes slides from a set of template presentations on, say, product information, sales performance, and strategy development.

Development of this presentation generator combines the use of a Microsoft Office COM add-in, the Microsoft .NET Framework, and VBA:

- An Office COM add-in is used to manage the user workflow for creating presentations.

- VBA is used to control the presentation template's customization wizard.

- .NET is used to build the managed COM add-in.

COM add-ins provide a central mechanism for extending Office applications. Instead of creating a separate add-in for each targeted Office application, all functions can be implemented within a single COM add-in and run within each desired application. This is a great way to share business rules and logic within Microsoft Office, and especially with applications that do not yet support .NET extensions—in such applications (like PowerPoint) VBA allows a developer to embed, within a document, business logic specific to that particular document.

Thus, one of the key take-aways of this chapter is that it shows how to create a managed COM add-in using Visual Studio 2003 targeted for PowerPoint, and hook it in to VBA code embedded inside an individual PowerPoint template file. The VBA code inside the document is used by the managed add-in to start the customization wizard included in the PowerPoint file. This wizard then walks the user through the steps required to create a new presentation.

The presentation generator will be demonstrated in the context of our fictional BravoCorp, which needs to streamline the development of Sales presentations.

Designing the Presentation Generator

To the user, the Presentation Generator is PowerPoint. They probably will not even be aware that the application is not a standard PowerPoint feature. This is because the application runs within PowerPoint and is available from the standard menu toolbar.

The user workflow is as follows:

1. The user opens PowerPoint and selects New PPT from a custom menu in PowerPoint's standard toolbar. The user is presented with a ListPresentations form.

2. The user selects the desired presentation template from a listing of available templates on their hard drive. This is the base template for the new, custom presentation. Once the user has selected the desired template and clicked OK, the template opens up in PowerPoint.

3. Immediately after the template opens in PowerPoint, the customization wizard (PPTWizard) is automatically invoked. Using this wizard-driven form, the user can choose to add other presentation templates into their base presentation if, for example, they are giving a more general presentation on a range of topics. Each selected general presentation is then used, along with the previously selected base presentation (selected in step 1) to create the whole. A useful customization for you to consider is to allow users to select only specific slides from these secondary templates.

4. The user then completes the wizard by entering information (such as presentation title, customer name, presenter name, etc.) that will be inserted into the completed presentation. Once the user clicks the Finish button, the presentation-creation process executes and the newly created presentation loads within the PowerPoint application window.

From a developer's viewpoint, the Presentation Generator is a desktop application with some client/server functionality thrown in. Hosted within PowerPoint, the Presentation Generator is a combination of a COM add-in, PowerPoint template files, and a SQL Server database.

The managed COM add-in serves as the solution's engine and extends PowerPoint (see Figure 2-1) by creating a custom menu for the add-in and responding to user-initiated events (such as when the user clicks the add-in's menu buttons). This add-in is the entry point to all the features and functionality available to the user when creating new presentations. This does not mean, however, that all of the code is contained within the add-in (part of the overall solution code is contained in an individual PowerPoint file).

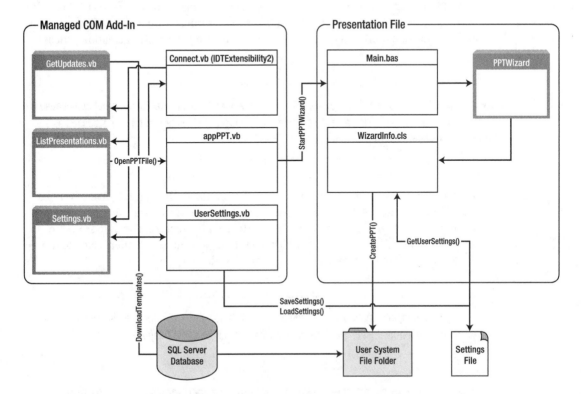

Figure 2-1. *The Presentation Generator architecture and object interaction*

A PowerPoint template file containing the Presentation Customization Wizard works in conjunction with the add-in to allow the user to customize their selected presentation. The wizard code is placed in the presentation template for ease of maintenance and updating. If the business rules change for a presentation, the file can be updated to reflect the changes, and it can be republished without requiring any updates to the add-in.

Here is what occurs behind the scenes from a code standpoint:

1. When the user selects the New PPT option from the menu, the ListPresentations form opens and lists all available templates in a list box control. Behind the scenes, the add-in uses the values stored in the UserSettings class to locate the file system folder storing the available templates, read their filenames, and fill the list box.

2. Once the user selects the desired template and clicks OK, the add-in calls the OpenPPT-File method available in the appPPT class to open the selected presentation template.

3. Immediately after the template opens in PowerPoint, the AfterPresentationOpen event of the COM add-in triggers and makes a call to the template's StartPPTWizard VBA method. This method resides in a VBA module named Main. As soon as StartPPTWizard

is invoked, the add-in ceases activity, and the remaining workflow is handled by code residing in the presentation template.

4. StartPPTWizard creates a instance of the WizardInfo class and opens the PPTWizard form (a VBA UserForm). WizardInfo reads the user settings (from an XML file stored on the user's file system) into memory for use during the presentation creation process.

■**Note** The location of the user-settings XML file must be known by the presentation template because it uses the folder location for saving a newly created presentation. The location of the file is passed as a parameter in the StartPPTWizard method.

---

5. As the user enters information into the wizard's controls, the WizardInfo class stores the data in memory. As soon as the user completes the wizard and clicks the Finish button, the CreatePPT method of the WizardInfo class executes. The data stored in memory is inserted into the presentation, and the presentation is then saved to the folder specified in the Presentation Generator settings.

■**Note** PowerPoint templates have an extension of .pot. From now on I will refer to these templates as PowerPoint templates, templates, or .pots. All three terms refer to the same things.

The COM add-in does not need to know the details of each template and its unique options or business rules. Embedding the wizard in the .pot file encapsulates its business rules and allows for easy deployment of updated or new templates.

The last component of the Presentation Generator is the backend SQL Server database. The Presentation Generator utilizes a single table from this database, and each row in the table contains a published presentation template approved for use by Bravo Corp employees.

The Business Scenario

As a first step toward building a set of sales tools, Bravo Corp decided to build the Presentation Generator to give their sales team the capability to automatically generate presentations based on a set of templates. Bravo Corp saw the need to give each team member quick access to the company's published presentations in order to decrease the time required to create a presentation. Using the Presentation Generator, the Bravo Corp sales team could quickly build presentation that included only the information the customer would be interested in.

Creating the Database

Before diving into creating the add-in, we need to first create the backend database.

■**Note** Sample scripts for creating the database are available as part of the book's source code. You can use them to create the database or you can follow the database design discussion in this section.

The code examples in this book use a SQL Server database named "BravoCorp". Not everyone has access to a SQL Server, and this poses a problem. However the Microsoft Data Engine (MSDE) is available with Office 2000 or later and with Visual Studio 6 or later. I recommend using a SQL Server database for the applications covered in this book, but if this is not an option, an MSDE database will work just fine.

■**Tip** For more information regarding MSDE, including how to install and configure it, visit the MSDE website at `http://www.microsoft.com/sql/msde/downloads/default.asp`. In addition, a 120 day trial version of SQL Server 2000 is available from Microsoft at `http://www.microsoft.com/sql/evaluation/trial/`. If you take the MSDE route, download a copy of MSDE Query—a utility tool allowing a developer to work with MSDE in a fashion similar to SQL Server. The basic version of MSDE Query is free and available at `http://www.msde.biz`.

To get started, we'll need to create a new database in SQL Server named "BravoCorp". Only the database name matters; you can leave all other properties at their defaults (size, file locations, etc.).

For the code in the Presentation Generator to run, a single table named `tblPresentations` is required. Create a new table using the schema specified in Table 2-1.

Table 2-1. *The Table Schema for* `tblPresentations`

Column Name	Data Type	Length	Allow Nulls
PresentationID	int	4	no
PresentationName	varchar	255	no
PresentationDesc	varchar	255	yes
PresentationBinary	image		yes

Before saving the table, set the following properties of the `PresentationID` column:

- Identity = yes

- Identity Seed = 1

- Identity Increment = 1

Your table should look similar to the one shown in Figure 2-2.

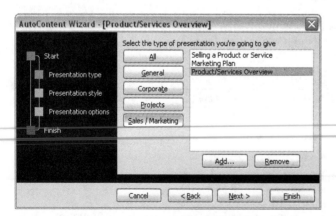

Figure 2-2. *The completed* tblPresentations *table*

Creating PowerPoint Templates

We need to create some sample PowerPoint presentation templates. The easiest way to create a set of sample templates is to use the PowerPoint AutoContent Wizard (see Figure 2-3).

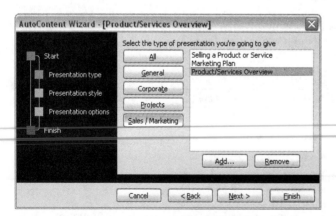

Figure 2-3. *The PowerPoint AutoContent Wizard*

With the wizard, create a Product/Services Overview presentation, and save it in the same folder you plan to use for this chapter's application. (I saved it in C:\Projects\Chapter02 using the filename `Company Overview.pot`.) This will be our base template, behind which we'll write the VBA code to control the customization wizard.

Tip If you are having trouble locating the AutoContent Wizard, try selecting File ➤ New from the menu. Depending on your version of PowerPoint (I am using PowerPoint 2003) either a dialog box will open that displays available templates (Office 2000) or the New Presentation Task Pane will become visible (Office XP or later). In both cases, the AutoContent Wizard is one of the templates listed. If all else fails, try searching for "AutoContent" in the PowerPoint Help file.

Create three more files as follows:

- `Event Management.pot`: Use the Project Overview presentation type.

- `Brainstorming Session.pot`: Use the Brainstorming Session presentation type.

- `Strategy Recommendation.pot`: Use the Strategy Recommendation presentation type.

These templates can be used to customize the base template presentation, and they will not contain any VBA code.

Caution The filenames are important as they will be relied upon later when building the `PPTWizard` form. If you use different filenames, make a note of them for use in the "Creating the PPTWizard Form" section later in the chapter.

With these tasks complete, we are ready to build the add-in.

Creating the Presentation Generator Add-In

A COM add-in is typically an in-process ActiveX .dll file (it can also be an out-of-process ActiveX .exe file). COM add-ins can be created using Visual Basic .NET, Visual Basic 6, or the Office Developer environment. This is by no means a complete list, as one could write a COM add-in using C# or C++, but we are focusing on Visual Basic here. The only requirement for a COM add-in is the implementation of the `IDTExtensibility2` interface (discussed later in the chapter).

In each case, the resulting COM add-in is a library of code that is registered on the system to load when the host applications are loaded (such as Word, PowerPoint, and Excel).

Note COM add-ins are called Shared add-ins in Visual Studio .NET. Since they are still COM libraries whether you create them with .NET or traditional Visual Basic, I will refer to them as COM add-ins.

The Presentation Generator COM add-in component acts as the engine of the entire solution. It creates the add-in's menu structure within PowerPoint, and it provides the capabilities allowing the user to specify settings for the add-in (the locations of the Template folder and where newly created presentations should be saved). Lastly, the add-in allows the user to connect to the SQL server database to download additional presentation templates. These are the steps for creating the add-in:

1. Create the add-in project in Visual Studio .NET: In this section, you will learn the basics of creating a managed code COM add-in. We will go step by step through the project setup, and we'll look at the project options presented in the project setup wizard.

2. Create the add-in code: This section explains how to build each of the classes and forms required by the Presentation Generator add-in. This section will show you how to

   - Implement the IDTExtensibility2 interface

   - Create custom toolbars within PowerPoint

   - Save user-specified settings to the user's local hard drive and then retrieve them for use

   - Use managed code (VB .NET) to call a custom VBA macro stored within a PowerPoint file

   - Listen for and respond to PowerPoint events within the add-in

Before we build the project, though, we need to look at the IDTExtensibility2 interface, which you will need to use for any COM add-in you build.

The IDTExtensibility2 Interface

Creating a COM add-in requires the implementation of the IDTExtensibility2 interface. This interface is called by the Office applications to perform such tasks as loading or unloading the add-in.

The IDTExtensibility2 interface requires that five specific events be implemented. Code is not required for every one of these events, but they do need to be present. These are the five events of the IDTExtensibility2 interface:

- OnConnection: This event is executed when the target application loads the add-in. It is the first event to execute and can be treated like an object's constructor method in that it is the best place for setting up the add-in's environment. It can be used for adding custom CommandBars, loading add-in settings, and so on. We use this method to create a reference to PowerPoint and to retrieve the application's user settings stored in the local file system.

- OnDisconnection: This is the last event executed, and it executes when the host application unloads the add-in. Like a deconstructor method, this event should be used to clean up the host application's environment. The PowerPoint Generator does not utilize this method.

- `OnStartupComplete`: This event executes once the target application has completed all of its startup routines and the `OnConnection` event has completed. This method is the best place for any code that interacts with objects in the host application's object model. For example, this event could be used to create a new document in the host application based on information automatically retrieved from a database. When this event fires, the host application will be fully loaded into memory and available to be accessed via code. This event only occurs if the add-in is set to load at startup. We use this method to create the add-in's toolbar structure within the host application.

- `OnBeginShutdown`: This event is executed upon the initialization of the target application's shutdown routines; it executes prior to `OnDisconnection`. This event is a good place for any code that will protect data in case of an unexpected application shutdown. For example, the event could be used to save the active document. In addition, this method is a good place for code that clears memory objects and references that are created and used by the add-in. It can be used for deleting custom `CommandBars` and restoring the host application to its original state. This event only occurs if the add-in is loaded when the host application is shut down. In this application, we use this method to delete the add-in's menu from the host application.

- `OnAddInUpdate`: This event is executed any time a COM add-in is loaded or unloaded. Typically the event is triggered by the user loading or unloading COM add-ins via the host application's COM add-ins dialog box. If your add-in depends on the presence of other COM add-ins, this event is the place to check and ensure that the required add-ins are still loaded in memory and to respond if they are not. This event is executed in all currently loaded add-ins, but it is not utilized by the PowerPoint Generator.

The Shared Add-In Extensibility project within Visual Studio .NET implements this interface automatically inside the `Connect.vb` class.

Creating the Add-In Project

One of the best reasons to use Visual Studio .NET to create COM add-ins is that it does the best job of any available development IDE of setting up the add-in. Performing this task within Visual Basic 6 is certainly more complicated, and the process is not nearly as automated. With VS .NET, most of the plumbing of the add-in is provided, leaving developers to focus their attention on writing the requisite business logic.

■Note Generally speaking, Visual Basic is a better choice than C# for creating COM add-ins in terms of the coding effort required. Office functions are jam-packed with optional parameters, and C# does not support optional parameters. Working around this issue requires a bit of extra effort and some really wordy function calls. To learn more, visit `http://msdn.microsoft.com/library/en-us/odc_vsto2003_ta/html/OffCSharp.asp`.

Let's begin writing the add-in application:

1. Open Visual Studio .NET and select File ➤ New ➤ Project (or press Ctrl+N on the keyboard).

2. In the New Project dialog box (see Figure 2-4), expand the Other Projects folder and select Extensibility Projects.

3. Select the Shared Add-In template, choose a location for the project files, and name the new project PPTGEN.

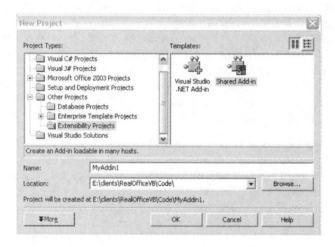

Figure 2-4. *Creating a new VBA add-in project*

4. Click OK. Visual Studio .NET initializes the Extensibility Wizard (see Figure 2-5).

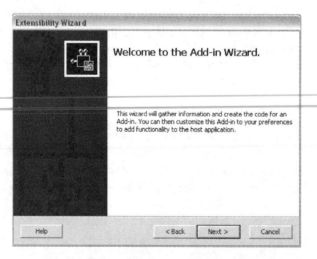

Figure 2-5. *Initializing the Shared add-in project wizard*

5. Click Next. In the Select a Programming Language window (see Figure 2-6), choose Create an Add-In Using Visual Basic. Click Next.

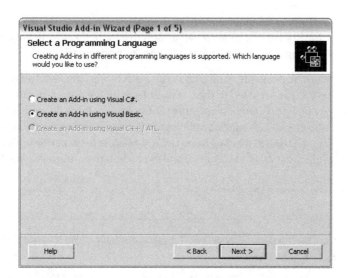

Figure 2-6. *Specifying Visual Basic as the add-in's language*

6. The Select an Application Host window appears (see Figure 2-7). You want this add-in to only load in PowerPoint, so uncheck all applications except Microsoft PowerPoint. Click Next.

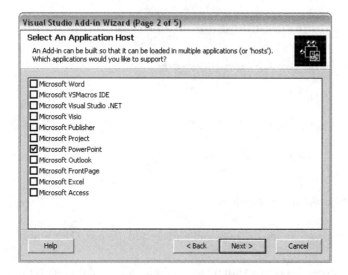

Figure 2-7. *Setting the add-in to load only in PowerPoint*

7. The Enter a Name and Description window displays. Give the add-in the name **PresentationGenerator** and enter **BravoCorp PowerPoint Presentation Generator** as the description. Click Next.

8. In the Choose Add-In Options window (see Figure 2-8), select the "I would like my Add-in to load when the host application loads" option to ensure the add-in always loads and is available within PowerPoint. Leave all other options unselected.

If the "My Add-in should be available to all users . . ." check box is checked, the user will not be able to see the add-in listed in the COM Add-Ins dialog box accessed from PowerPoint's Tools ➤ COM Add-Ins menu because Office applications list add-ins on a per user basis. (If the add-in is made available to all users, a registry entry is created inside HKEY_LOCAL_MACHINE instead of HKEY_LOCAL_USER.) By leaving this option unchecked, you provide the user with some control over when the add-in is available or unavailable.

■Tip The COM Add-Ins menu button is not visible by default. It must be manually added by customizing PowerPoint's CommandBars (Tools ➤ Customize).

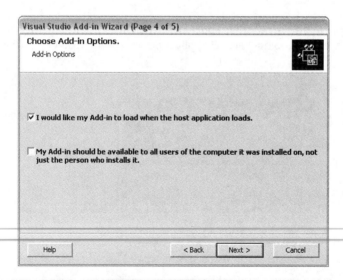

Figure 2-8. *Specifying the add-in's options*

9. Click Next. The Summary window displays all the selected options. Click Finish.

The completed new project is created within Visual Studio .NET, and the Solution Explorer should resemble Figure 2-9. Notice that two projects have been created by the wizard. The first is the add-in project, and it is the basic shell that will interface with PowerPoint.

The second project is the setup (or installation) project for the add-in. The setup project creates the necessary Windows installer files used to deploy the add-in on a user's system.

Figure 2-9. *The add-in project displayed in the Solution Explorer*

We will not be adding or modifying code in this setup project. Just know that this project's main feature is the registry key needed for proper installation. The key is automatically created with the project and can be viewed by right-clicking on the `PresentationGeneratorSetup` project and selecting View ➤ Registry from the pop-up menu. (In Figure 2-9, the setup program is the node labeled "PPTGENSetup".) Once opened, you can navigate in a window that resembles the Windows Registry Editor and view the keys that will be installed by the setup project.

All that remains in this first step is to make sure the add-in references the libraries it will need. We will be adding code to work with Windows forms and the file system, and both of these namespaces are already available. The add-in will also utilize PowerPoint's objects throughout its code, so it requires a project reference to the PowerPoint library. This reference needs to be added to the project or the code will not compile when it is completed.

■**Caution** Once the PowerPoint reference is created, delete the references to `Microsoft.Office.Core` or `Office`. These references point to the same files causing ambiguous reference errors when attempting to compile the add-in.

To add this reference follow these steps:

1. Select Tools ➤ Add Reference.

2. The Add Reference dialog box will be displayed (see Figure 2-10). Select the COM tab.

3. Scroll down the COM listing, select the Microsoft PowerPoint 11.0 Object Library (PowerPoint 2003's library), and click Select.

Note If you are using PowerPoint 2002, select the Microsoft PowerPoint 10.0 Object Library. For Power-Point 2000, select the Microsoft PowerPoint 9.0 Object Library.

4. Make sure the Selected Components section lists the PowerPoint library. Click OK.

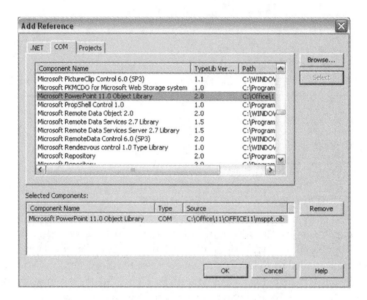

Figure 2-10. *Adding a reference to the PowerPoint library*

Required Components of the Presentation Generator Add-In

There are six components of the Presentation Generator add-in:

- appPPT: This is a public class used to maintain a reference to PowerPoint and respond to PowerPoint events. This class contains code that responds to certain PowerPoint application events available within the PowerPoint object model.

- Settings: This form allows users to update their settings. For example, in addition to maintaining database-access settings, the add-in allows the user to specify storage locations for downloaded templates as well as newly authored, template-based presentations. These settings give the user control of their file system instead of defaulting to "My Documents" or Office's templates folder. The settings are stored locally within an XML file.

- UserSettings: This is a public class that handles the XML file reading and writing tasks required to set and retrieve the settings specified in the Settings form. This class writes the settings values to an XML file on the user's system. In addition, the class retrieves the settings from the XML file for use within the add-in.

- `GetUpdates`: This form retrieves all published presentations from a SQL Server and stores them on the user's file system. This form is available from the add-in's menu (integrated as part of the standard PowerPoint menu) and contains code for connecting to the template database and downloading available templates to the user-specified template folder.

- `ListPresentations`: This form lists all presentation templates available for selection and use by the user. When the user selects a template, it is loaded into PowerPoint and integrated into the currently active PowerPoint presentation.

- `Connect`: This public class is the entry point to the add-in. It inherits the `IDTExtensibility2` interface and implements its five required methods. The add-in's registry entry refers to this class, so it is called by PowerPoint when loading the Presentation Generator.

The instructions for creating or modifying each of these forms and classes appear in the following sections.

Creating the appPPT Class

The PowerPoint Generator needs a mechanism for responding to PowerPoint events (like the `AfterPresentationOpen` event), and the `appPPT` class fulfills this need. It is designated as a shared class in order to ensure that the accessible variables within the class maintain the same values across all objects in the add-in. Designating the class as shared also means we do not have to create an instance of the class in order to use its properties and methods.

Create the class by selecting Project ➤ Add Class from the Visual Studio menu. From the Add New Item dialog box, select the Class icon. Name the class **appPPT.vb** and click OK.

■**Note** Make sure PPTGEN is the active project within Visual Studio's Solution Explorer window.

Imports Directives

You will be accessing the Microsoft PowerPoint elements within this class, so insert the following line of code in the Imports Directives section of the class:

```
Imports PowerPoint = Microsoft.Office.Interop.PowerPoint
```

Variable Declarations

The `appPPT` class has only a single private field that contains the reference to the host PowerPoint application. At the top of the class declaration, insert the following line:

```
Private Shared WithEvents m_appPPT As PowerPoint.Application
```

Notice that the m_appPPT variable is declared using both the Shared and WithEvents keywords. Because the class is a shared class, all elements within the class must be designated as shared too. The WithEvents keyword tells the compiler we want to be notified of any event raised by the variable's object.

Property Procedures and Methods

In order to expose the class-level PowerPoint variable to the other objects of the add-in, the following property procedure is required:

```
Public Shared Property App() As PowerPoint.Application
  Get
    App = m_appPPT
  End Get
  Set(ByVal Value As PowerPoint.Application)
    m_appPPT = Value
  End Set
End Property
```

The appPPT class contains only two functions: Setup and Shutdown. These two functions are as follows:

```
Public Shared Function Setup(ByVal oApp As PowerPoint.Application) _
  As Boolean
  'store reference to PowerPoint in class variable
  m_appPPT = oApp
End Function

Public Shared Function ShutDown()
  'Close Powerpoint and clear its reference
  m_appPPT.Quit()
  m_appPPT = Nothing
End Function
```

As their names imply, these two functions handle the details of setting up and shutting down the class. The Setup function stores the PowerPoint application variable within the class for further use. The Shutdown function first stops the PowerPoint application and frees the Power-Point variable.

The purpose of this class is to respond to PowerPoint events, but of the many events provided by PowerPoint, this add-in only needs to respond to the AfterPresentationOpen event. This event triggers after a presentation has successfully opened within PowerPoint.

The reason we want to capture this event is to present a wizard that allows the user to select templates and create a custom presentation. Each Bravo Corp presentation template contains a public VBA method named StartPPTWizard (discussed later in this chapter). When called by the add-in, StartPPTWizard loads the wizard form (a VBA UserForm) contained within the template.

Insert the following code into the AfterPresentationOpen event:

```
Private Shared Sub m_appPPT_AfterPresentationOpen(ByVal Pres _
  As PowerPoint.Presentation) Handles m_appPPT.AfterPresentationOpen

  'Store the name of the VBA macro
  'contained in the template
  Dim strMacroName As New String("!StartPPTWizard")
  'Create variable containing the location of the
  'settings file
  Dim aryParams() = {UserSettings.SettingsPath}

  'combine the VBA macro name with the
  '.PPT filename in order to call the macro
  strMacroName = strMacroName.Concat(m_appPPT.ActivePresentation.Name, _
    strMacroName.ToString)
  'Call the macro
  m_appPPT.Run(strMacroName.ToString, aryParams)

End Sub
```

The code begins by building a string to call the presentation's StartPPTWizard method. This call uses the normal VB syntax of *ObjectName!MethodName*. In this case, the object name is the name of the presentation file running within PowerPoint. The Run method of the PowerPoint application object provides the bridge needed for our add-in to call functions inside Power-Point. The Run method calls a Visual Basic procedure, which could be a procedure within a module, a loaded add-in, or a loaded presentation.

Since we cannot rely on every presentation having the same presentation name, we need to retrieve the active presentation's name and concatenate it to the method name. We do this by utilizing the Name property of the ActivePresentation object. The Name property returns only the filename of the presentation currently open in the PowerPoint application window. The last line calls PowerPoint's Run method, passing the strMacroName variable containing the newly concatenated method name.

Creating the Settings Form and the UserSettings Class

In any good application architecture it is best not to hard-code any of the settings used by the application, as they may change over time. Accordingly, the add-in's user settings are stored on the user's system within an XML file. By providing the user a way to change these settings, we avoid having to redeploy the add-in if the template database is moved to a new server or when the user's password changes.

The Presentation Generator add-in relies on the values listed in Table 2-2. To provide the user with the ability to update these settings, we will build a worker class named UserSettings and a form for interfacing with the user.

Table 2-2. *The Presentation Generator User Settings*

Setting Name	Purpose
TemplatesFolder	Location for storing downloaded templates
SaveFolder	Location for saving newly created presentation
ServerName	Name or IP address of the SQL Server running the templates database
UserName	The user's account name for accessing the database
Password	The user's password for accessing the database
DatabaseName	The name of the templates database residing on the specified server

There are a couple of points to keep in mind about these settings:

- TemplatesFolder: Instead of defaulting to Office's standard template folder location (\Program Files\Microsoft Office\Templates\1033), the add-in maintains its own user-specified location. Some users prefer to store files in one or two main parent folders (like My Documents) for ease of access and backup, and this setting allows for such a file system strategy.

- SaveFolder: This setting is not necessarily needed, as PowerPoint maintains a Default File Location setting (Tools ➤ Options ➤ File Locations). The SaveFolder setting exists to make the add-in user friendly while not affecting the PowerPoint application options.

■**Caution** For convenience in developing and testing the Presentation Generator add-in, the username and password required to connect to the database are included as part of the add-in's user settings. Before deploying the actual solution, you could extend the solution by encrypting the user settings before saving them to the file system. Encrypting the settings information would help prevent exposing the contained security information to curious individuals.

Building the Settings Form

Add a new form to the project and name it **Settings.vb**. Set the width of the form to 448 pixels and the height to 360 pixels. Set the Text property to **Presentation Generator Settings** and the StartPosition to **CenterScreen**.

From the toolbox, drag and drop the following controls:

- 2 GroupBox controls

- 6 TextBox controls

- 6 Label controls

- 4 Button controls

Figure 2-11 shows how to lay out each of the controls on the form.

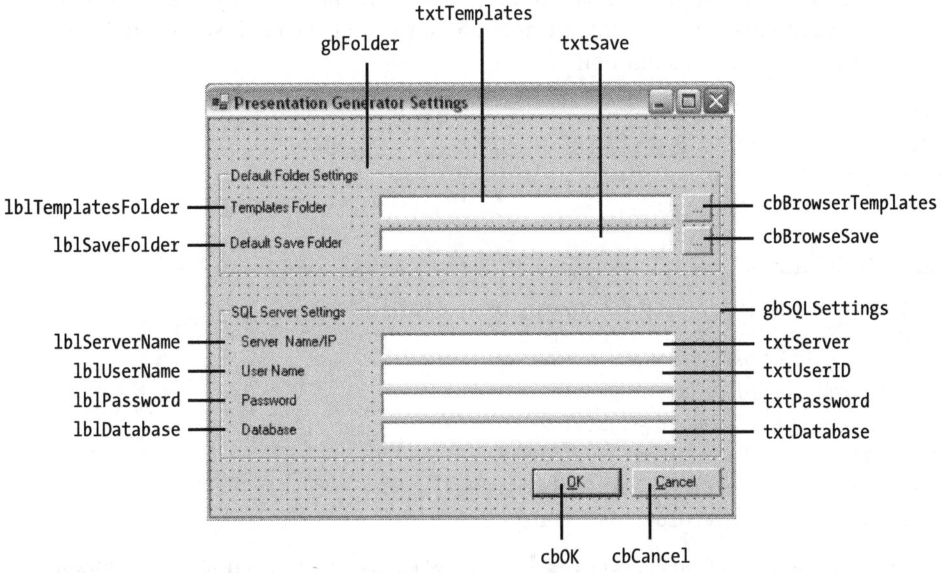

Figure 2-11. *The Presentation Generator* Settings *form at design time*

The code behind this form will make more sense if we create the UserSettings class first. The UserSettings class performs the majority of the work for the Settings form (which really just displays the information provided by UserSettings).

■Tip The need for application accessibility continues to increase. In fact, at times it is even required by some organizations (such as the United States Federal Government). An effective method for providing at least a base level of accessibility is to provide ToolTips for every control on the form. Not only will ToolTips provide for users with special needs, they also help to inform novice-level users of each control's purpose.

Creating the UserSettings Class

We need to somehow store the user settings in memory for use at run time, and we need a mechanism for saving and retrieving the settings to and from the file system. To accomplish all of these tasks, we will build a class called UserSettings.

The UserSettings class has the sole purpose of handling the values specified in the Settings form. It does the following:

- Exposes public variables that contain each user setting value

- Handles the details of saving the user settings to the file system

- Handles the details of retrieving the user settings from the file system

Add a new class to the project and name it **UserSettings.vb**.

Imports Directives

The UserSettings class will save the user settings as an XML file on the file system as well as rely on the application's environment information, so you will need to insert the following lines of code above the class definition:

```
Imports System.XML
Imports System.Environment
Imports System.IO
```

Variable Declarations

The UserSettings class defines the following private variables:

```
Private Shared m_strDatabaseName As String
Private Shared m_strUserName As String
Private Shared m_strPassword As String
Private Shared m_strServerName As String
Private Shared m_strTemplatesFolder As String
Private Shared m_strSaveFolder As String
```

Notice that each variable is declared using the Shared keyword. We use this keyword here because, as with the appPPT class, we want the values to remain the same across all instances of the UserSettings class.

In order to read and write these variables, we need a corresponding Property procedure for each one. Each Property procedure must be declared as Public and Shared.

The DatabaseName Property

The DatabaseName property is a read/write property representing the name of the Bravo Corp database containing the published presentations:

```
Public Shared Property DatabaseName() As String
  Get
    Return m_strDatabaseName
  End Get
  Set(ByVal Value As String)
    m_strDatabaseName = Value
  End Set
End Property
```

The UserName Property

The UserName property is a read/write property representing the Windows or SQL Server username needed to access the Bravo Corp database:

```
Public Shared Property UserName() As String
  Get
    Return m_strUserName
```

```
End Get
  Set(ByVal Value As String)
    m_strUserName = Value
  End Set
End Property
```

The Password Property

The Password property is a read/write property representing the password assigned to the username for accessing the Bravo Corp database:

```
Public Shared Property Password() As String
  Get
    Return m_strPassword
  End Get
  Set(ByVal Value As String)
    m_strPassword = Value
  End Set
End Property
```

The ServerName Property

The ServerName property is a read/write property representing the Windows or SQL Server username needed to access the Bravo Corp database:

```
Public Shared Property ServerName() As String
  Get
    Return m_strServerName
  End Get
  Set(ByVal Value As String)
    m_strServerName = Value
  End Set
End Property
```

The TemplatesFolder Property

The TemplatesFolder property is a read/write property representing the user's file system folder for storing Bravo Corp presentation templates:

```
Public Shared Property TemplatesFolder() As String
  Get
    Return m_strTemplatesFolder
  End Get
  Set(ByVal Value As String)
    m_strTemplatesFolder = Value
  End Set
End Property
```

The SaveFolder Property

The SaveFolder property is a read/write property representing the user's file system folder for storing all presentations created by the user:

```
Public Shared Property SaveFolder() As String
  Get
    Return m_strSaveFolder
  End Get
  Set(ByVal Value As String)
    m_strSaveFolder = Value
  End Set
End Property
```

For each private class variable, you now have a read/write Property procedure that is available throughout the add-in without requiring an instance of the class.

Custom Methods

The UserSettings class contains two functions that handle its file system input/output needs: SaveSettings and LoadSettings. These functions must know where the settings file is located in order to do their job. We will handle this with a constant. Insert the following line of code in the variable declarations section of the class:

```
Private Const SETTINGS_XML_FILE_NAME As String = "\pptgen.xml"
```

The SaveSettings function is used to save the values of the class variables to an XML file. This is done to save the application's state, and it is important because a user will quickly become annoyed with the application if it does not remember their settings and requires the user to set them every time it is run.

To create the SaveSettings function, insert the following lines of code:

```
Public Shared Function SaveSettings() As Boolean
  Try
    Dim strPath As String
    strPath = strPath.Concat(m_strSettingsPath, SETTINGS_XML_FILE_NAME)
    'set the settings path variable just in case
    m_strSettingsPath = strPath
    Dim xtwSettings As New XmlTextWriter(strPath.ToString, _
      System.Text.Encoding.UTF8)
      'Set XML Writer Settings
    With xtwSettings
      .Formatting = Formatting.Indented
      .Indentation = 2
      .QuoteChar = """"

      'This creates the ?XML line and identifies
      'the doc as an XML document
```

```
        .WriteStartDocument(True)
        .WriteComment("User Settings from the Bravo Powerpoint Add-In")

        'Begin writing each setting to the XML file as
        'Attributes of a single XML Element
        .WriteStartElement("BravoPowerPointUserSettings")
        .WriteAttributeString("UserName", UserSettings.UserName)
        .WriteAttributeString("Password", UserSettings.Password)
        .WriteAttributeString("SaveFolder", UserSettings.SaveFolder)
        .WriteAttributeString("TemplatesFolder", UserSettings.TemplatesFolder)
        .WriteAttributeString("ServerName", UserSettings.ServerName)
        .WriteAttributeString("DatabaseName", UserSettings.DatabaseName)
        .WriteEndElement()

        .WriteEndDocument()
        .Close()
    End With

    Return True
  Catch ex As Exception
    Return False
  End Try
End Function
```

In the preceding code, SaveSettings is defined as a shared, public function, and it uses an XmlTextWriter to output the values of the UserSettings class to an XML file. The method then creates the XmlTextWriter (variable xtwSettings) by passing the SETTINGS_XML_FILE_NAME constant to its constructor as the filename. The second argument of the constructor specifies an encoding value for the file. The UTF8 value will result in a file encoded with the UTF-8 Unicode characters.

The XmlTextWriter indents each level of child elements by two spaces. Each attribute value will be enclosed in double quotes. The XML file is created through the following workflow:

1. The XML document is written one line at a time.

2. The file is specified as an XML document by using the WriteStartDocument method to insert the XML declaration line. In addition, the WriteComment method is used to add a description to the file.

3. The file's only element is inserted using the WriteElement method.

4. Each attribute is written to the document using the passed element name and value.

5. Once all the values are inserted in the document, the function closes the element tag, the XML document, and the XmlTextWriter.

If no errors occurred, the function returns True; otherwise the error handler will catch any exceptions and return a False Boolean value. When the SaveSettings function successfully creates the PPTGEN.xml document, it should look like what is shown in Figure 2-12.

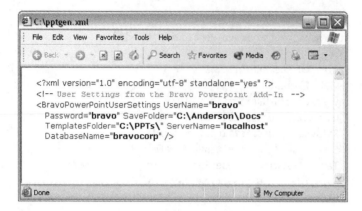

Figure 2-12. *The* PPTGEN.xml *document*

The LoadSettings function is essentially the startup routine of the UserSettings class, similar in nature to the Setup function of the appPPT class. Insert the following code into the UserSettings class:

```
Public Shared Function LoadSettings(ByVal FilePath As String) As Boolean
  Try
  'if the settings file exists, we know we are okay
    m_strSettingsPath = FilePath
    'create full path to settings file
    Dim strPath As String
    strPath = strPath.Concat(FilePath, SETTINGS_XML_FILE_NAME)
    'Test for the existence of the settings file
    Dim fi As New FileInfo(strPath)
    If fi.Exists Then
      'open the settings file for reading into memory
      Dim xtrSettings As New XmlTextReader(strPath.ToString)
      'move through the XML content and fill variables
      With xtrSettings
        .MoveToContent()
        m_strTemplatesFolder = .GetAttribute("TemplatesFolder")
        m_strSaveFolder = .GetAttribute("SaveFolder")
        m_strDatabaseName = .GetAttribute("DatabaseName")
        m_strServerName = .GetAttribute("ServerName")
        m_strUserName = .GetAttribute("UserName")
        m_strPassword = .GetAttribute("Password")

        .Close()
        Return True
      End With
    Else
```

```
      'Settings do not exist so alert the user...
      MsgBox("The Presentation Generator settings file does not exist." & _
      vbCrLf & vbCrLf & _
      "Please set your settings now.", MsgBoxStyle.Information, _
      "Settings Not Found")
      m_strSettingsPath = FilePath
    End If
  Catch ex As Exception
    Return False
  End Try
End Function
```

The LoadSettings function attempts to open the PPTGEN.xml file on the user's file system as follows:

1. A check is performed to ensure the settings file exists. If it does, the code continues to step 2. If the settings file is not found in the expected location, the user receives an alert and then is shown the Settings form so they can specify their settings.

2. The XMLTextReader uses the constant value SETTINGS_XML_FILE_NAME to locate the XML file on the system.

3. After assigning the contents of the file to the xtrSettings variable, the contents of the file are loaded into memory by calling the MoveToContent method.

4. The GetAttribute method is then called to retrieve the values for each of the six user settings, and it stores them in the private, class-level variables.

5. The file is then closed and the function returns a value of True.

6. If an error occurs while trying to open the XML file or while attempting to retrieve an attribute's value, the exception handler kicks in and the function will return a value of False.

Completing the Settings Form

With the UserSettings class complete, we are now ready to build the Settings form. We need to add code to the Settings form to call the UserSettings class's methods. In addition, we need to add code that will allow the user to select file system folders.

Imports Directives

This form will need the following Imports statements in its Directives section:

```
Imports System.Data.SqlClient
Imports System.IO
Imports System.Drawing
```

The Settings_Load Event

Before the Settings form is displayed to the user, the user settings need to be retrieved from the file system and inserted into their related TextBox controls. The form's Load event is the best place for this to occur:

```
Private Sub Settings_Load(ByVal sender As System.Object, _
  ByVal e As System.EventArgs) Handles MyBase.Load
  LoadSettings()
End Sub
```

The LoadSettings Method

Utilizing the UserSettings class, the values for each TextBox control on the form are easily filled by matching them with their related UserSettings property as follows:

```
Private Function LoadSettings()
  Try
    txtTemplates.Text = UserSettings.TemplatesFolder
    txtSave.Text = UserSettings.SaveFolder
    txtDatabase.Text = UserSettings.DatabaseName
    txtServer.Text = UserSettings.ServerName
    txtUserID.Text = UserSettings.UserName
    txtPassword.Text = UserSettings.Password
  Catch ex As Exception
    MsgBox(ex.GetBaseException)
  End Try
End Function
```

The BrowseForFolder Method

One of the two main purposes of the Settings form is to allow the user to specify where the presentation templates and completed presentations should be stored. This task is handled by the BrowseForFolder method:

```
Private Function BrowseForFolder(ByVal FolderType As String) As String
  Dim fdPath As New Windows.Forms.FolderBrowserDialog
  Dim strTitle As String
  Dim strSelectedPath As String

  Try
    strTitle = "Select the "
    strTitle = strTitle.Concat(strTitle, FolderType.ToUpper)
    strTitle = strTitle.Concat(strTitle, " for your Bravo Presentations")

    With fdPath
      .Description = strTitle
      .ShowNewFolderButton = True
```

```
  If .ShowDialog() = DialogResult.OK Then
    strSelectedPath = .SelectedPath
      strSelectedPath = strSelectedPath.Concat(strSelectedPath, "\")
    Return strSelectedPath.ToString
  Else
    Return ""
  End If

End With

Catch ex As Exception

Finally
  fdPath = Nothing
  strSelectedPath = Nothing

End Try

End Function
```

The BrowseForFolder function handles the task of displaying a FolderBrowserDialog object by completing the following steps:

1. The function accepts a string parameter (FolderType) which is used to build the title for the FolderBrowserDialog.

2. Before displaying the FolderBrowserDialog window, the ShowNewFolderButton property is set to True. This allows the user to create new file system folders using a toolbar button displayed in the FolderBrowserDialog window.

3. The form is displayed and code determines whether the user clicked the OK button. If the OK button was clicked, the path of the selected folder is appended with the backslash character, and the modified path value is returned as the value of the function. If the form is closed without clicking the OK button, an empty string is returned.

The cbBrowseTemplates_Click and cbBrowseSave_Click Events

To call BrowseForFolders, insert this code into the Click events of the cbBrowseTemplates and cbBrowseSave buttons:

```
Private Sub cbBrowseTemplates_Click(ByVal sender As System.Object, _
  ByVal e As System.EventArgs) Handles cbBrowseTemplates.Click
  txtTemplates.Text = BrowseForFolder("Templates Folder")
End Sub

Private Sub cbBrowseSave_Click(ByVal sender As System.Object, _
  ByVal e As System.EventArgs) Handles cbBrowseSave.Click
  txtSave.Text = BrowseForFolder("Save Folder")
End Sub
```

When the user clicks one of the browse buttons, the BrowseForFolder function is called and, depending on which button was clicked, the txtTemplates or txtSave text box is updated with the returned value.

The SaveSettings Method

When the form closes, one of two actions takes place. If the OK button is clicked, the User-Settings class properties are updated to reflect the values of the Settings form. In addition, the UserSettings.SaveSettings method is called in order to write the settings values to the file system. This will make the updated settings available to any presentation created while the add-in is running. If the Cancel button is clicked, the form is closed and nothing happens. Any changes made while the Settings form was open are disregarded.

The SaveSettings function is a mirror image of the LoadSettings function. The values of the TextBox controls on the Settings form are used to update their related properties in the UserSettings class as follows:

```
Private Function SaveSettings()
  Try
    UserSettings.TemplatesFolder = txtTemplates.Text
    UserSettings.SaveFolder = txtSave.Text
    UserSettings.DatabaseName = txtDatabase.Text
    UserSettings.ServerName = txtServer.Text
    UserSettings.UserName = txtUserID.Text
    UserSettings.Password = txtPassword.Text
    UserSettings.SaveSettings(UserSettings.SettingsPath())
  Catch ex As Exception
    MsgBox(ex.GetBaseException)
  End Try
End Function
```

The cbOK_Click and cbCancel_Click Events

Insert the following code into the cbOK button's Click event to call the SaveSettings function:

```
Private Sub cbOK_Click(ByVal sender As System.Object, _
  ByVal e As System.EventArgs) Handles cbOK.Click
  Try
    SaveSettings()
  Catch ex As Exception
    MsgBox(Err.Description, MsgBoxStyle.Exclamation, "Critical Error")
  Finally
    Me.Close()
  End Try
End Sub
```

In the cbCancel button's Click event, insert the following code to close the form:

```
Private Sub cbCancel_Click(ByVal sender As System.Object, _
  ByVal e As System.EventArgs) Handles cbCancel.Click
```

```
  Me.Close()
End Sub
```

Creating the GetUpdates Form

Bravo Corp publishes new presentation templates to a SQL Server database as soon as they are approved for publication. In addition, existing presentation templates are reviewed and updated on a regular basis to ensure that they remain accurate and relevant.

The GetUpdates form (see Figure 2-13) provides the capability to download the published templates from the SQL Server specified in the Settings form. For the purposes of this book, the form has been simplified to download all the templates, no matter what. There is no logic to determine which files in the database already exist on the file system. Nor is there any logic to determine whether a file existing in the user's file system has an update on the server to be downloaded. This is okay for our scope, as we are not dealing with a significant amount of data. For a production scenario, you should consider adding these features.

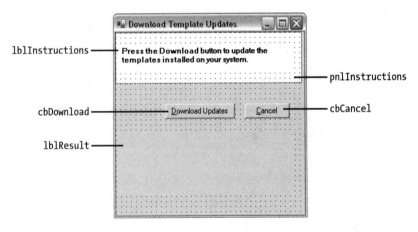

Figure 2-13. *The* GetUpdates *form in design mode*

The GetUpdates form downloads the presentations from the SQL Server by establishing a connection to the database, opening a recordset of the tblPresentations table, and saving the presentation binaries to the user's file system.

Building the GetUpdates Form

To build the GetUpdates form, add a new form to the project and name it **GetUpdates.vb**. Add the following controls from the toolbox:

- 1 Panel

- 2 Buttons

- 2 Labels

Lay out each of the controls as shown in Figure 2-13. Set the width and height of the form to 300 pixels. Set the Text property to **Download Template Updates** and change the form's StartPosition to **CenterScreen**.

The Panel is purely aesthetic and provides the backdrop for a Label containing the form's instructions, while the Download Updates (cbDownload) and Cancel (cbCancel) Buttons initiate the code within the form. The other Label displays the results created by the update function.

Coding the GetUpdates Form

Open the code window of the GetUpdates form by selecting View ➤ Code from the menu, and add the code in the following sections.

Imports Directives

Add the following lines of code to import the following assemblies into the GetUpdates form:

```
Imports System.Data.SqlClient
Imports System.IO
Imports System.Drawing
```

The cbCancel_Click Method

Insert this function into the form's module to cancel the process when the Cancel button is clicked:

```
Private Sub cbCancel_Click(ByVal sender As System.Object, _
  ByVal e As System.EventArgs) Handles cbCancel.Click

  Me.Close()
End Sub
```

The DownloadTemplates Method

The DownloadTemplates function is the exciting part of the form. Insert the following block of code into the form's module:

```
Private Function DownloadTemplates() As Boolean
  Dim cnnPPT As New SqlConnection
  Dim daPPT As New SqlDataAdapter("Select * From tblPresentations", _
    cnnPPT)
  Dim dsPPTs As New DataSet
  Dim dtPPTs As DataTable
  Dim drPPTRecord As DataRo
  Dim btPPTBinary() As Byte
  Dim iPPTSize As Long
  Dim strCnn As String
  Try
    'Create connection string
    strCnn = "Server=" & UserSettings.ServerName
    strCnn = strCnn.Concat(strCnn, ";uid=" & UserSettings.UserName)
```

```
     strCnn = strCnn.Concat(strCnn, ";pwd=" & UserSettings.Password)
     strCnn = strCnn.Concat(strCnn, ";database=" & _
       UserSettings.DatabaseName)

     cnnPPT.ConnectionString = strCnn.ToString
     cnnPPT.Open()
     'Fill the dataset with presentation templates
     daPPT.Fill(dsPPTs, "tblPresentations")

     'Loop through all records and save to the default Save location
     For Each drPPTRecord In dsPPTs.Tables("tblPresentations").Rows
       btPPTBinary = drPPTRecord("PresentationBinary")

       Dim strPath As String = UserSettings.TemplatesFolder
       strPath = strPath.Concat(strPath, _
       drPPTRecord("PresentationName").ToString)

       Dim fsFile As New FileStream(strPath, FileMode.Create)
       iPPTSize = UBound(btPPTBinary)
       fsFile.Write(btPPTBinary, 0, iPPTSize)
       fsFile.Close()
       fsFile = Nothing
     Next drPPTRecord

     Return True


   Catch ex As Exception
     Return False
   Finally

     cnnPPT.Close()

     drPPTRecord = Nothing
     dsPPTs = Nothing
     dtPPTs = Nothing
     daPPT = Nothing
     cnnPPT = Nothing
   End Try
End Function
```

This function connects to the database's template table (tblPresentations) and downloads all available templates to the user's file system. The function follows this workflow:

1. The function builds a data-connection string for connecting with the SQL Server database named in the UserSettings class.

2. A Dataset object is created and filled with all the records in the tblPresentations table.

3. The Dataset containing the bits we need is saved to the hard drive with a For...Each statement that loops through each record in the tblPresentations table. Each presentation binary is written to the user's templates folder. The binary is stored in a Byte variable type in order to process this information later in the function.

4. A string variable is built containing the user's specified templates file path and the template's filename.

5. Using the path, a FileStream object is opened in Create file mode. This file mode creates a new file using the specified path. If the file already exists, it will be overwritten automatically. Because we are downloading the most current presentation template binaries, we want any existing templates with the same filenames to be overwritten.

6. The code determines the size of the current record's PresentationBinary field. The size value is passed to a FileStream object that writes the binary to the file system and closes the stream.

7. If no errors occur, the function returns a value of True. If an error does occur along the way, the exception handler captures the error and the function will return a value of False.

8. Finally, all the variables are closed and are set to Nothing.

The GetUpdates_Load Method

Before the GetUpdates form displays to the user, it needs to be resized in order to hide the lblResult control (since the control should only be visible after attempting the template download process). The form's Load event is the best place to take care of this task.

```
Private Sub GetUpdates_Load(ByVal sender As Object, _
  ByVal e As System.EventArgs) Handles MyBase.Load

  Me.Size = New Size(300, 175)
End Sub
```

The cbDownload_Click Event

The last bit of code needed for the form will call the DownloadTemplates function and display the results of the task to the user. Insert the following code block:

```
Private Sub cbDownload_Click(ByVal sender As System.Object, _
  ByVal e As System.EventArgs) Handles cbDownload.Click

  If DownloadTemplates() Then
    lblResult.Text = "Templates downloaded to the folder path " & _
      UserSettings.TemplatesFolder & "."
    lblResult.Visible = True
  Else
    lblResult.Text = "An error occurred attempting to update your templates."
```

```
    lblResult.Visible = True
  End If

  Me.Size = New Size(300, 300)
End Sub
```

The first If statement wraps the DownloadTemplates function call in order to properly branch processing based on the returned Boolean value. Whatever the results (success or failure) lblResult's Text property is updated, the label is displayed, and the form is heightened to display the label (see Figure 2-14).

Figure 2-14. *The* GetUpdates *form displaying the update results*

Creating the ListPresentations Form

When users want to create a new presentation, they select the desired template from a listing of available presentation templates on their hard drive. For the purposes of our scenario, the user is limited to selecting a single presentation from the ListPresentations form. After the user selects a presentation and clicks the OK button, the presentation is loaded into Power-Point and the add-in calls the file's Presentation Customization Wizard (more on this later in the "Tying the Pieces Together" section at the end of this chapter).

Building the ListPresentations Form

Add a new form to the project and name it **ListPresentations.vb**. Change the following settings from their default values:

- Text = "Available PowerPoint Templates"

- Size.Width = 300

- Size.Height = 300

- StartPosition = "CenterScreen"

Add the following controls from the toolbox, laying them out as shown in Figure 2-15:

- 1 ListBox control

- 2 Button controls

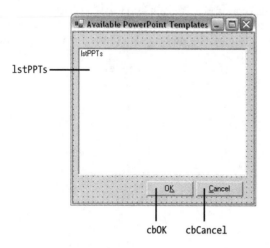

Figure 2-15. *Design view of the* ListPresentations *form*

Coding the ListPresentations Form

The ListPresentations form needs the following lines in its Imports Directive section:

```
Imports MSC = Microsoft.Office.Core
Imports Microsoft.Office.Interop.PowerPoint
Imports System.IO
```

The cbOK Button

The cbOK button builds the file path of the selected template and opens the file by calling the OpenPPTFile function. The form is then closed if the file was opened successfully. If any problems arise, such as the file failing to open, an error message is displayed. The cbOK button's Click event looks like this:

```
Private Sub cbOK_Click(ByVal sender As System.Object, _
  ByVal e As System.EventArgs) Handles cbOK.Click
  'Use the Templates folder specified in the user settings
  Dim strSelectedPath As String = UserSettings.TemplatesFolder

  Try
    strSelectedPath = strSelectedPath.Concat(strSelectedPath, _
      lstPPTs.SelectedItem)
    'Open the file at the specified path
```

```
    OpenPPTFile(strSelectedPath)
    Me.Close()
  Catch ex As Exception
    MsgBox(Err.GetException)
  Finally

  End Try
End Sub
```

The OpenPPTFile Function

The OpenPPTFile function opens the specified presentation file by calling PowerPoint's App.Presentations.Open method. This method is accessible using the PowerPoint object available through the appPPT shared class. The code for the OpenPPTFile function is as follows:

```
Private Function OpenPPTFile(ByVal strFilePath As String) as Boolean
  Try
    'open the file using PowerPoint's Open method
    AppPPT.App.Presentations.Open(strFilePath.ToString, MsoTriState.msoFalse, _
      MsoTriState.msoTrue)

  Catch ex As Exception
    Return False
  End Try
End Function
```

Initializing the Form

When the form is loaded, the lstPPTs ListBox control is filled with the names of all available templates. Using a DirectoryInfo object, the function retrieves the filenames of all .pot files from the UserSettings.TemplatesFolder and adds them to lstPPTs.

```
Private Sub listPresentations_Load(ByVal sender As System.Object, _
  ByVal e As System.EventArgs) Handles MyBase.Load
  'Need a DirectoryInfo object for accessing folder properties
  Dim diFolder As New DirectoryInfo(UserSettings.TemplatesFolder)
  Dim fiPPT As FileInfo
  Try
    'move through each template in the folder and
    'load their names into the ListBox
    For Each fiPPT In diFolder.GetFiles("*.pot")
      lstPPTs.Items.Add(fiPPT.Name)
    Next

  Catch ex As Exception
    MsgBox(Err.GetException)
  End Try
End Sub
```

The cbCancel Button

Clicking the cbCancel button will cancel the entire process and close the form without any action taking place:

```
Private Sub cbCancel_Click(ByVal sender As System.Object, _
  ByVal e As System.EventArgs) Handles cbCancel.Click

  Me.Close()
End Sub
```

Creating the Connect Class

The Connect class, through the implementation of the IDTExtensibility2 interface, is the gateway between our add-in and the host application (PowerPoint in this case). In addition to bridging the connection between our add-in and PowerPoint, the Connect class also acts as the messenger for objects within the add-in waiting to respond to events.

The Connect class is the starting point for the add-in, but I have saved it for the last part of our add-in discussion. It makes more sense to discuss it here because the objects and functions called within the Connect class now exist, and the context of the code is easier to understand.

The Declarations Section

The Extensibility Project Wizard automatically declared two objects that are available within the entire class. These objects will contain references to the host application and to the add-in itself. You do not need to add these lines since they already exist; they are listed here for completeness.

```
Dim applicationObject as Object
Dim addInInstance As Object
```

The Presentation Generator creates a custom Office CommandBar to initiate each of the four processes defined by the add-in. In addition, we need to capture the Click event of each command button. Declare four public command bar button variables utilizing the WithEvents keyword. In addition, create one public pop-up style command bar. Again, declare the variable utilizing the WithEvents keyword in order to capture its events.

```
Dim cbbBravoMenu As CommandBarPopup
Dim WithEvents cbbNewPPTFromTemplate As CommandBarButton
Dim WithEvents cbbSaveBravoPPT As CommandBarButton
Dim WithEvents cbbGetUpdates As CommandBarButton
Dim WithEvents cbbSettings As CommandBarButton
```

The IDTExtensibility2 Events

The IDTExtensibility2 interface requires the implementation of the following five events. There is no requirement that all five events contain code, just that all five exist. The Presentation Generator add-in responds to four of the five interface events.

OnConnection Event

The OnConnection event is the first event of the add-in that executes. It is called by the host application upon loading the add-in, so it is the best location for any code that sets up the add-in for use by the user. In the OnConnection event insert the following code:

```
Public Sub OnConnection(ByVal application As Object, ByVal connectMode As _
  Extensibility.ext_ConnectMode, ByVal addInInst As Object, ByRef custom As _
  System.Array) Implements Extensibility.IDTExtensibility2.OnConnection

  appPowerPoint = application
  AppPPT.Setup(application)
  UserSettings.LoadSettings(System.Windows.Forms.Application.StartupPath)
  addInInstance = addInInst
End Sub
```

The beginning of this event starts by setting the class-level reference to the host application (appPowerPoint). The next two lines initialize the appPPT and UserSettings classes by calling their setup functions. The last line creates a class-level variable of our add-in.

OnStartupComplete Event

Because this add-in is set to load at startup, the OnStartupComplete event will always fire. This makes this event a good location for the code that sets up the add-in's custom menu. We need to create a new menu along with four command buttons in order to operate the add-in. Insert the following lines of code into the OnStartupComplete event.

```
Public Sub OnStartupComplete(ByRef custom As System.Array) Implements _
  Extensibility.IDTExtensibility2.OnStartupComplete

  Dim cbCommandBars As CommandBars
  Dim cbMenuBar As CommandBar
  Dim iToolsMenuPosition As Integer

  cbCommandBars = appPowerPoint.CommandBars
  cbMenuBar = cbCommandBars.Item("Menu Bar")

'Find the position of the Tools menu; we want the Bravo Tools to be next to it.
  iToolsMenuPosition = cbCommandBars.Item("Menu Bar").Controls("Tools").Index
  iToolsMenuPosition = iToolsMenuPosition + 1
  cbbBravoMenu = cbMenuBar.Controls.Add(Type:=MsoControlType.msoControlPopup, _
    before:=iToolsMenuPosition)

  With cbbBravoMenu
    .Caption = "&Bravo Tools"

    '=========Create New PPT Button============
    cbbNewPPTFromTemplate = .Controls.Add(1)
    With cbbNewPPTFromTemplate
```

```
        .Caption = "Ne&w PPT..."
        .Style = MsoButtonStyle.msoButtonCaption
        .Tag = "Generate New Presentation from Template"
        .OnAction = "!<SalesPresentationGenerator.Connect>"
        .Visible = True
    End With


    '=========Create cbbSaveBravoPPT Button============
    cbbSaveBravoPPT = .Controls.Add(1)
    With cbbSaveBravoPPT
      .Caption = "&Save Presentation..."
      .Style = MsoButtonStyle.msoButtonCaption
      .Tag = "Save Bravo Presentation to Bravo Folder"
      .OnAction = "!<SalesPresentationGenerator.Connect>"
      .Visible = True
    End With


    '=========Create Update Database Button============
    cbbGetUpdates = .Controls.Add(1)
    With cbbGetUpdates
      .Caption = "&Update Local Templates"
      .Style = MsoButtonStyle.msoButtonCaption
      .Tag = "Get the latest templates from Headquarters."
      .OnAction = "!<SalesPresentationGenerator.Connect>"
      .Visible = True
    End With


    '=========Create Settings Button============
    cbbSettings = .Controls.Add(1)
    With cbbSettings
      .Caption = "Se&ttings..."
      .Style = MsoButtonStyle.msoButtonCaption
      .Tag = "Change Add-In Settings."
      .OnAction = "!<SalesPresentationGenerator.Connect>"
      .Visible = True
    End With

  End With

  cbMenuBar = Nothing
  cbCommandBars = Nothing
End Sub
```

The purpose of the procedure is to set up the add-in's menu structure by adding a new set of buttons to the standard PowerPoint menu:

1. The procedure creates the variables that will be used for creating the Bravo Tools menu and related buttons.

2. Using a reference to the PowerPoint CommandBars object, we navigate to the CommandBar named Menu Bar. The Menu Bar CommandBar is the main menu of any Office application, and it contains the standard menus of File, Edit, View, and so on.

3. The function uses the Menu Bar reference to locate the position of the Tools menu. The Bravo Tools menu is placed immediately to the right of the Tools menu by incrementing the value of iToolsMenuPosition by 1 and assigning this as the index value for the new Bravo Tools menu control. The Bravo Tools menu is created as a pop-up menu type (the same type as for all menu controls on the Menu Bar).

Tip The constant, msoControlPopup, is part of the Microsoft.Office.Core namespace. More specifically, it is part of the Microsoft.Office.Core.msoControlType namespace. These constants are easy enough to call when developing within an Office application because they are an Office-level constant; however, it takes some investigating when coding in Visual Studio. The quickest way to find out how to reference these constants in VB .NET is to search for them with the Object Browser found within the Office application's VB IDE. A quick search for msoControlPopup shows it to be a child of msoControlType.

---

4. The code creates the four CommandBar buttons of the add-in. Each button is created by performing the following steps:

   a. The Add method of the newly created Bravo Tools menu is called (in our case, the tools menu variable is cbbBravoMenu).

   b. The Caption property is set to something useful for the user.

   c. The button's Style property is set to msoButtonCaption so that only a description is displayed.

   d. The Tag property is given a unique string. This is good practice anytime you are creating CommandBar buttons, because the tag provides additional information about the button.

   e. The OnAction property is set to run the add-in's Connect class. This property connects the button to the programmatic identifier of the add-in. In effect, this causes the button to look to the add-in's Connect class for the code the button executes.

   f. The Visible property is set to True (just to be sure).

   g. The variables are cleaned up.

OnBeginShutdown Event

The OnBeginShutdown event executes when the host application initiates its shutdown process. Using this event, we want to return PowerPoint to its original state. Insert the following block of code:

```
Public Sub OnBeginShutdown(ByRef custom As System.Array) _
  Implements Extensibility.IDTExtensibility2.OnBeginShutdown

  cbbNewPPTFromTemplate.Delete()
  cbbGetUpdates.Delete()
  cbbSettings.Delete()
  cbbBravoMenu.Delete()
  AppPPT.ShutDown()

  cbbGetUpdates = Nothing
  cbbSettings = Nothing
  cbbNewPPTFromTemplate = Nothing
End Sub
```

As you can see, nothing out of the ordinary is taking place here. The first section of the code deletes each CommandBar Button and then the CommandBar Menu. In addition, we call the ShutDown method of the appPPT shared class to release the reference we have held to Power-Point. The second section of the procedure handles the usual variable cleanup.

OnDisconnection Event

The OnDisconnection event executes when the add-in is unloaded. An add-in is always unloaded when the host application is closed and OnDisconnection is the last event the add-in has a chance to respond to. All we want to do is release our reference to PowerPoint. Insert the following line into the OnDisconnection event:

```
Public Sub OnDisconnection(ByVal RemoveMode As Extensibility.ext_DisconnectMode, _
  ByRef custom As System.Array) _
  Implements Extensibility.IDTExtensibility2.OnDisconnection

  appPowerPoint = Nothing
End Sub
```

This code releases the class's reference to PowerPoint and makes for a clean shutdown.

OnAddInsUpdate Event

Since the Presentation Generator add-in does not need to respond to changes in the host application's add-ins collection, we will leave this event blank.

The Custom Methods

To complete the add-in's interface with PowerPoint, you need to add code to each command bar Button's Click event. We are able to respond to each button's events because we declared each one using the WithEvents keyword.

cbbNewPPTFromTemplate_Click

The ListPresentations form is opened by the cbbNewPPTFromTemplate command bar Button's Click event as follows:

```
Private Sub cbbNewPPTFromTemplate_Click(ByVal Ctrl As _
  Microsoft.Office.Core.CommandBarButton, ByRef CancelDefault As Boolean) _
  Handles cbbNewPPTFromTemplate.Click

  Dim frmList As New ListPresentations
  frmList.Show()
End Sub
```

cbbGetUpdates_Click

The cbbGetUpdates CommandBar Button's Click event opens the GetUpdates form as follows:

```
Private Sub cbbGetUpdates_Click(ByVal Ctrl As _
  Microsoft.Office.Core.CommandBarButton, ByRef CancelDefault As Boolean) _
  Handles cbbGetUpdates.Click

  Dim frmDBF As New GetUpdates
  frmDBF.Show()
End Sub
```

cbbSettings_Click

The cbbSettings command-bar button's Click event opens the Settings form as follows:

```
Private Sub cbbSettings_Click(ByVal Ctrl As _
  Microsoft.Office.Core.CommandBarButton, ByRef CancelDefault As Boolean) _
  Handles cbbSettings.Click

  Dim frmSettings As New Settings
  frmSettings.Show()
End Sub
```

Each of the two Click events simply opens a form by declaring a variable of the form class it will open and calls the Show method of the form variable to display the form.

cbbSaveBravoPPT_Click

The cbbSaveBravoPPT command-bar button is a bit more complex, but still easy enough. Insert the following block of code:

```
Private Sub cbbSaveBravoPPT_Click(ByVal Ctrl As _
  Microsoft.Office.Core.CommandBarButton, ByRef CancelDefault As Boolean) _
  Handles cbbSaveBravoPPT.Click
```

```
Dim sfdFile As New SaveFileDialog
With sfdFile
  .Title = "Save Bravo Presentation"
  'Change the FileDialog's initial folder to the one
  'specified in the UserSettings
  .InitialDirectory = UserSettings.SaveFolder
  .Filter = "PowerPoint files (*.ppt)|*.ppt|All files (*.*)|*.*"
  'Set .ppt as the default type (the first filter)
  .FilterIndex = 1
  'notify user if the file exists
  .OverwritePrompt = True
  'Restore the initial directory settings back to the user's default.
  .RestoreDirectory = True
  If .ShowDialog() = DialogResult.OK Then
    Dim bExists As Boolean = .CheckFileExists()
    If Not bExists Then
      'Use PowerPoint's save function to save file to location just specified
      AppPPT.App.ActivePresentation.SaveAs(.FileName, _
          PowerPoint.PpSaveAsFileType.ppSaveAsPresentation, -2)
    End If
  End If
End With
End Sub
```

In this code a SaveFileDialog variable is declared to allow the user to select a save location for the file. Before displaying the save dialog box to the user, the SaveFileDialog's initial directory is set to the default save location specified in the user settings. In addition, the SaveFileDialog is given a relevant title, is set to alert the user to a potential file overwrite, and is set to restore the default initial directory.

The presentation saves to the user's specified Save folder by calling the PowerPoint application's SaveAs method.

Compiling the Presentation Generator Add-In

The next section discusses how to build a sample presentation template that includes the wizard that guides a user through the presentation creation process.

Before jumping into that section, though, go ahead and compile the Presentation Generator add-in to ensure that it is working properly. Edit the solution's configuration to include the setup project in the build process (see Figure 2-16). After the build completes successfully, you will need to install the add-in by executing the Setup program. Just right-click on the Setup project from within Visual Studio and select Install.

Press F5 to run the add-in and test it. If you see the Bravo Tools menu after PowerPoint loads, everything is working correctly.

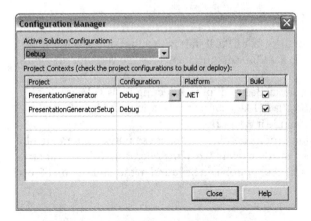

Figure 2-16. *Configuring the Presentation Generator's compilation settings*

Creating the Presentation Customization Wizard

Each presentation template is a self-contained application of its own. Working hand-in-hand with the PowerPoint add-in, the template is, in effect, the second act of our two-part application.

One of the main goals for the Presentation Generator application was to streamline the creation of presentation content and enable the sales staff to generate a presentation for the intended audience. Once a presentation has been selected, it is loaded into PowerPoint and the Presentation Customization Wizard walks the user through the steps to set any necessary options. When the user completes the wizard or clicks the Finish button, the selected presentation is completed and displayed to the user. The intention is that the salesperson will have about 95 percent of their work completed when they're finished with the wizard, and only minor tweaking will be required of them.

These are the components of the Presentation Customization Wizard:

- WizardInfo class: This class contains the properties and methods used to create the presentation. We will look at how to build a class to store user input values (entered via the PPTWizard form) in memory. In addition, this class discusses how to read the titles of each PowerPoint slide to create an "agenda" slide, as well as how to read the contents of an XML file into memory.

- Main module: This module contains the public procedure used to call the wizard. In creating this module, we will see more about how a VBA method can be called from VB .NET code. The discussion here also explains how to read parameters passed from the calling VB .NET code and use them in VBA.

- PPTWizard form: This is the wizard form used to collect and retrieve custom options for the presentation. We will build a fully functioning wizard form that walks the user through a multi-step process. We will also see how to use the WizardInfo class to store the user-entered values until the process is complete.

Creating the WizardInfo Class

The WizardInfo class is the workhorse of the wizard. We'll start with it, because it will help everything else fall into place. WizardInfo is a VBA class tucked inside a PowerPoint presentation file.

To create the class, open the Office Visual Basic editor by selecting Tools ➤ Macro ➤ Visual Basic Editor (you can also use the Alt+F11 keyboard combination) and insert a new class module into the file's VBA project (name it **WizardInfo**).

The WizardInfo class reads the information contained in the Presentation Generator add-in's XML settings file. Therefore, we need to add a reference to the Microsoft XML v5.0 library. In the Office Visual Basic editor, the References option can be found in the Tools menu (Tools ➤ References).

■**Note** The PPTGEN.xml file requires at least version 4.0 of the Microsoft XML library. You may need to download these files if you are using a previous version of Office. The Microsoft XML libraries can be downloaded at http://msdn.microsoft.com/XML/XMLDownloads/default.aspx.

This class encapsulates all the properties and functions needed to create a Bravo Corp custom presentation. It is utilized by the PPTWizard form to fill the wizard form with the user's choices. When the wizard is completed, this class performs all the steps necessary for completing the presentation and displaying the final result to the user.

The WizardInfo Class's Declaration Section

The WizardInfo class contains the following variable declarations:

```
Private m_strPresenterName As String
Private m_fBravoStaff As Boolean
Private m_strPartnerCompany As String
Private m_strClientName As String
Private m_fIncludeAgenda As Boolean
Private m_strPPTTitle As String
Private m_strTemplatesFolder As String
Private m_strChosenPPTS As New Collection
Private m_iCount As Long
```

The WizardInfo Class's Properties

The WizardInfo class has six read/write properties, two read-only properties, and one write-only property.

PresenterName

The PresenterName property contains the name of the presenter, whether the person is a Bravo Corp staff member or a third party:

```
Public Property Get PresenterName() As String
  PresenterName = m_strPresenterName
End Property

Public Property Let PresenterName(ByVal strValue As String)
  m_strPresenterName = strValue
End Property
```

IsBravoStaff

The IsBravoStaff property indicates whether or not the presenter is a Bravo Corp staff member:

```
Public Property Get IsBravoStaff() As Boolean
  IsBravoStaff = m_fBravoStaff
End Property

Public Property Let IsBravoStaff(ByVal fValue As Boolean)
  m_fBravoStaff = fValue
End Property
```

PartnerCompany

The PartnerCompany property contains the company name of the presenter:

```
Public Property Get PartnerCompany() As String
  PartnerCompany = m_strPartnerCompany
End Property

Public Property Let PartnerCompany(ByVal strValue As String)
  m_strPartnerCompany = strValue
End Property
```

ClientName

The ClientName property contains the name of the client being presented to:

```
Public Property Get ClientName() As String
  ClientName = m_strClientName
End Property

Public Property Let ClientName(ByVal strValue As String)
  m_strClientName = strValue
End Property
```

IncludeAgenda

The IncludeAgenda property indicates whether or not an agenda slide should be inserted at the beginning of the presentation:

```
Public Property Get IncludeAgenda() As Boolean
  IncludeAgenda = m_fIncludeAgenda
End Property

Public Property Let IncludeAgenda(ByVal fValue As Boolean)
  m_fIncludeAgenda = fValue
End Property
```

Title

The Title property contains the title for the presentation:

```
Public Property Get Title() As String
  Title = m_strPPTTitle
End Property

Public Property Let Title(ByVal strValue As String)
  m_strPPTTitle = strValue
End Property
```

NewSelection

The NewSelection property is a write-only property that inserts a new topic selection into the chosen topics collection (m_strChosenPPTS):

```
Public Property Let NewSelection(ByVal strValue As String)
  m_strChosenPPTS.Add strValue, strValue
  m_iCount = m_iCount + 1
End Property
```

GetSelection

GetSelection is a read-only property that returns the name of the specified topic from the chosen topics collection:

```
Public Property Get GetSelection(Index As Long) As String
  GetSelection = m_strChosenPPTS(Index)
End Property
```

TotalSelections

TotalSelections is a read-only property that provides the total number of topics selected:

```
Public Property Get TotalSelections() As Long
  TotalSelections = m_iCount
End Property
```

The WizardInfo Class's Methods

The WizardInfo class contain several methods, each of which are described in the following sections.

Class_Initialize

When initialized, the WizardInfo class sets its internal topic counter equal to 0. In addition, it calls the GetUserSettings function to determine if the user-settings file exists.

```
Private Sub Class_Initialize()
  m_iCount = 0
 'Verify user settings exist
  If Not GetUserSettings Then
    'No settings were found, notify the user
    MsgBox "There is an issue with the User Settings file stored at " & _
      strSettingsPath & vbCrLf & vbCrLf & _
      "Set the user settings file location using Bravo Tools Settings menu.", _
      vbCritical, "Configuration Error"
  End If
End Sub
```

GetUserSettings

The GetUserSettings function opens the user-settings file and retrieves the value for the presentation templates folder. This function is called by the Class_Initialize method:

```
Private Function GetUserSettings() As Boolean
  Dim xmlDoc As New MSXML2.DOMDocument40
  Dim objNodeMap As IXMLDOMNamedNodeMap
 'Attempt to load the document specified by
 'the strSettingsPath variable
  If xmlDoc.Load(strSettingsPath) = True Then
    Set objNodeMap = xmlDoc.documentElement.Attributes

    m_strTemplatesFolder = objNodeMap.getNamedItem("TemplatesFolder").Text

    GetUserSettings = True
  Else
  'If the Load method failed, the document
  'probably does not exist at the specified location
    GetUserSettings = False
  End If
End Function
```

EraseSelections

The EraseSelections function removes all selected topics from the chosen topics collection.

```
Public Function EraseSelections() As Boolean
  Dim i As Long
  'Reset the string containing user selections
  'If the count is >0 we know selections were made
  If m_strChosenPPTS.Count > 0 Then
    'The array is 1-based array
    For i = 1 To m_strChosenPPTS.Count
      m_strChosenPPTS.Remove (1)
    Next i
  End If
End Function
```

CreatePPT

The CreatePPT function creates the presentation.

```
Public Function CreatePPT() As Boolean
  Dim strPath As String
  Dim i As Long
  Dim pptInsert As Presentation
  Dim pptFile As Presentation
  Dim sld As Slide
  'We are assuming the current file is the one needing the template slides
  Set pptFile = Application.ActivePresentation

  strPath = m_strTemplatesFolder
  'Loop through all selections in the array and...\
  '1 - open each presentation
  '2 - copy and paste each slide into the active presentation
  '3 -- close each presenation
  For i = 1 To m_strChosenPPTS.Count
    Set pptInsert = Presentations.Open(strPath & Me.GetSelection(i), _
      msoTrue, msoFalse, msoFalse)

    For Each sld In pptInsert.Slides
      sld.Copy
      pptFile.Slides.Paste
    Next sld

    pptInsert.Close
    Set pptInsert = Nothing
  Next i
  'Create a title slide at the beginning of the presentation
  CreateTitleSlide
```

```
'include an agenda if option selected by the user
If m_fIncludeAgenda Then
  CreateAgendaSlide
End If
End Function
```

As shown previously, the first step in the `CreatePPT` method is to assign variable references to the `ActivePresentation` and to the templates folder:

```
Set pptFile = Application.ActivePresentation
strPath = m_strTemplatesFolder
```

Then the selected presentation topics are retrieved using a `For...Each` loop:

```
For i = 1 To m_strChosenPPTS.Count
  Set pptInsert = Presentations.Open(strPath & Me.GetSelection(i), _
    msoTrue, msoFalse, msoFalse)

  For Each sld In pptInsert.Slides
    sld.Copy
    pptFile.Slides.Paste
  Next sld

  pptInsert.Close
  Set pptInsert = Nothing
Next i
```

The loop starts by opening the presentation that contains the selected topic. Next, another `For...Each` loop retrieves each slide within the topic presentation and copies its slides into the active presentation. By inserting the slides in this manner, all copied slides will retain the slide master design of the active presentation. The topic presentation is then closed and set to Nothing and the loop moves to the next topic.

■**Note** Slide masters are special slides within PowerPoint that contain the design elements for a presentation—elements such as fonts, color schemes, and images. Any elements specified or included in the slide master are automatically copied to a new slide created within the presentation. For more information about slide masters, visit `http://www.microsoft.com/Education/UseSlideMaster.aspx`.

Finally, a title slide is inserted, and if the `m_fIncludeAgenda` flag is set to True, an agenda slide is inserted as well:

```
CreateTitleSlide
If m_fIncludeAgenda Then
  CreateAgendaSlide
End If
```

CreateTitleSlide

The CreateTitleSlide function inserts a PowerPoint title slide at the beginning of the presentation:

```
Private Function CreateTitleSlide()
'Create a Title slide at beginning of the presentation
'using the specified user name
  Dim strSubTitle As String
  strSubTitle = "Presented by "
  strSubTitle = strSubTitle & m_strPresenterName & vbCrLf
  strSubTitle = strSubTitle & "of" & vbCrLf
  If m_fBravoStaff Then
    strSubTitle = strSubTitle & "BravoCorp"
  Else
   'If a different company name is provided, use it instead
    strSubTitle = strSubTitle & m_strPartnerCompany
  End If

  With ActivePresentation
  'Add a Title slide to the front of the ppt
    .Slides.Add 1, ppLayoutTitle
    'Add two TextRange shapes and fill with the specified Title and Subtitle
    .Slides(1).Shapes(1).TextFrame.TextRange = m_strPPTTitle
    .Slides(1).Shapes(2).TextFrame.TextRange = strSubTitle
  End With
End Function
```

As shown in the preceding code, the method begins by building a string to insert into the slide. This string consists of the presenter's name and their company name:

```
Dim strSubTitle As String
strSubTitle = "Presented by "
strSubTitle = strSubTitle & m_strPresenterName & vbCrLf
strSubTitle = strSubTitle & "of" & vbCrLf
If m_fBravoStaff Then
  strSubTitle = strSubTitle & "BravoCorp"
Else
  strSubTitle = strSubTitle & m_strPartnerCompany
End If
```

Then a slide with two TextFrame shapes is inserted at the beginning of the presentation. The presentation's title is inserted into the first, and the presenter's information is inserted into the second:

```
With ActivePresentation
  .Slides.Add 1, ppLayoutTitle
  .Slides(1).Shapes(1).TextFrame.TextRange = m_strPPTTitle
  .Slides(1).Shapes(2).TextFrame.TextRange = strSubTitle
End With
```

CreateAgendaSlide

The CreateAgendaSlide method inserts an agenda slide using the titles of each presentation slide as the content. This method is called by the CreatePPT method:

```
Private Function CreateAgendaSlide()
  'Read each slide title and use to create
  'A Table of Contents slide after the presentation's
  'Title slide
  Dim ppt As Presentation
  Dim sldAgenda As Slide

    Set sldAgenda = ActivePresentation.Slides.Add(2, ppLayoutText)
  With sldAgenda
    .Shapes(1).TextFrame.TextRange = "Today's Agenda for " & m_strClientName
    .Shapes(2).TextFrame.TextRange = GetSlideTitles
  End With
End Function
```

The CreateAgendaSlide method begins by inserting a new slide into the currently active presentation. Next, two TextFrame objects are inserted: the first contains a title for the agenda slide that includes the client's name, and the second calls the GetSlideTitles method to retrieve a bulleted list of all slide titles in the presentation.

GetSlideTitles

The GetSlideTitles method returns a string containing the titles of all slides that contain a title:

```
Private Function GetSlideTitles() As String
'Move through each slide, grab the title, and create a TOC slide
  Dim strSlideTitles As String
  Dim sld As Slide
  Dim iStart As Integer

  strSlideTitles = ""
  'If an agenda slide will be created, start at Slide #3, else start at #2
  If m_fIncludeAgenda Then
    iStart = 3
  Else
    iStart = 2
  End If
  'Go through each slide and grab the title
  'Skip the title and agenda slides (they should exist by now)
  For Each sld In ActivePresentation.Slides
    Select Case sld.SlideIndex
```

```
        Case Is >= iStart
        'We only want slides that have a title
        'Identified by the HasTitle property
          If sld.Shapes.HasTitle Then
            strSlideTitles = strSlideTitles & sld.Shapes.Title.TextFrame.TextRange.Text
            strSlideTitles = strSlideTitles & vbCrLf
          End If
        Case Else

      End Select
    Next sld

  GetSlideTitles = strSlideTitles
End Function
```

As shown in the previous listing, the method begins by determining whether the slide contains an agenda slide:

```
If m_fIncludeAgenda Then
  iStart = 3
Else
  iStart = 2
End If
```

The iStart variable is set to the number of the first slide that contains presentation content.

Next, using a For...Each loop, the method loops through each slide in the presentation. If the index number of the slide is equal to or greater than iStart, it is checked to see if it contains a title shape. If so, the text inside the shape is added to strSlideTitles:

```
For Each sld In ActivePresentation.Slides
  Select Case sld.SlideIndex

    Case Is >= iStart
      If sld.Shapes.HasTitle Then
        strSlideTitles = strSlideTitles & sld.Shapes.Title.TextFrame.TextRange.Text
        strSlideTitles = strSlideTitles & vbCrLf
      End If
    Case Else

  End Select
Next sld
```

Finally, the function returns the value of strSlideTitles:

```
GetSlideTitles = strSlideTitles
```

Creating the PPTWizard Form

The PPTWizard form functions the way you would expect any wizard to function. The user is presented with series of tabbed windows that display different options for creating the presentation. These options can be broken down into the following three categories:

- **Presentation information**: These options allow the user to include additional published presentation templates as part of the completed presentation. The user can also specify a title for the created presentation and designate whether they would like to have an agenda slide included at the beginning of the presentation.

- **Client information**: The only available option here is the name of the client targeted to receive the presentation. This information is used to build the presentation's title slide.

- **Presenter information**: These options allow the user to include information regarding the individual charged with delivering the presentation (name and company name).

Figures 2-17 through 2-19 show the three windows of the wizard to help you understand how the form is built. Each figure illustrates how to name and lay out the controls on the PPTWizard form.

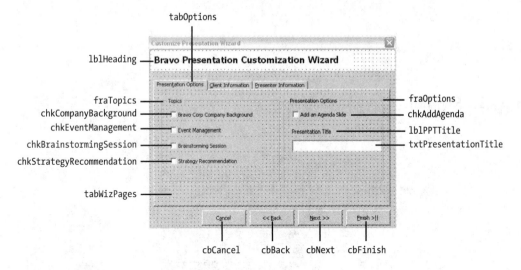

Figure 2-17. *The* PPTWizard *Presentation Options tab*

For the most part, the wizard form is straightforward, but there is one caveat. Each of the CheckBox controls within the Topics frame of Figure 2-17 use the Tag property to store the related presentation template's filename. For example the CheckBox labeled "Bravo Corp Company Background" has a Tag property of "Company Overview.pot". When building your form, you will want to match each Topic CheckBox control with the name of a file you created at the beginning of this chapter. Table 2-3 shows this relation.

Table 2-3. *The Presentation Template Files and Their* PPTWizard *Form Controls*

Template Filename	Form Control Name	Tag Value
Company Overview.pot	chkCompanyBackground	"Company Overview.pot"
Event Management.pot	chkEventManagement	"Event Management.pot"
Brainstorming Session.pot	chkBrainstormingSession	"Brainstorming Session.pot"
Strategy Recommendation.pot	chkStrategyRecommendation	"Strategy Recommendation.pot"

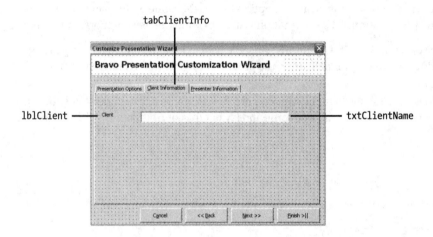

Figure 2-18. *The* PPTWizard *Client Information tab*

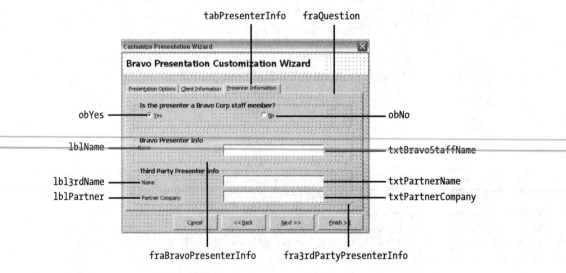

Figure 2-19. *The* PPTWizard *Presenter Information tab*

The PPTWizard Declaration Section

The PPTWizard form has the following variable declaration:

```
Dim wiInfo As WizardInfo
```

This variable represents an instance of the WizardInfo class used within the form to store the selected wizard options.

The PPTWizard Methods

The following sections describe the methods within the PPTWizard form.

UserForm_Initialize

The UserForm_Initialize event occurs after the form is loaded but before it is visible in the active window. This makes it a good place to set up the form.

```
Private Sub UserForm_Initialize()
  Set wiInfo = New WizardInfo
  GetFormCaption
  obYes.Value = 1
'Fill the ppt's author property - to signify it is an authored presentation
  txtBravoStaffName.Text = _
    Application.ActivePresentation.BuiltInDocumentProperties("author")
End Sub
```

Within this event, a new instance of the WizardInfo class is created, and the values for the form's caption and the obYes control are set. The txtBravoStaffName control's value is set to the presentation's Author document property.

cbCancel_Click

The cbCancel_Click event closes the form without any processing.

```
Private Sub cbCancel_Click()
  Unload Me
End Sub
```

cbBack_Click

If the user is not in the first tab, the cbBack_Click event moves the user to the previous tab.

```
Private Sub cbBack_Click()
  If tabWizPages.Value > 0 Then
    tabWizPages.Value = tabWizPages.Value - 1
  End If
End Sub
```

cbNext_Click

If the user is not in the last tab, the cbNext_Click event moves the user to the next tab. If the user is in the last tab, the presentation-building process begins and the form is unloaded.

```
Private Sub cbNext_Click()
  If tabWizPages.Value < tabWizPages.Pages.Count - 1 Then
     tabWizPages.Value = tabWizPages.Value + 1
     GetFormCaption
  Else
     wiInfo.CreatePPT
     Unload Me
  End If
End Sub
```

cbFinish_Click

The cbFinish_Click event begins the presentation-building process and unloads the form.

```
Private Sub cbFinish_Click()
  wiInfo.CreatePPT
  Unload Me
End Sub
```

obYes_Click and ObNo_Click

The obYes_Click and obNo_Click events call the DisplayPresenterInfo function, passing the value of the obYes radio button.

```
Private Sub obNo_Click()
  DisplayPresenterInfo (obYes.Value)
End Sub
```

```
Private Sub obYes_Click()
  DisplayPresenterInfo (obYes.Value)
End Sub
```

Both Click events pass the value of obYes as the argument for DisplayPresenterInfo. If the user specifies they would like to include the presenter's information in the presentation, obYes will be selected, and its value will be True. If the user does not want to include presenter information, obYes will not be selected (obNo will be selected instead), and the value of obYes will be False.

DisplayPresenterInfo

The DisplayPresenterInfo procedure takes the value of the passed variable to determine which controls to display on the Presenter Info tab. If the presenter is not a Bravo Corp employee, additional fields need to be displayed. The `DisplayPresenterInfo` method is called by the `obYes_Click` and `obNo_Click` events.

```
Private Sub DisplayPresenterInfo(fBravoStaff As Boolean)
  If fBravoStaff Then
    fra3rdPartyPresenterInfo.Visible = False
  With fraBravoPresenterInfo
    .Visible = True
    .Top = 66
    .Left = 12
  End With
  Else
   fraBravoPresenterInfo.Visible = False
   With fra3rdPartyPresenterInfo
    .Visible = True
    .Top = 66
    .Left = 12
   End With
  End If
End Sub
```

GetFormCaption

The `GetFormCaption` function sets the form's caption to reflect the current step displayed by the wizard. It is called by the `tabWizPages_Change` event as well as the `UserForm_Initialize` event.

```
Public Function GetFormCaption() As String
  Dim strCaption As String
  strCaption = "Custom Presentation Wizard"

  With PPTWizard
    .Caption = strCaption & " " & "Step " & !tabWizPages.Value + 1
  End With
End Function
```

tabWizPages_Change

The `tabWizPages_Change` event executes each time the user changes tabs within the wizard.

```
Private Sub tabWizPages_Change()
  Dim ctl As Control
  'Update the data from the Options tab
  wiInfo.EraseSelections
    For Each ctl In tabWizPages.Pages("tabOptions").Controls
      If TypeOf ctl Is CheckBox Then
        Select Case Len(ctl.Tag)
```

```
               Case Is > 0
                  If ctl.Value Then wiInfo.NewSelection = ctl.Tag
               Case Else

            End Select

         End If
      Next ctl

      wiInfo.IncludeAgenda = chkAddAgenda.Value
      wiInfo.Title = txtPresentationTitle.Value

   'Data from the Client Info tab
      wiInfo.ClientName = txtClientName.Value

   'Data from the Presenter Info tab
      If obYes.Value Then
         wiInfo.IsBravoStaff = True
         wiInfo.PresenterName = txtBravoStaffName.Text
         wiInfo.PartnerCompany = ""
      Else
         wiInfo.IsBravoStaff = False
         wiInfo.PresenterName = txtPartnerName.Text
         wiInfo.PartnerCompany = txtPartnerCompany.Text
      End If
      DisplayPresenterInfo (obYes.Value)
      GetFormCaption
End Sub
```

The preceding method begins by erasing any previously selected presentation topics, and then it inserts the current topic selections into the wiInfo class:

```
wiInfo.EraseSelections
For Each ctl In tabWizPages.Pages("tabOptions").Controls
   If TypeOf ctl Is CheckBox Then
      Select Case Len(ctl.Tag)

         Case Is > 0
            If ctl.Value Then wiInfo.NewSelection = ctl.Tag
         Case Else

         End Select

   End If
Next ctl
```

The loop checks the type of control to ensure it is a CheckBox before reading the Tag property of the control. If the Tag is not blank, the value is added as a NewSelection of the wiInfo class.

The next step is to update the `wiInfo` class with the values from all fields on the form. These lines of code go through all the controls on all the tabs and update their corresponding values within `wiInfo`:

```
wiInfo.IncludeAgenda = chkAddAgenda.Value
wiInfo.Title = txtPresentationTitle.Value

'Data from the Client Info tab
  wiInfo.ClientName = txtClientName.Value

'Data from the Presenter Info tab

  If obYes.Value Then
    wiInfo.IsBravoStaff = True
    wiInfo.PresenterName = txtBravoStaffName.Text
    wiInfo.PartnerCompany = ""
  Else
    wiInfo.IsBravoStaff = False
    wiInfo.PresenterName = txtPartnerName.Text
    wiInfo.PartnerCompany = txtPartnerCompany.Text
  End If
```

Finally, the correct fields in the Presenter Info tab are made visible, and the form's caption is updated:

```
DisplayPresenterInfo (obYes.Value)
GetFormCaption
```

Creating the Main Module

The `Main` module contains a single, public procedure named `StartPPTWizard`:

```
Public Sub StartPPTWizard()
  Load PPTWizard
  PPTWizard.Show
End Sub
```

This procedure initializes the Presentation Customization Wizard by loading and then displaying the `PPTWizard` form. This simple procedure actually does much more than display the `PPTWizard` form; it also serves as the connection between the presentation template's wizard application and the PowerPoint Presentation Generator add-in. This link is discussed in the following section.

Tying the Pieces Together

Now that all the pieces are built, there is one small but very significant step left. In order for the add-in to initiate the Presentation Customization Wizard within the presentation template, it needs to respond to a PowerPoint event and call the StartPPTWizard procedure, which is found within the Main module of the template. Figure 2-20 illustrates this process.

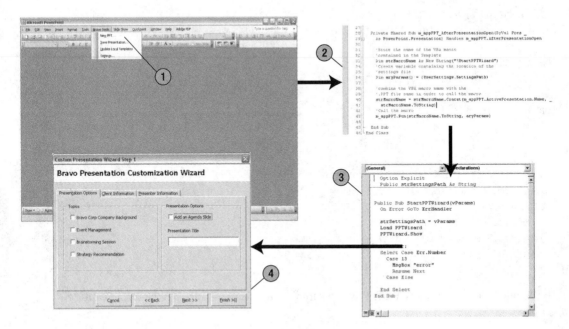

Figure 2-20. *How the add-in and the wizard work together*

Starting the Wizard from the Add-In

Calling the PPTWizard procedure from the add-in turns out to be an easy task. If you remember, the appPPT class residing inside the Presentation Generator add-in responds to PowerPoint's AfterPresentationOpen event. For convenience, here is the code for this event:

```
Private Shared Sub m_appPPT_AfterPresentationOpen(ByVal Pres As Presentation) _
   Handles m_appPPT.AfterPresentationOpen

   'Store the name of the VBA macro
   'contained in the template
   Dim strMacroName As New String("!StartPPTWizard")
   'Create a variable containing the location of the
   'settings file
   Dim aryParams() = {UserSettings.SettingsPath}

   'Combine the VBA macro name with the
   '.PPT filename in order to call the macro
   strMacroName = strMacroName.Concat(m_appPPT.ActivePresentation.Name, _
      strMacroName.ToString)
```

```
'Call the macro
m_appPPT.Run(strMacroName.ToString, aryParams)
End Sub
```

The AfterPresentationOpen event occurs, as its name implies, immediately after a presentation is opened within PowerPoint. By responding to this event, the add-in is able to respond to any recently opened presentation. In the case of this chapter's code, the AfterPresentationOpen event calls the newly opened template's StartPPTWizard procedure using PowerPoint's Run method.

■**Note** Not all files opened in PowerPoint will contain the StartPPTWizard procedure (only Bravo Corp templates will contain it). The add-in will always attempt to call the StartPPTWizard procedure, but the call will be ignored if the file is not "wizard-enabled" and lacks this function.

Summary

In this chapter, you learned how to build a Shared/COM add-in to customize the PowerPoint user experience and combine it with custom VBA code encapsulated within a PowerPoint presentation. The end result is a powerful tool that helps extend PowerPoint by automating a common business scenario—creating sales and marketing decks. In addition to creating a COM add-in, you also learned how to build a VBA wizard application within a PowerPoint template file using VBA UserForms. You also learned how to connect the add-in and the wizard by creating a "hook" inside the COM add-in that initiates any template file that contains the StartPPTWizard VBA procedure.

By combining an add-in engine with custom business logic that resides inside a file, you can easily extend this scenario beyond the example in this chapter to include multiple files with different purposes. Custom wizards could be created for each department that incorporates published presentations and custom business rules.

■ ■ ■

CHAPTER 3

Document Generator

Automating Document Creation Using Word, Outlook, and a COM Add-In

This chapter will illustrate how to combine Word and Outlook to automate the document-creation process. By wrapping all the necessary logic into a managed COM add-in hosted within Outlook, the Document Generator can churn out frequently used documents in the blink of an eye.

The Document Generator helps automate the creation of typical business documents such as contracts, work orders, or letters, where standard documents need to have specific client information inserted into them. After the documents are created and approved, the Document Generator attaches them to an email so they are ready to be sent out. The example in this chapter will focus on documents typically created at Bravo Corp once they win business from a new client. Of course, the Document Generator is not limited to this scenario and could be extended to generate any Word document within any number of scenarios.

To build this Document Generator, we will use the Word and Outlook object models, the COM add-in IDTExtensibility2 interface, and the .NET Framework:

- The Word object model is used to manipulate Word documents and fill them with client-related data.

- The Outlook object model is used to build the add-in's toolbar, read contact records, and create an email that includes the newly created documents to be sent to the selected client.

- The IDTExtensibility2 interface is used to create a managed COM add-in that will load inside Microsoft Outlook.

- The .NET Framework is used to build the forms, classes, and business logic required by the add-in.

In the process of building this chapter's sample application, you will learn how to build a managed COM add-in that runs within Microsoft Outlook. In addition, this chapter demonstrates how to use VB .NET to read and manipulate Outlook data items (in this case, Outlook contact records). Finally, you will learn the secret of inserting text into a Word document in prespecified locations using Word bookmarks and data from an Outlook contact item.

The document generator will be demonstrated in the context of our fictional BravoCorp, who need to decrease the document creation cycle time as well as decrease the risk of data errors associated with the targeted document.

User Workflow

When a user creates a document with the Document Generator, the workflow follows the process shown in Figure 3-1.

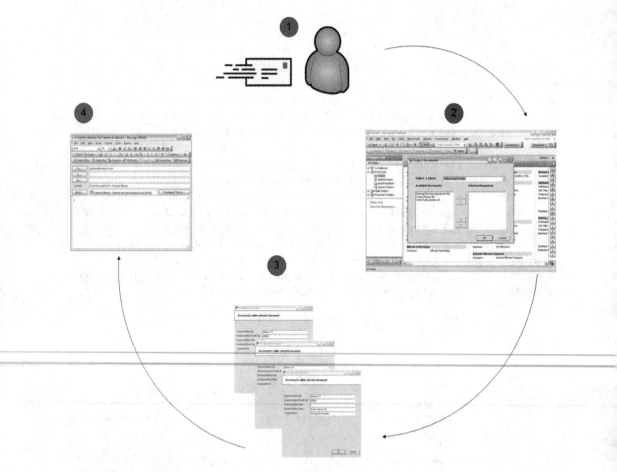

Figure 3-1. *The Document Generator user-process workflow*

1. A user receives an email request, or notification of an event, that requires the generation of a standard document. This might be a request for a Status Report document on a current client project, or notification that a new client account has been won and that a Services Agreement document is needed.

2. With Microsoft Outlook open, the user initiates the document-creation process by selecting Create Project Documents from a custom Word menu. The Documents form lists all project documents available for generation. These documents have been previously downloaded from a central repository, such as a SQL Server database, and stored on the local file system within the Templates folder specified in the add-in's Settings form.

   The user selects the desired document or documents that they wish to create. In order to insert client information into the documents, the desired client is selected from the Select a Client combo box found at the top of the Project Documents form.

3. When the user clicks OK on the Project Documents form, each selected Word document template opens inside a DocumentProcessor form. Within each Word template, several bookmarks define areas within the document template where client data will be inserted. For each bookmark in the template, the DocumentProcessor form allows the user to generate a corresponding label and text box, filled with the client information specified in step 2.

4. Once the user okays the information to be inserted into each selected document, the DocumentProcessor form inserts the client information into the targeted template document and saves the document to the Save folder specified in the add-in's Settings form. The process completes with the creation of an Outlook email item containing each of the newly created documents as attachments. The To field of the email is populated using the client's email address, and the Attachments field contains a listing of the attached documents. All that is left for the user to do is review the documents, add some content to the body of the email, and click Send.

■**Note** The Document Generator add-in could be improved by walking the user through each document location where data was inserted or text was changed. In addition, the code could be extended to include logic for better error handling, security, and document template editing.

Designing the Document Generator

From a coding point of view, the Document Generator is a COM add-in hosted within Microsoft Outlook. Like the Presentation Generator, the Document Generator is a rich client utilizing the features of Microsoft Office and the Windows operating system. The add-in is the main component of the application, and it handles all interaction with the other components that make up the add-in solution (including the user!).

The add-in is composed of five major pieces (see Figure 3-2):

- **Document Generator add-in**: This is the dynamic-link library containing the class implementing the IDTExtensibility2 interface and all other forms and classes required for the add-in to function.

- **Microsoft Outlook**: This is the host application for the COM add-in, and it is the primary user interface.

- **Microsoft Word**: Word is used by the COM add-in to create Word documents from the add-in's document templates.

- **SQL Server database**: Published Word document templates are stored within a table of a SQL Server database. This table stores the actual binaries of the templates, and its contents are available for users to download at any time.

- **Word Document templates**: Word documents are the end product of the add-in. Each document contains bookmarks specifying text placeholders for inserting content specific to a client.

The Document Generator add-in implements four processes, which are numbered in Figure 3-2. As you can see, some pieces are involved in multiple processes. These are the processes:

- **Load the add-in (process 1)**: The add-in loads within the host application. During this process the Connect and appOutlook classes set up the host environment by creating a reference to Outlook's Application object as well as creating the add-in's custom menu. Once completed, the add-in is ready to initiate the document-generation process discussed previously in the user workflow section.

- **Get updates (process 2)**: The GetUpdates process connects to the Document Templates table residing within the SQL Server database and downloads all available document templates. The add-in saves each template file in the file system folder specified as the Templates folder in the user settings. This process should be initiated by the user on a regular basis to ensure they have the most current document templates on their system.

- **Specify user settings (process 3)**: This process allows the user to specify or update the add-in's user settings. The Settings form and the UserSettings class interact to capture the data input by the user and store the settings in an XML file in the user's file system. In addition, this process captures the location of the Clients folder within Outlook (a contact-type folder). The client records listed in the combo box are pulled from a Microsoft Outlook Contacts folder specified in the add-in's user settings. These settings must be set prior to initiating the document-generation process.

Note The add-in's settings file is not specific to a single user. The settings specified in the Settings form affect all users of the machine in question. However, the add-in could be extended to create different settings files based on the current Windows user account.

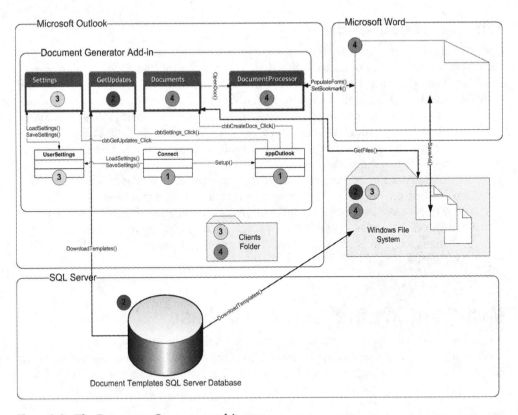

Figure 3-2. *The Document Generator architecture*

- **Generate the documents (process 4):** This is the main process of the add-in, and it was described in the user workflow section. After receiving an email request or event notification, the user selects the documents they want to create from a list presented in the Documents form. The form scans the add-in's Templates folder to fill a list box on the form with the name of each available template residing in the folder. The form also fills a combo box with all contact records found in the add-in's specified Clients folder in Outlook.

  Once the user selects the documents, the Documents form goes through each selected document and processes it using the DocumentProcessor form. The DocumentProcessor dynamically creates and places controls on its canvas. Each of these controls corresponds to a bookmark in the document. Once the controls exist on the Document-Processor, client data is inserted into each of them. The user then has the opportunity to review the presented data and approve it by clicking OK. With each approval, the DocumentProcessor inserts the values from the DocumentProcessor into the document, which is then saved to the file system.

  Once each selected template has been processed, the add-in creates a new Outlook email, attaches each generated document, and addresses the email to the client.

The Business Scenario

Bravo Corp account managers (AMs) are the intermediaries between the clients and the Bravo Corp event team. AMs spend a large chunk of their time authoring documents, and in recent years they have voiced the need for document-authoring automation tools to reduce the time spent on these documents and increase their time in front of clients. No matter what type of event is involved, hundreds of documents are generated to properly communicate and manage all the event details. From service contracts to work authorizations, from exhibit hall layouts to booth designs, an AM spends each day shuffling paper and communicating with both the project team and the client.

Because each document type remains largely the same each time it is used, the decision was made to create the Document Generator, which could use document templates that contained approved standard language, and automatically enter the client information into each document when it is generated. Not only would such a tool save time, it would reduce errors and, in the long run, increase customer satisfaction and loyalty due to the high quality of services delivered.

Modifying the BravoCorp Database

For the code in this application to execute without a hitch, a new table named tblDocuments needs to be added to the BravoCorp database. This is the central location where the approved document templates are stored. Create a new table using the schema specified in Table 3-1.

Table 3-1. *The Table Schema for* tblDocuments

Column Name	Data Type	Length	Allow Nulls
DocumentID	int	4	no
DocumentName	varchar	255	no
DocumentDesc	varchar	255	yes
DocumentBinary	image		no

Before saving the table, you need to set the following properties of the DocumentID column:

- Identity = yes

- Identity Seed = 1

- Identity Increment = 1

Once that is done, save the table.

Creating the Word Templates

Once Bravo Corp has won a new account for event-management services, the account manager needs to create three documents and send them to the client:

- **General Services Agreement**: This document contains the contract details between Bravo Corp and the client.

- **Services Work Authorization**: This document contains authorization approvals for individual work orders issued by the client. This document is a template sent to the client, with their account information already filled in, for the client's use when requesting additional services.

- **Status Report**: This document contains details relating to the project's status. This document is sent to the client as an example of the status reports they will receive as the event progresses.

You can create these documents yourself within Word, or you can download them from the downloads section of the Apress web site (http://www.apress.com). If you choose to build the document templates yourself, do not worry about having content applicable to the documents listed previously—it is only the documents' bookmarks that really matter for the code examples to work as intended.

You will need to place a number of text placeholders (bookmarks) into each template document, using Word's Bookmark object. Like bookmarks in the physical world, Word bookmarks mark a placeholder in a document for future reference.

In the case of Bravo Corp, bookmarks are inserted into every published Word template by the Bravo Documents team to mark insertion points for client data. Where possible, the bookmark names match up with the properties of an Outlook ContactItem. For example, the company field of a ContactItem form in Outlook is named "CompanyName". Any document that needs to automatically include the company name of a selected contact will have a bookmark named "CompanyName". You will learn how this works later in the chapter.

■Caution When utilizing this strategy of mapping bookmark names to ContactItem properties, be aware that changing bookmark names can cause you to easily get out of sync and waste all kinds of time debugging. If you find that data is not inserting into your document as you expect, check the bookmark names first. This is an issue during development, but it has a low risk of occurring at run time (primarily because the user will not have a chance to edit the document until the bookmarks have been filled with data).

For each document you create, insert the following bookmarks:

- CompanyName

- BusinessAddress

- BusinessAddressCity

- BusinessAddressState

- BusinessAddressPostalCode

To insert a bookmark:

1. Highlight some text within the document that will act as a placeholder.

2. Select Insert ➤ Bookmark from the main menu within Word.

3. The Bookmark dialog box is displayed (see Figure 3-3). Insert a name for the selected text in the Bookmark Name field, and click the Add button at the bottom of the dialog box.

Repeat this process until you have added all the bookmarks.

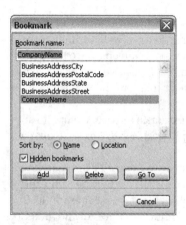

Figure 3-3. *Inserting bookmarks into the Word documents*

Setting up the Outlook Data File

The Document Generator uses Outlook contact items as records containing client information. This is the information we will use at run time to insert text into the document templates selected by the user. I recommend downloading the Bravo Corp Clients Outlook data file from the Apress web site. The data file can easily be recreated because it is an imported version of the Northwind Access database (and as we have discussed before, Northwind is included with Office and Visual Studio).

To import the Northwind database, follow these steps:

1. Open Outlook and create a new Outlook data file by selecting File ➤ New ➤ Outlook Data File from the menu.

2. Select Office Outlook Personal Folders File from the New Outlook Data File window. Click OK.

3. Select the folder on your file system where the new personal folders file should be stored (for example, C:\Projects\Chapter03), and name the file **BravoCorp.pst**. Click OK.

4. In the Create Microsoft Personal Folders dialog box, enter **Bravo Clients** in the Name field (see Figure 3-4). Leave all other fields at their default values. Click OK.

Figure 3-4. *Creating the Bravo Clients Outlook data file*

5. Right-click on the newly created Bravo Corp folder in the Navigation Pane and select the New Folder option.

6. In the Create New Folder dialog box (see Figure 3-5), enter **Clients** in the name field. Select Contact Items from the Folder Contains drop-down box. Click OK.

Figure 3-5. *Creating the Bravo Clients Outlook folder*

7. From the main menu, select File ➤ Import and Export.

8. The Import Export Wizard window is displayed. Select Import from Another Program or File. Click Next.

9. Select Microsoft Access from the Select File Type to Import From list.

10. In the Import a File window (see Figure 3-6), browse to the location of the Northwind.mdb file on your system. If you installed Microsoft Office to its default location, this file is located at C:\Program Files\Microsoft Office\OFFICE11\SAMPLES. In the Options section of the dialog box, select the Do Not Import Duplicate Items option, and click Next.

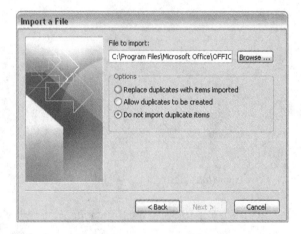

Figure 3-6. *Importing the Northwind sample data*

11. The Import a File window changes to display a tree view of your Outlook folder structure. Select the Clients folder created in step 4 to specify it as the target folder for the imported records. Click Next.

12. Select the Import Customers into Folder:Clients check box and click the Map Custom Fields button.

13. In the Map Custom Fields window (Figure 3-7), drag and drop the items listed in Table 3-2 from the From area into the To area. Click OK.

14. Click Finish to initiate the import process. A progress dialog box will show the progress of the import process. Once the import completes, the progress dialog box disappears and the focus returns to Outlook. If the import was successful, the contents of the Clients folder will resemble Figure 3-8.

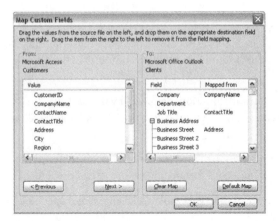

Figure 3-7. *Mapping Northwind customer values to Outlook contact fields*

Table 3-2. *Import Field Mappings*

Northwind Field Name	Contact Field Name
CompanyName	Company
Address	Business Street
City	Business City
Region	Business State
Postal Code	Business Postal Code
Fax	Business Fax
Phone	Business Phone

Now that you have some sample client records for the add-in to work with, we can build the Document Generator.

	Last Name	First Name	Company	File As	Business Phone	Business Fax
		Click here to ...				
	Accorti	Paolo	Franchi S.p.A.	Accorti, Paolo	(011) 498-8260	(011) 498-8261
	Afonso	Pedro	Comércio Mineiro	Afonso, Pedro	(11) 555-7647	
	Anders	Maria	Alfreds Futterkiste	Anders, Maria	(030) 007-4321	(030) 007-6545
	Angel Paolino	Miguel	Tortuga Restaurante	Angel Paolino, Miguel	(5) 555-2933	
	Ashworth	Victoria	B's Beverages	Ashworth, Victoria	(171) 555-1212	
	Batista	Bernardo	Que Delícia	Batista, Bernardo	(21) 555-4252	(21) 555-4545
	Bennett	Helen	Island Trading	Bennett, Helen	(198) 555-8888	
	Berglund	Christina	Berglunds snabbköp	Berglund, Christina	0921-12 34 65	0921-12 34 67
	Bergulfsen	Jonas	Santé Gourmet	Bergulfsen, Jonas	07-98 92 35	07-98 92 47
	Bertrand	Marie	Paris spécialités	Bertrand, Marie	(1) 42.34.22.66	(1) 42.34.22.77
	Braunschweiger	Art	Split Rail Beer & Ale	Braunschweiger, Art	(307) 555-4680	(307) 555-6525
	Brown	Elizabeth	Consolidated Holdings	Brown, Elizabeth	(171) 555-2282	(171) 555-9199
	Camino	Alejandra	Romero y tomillo	Camino, Alejandra	(91) 745 6200	(91) 745 6210
	Cartrain	Pascale	Suprêmes délices	Cartrain, Pascale	(071) 23 67 22 20	(071) 23 67 22 21
	Carvalho	Lúcia	Queen Cozinha	Carvalho, Lúcia	(11) 555-1189	
	Chang	Francisco	Centro comercial Moctezuma	Chang, Francisco	(5) 555-3392	(5) 555-7293
	Citeaux	Frédérique	Blondesddsl père et fils	Citeaux, Frédérique	88.60.15.31	88.60.15.32
	Cramer	Philip	Königlich Essen	Cramer, Philip	0555-09876	
	Crowther	Simon	North/South	Crowther, Simon	(171) 555-7733	(171) 555-2530
	Cruz	Aria	Familia Arquibaldo	Cruz, Aria	(11) 555-9857	
	de Castro	Isabel	Princesa Isabel Vinhos	de Castro, Isabel	(1) 356-5634	
	Devon	Ann	Eastern Connection	Devon, Ann	(171) 555-0297	(171) 555-3373
	Dewey	Catherine	Maison Dewey	Dewey, Catherine	(02) 201 24 67	(02) 201 24 68
	Domingues	Anabela	Tradição Hipermercados	Domingues, Anabela	(11) 555-2167	(11) 555-2168
	Fernández	Guillermo	Pericles Comidas clásicas	Fernández, Guillermo	(5) 552-3745	(5) 545-3745
	Feuer	Alexander	Morgenstern Gesundkost	Feuer, Alexander	0342-023176	

Figure 3-8. *The new Bravo Corp Clients folder*

Creating the Add-In

The Document Generator add-in is self-sufficient in terms of code. Unlike the Presentation Generator, this add-in does not rely on any code contained in other components. The following objects constitute the add-in:

- appOutlook: This class contains all the Outlook functions required by the add-in. This includes functions that respond to Outlook and set up the add-in's Outlook interface (the CommandBar buttons).

- Documents: This form lists document templates available for creating documents, and it kicks off any additional processing. The Documents form is the main form of the add-in.

- DocumentProcessor: This form allows the user to insert bookmark values for a specified Word document.

- Settings: This form allows the user to change settings, and it calls the UserSettings methods for retrieving and saving the add-in's settings.

- UserSettings: This class contains the methods for storing and retrieving the add-in's user settings.

- GetUpdates: This form retrieves all published presentations from a SQL Server and stores them on the user's file system.

- Connect: This class implements the IDTExtensibility2 interface.

The appOutlook Class

Since Microsoft Outlook is the host application for the Document Generator, the add-in will make great use of the objects and methods available in Outlook. The main purpose of the appOutlook class is to create the Bravo Tools CommandBar menu and set up the necessary event sinks that will be used to initiate the processes implemented within the add-in (such as generating documents, specifying settings, and downloading document templates). In addition, this class provides Outlook-specific utility methods needed by the other classes in the project. For example, appOutlook provides methods for selecting an Outlook Contacts folder, listing ContactItem records, retrieving a specified ContactItem record, and creating an email (MailItem).

The appOutlook class illustrates how to create a shared class that is accessible by all other project objects (form and classes) without requiring an object instance. The class includes logic for building a custom toolbar in Outlook's standard menu bar, for accessing Outlook folders and contact records, and for creating an email prepopulated with data from a contact record.

With Visual Studio .NET open, create a new Shared Add-In project and name it **Document-Generator**. Add a class, and name it **appOutlook**.

■**Note** See Chapter 2 for detailed steps on how to create this type of project.

Complete the remaining Setup Wizard steps as follows:

1. In the Select a Programming Language window, choose Create an Add-In using Visual Basic. Click Next.

2. The Select an Application Host window appears. You want this add-in to only load in Outlook, so uncheck all applications except Microsoft Outlook. Click Next.

3. The Enter a Name and Description window displays. Name the add-in **Document-Generator**, and set the description to **BravoCorp Document Generator**. Click Next.

4. In the Choose Add-In Options window, select the "I would like my Add-in to load when the host application loads" option. Leave all other options unselected.

5. Click Next. The Summary window displays all the selected options. Click Finish.

After Visual Studio creates the project, add the following references:

- Microsoft Outlook 11.0 Object Library (COM tab)

- Microsoft Word 11.0 Object Library (COM tab)

- System.XML.dll (.NET tab)

- System.Windows.Forms.dll (.NET tab)

Imports Directives

The appOutlook class encapsulates all methods that access Outlook objects or call Outlook methods. We are making this a shared class to ensure that the methods and data of the class are shared by all other objects while the add-in is loaded. In addition to Outlook, the class will work with Office CommandBar objects and Windows Forms.

Insert the following lines of code into the Imports section of the class:

```
Imports OL = Microsoft.Office.Interop.Outlook
Imports Microsoft.Office.Core
Imports System.Windows.Forms
```

The Outlook namespace is prefixed with "OL" to prevent naming conflicts between the Outlook and Office namespaces. Assigning a prefix like this is a good practice anytime there is a chance for naming conflicts among the different namespace objects.

Variable Declarations

The appOutlook class requires six class-level variables to be used throughout the class. Insert the following lines in the Declarations section of the class.

```
Private Shared appOL As OL.Application
Private Shared fldClients As OL.MAPIFolder
Private Shared cbbBravoMenu As CommandBarPopup
Private Shared WithEvents cbbCreateDocs As CommandBarButton
Private Shared WithEvents cbbSettings As CommandBarButton
Private Shared WithEvents cbbGetUpdates As CommandBarButton
```

The appOL variable is a reference to the Outlook application and is used by the class's methods to call Outlook objects and functions. The fldClients variable contains a reference to the Outlook folder containing the Bravo Corp client records. The cbbBravoMenu variable is the Office CommandBar button that serves as the Bravo Tools menu. Both cbbCreateDocs and cbbSettings are Office CommandBars with event sinks that will allow the add-in to respond to their Click events and execute the code we attach later in this section.

The Class Methods

The appOutlook class is a shared class containing several methods that handle the Outlook "plumbing" for the other objects in the add-in. The class is set up as a shared class to make it easy to use. Since it is shared, there is no need to instantiate it prior to calling its methods. (I like to avoid typing as much as possible, and this strategy helps achieve this goal.)

Okay, let's get going and create the methods of the appOutlook class.

Setup

Prior to being used in the add-in, appOutlook needs to set up its environment. This is achieved by creating references in memory to the host Outlook application (appOL) and the location within Outlook of the Clients folder (fldClients), and by calling the SetupBravoMenu routine that will create the Bravo Tools menu.

The procedure looks like this:

```
Friend Shared Sub Setup(ByVal oApp As OL.Application, _
  ByVal EntryID As String, ByVal StoreID As String)

  appOL = oApp
  fldClients = GetFolder(EntryID, StoreID)
  SetupBravoMenu()
End Sub
```

This procedure takes the passed Outlook Application object and stores it for use within the class. The Connect class also has a reference to the Outlook host, and we could have changed that reference so that it was available to appOutlook. The problem with that strategy is that it would break the principle of encapsulation.

The GetFolder method is called to set a reference to the Clients folder. Don't worry about the EntryID and StoreID parameters for now—they will be explained fully just ahead. The last thing here is the call to the SetupBravoMenu function, which adds the Bravo Tools menu to the Outlook application's main menu.

Shutdown

Since we have a Setup method to handle the class's initialization, let's go ahead and create the related Shutdown method before moving on to the remaining functions. The Shutdown method could just as easily be called "JanitorialServices" because its sole purpose is to clean up all referenced objects and close Outlook. Insert the Shutdown method as follows:

```
Friend Shared Sub ShutDown()
  appOL.Quit()
End Sub
```

This one line of code does a lot of stuff, the most important of which is the closing of any open Outlook windows and the logging off of the user session.

SetupBravoMenu

The SetupBravoMenu method handles the task of creating the add-in's menu (see Figure 3-9). Sounds simple, right? It is, but as it turns out, this is the longest function of the class.

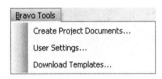

Figure 3-9. *The Document Generator's Bravo Tools menu*

Take a look at the whole function before we step through each section:

```
Private Shared Function SetupBravoMenu()
  Dim cbCommandBars As CommandBars
  Dim cbMenuBar As CommandBar

  ' Outlook has the CommandBars collection on the Explorer object.
  cbCommandBars = appOL.ActiveExplorer.CommandBars
  cbMenuBar = cbCommandBars.Item("Menu Bar")
  cbbBravoMenu = cbMenuBar.FindControl(tag:="Bravo Tools")
  If cbbBravoMenu Is Nothing Then
    cbbBravoMenu = cbMenuBar.Controls.Add( _
      Type:=MsoControlType.msoControlPopup, _
      Before:=6, Temporary:=True)

    With cbbBravoMenu
      .Caption = "&Bravo Tools"
      .Tag = "Bravo Tool"
      .TooltipText = "Bravo Crop Tools Menu"
      .OnAction = "!<DocumentGenerator.Connect>"
      .Visible = True
      'Create Documents Button
      cbbCreateDocs = .Controls.Add( _
        Type:=MsoControlType.msoControlButton, _
        Temporary:=True)

    With cbbCreateDocs
        .Caption = "Create Project Documents..."
        .Style = MsoButtonStyle.msoButtonCaption
        .Tag = "Create a set of Project Documents to send to a client."
        .OnAction = "!<DocumentGenerator.Connect>"
        .Visible = True
```

```
            End With
            'Settings Button
            cbbSettings = .Controls.Add( _
              Type:=MsoControlType.msoControlButton, _
              Temporary:=True)
            With cbbSettings
              .Caption = "User Settings..."
              .Style = MsoButtonStyle.msoButtonCaption
              .Tag = "Change the Document Generator User Settings."
              .OnAction = "!<DocumentGenerator.Connect>"
              .Visible = True
            End With
            'Download Updates Button
            cbbGetUpdates = .Controls.Add( _
              Type:=MsoControlType.msoControlButton, _
              Temporary:=True)
             With cbbGetUpdates
              .Caption = "Download Templates..."
              .Style = MsoButtonStyle.msoButtonCaption
              .Tag = "Download additional Document Templates..."
              .OnAction = "!<DocumentGenerator.Connect>"
              .Visible = True
            End With
          End With
        End If

End Function
```

The first section of the function handles the process of adding a button to Outlook's menu bar `CommandBar`. You can add the button to any of the menu bars in Outlook or you could even create a new `CommandBar` specifically for the add-in. I chose the first strategy:

```
' Outlook has the CommandBars collection on the Explorer object.
  cbCommandBars = appOL.ActiveExplorer.CommandBars
  cbMenuBar = cbCommandBars.Item("Menu Bar")
  cbbBravoMenu = cbMenuBar.FindControl(tag:="Bravo Tools")
  If cbbBravoMenu Is Nothing Then
    cbbBravoMenu = cbMenuBar.Controls.Add( _
      Type:=MsoControlType.msoControlPopup, _
      Before:=6, Temporary:=True)
    ...
  End if
```

Note I like to incorporate add-in menus as part of the host application's main menu because it conserves space and is less likely to confuse a user.

The `SetupBravoMenu` method determines whether the menu already exists, and if it does not, the Bravo Tools menu is added to the menu bar and its properties are set.

Notice that the Bravo Tools `CommandBar` button's `Temporary` property is set to True. This means the button will be removed automatically when Outlook is shut down. In addition, the `Before` property is set to 6, which positions the Bravo Tools menu between the default positions of the Tools and Actions buttons (assuming no menu customizations by the user).

■Note There are advantages and disadvantages to setting the `Temporary` parameter to either True or False. The advantage of a temporary `CommandBarButton` is that there is no need to write code to remove the add-in's buttons upon disconnection with the host application. The disadvantage is that the `CommandBar` must be created each time the application loads the add-in. In addition, if the user moves the `CommandBar`, the new location will not be saved between application sessions.

Once created, the newly added command bar button's `Caption`, `Tag`, `ToolTipText`, and `OnAction` properties are set:

```
With cbbBravoMenu
  .Caption = "&Bravo Tools"
  .Tag = "Bravo Tool"
  .TooltipText = "Bravo Crop Tools Menu"
  .OnAction = "!<DocumentGenerator.Connect>"
  .Visible = True
. . .
End With
```

If you remember from Chapter 2, the `OnAction` property is set to the add-in project's `Connect` class. This tells the command button to run the Document Generator add-in each time the button is clicked.

■Tip The `OnAction` property needs to contain the program ID of the add-in and the name of its class containing the `IDTExtensibility2` interface (the `Connect` class in this case). Instead of using the project name here, you could use reflection to discover the add-in's name and insert it as the value for the `OnAction` property.

Now that we have a menu control, let's add some buttons to it. The remainder of the procedure adds the two `CommandBarButton` objects, `cbbCreateDocs` and `cbbSettings`, to `cbbBravoMenu` and sets their properties. Like the Bravo Tools menu, both of these buttons are set as temporary CommandBar buttons.

```
'Settings Button
  cbbSettings = .Controls.Add( _
    Type:=MsoControlType.msoControlButton, _
    Temporary:=True)
```

```
  With cbbSettings
    .Caption = "User Settings..."
    .Style = MsoButtonStyle.msoButtonCaption
    .Tag = "Change the Document Generator User Settings."
    .OnAction = "!<DocumentGenerator.Connect>"
    .Visible = True
  End With
  'Download Updates Button
  cbbGetUpdates = .Controls.Add( _
    Type:=MsoControlType.msoControlButton, _
    Temporary:=True)
  With cbbGetUpdates
    .Caption = "Download Templates..."
    .Style = MsoButtonStyle.msoButtonCaption
    .Tag = "Download additional Document Templates..."
    .OnAction = "!<DocumentGenerator.Connect>"
    .Visible = True
  End With
End With
```

GetFolder

The GetFolder function returns a reference to a folder in the Outlook folder hierarchy that matches the passed MAPI FolderID (EID argument) and MAPI StoreID (SID argument).

```
Private Shared Function GetFolder(ByVal EID As String, _
  ByVal SID As String) As OL.MAPIFolder

  Dim nsMAPI As OL.NameSpace
  Dim fld As OL.MAPIFolder
  Try
    nsMAPI = appOL.Application.GetNamespace("MAPI")
    fld = nsMAPI.GetFolderFromID(EID, SID)

    Return fld
  Catch ex As Exception

  End Try
End Function
```

Each folder within Outlook has a unique identification number, much like a record in a database table. In addition, every data store within Outlook has a unique number as well. The GetFolderFromID method utilizes these two identifiers to find the desired folder and return a reference to it.

The importance of the StoreID (SID) is increased in situations where multiple data stores (multiple .pst files) are open within Outlook. If the StoreID is not provided as an argument to GetFolderFromID, Outlook will assume you want to look in the default data file. In this sample application, the desired folder would not be found without the StoreID, since the Clients folder resides in the BravoCorp.pst file instead of the default Outlook data store.

PickContactsFolder

The Document Generator relies on the existence of an Outlook Contacts folder for storing client records. Since we want to be nice and flexible, we will build some logic that allows the user to pick any folder in the Outlook folder hierarchy whose default item type is ContactItem.

```
Friend Shared Function PickContactsFolder() As String()
    Dim nsMAPI As OL.NameSpace
    Dim fld As OL.MAPIFolder
    Dim str(2) As String
    nsMAPI = appOL.Application.GetNamespace("MAPI")

    Do

      fld = nsMAPI.PickFolder
      If fld Is Nothing Then
        Exit Function
      End If

      If fld.DefaultItemType <> OL.OlItemType.olContactItem Then
        MsgBox("Please pick a folder containing Contact Items.")
      Else
        str(0) = fld.FolderPath
        str(1) = fld.EntryID
        str(2) = fld.StoreID
        Return str
      End If
    Loop While fld.DefaultItemType <> OL.OlItemType.olContactItem
End Function
```

In this function, the PickFolder method displays the Select Folder dialog box (see Figure 3-10) by using the MAPI namespace (currently the only namespace available within Outlook).

```
Dim nsMAPI As OL.NameSpace
Dim fld As OL.MAPIFolder
Dim str(2) As String
nsMAPI = appOL.Application.GetNamespace("MAPI")

Do

  fld = nsMAPI.PickFolder
```

This dialog box contains a tree view of all Outlook folders and makes it simple for a user to select an Outlook folder. The code pauses until the user selects a folder and closes the form (or until they just click Cancel). PickFolder then returns a string array containing the information needed to retrieve the selected folder at any time.

Figure 3-10. *Specifying a Contacts folder*

If a folder was not selected, `fld` equates to Nothing and the function exits. However, if a folder is selected, the folder type is checked to ensure it contains `ContactItems` before returning the folder as the value of the method. If the folder does not contain `ContactItems`, the user is notified and the `PickFolder` dialog box is displayed again.

```
If fld Is Nothing Then
    Exit Function
  Else
    If fld.DefaultItemType <> OL.OlItemType.olContactItem Then
      MsgBox("Please pick a folder containing Contact Items.")
    Else
      str(0) = fld.FolderPath
      str(1) = fld.EntryID
      str(2) = fld.StoreID
      Return str
    End If
End If
```

Once the user selects a folder that includes contact records, `PickContactsFolder` builds an array and stores the folder's path, unique EntryID, and unique data StoreID within it. The latter two properties are needed to access the specified folder and retrieve contact records with code. The `FolderPath` property is captured in order to present the user with meaningful information in the `Settings` form.

```
str(0) = fld.FolderPath
str(1) = fld.EntryID
str(2) = fld.StoreID
```

Note The preceding strategy provides a user-friendly way of providing feedback about which folder was selected. For accessing the selected folder with code, the `EntryID` and `StoreID` properties are required. Both of these properties are unique numbers that would have no meaning to the user if they were to see them. For example, if I were to select my default Contacts folder as the location of my Bravo Corp Clients folder, the `FolderPath` property would be `\\Mailbox - Ty Anderson\Contacts`, while the EntryID alone would be `00000000B28A083623C8384C9BA5416A6BB5CB1F021133153D33458BFD49865931EEA8BCA8F40000000000740000`.

The entire folder-selection process is wrapped inside a loop that continues until the user selects a folder whose default item type is `ContactItem`.

```
Do
  . . .
Loop While fld.DefaultItemType <> OL.OlItemType.olContactItem
```

Caution Be careful when using the EntryID and StoreID of an Outlook item. If an item is moved from one data store to another, both properties will change because the MAPI store will generate new values. A good example of this scenario is moving an email item from the Inbox to a folder in a separate Outlook data file (.pst). This situation could cause problems if you do not allow for these changes. For example, in this add-in, if the user were to change the location of the Bravo Corp Clients folder after selecting it in the Settings form, the add-in would not be able to access it. In order for the add-in to again function properly, the user would need to update the location of the Bravo Corp Clients folder in the Settings form. You could reduce the risk of this situation occurring by enhancing the sample application to monitor changes to the Outlook folder hierarchy and alert the user if they moved a folder specified in the Settings form.

ListContacts

To put the items residing in the specified Contacts folder to good use, we'll add a helper function named `ListContacts`. This handles all the details of rummaging through the client records and adding them to a list in a `ComboBox`. The function accepts a `ComboBox` type variable and fills it with the names of client contacts:

```
Friend Shared Function ListContacts(ByVal ctl As ComboBox)
  Dim fld As OL.MAPIFolder
  Dim itms As OL.Items
  Dim itm As OL.ContactItem
  Dim strName As String
  Dim i As Integer

  itms = fldClients.Items
  itms.Sort("[LastName]", False)
```

```
For i = 1 To itms.Count
  itm = itms(i)
  strName = itm.FirstName & " " & itm.LastName
  ctl.Items.Add(strName)

Next i
End Function
```

ListContacts begins by creating a reference to the fldClients.Items collection. This provides easy access to the contact records stored in the add-in's Bravo Corp Clients folder; remember, this is the folder specified by the user in the Settings form. The contents of the folder are sorted by LastName in order to present the data in a manner expected by the user. The ListContacts method finishes by looping through each item and adding items to the passed ComboBox control. The items are listed in LastName, FirstName format.

GetContact

So far we have specified which folder contains the client contact records, and we've filled a ComboBox full of these client records. Now we need a method for retrieving the client record selected in the ComboBox.

The GetContact method accepts a single string (the name of a client) as a parameter and returns an Outlook ContactItem:

```
Friend Shared Function GetContact(ByVal ContactName As String) _
  As OL.ContactItem

  Dim itms As OL.Items
  Dim itm As OL.ContactItem

  itms = fldClients.Items
  itm = itms(ContactName)

  Return itm

End Function
```

Using the class's reference to the Clients folder, the method uses the folder's Items collection and the ContactName variable to retrieve the related ContactItem. GetContact returns the retrieved item as its value.

■Caution When searching for a ContactItem, be sure to use a name in the *FirstName LastName* format. This can be a problem because ListContacts fills a ComboBox in the *LastName, FirstName* format. If the preceding code used this second format, the desired contact would not be found.

CreateEmail

Once the user selects a client record, they will probably want to send the selected client an email, a situation handled quite nicely by the CreateEmail method.

The CreateEmail method creates an Outlook MailItem filled with data from the selected client record, and it attaches the documents created earlier in the document-generation process.

```
Friend Shared Sub CreateEmail(ByVal FileNames() As String, _
  ByVal ClientName As String)

  Dim mi As OL.MailItem
  Dim ci As OL.ContactItem
  Dim i As Integer
  Dim TotalCount As Integer

  TotalCount = FileNames.GetUpperBound(0)
  ci = GetContact(ClientName)
  mi = appOL.CreateItem(OL.OlItemType.olMailItem)
  mi.To = ci.Email1Address
  mi.Subject = "Event Documents for " & ci.CompanyName

  For i = 0 To TotalCount - 1
    mi.Attachments.Add(FileNames(i))
  Next

  mi.Display()

End Sub
```

The method begins by determining the size of the passed string array. This size is used in the loop that completes the procedure:

```
TotalCount = FileNames.GetUpperBound(0)
```

The UpperBound property lets the procedure know how many documents have been created. This number is useful later in the procedure when the documents are attached to the email.

Next, the procedure calls the GetContact method to retrieve the desired ContactItem. CreateEmail then uses the class's Outlook Application object to create a new MailItem and fill its properties.

```
ci = GetContact(ClientName)
mi = appOL.CreateItem(OL.OlItemType.olMailItem)
mi.To = ci.Email1Address
mi.Subject = "Event Documents for " & ci.CompanyName
```

The email's To field is set to the ContactItem's email address, while the Subject field includes the company name from the contact record.

Before displaying the MailItem, the procedure loops through the filenames contained in the passed string array. Each string in the array is used to add a new attachment to the email.

```
For i = 0 To TotalCount - 1
  mi.Attachments.Add(FileNames(i))
Next
```

To finish things off, the procedure displays the newly minted MailItem to the user (see Figure 3-11), and they can take whatever action is required (send the email, edit the email body, edit the attachments, etc.).

```
mi.Display()
```

■**Tip** This example utilizes the Display method in order to give the user a chance to review the end results of the document-generation process and ensure that everything completed to their satisfaction. The process could be automated completely by calling the created MailItem's Send method instead.

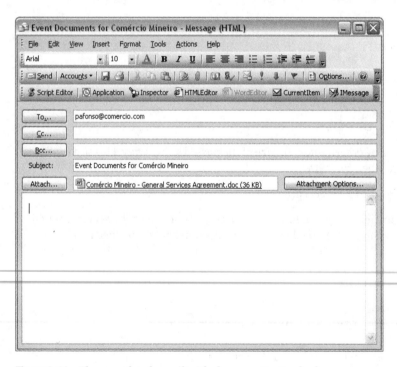

Figure 3-11. *The completed email with documents attached*

cbbCreateDocs_Click

There is one more thing to accomplish. If you remember, we declared three class-level variables at the beginning of the appOutlook class named cbbCreateDocs, cbbSettings, and cbbGetUpdates using the WithEvents keyword. Each of these variables represents a button on the add-in's CommandBar and needs code to respond to each button's Click event. We'll look at them in this and the next couple sections.

The cbbCreateDocs button starts the whole document-generation process. It is the most popular button of the Document Generator add-in, but the only heavy lifting involves the appearance of the Documents form.

The Click event for the cbbCreateDocs CommandBar looks like this:

```
Private Shared Sub cbbCreateDocs_Click(ByVal Ctrl As _
  Microsoft.Office.Core.CommandBarButton, ByRef CancelDefault As Boolean) _
  Handles cbbCreateDocs.Click

  Dim frmDocuments As New Documents
  frmDocuments.Show()

End Sub
```

Easy enough? We just declare a variable of type Documents, and then we call its Show method.

cbbSettings_Click

The cbbSettings button is also very popular with users. When the user clicks this button, they will be shown the Settings form, which allows them to customize the settings for the add-in.

The Click event for cbbSettings looks like this:

```
Private Shared Sub cbbSettings_Click(ByVal Ctrl _
  As Microsoft.Office.Core.CommandBarButton, ByRef CancelDefault As Boolean) _
  Handles cbbSettings.Click

  Dim frmSettings As New Settings
  frmSettings.Show()

End Sub
```

cbbGetUpdates_Click

The cbbGetUpdates button is just like the last two buttons, except that it displays the GetUpdates form. Here's the code for the cbbGetUpdates_Click event:

```
Private Shared Sub cbbGetUpdates_Click(ByVal Ctrl _
  As Microsoft.Office.Core.CommandBarButton, _
  ByRef CancelDefault As Boolean) Handles cbbGetUpdates.Click
```

```
    Dim frm As New GetUpdates
    frm.ShowDialog()
End Sub
```

The Documents Form Class

We need a form to act as the primary user interface of the add-in—the Documents form. This form needs to be simple enough that it will not confuse the user but powerful enough to control the document-creation process. The form will control these processes:

- **Retrieve a listing of available document templates**: The code retrieves a listing of documents that reside in a Windows file system folder and then use that data to fill list box controls on the form.

- **Allow the user to select templates for creation**: We will use two list box controls and four button controls to give the user the ability to select and deselect listed documents for document generation.

- **Generate the selected documents**: We will instantiate the form and invoke its methods much as we would with a class lacking a user interface.

Here is how the Documents form does its job:

1. The user selects the desired documents from a list of available document templates. These templates reside in a folder specified by the user in the Settings form (discussed later).

2. A client record is selected from a ComboBox filled with the names of all Bravo Corp clients. (This is our little appOutlook class already at work.)

3. These selections are passed to the DocumentProcessor form (which we will create shortly) for document creation.

Now that you know what the Documents form does, let's create it. Add a new form to the project, and name it **Documents.vb**. The form contains

- 3 Label controls: lblClients, lblAvailableDocs, lblSelectedDocs

- 2 ListBox controls: lstAvailableDocs, lstSelectedDocs

- 1 ComboBox control: cboClients

- 6 Button controls: cbSelectOne, cbRemoveOne, cbSelectAll, cbRemoveAll, cbOk, and cbCancel

Draw each of these controls onto the Documents form according to the layout shown in Figure 3-12.

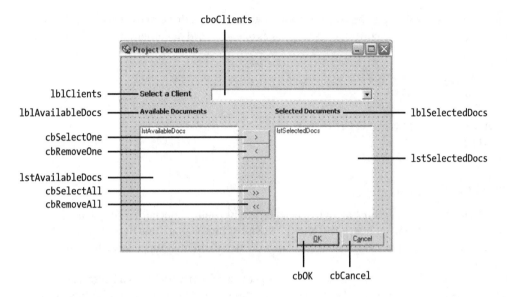

Figure 3-12. *The* Documents *form control layout*

Imports Directives

The Documents form will make use of the Windows file system, so edit the form's Imports section as follows:

```
Imports System.IO
Imports System.Windows.Forms
```

The System.IO namespace provides everything we need for opening, reading, and closing files stored on the user's system. The System.Windows.Forms namespace handles all details of creating Windows forms, and it is automatically added when you create a new form.

Methods

As mentioned just a moment ago, the Documents form has three main objectives: list the available templates, allow the user to select the documents they wish to create and specify the target client, and create the selected documents. We achieve this through the use of four custom functions and by responding to eight control or form events. The custom methods are called in the events, so we will begin by writing them.

GetFiles

The Documents form needs to retrieve a list of available document templates on the user's machine, and we'll use a function called GetFiles to do this. GetFiles takes a look in the

Templates folder specified in the user settings, and as it loops through the files in the folder, it fills the passed ListBox control with the names of each Word document it finds. Take a look:

```
Private Function GetFiles(ByVal ctl As ListBox)
  Dim diFolder As New DirectoryInfo(UserSettings.TemplatesFolder)
  Dim fi As FileInfo

  For Each fi In diFolder.GetFiles("*.dot")
    ctl.Sorted = True
    ctl.Items.Add(fi.Name)
  Next
End Function
```

There really isn't anything all that special here. The method declares a couple of variables, assigns values to them, and performs a loop. The most interesting thing here is the FileInfo typed variable named fi. Using this type of object, just about anything related to a file is at your fingertips.

We kill two birds with one stone by declaring the diFolder variable as a DirectoryInfo class and assigning it the path of the user's Templates folder. The DirectoryInfo object will return a collection of files of any type you specify by calling its GetFiles method and specifying which file extensions to retrieve. Using the returned collection of files, GetFiles loops through all files in the Templates folder and adds the name of each Word document template file (files with a .dot extension) to the ListBox that was passed as a method argument.

The end result is a ListBox filled with Word template filenames.

Note The .NET Framework provides several objects for manipulating files and directories, and there is a lot of overlap. To learn more about the file system–related classes available in the .NET Framework, look up the Directory, FileInfo, File, and Path classes, in addition to the DirectoryInfo class, in the .NET Framework documentation.

MoveSelected

So we have a ListBox filled with filenames of available templates. What we need now is a method to move them from one control to another and that allows the user to select the documents they want to create.

The MoveSelected method moves the selected items from one ListBox to another. All it needs to know is which control is the source and which is the destination.

```
Private Function MoveSelected(ByVal SourceList As ListBox, _
  ByVal TargetList As ListBox) As Boolean
  Try
    TargetList.Items.Add(SourceList.SelectedItem)
    SourceList.Items.Remove(SourceList.SelectedItem)
    Return True
```

```
   Catch ex As Exception
      Return False
   End Try
End Function
```

Using the Items collection of each ListBox, we either add the SelectedItem from the SourceList or remove it. It all depends on whether the ListBox is the target or the source. MoveSelected returns a Boolean value based on whether or not the operation was successful.

I like the simplicity of this function. Not only is it simple, it is primed for reuse in another project because of its generic nature.

MoveAll

The MoveAll method moves all items, with no regard for which items are currently selected, from one ListBox control to another. It is the same as the MoveSelected function, but different. See for yourself:

```
Private Function MoveAll(ByVal SourceList As ListBox, _
   ByVal TargetList As ListBox) As Boolean

   Try
      Dim si

      For Each si In SourceList.Items
         TargetList.Items.Add(si)

      Next
      SourceList.Items.Clear()
      Return True

   Catch ex As Exception
      Return False
   End Try

End Function
```

Just like MoveSelected, this function accepts a source and destination ListBox as parameters. Using a generic object (si), a loop is implemented to add new items to the TargetList by cycling through each item in the SourceList's Items collection. Once each and every item from the SourceList has been successfully added to the target control, the SourceList's Items collection is cleared of all items.

Tip Because you are incredibly smart, I know you noticed that when I declared the si variable in the previous chunk of code, I did not assign a type. This is simply because I am unaware of an Item type for a ListBox control. Since VB .NET is fully object oriented, I just declared si as a generic object and moved on. Notice how it works just fine (but the purists out there will be sure to inform you of the performance hit, blah!).

GenerateDocs

Let's quickly review our user scenario up to this point. The user needs to send their client some new documents relevant to their event. The account manager has opened the Documents form by clicking the cbbCreateDocs command bar button in the Bravo Tools menu.

Once the Documents form was opened, the account manager picked at least one available document template for creation. These selections are now sitting in the lstSelectedDocs control. In addition, the user (still the account manger here) has used the cboClients combo box to specify which client will receive these documents. In Figure 3-2, which outlined the whole process, we are in step 3.

The GenerateDocs method handles the task of running the DocumentProcessor class against each selected document template in the lstSelectedDocs control. I will attempt to run through this fairly quickly so we can move on to the DocumentProcessor, but stay with me because this stuff is important.

Take a minute to read through GenerateDocs before I explain what it does:

```
Private Sub GenerateDocs()

  Dim i As Integer
  Dim strClient As String
  Dim strFile As String
  Dim strFiles(lstSelectedDocs.Items.Count) As String

  strClient = cboClients.SelectedItem
  Try
    For i = 0 To lstSelectedDocs.Items.Count - 1
      Dim dp As New DocumentProcessor
      strFile = lstSelectedDocs.Items(i)

      With dp
        .Client = appOutlook.GetContact(strClient)
        .FileName = strFile.ToString
        .OpenPath = UserSettings.TemplatesFolder
        .SavePath = UserSettings.SaveFolder
        .OpenDoc()
        .PopulateForm()
        .ShowDialog()
        'Populate String Array.  These will be inserted as
        'Attachments to an email.
        If .DocSaved Then
          strFiles(i) = .SavePath & "\" & .SavedFileName
        End If
        .Visible = False
        .Dispose()

      End With
```

```
    Next
  Catch ex As Exception
    MsgBox(ex.Message)
  End Try


  appOutlook.CreateEmail(strFiles, strClient)
End Sub
```

At first glance, this looks like a lot of code, and it is. However, it really is quite simple. We start by first declaring some working variables, the most notable being a `String` array. Notice the use of the source control's `Items.Count` property to set the array's size:

```
Dim i As Integer
Dim strClient As String
Dim strFile As String
Dim strFiles(lstSelectedDocs.Items.Count) As String
```

This sets the array's size to the number of items that have been selected, and it helps avoid the need to use `ReDim` later.

Next, we store the value of the client name selected from `cboClients`:

```
strClient = cboClients.SelectedItem
```

And then we start a loop to process each selection. Within the loop, each selected item is handed off to an instance of the `DocumentProcessor` class, which handles the actual document-creation details. A `String` is set to the value of the current item referenced in the loop:

```
For i = 0 To lstSelectedDocs.Items.Count - 1
  Dim dp As New DocumentProcessor
  strFile = lstSelectedDocs.Items(i)
  . . .
Next
```

Next, we set up the `DocumentProcessor` form prior to displaying it.

```
With dp
  .Client = appOutlook.GetContact(strClient)
  .FileName = strFile.ToString
  .OpenPath = UserSettings.TemplatesFolder
  .SavePath = UserSettings.SaveFolder
  .OpenDoc()
  .PopulateForm()
  .ShowDialog()
  . . .
End With
```

We set the `Client` property to an Outlook `ContactItem` representing the selected client. The `OpenPath` and `SavePath` properties are set to the user-defined add-in values.

Next, the document is opened and a call is made to PopulateForm. This method scans the open Word document for any existing bookmarks. If it finds any, it creates a series of text boxes and labels on the DocumentProcessor form, each representing a single bookmark. Finally, the DocumentProcessor form opens as a dialog box, and the function waits for the user to do their thing and close the form.

Upon the user's completing the DocumentProcessor (or canceling out), GenerateDocs first determines whether the document was saved by checking the DocSaved property of the DocumentProcessor. If the document has been saved, the path and filename are added to strFiles:

```
If .DocSaved Then
  strFiles(i) = .SavePath & "\" & .SavedFileName
End If
```

Finally, the DocumentProcessor form is hidden and disposed of:

```
.Visible = False
.Dispose()
```

Wrapping things up, the appOutlook class's CreateEmail method is passed the strFiles array so it can create and display a new email addressed to the client with the newly created documents attached:

```
appOutlook.CreateEmail(strFiles, strClient)
```

Form and Control Events

We now have all the functions needed to make the process happen. The next step is to hook our functions to the appropriate forms and control events required to put the code in motion.

The Documents form implements eight form-event methods. Let's take them in a logical order, starting with the loading of the Documents form.

Documents_Load

The Documents_Load event prepares the form by filling the lstAvailableDocs and cboClients controls with data, as follows:

```
Private Sub Documents_Load(ByVal sender As System.Object, _
  ByVal e As System.EventArgs) Handles MyBase.Load

  GetFiles(lstAvailableDocs)
  appOutlook.ListContacts(cboClients)

End Sub
```

cboClients_Click

The cboClients_Click event adds a little user-friendly interaction by reversing the current state of the ComboBox control's DroppedDown property:

```
Private Sub cboClients_Click(ByVal sender As System.Object, _
  ByVal e As System.EventArgs) Handles cboClients.Click

  cboClients.DroppedDown = Not cboClients.DroppedDown

End Sub
```

This method allows the user to simply click on the control to view or hide the control's contents. It provides the user with an extra bit of usability because they are not required to navigate to and click the control's down arrow to cause it to display its contents.

cbSelectOne_Click

The cbSelectOne_Click event calls the MoveSelected method to move the selected item from lstAvailableDocs to lstSelectedDocs:

```
Private Sub cbSelectOne_Click(ByVal sender As System.Object, _
  ByVal e As System.EventArgs) Handles cbSelectOne.Click

  MoveSelected(lstAvailableDocs, lstSelectedDocs)

End Sub
```

cbRemoveOne_Click

The cbRemoveOne_Click event calls the MoveSelected method to move the selected item from lstSelectedDocs to lstAvailableDocs:

```
Private Sub cbRemoveOne_Click(ByVal sender As System.Object, _
  ByVal e As System.EventArgs) Handles cbRemoveOne.Click

  MoveSelected(lstSelectedDocs, lstAvailableDocs)

End Sub
```

cbSelectAll_Click

The cbSelectAll_Click event calls the MoveAll method to move the selected item from lstAvailableDocs to lstSelectedDocs:

```
Private Sub cbSelectAll_Click(ByVal sender As System.Object, _
  ByVal e As System.EventArgs) Handles cbSelectAll.Click

  MoveAll(lstAvailableDocs, lstSelectedDocs)

End Sub
```

cbRemoveAll_Click

The cbRemoveAll_Click event calls the MoveAll method to move the selected item from lstSelectedDocs to lstAvailableDocs:

```
Private Sub cbRemoveAll_Click(ByVal sender As System.Object, _
  ByVal e As System.EventArgs) Handles cbRemoveAll.Click

  MoveAll(lstSelectedDocs, lstAvailableDocs)

End Sub
```

cbOK_Click

The cbOK_Click event calls the GenerateDocs method and, upon its completion, closes the Documents form:

```
Private Sub cbOK_Click(ByVal sender As System.Object, _
  ByVal e As System.EventArgs) Handles cbOK.Click

  GenerateDocs()
  Me.Close()

End Sub
```

cbCancel_Click

The cbCancel_Click event closes the form without any further processing:

```
Private Sub cbCancel_Click(ByVal sender As System.Object, _
  ByVal e As System.EventArgs) Handles cbCancel.Click

  Me.Close()

End Sub
```

And so, just like that, we have completed the Documents form.

The DocumentProcessor Form Class

Next on the agenda is the DocumentProcessor form, which is controlled by the Documents form. The DocumentProcessor form creates a new document and fills it with details from a specified client record.

These are the steps involved:

1. The Word document template is opened.

2. The document's Bookmarks collection is read.

3. The DocumentProcessor is populated with controls representing each Bookmark.

4. The values from the form's controls are inserted into their corresponding Bookmark within the document.

5. The document is saved to the UserSettings.SaveFolder path.

In building the DocumentProcessor form, we will look at how to manipulate Word documents and insert data from an Outlook contact item within the document, inserting values inside bookmarks that already exist inside the document. In addition we will see how to dynamically add controls to the form at run time to match the number of bookmarks found inside the document.

The DocumentProcessor form is completely subordinate to the Documents form and is not accessed from anywhere else within the project. In addition, the DocumentProcessor only handles one document at a time.

At design time, the form contains the following controls (see Figure 3-13):

- 1 Panel control: pnlTitle

- 1 Label control: lblTitle

- 2 Button controls: cbOK, cbCancel

More controls will be added at run time to allow the user to enter values for the document's bookmarks (see Figure 3-14 for the runtime version). Add a new form to the project and name it "DocumentProcessor". Using Figure 3-13 as a guide, lay out the controls in a similar manner.

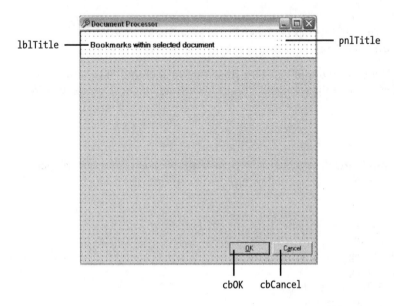

Figure 3-13. *The* DocumentProcessor *form control layout*

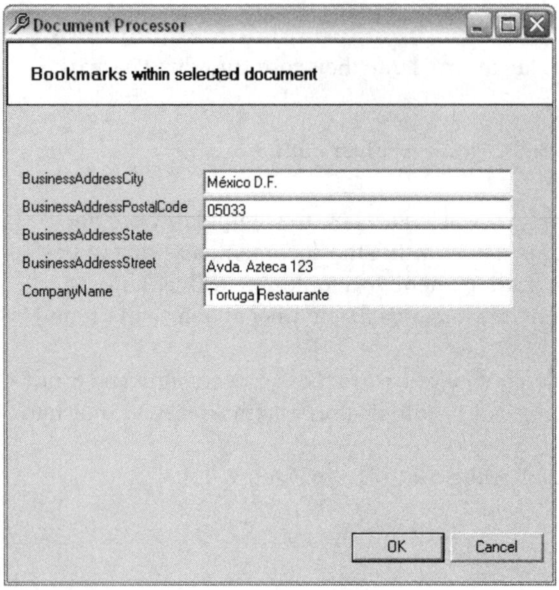

Figure 3-14. *The* DocumentProcessor *form at run time*

Imports Directives

This form will make use of Microsoft Word and Outlook. Edit the Imports section of the DocumentProcessor form class to look just like this:

```
Imports W = Microsoft.Office.Interop.Word
Imports OL = Microsoft.Office.Interop.Outlook
Imports Frm = System.Windows.Forms
```

This puts Word and Outlook at our mighty little fingertips. In addition, since some of the objects in the namespaces may conflict, I added a prefix to each statement so we can qualify the objects later on.

Variable Declarations

We are going to need several variables for the different tasks the DocumentProcessor will perform. For now, just go ahead and insert the following lines of code into the class.

```
Private m_appW As W.Application
Private m_Doc As W.Document
Private m_OpenPath As String
Private m_SavePath As String
Private m_FileName As String
Private m_SavedPathAndFileName As String
Private m_Contact As OL.ContactItem
Private m_Documents As System.Windows.Forms.ListBox
Private m_WordIsRunning As Boolean
Private m_DocSaved As Boolean
```

Since all of these are declared as `Private` class variables, we need to add a property procedure for each one that we want to expose to other classes in the project. We could have just declared them all as `Public` fields, but we have the time to be purists and do this correctly (or at least I do). Besides, some of the variables need to be defined as read-only properties of the class, and we need a correct property procedure to accomplish this.

Properties

Unlike the other classes we have created for this project, the `DocumentProcessor` class already has several properties (and methods). In addition to the properties available to any class inherited from the `System.Windows.Forms.Form` class, though, the `DocumentProcessor` needs the custom properties described in the following sections. These property methods expose the class variables for access by other classes.

■Note The fact that there are already properties and methods for the form is not a big deal at all. A form is just a class with a visual aspect to it. Don't freak out later when you hit that "." and IntelliSense lists a couple dozen or more properties than the custom properties we are about to create.

GetBookmarks

GetBookmarks is a read-only property that returns the Bookmarks collection of the m_Doc variable.

```
Public ReadOnly Property GetBookmarks() As W.Bookmarks
  Get
    If Not m_Doc Is Nothing Then
      Return m_Doc.Bookmarks()
    End If
  End Get
End Property
```

DocSaved

The DocSaved property is a read-only property that returns the value of the m_DocSaved class variable. This property is set to True upon the successful completion of the SaveDoc method (discussed in the next section covering the class's methods).

```
Public ReadOnly Property DocSaved() As Boolean
  Get
    Return m_DocSaved
  End Get
End Property
```

This property allows any object using the `DocumentProcessor` class to determine whether the document was saved and to respond appropriately.

FileName

The `FileName` property is a read/write property representing the name of the file to be processed:

```
Public Property FileName() As String
  Get
    Return m_FileName
  End Get
  Set(ByVal Value As String)
    m_FileName = Value
  End Set
End Property
```

In our scenario, the filename is one of the selected Word documents stored in the Templates folder.

OpenPath

The `OpenPath` property is a read/write property representing the folder where the document defined in the `FileName` property resides:

```
Public Property OpenPath() As String
  Get
    Return m_OpenPath
  End Get
  Set(ByVal Value As String)
    m_OpenPath = Value
  End Set
End Property
```

SavePath

The `SavePath` property is a read/write property storing the folder location where the completed document should be saved:

```
Public Property SavePath() As String
  Get
    Return (m_SavePath)
  End Get
  Set(ByVal Value As String)
    m_SavePath = Value
  End Set
End Property
```

SavedFileName

The `SavedFileName` property is a read-only property that stores the name of the file after it has been saved to the `SavePath` location:

```
Public ReadOnly Property SavedFileName() As String
  Get
    Return m_SavedPathAndFileName
  End Get
End Property
```

The m_SavedPathAndFileName variable is updated in the SaveDoc method (discussed shortly).

Client

The Client property is a read/write property representing the Outlook ContactItem containing the client's contact information:

```
Public Property Client() As OL.ContactItem
  Get
    Client = m_Contact
  End Get
  Set(ByVal Value As OL.ContactItem)
    m_Contact = Value
  End Set
End Property
```

Methods

The DocumentProcessor class has six custom methods, each handling a different aspect of creating a new Word document. In addition to these methods, the New and Dispose methods are customized just a tad for our specific purposes.

New

Before the form displays itself to the user, you will want to properly set up its environment. The New method is a great location for this code, as it is the class's constructor method.

Tip A constructor method runs anytime a new instance of the class is instantiated. All this means to you and me is that the constructor is the perfect place for code that needs to run each time the class is created.

Edit the form's New method to include our custom logic for opening Microsoft Word. The new New method should look like this:

```
Public Sub New()
  MyBase.New()

  'This call is required by the Windows Form Designer.
  InitializeComponent()
```

```
'Add any initialization after the InitializeComponent() call
Try
  m_appW = GetObject(, "Word.Application")
  m_WordIsRunning = True
Catch ex As Exception
  If Err.Number = 429 Then
    m_appW = CreateObject("Word.Application")
    m_WordIsRunning = False
  Else
    Throw New System.Exception("Microsoft Word Automation error.")
  End If
End Try
End Sub
```

To function properly, the DocumentProcessor really needs Word to be running. Word does not have to be visible and the center of the user's attention—it just needs to be running as a process on the user's machine. The tricky part about this is that the user might have already opened Word and started updating their resume (at least, that's what people do in my office). Before creating a new instance of Word, the method determines whether or not Word is currently running:

```
'Add any initialization after the InitializeComponent() call
Try
  m_appW = GetObject(, "Word.Application")
  m_WordIsRunning = True
```

The class name of Word is passed to the GetObject function to check for an existence of Word running in the operating system. If one is found, a flag is set to remind us later that this was the case. This little nugget of info will be useful later in the Dispose method.

Note Anytime you use GetObject or CreateObject, VB .NET creates a wrapper object to handle the calls to the COM object. This is known as an *interop* assembly. If an interop assembly already exists, it is used. If not, Visual Studio asks if you would like it to create one.

If Word is not running, the code will trip an error that the following Catch block handles quite nicely:

```
Catch ex As Exception
  If Err.Number = 429 Then
    m_appW = CreateObject("Word.Application")
    m_WordIsRunning = False
  Else
    Throw New System.Exception("Microsoft Word Automation error.")
  End If
```

Error number 429 ("Cannot Create ActiveX Component") occurs if Word is already running as a Windows process. If it isn't, CreateObject (GetObject's sister function) opens Word and creates a reference to it in the code.

Once Word opens successfully, the m_WordIsRunning flag is set to False, specifying that Word was initialized by the DocumentProcessor form. If any other error occurred, a custom exception is thrown.

Note To learn more about GetObject and CreateObject, read the article on MSDN titled "Using the CreateObject and GetObject Functions" (http://msdn.microsoft.com/library/en-us/modcore/html/deconUsingCreateObjectGetObjectFunctions.asp).

Dispose

Because the form's New method contains customized logic for creating the Word application, the Dispose method is the proper location for the custom code needed to release the form's reference to Word. The Dispose method's definition is as follows:

```
Protected Overloads Overrides Sub Dispose(ByVal disposing As Boolean)
  If disposing Then
    If Not (components Is Nothing) Then
      components.Dispose()
    End If
  End If

  If m_WordIsRunning Then
    m_Doc.Close()
  Else
    m_Doc.Close()
    m_appW.Quit()
  End If

  MyBase.Dispose(disposing)
End Sub
```

Before closing Word, the method uses the flag set in the New method to determine whether the DocumentProcessor started Word. If so, only the newly created document is closed and Word is left running:

```
If m_WordIsRunning Then
  m_Doc.Close()
```

Closing the document and keeping Word open restores Word to the state it was in prior to the DocumentProcessor taking control.

If Word was started by the DocumentProcessor, both the document and the Word application are closed and removed from memory:

```
Else
  m_Doc.Close()
  m_appW.Quit()
End If
```

The class cleans up after itself pretty well, don't you think? The real heavy lifting, however, is in the following six methods that work directly with a specific Word document.

OpenDoc

The OpenDoc method opens the Word document by combining the DocumentProcessor's OpenPath and FileName properties and calling Word's Open function:

```
Public Function OpenDoc() As Boolean
  Try
    With m_appW
      .DisplayAlerts = W.WdAlertLevel.wdAlertsNone
      .Documents.Open(m_OpenPath & "\" & m_FileName)
      m_Doc = .ActiveDocument
      .DisplayAlerts = W.WdAlertLevel.wdAlertsAll
    End With
    Return True
  Catch ex As Exception
    Return False

  End Try
End Function
```

Before actually attempting to open the file, the function turns off Word's DisplayAlerts property. This avoids the situation where Word pops up a message to the user by displaying a dialog box. This would only confuse the user, so it is turned off while an attempt is made to open the document:

```
.DisplayAlerts = W.WdAlertLevel.wdAlertsNone
.Documents.Open(m_OpenPath & "\" & m_FileName)
```

If the document opens successfully, it is stored for use within the class, and the alerts are reactivated:

```
m_Doc = .ActiveDocument
.DisplayAlerts = W.WdAlertLevel.wdAlertsAll
```

PopulateForm

We now have an opened Word document ready for action. The next thing we need to do is populate the DocumentProcessor form with a series of TextBox controls representing each Bookmark in the document.

The PopulateForm method does just that; it reads the Bookmarks collection contained in the referenced document and creates corresponding Label and TextBox controls on the DocumentProcessor form. As each TextBox is created, it is filled with corresponding data from m_Contact.

```
Public Sub PopulateForm()
  Dim bm As W.Bookmark
  Dim i As Integer
  Dim iTop As Integer
  Dim itms As OL.ItemProperties
  Dim itm As OL.ItemProperty
  Dim val As String

  Try
    iTop = pnlTitle.Top + 100
    itms = m_Contact.ItemProperties

    For Each bm In m_Doc.Bookmarks
      Dim lbl As New Windows.Forms.Label
      Dim txt As New Windows.Forms.TextBox

      With lbl
        .Text = bm.Name
        .Left = 10
        .Width = 150
        .Top = iTop
        .Visible = True
      End With

      If PropertyExists(m_Contact, bm.Name) Then
        itm = itms(bm.Name)
        val = itm.Value
      Else
        val = ""
      End If

      With txt
        .Name = bm.Name
        .Text = val
        .Width = 250
        .Left = lbl.Width + 10
        .Top = iTop
        .Visible = True
      End With

      Me.Controls.Add(txt)
      Me.Controls.Add(lbl)
```

```
    iTop = iTop + 22
  Next

Catch ex As Exception
  Throw New System.Exception("An exception has occurred.")
End Try
End Sub
```

The trick to this method is synchronizing the creation of the TextBox controls (and their data population) with the reading of the Bookmark items within the document. The first step is to do a little prep work. The method uses a counter variable to position each newly created control. The first control will be positioned 100 pixels below pnlTitle:

```
iTop = pnlTitle.Top + 100
```

■**Tip** If you want the controls closer together or farther apart, simply adjust the value to meet your specifications.

To simplify the code, the properties of m_Contact are stored in an Outlook ItemProperties typed variable:

```
itms = m_Contact.ItemProperties
```

Now the method is ready to work. We have a ContactItem and we have a mechanism for positioning the controls. We are ready to read the bookmarks and build the form. For each Bookmark in the Word document, a new Label and TextBox are dimensioned as follows:

```
For Each bm In m_Doc.Bookmarks
  Dim lbl As New Windows.Forms.Label
  Dim txt As New Windows.Forms.TextBox
```

The new Label control's properties are set as follows:

```
With lbl
  .Text = bm.Name
  .Left = 10
  .Width = 150
  .Top = iTop
  .Visible = True
End With
```

The Text property is set equal to the Bookmark name. This will help the user understand what information to enter into the corresponding TextBox.

Before setting the properties of the TextBox, a quick check is performed to determine whether the ContactItem has a property with the same name as the current Bookmark:

```
If PropertyExists(m_Contact, bm.Name) Then
   itm = itms(bm.Name)
   val = itm.Value
Else
   val = ""
End If
```

If the corresponding property exists, the value is read and stored for use in the setup of the TextBox control:

```
With txt
   .Name = bm.Name
   .Text = val
   .Width = 250
   .Left = lbl.Width + 10
   .Top = iTop
   .Visible = True
End With
```

Notice that the TextBox is named after the current Bookmark. This is important later, when the form attempts to update the document's Bookmark collection with the values entered by the user.

With all their properties set, the Label and TextBox are added to the form, the counter is updated to the next position, and the loop moves to the next Bookmark item:

```
   Me.Controls.Add(txt)
   Me.Controls.Add(lbl)

   iTop = iTop + 22
Next
```

Upon successful completion of PopulateForm, the DocumentProcessor form is ready to show itself off to the user. In this project, the Documents form displays DocumentProcessor in the following lines:

```
Dim dp As New DocumentProcessor
   . . .
dp.ShowDialog()
```

This call is part of the Documents form's GenerateDocs method, discussed earlier in the chapter.

PropertyExists

One thing to be careful of anytime you are referencing an Outlook item's properties is the fact that the property may not exist. A neat and clean strategy for handling this possibility is to create a helper function to check for the existence of a specified property name. If the property exists, the function returns True, and if the property does not exist, False is returned. This is exactly why PropertyExists, um, exists.

```
Private Function PropertyExists(ByVal Contact As OL.ContactItem, _
  ByVal PropertyName As String) As Boolean

  Dim prop As OL.ItemProperty
  prop = Contact.ItemProperties(PropertyName)

  If Not prop Is Nothing Then
    Return True
  Else
    Return False
  End If

End Function
```

Making great use of the passed Outlook ContactItem, PropertyExists attempts to retrieve a property that matches the passed PropertyName argument:

```
Dim prop As OL.ItemProperty
prop = Contact.ItemProperties(PropertyName)
```

If the property is not found, the prop variable will contain Nothing. We can test for this and return either True or False to specify whether the property was found or not:

```
If Not prop Is Nothing Then
  Return True
Else
  Return False
End If
```

UpdateBookMarks

After the user inserts values into the form's text boxes and clicks the OK button, we need a mechanism for updating the bookmarks in the document. In addition, we need to be careful and only process TextBox objects.

The UpdateBookMarks method loops through the Controls collection of the Document-Processor form. If the control is a TextBox, the SetBookmark method is called:

```
Private Sub UpdateBookMarks()
  Dim ctl As Frm.Control

  For Each ctl In Me.Controls
    If TypeOf (ctl) Is Frm.TextBox Then
      SetBookmark(ctl)
    End If
  Next

End Sub
```

With a simple check of each control's type, we avoid the nasty situation of accidentally passing a non-TextBox control to SetBookMark.

SetBookMark

SetBookMark accepts a TextBox control as an argument and uses it to fill the Bookmark of the same name within the Word document:

```
Private Sub SetBookMark(ByVal txt As Frm.TextBox)
  Dim rng As W.Range
  Dim str As String
  str = txt.Name.ToString

  If m_Doc.Bookmarks.Exists(str) Then
    rng = m_Doc.Bookmarks(str).Range
    rng.InsertBefore(txt.Text)
  End If

End Sub
```

Before inserting any text into the Bookmarks Range object, the method checks to make sure the Bookmark exists within the Bookmarks collection. If it does exist, the text within txt is inserted using the InsertBefore method of the Bookmark.

■**Caution** When updating the Text property of Bookmark's Range object, understand that the bookmark will be destroyed. This is okay as long as the bookmarks are not needed in the future. However, if they may be required, they can easily be created when the Text is updated by calling the Add method of the Bookmarks collection.

If a particular string needs to be inserted throughout the document, the best strategy is to create one bookmark in the document and then insert REF fields anywhere the bookmark value should be repeated. A REF field is what's known as a *field code*, and it is used to refer to the value of a bookmark residing in the document. For example, if you have a bookmark that contains a client name, and you want that value duplicated in several locations throughout the document, you would insert several REF fields that refer to the bookmark. Using REF fields is easier than creating several bookmarks that will contain the same information. Another benefit of REF fields is that any time the referenced bookmark changes, the REF field automatically updates to show the new bookmark value.

To insert a REF field, select Insert ➤ Fields from the main menu, REF from the Field Names listing, and then select the desired bookmark from the Field Properties listing (this is not applicable, though, if the referenced bookmark is actually destroyed).

▪Tip To avoid any issues related to referring to a bookmark in code, insert at least one character (a space will do) into each `Bookmark` within the document template. Then insert REF fields for duplicating the `Bookmark` as desired throughout the document. Then, in the code, call the `InsertBefore` method of the `Bookmark` object to insert text at the beginning of the `Bookmark`'s `Range`. This will leave the `Bookmark` intact for future use.

SaveDoc

Thanks to our two previous bookmark methods, we now have an updated document filled with custom values. All that's left to make this a whiz-bang class is to actually save the document somewhere. The `SaveDoc` method will save the updated document to the folder specified in the class's `SavePath` property:

```
Private Function SaveDoc() As String
  Try
    m_appW.ActiveDocument.Fields.Update()
    m_appW.ActiveDocument.SaveAs(m_SavePath & "\" & _
      m_Contact.CompanyName & " - " & m_FileName)

    m_SavedPathAndFileName = m_Contact.CompanyName & " - " & m_FileName
    m_DocSaved = True

  Catch ex As Exception
    m_DocSaved = False
  End Try

End Function
```

In case the document contains any REF fields linked to bookmarks, the method calls the `Field` collection's `Update` method:

```
m_appW.ActiveDocument.Fields.Update()
```

Next, the document is saved to the specified save location, m_SavedPathAndFileName is updated with the full path and filename of the saved document, and DocSaved flag is set to True:

```
m_appW.ActiveDocument.SaveAs(m_SavePath & "\" & _
  m_Contact.CompanyName & " - " & m_FileName)

m_SavedPathAndFileName = m_Contact.CompanyName & " - " & m_FileName
m_DocSaved = True
```

If any error occurs along the way, the DocSaved flag is set to False:

```
Catch ex As Exception
  m_DocSaved = False
```

Form and Control Events

Everything's almost all set now. All that remains to complete the class is to call the appropriate methods from the form's two Button objects.

cbOK_Click

The OK Button is the spark that kicks everything off. To get things going, it calls the Update-BookMarks method. It then saves the document and closes the form.

```
Private Sub cbOK_Click(ByVal sender As System.Object, _
  ByVal e As System.EventArgs) Handles cbOK.Click

  UpdateBookMarks()

  Me.SaveDoc()
  Me.Close()
End Sub
```

cbCancel_Click

The Cancel Button isn't exactly exciting, but it would really annoy the user if we didn't have it. So here it is:

```
Private Sub cbCancel_Click(ByVal sender As System.Object, _
  ByVal e As System.EventArgs) Handles cbCancel.Click

  Me.Close()
End Sub
```

The Settings Form

We've now completed all the new material in this chapter, but we have two more classes to create, both of which will be familiar from Chapter 2: Settings and GetUpdates. We'll take a quick run through them, highlighting any differences from the versions in Chapter 2.

The Settings form is a copy of the Settings form in Chapter 2, but it has been slightly modified. In addition to specifying a folder location and database settings, this version captures the location of an Outlook folder. This allows the user to specify the location of the folder containing Bravo Corp Client contact items.

In creating this form, we will look at how to save user settings to the file system and how to retrieve and load them into memory when the add-in initializes. The key difference in this version of the form (as compared with Chapter 2's Settings form) is the addition of a field allowing the user to select an Outlook folder containing contact items. The discussion of this new field explains the intricacies of storing folder information that can be used to quickly identify and retrieve the folder in code.

Figure 3-15 illustrates the modified version of the Settings form. The modifications require a GroupBox control (gbOutlook), a Label control (lblFolderID), a TextBox control (txtClientsFolder), and a Button control (cbPickFolder).

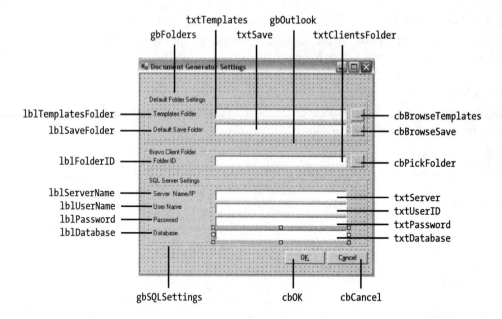

Figure 3-15. *The modified* Settings *form*

Variable Declarations

The Settings form now has two class-level variables:

```
Private entryID As String
Private storeID As String
```

These variables store the selected folder's MAPI data store EntryID and StoreID values.

Methods

The SaveSettings and LoadSettings methods are slightly modified from their Chapter 2 versions to include the new settings.

SaveSettings

The modified parts of the SaveSettings method are shown in bold:

```
Private Function SaveSettings()
  Try
    UserSettings.TemplatesFolder = txtTemplates.Text
    UserSettings.SaveFolder = txtSave.Text
    UserSettings.DatabaseName = txtDatabase.Text
    UserSettings.ServerName = txtServer.Text
    UserSettings.UserName = txtUserID.Text
    UserSettings.Password = txtPassword.Text
```

```
    UserSettings.ClientsFolderPath = txtClientsFolder.Text
    UserSettings.EntryID = EntryID
    UserSettings.StoreID = StoreID
    UserSettings.SaveSettings()
  Catch ex As Exception
    MsgBox(ex.Message)
  End Try

End Function
```

LoadSettings

The modified parts of the LoadSettings method are shown in bold:

```
Private Function LoadSettings()
  Try
    txtTemplates.Text = UserSettings.TemplatesFolder
    txtSave.Text = UserSettings.SaveFolder
    txtDatabase.Text = UserSettings.DatabaseName
    txtServer.Text = UserSettings.ServerName
    txtUserID.Text = UserSettings.UserName
    txtPassword.Text = UserSettings.Password
    txtClientsFolder.Text = UserSettings.ClientsFolderPath
    entryID = UserSettings.EntryID
    storeID = UserSettings.StoreID
  Catch ex As Exception
    MsgBox(ex.Message)
  End Try
End Function
```

Events

A single event is needed for the cbPickFolder event:

```
Private Sub cbPickFolder_Click(ByVal sender As System.Object, _
  ByVal e As System.EventArgs) Handles cbPickFolder.Click

  Dim str() As String

  str = appOutlook.PickContactsFolder()
  txtClientsFolder.Text = str(0)
  EntryID = str(1)
  StoreID = str(2)

End Sub
```

The appOutlook.PickContactsFolder method displays a dialog box (shown in Figure 3-10) allowing the user to select an Outlook folder. PickContactsFolder returns a string array containing the folder path, MAPI EntryID, and MAPI StoreID, and the procedure uses these values to update txtClientsFolder with the FolderPath, while the EntryID and StoreID values are stored within the class.

The UserSettings Class

The UserSettings class is a slightly modified copy of the version included with the Presentation Generator of Chapter 2. This class shows how to use XML to store the user's settings information on their file system. The class also shows how to read an XML file's contents and load its data inside a shared class, where the data is available to all other objects in the project without requiring a UserSettings object instance. I will not provide a discussion of this class except to explain the new code required to save the Outlook folder information: the Bravo Corp Clients folder.

Three properties need to be saved from the Outlook folder selected in the Settings form: the FolderPath, EntryID, and StoreID. The FolderPath provides meaningful information to the user regarding the folder they selected (the path of the folder selected). The latter two properties are what really matter to the add-in because together they identify the specified folder when calling appOutlook.GetFolder.

Variable Declarations

The following variables are added to the declarations section:

```
Private Shared m_strEntryID As String
Private Shared m_strStoreID As String
Private Shared m_strClientsFolderPath As String
```

In addition, the SETTINGS_XML_FILE_NAME constant needs a different value:

```
Private Const SETTINGS_XML_FILE_NAME As String = "\docgen.xml"
```

Property Procedures

The new properties for the UserSettings class are described in the following sections.

ClientsFolderPath

The ClientsFolderPath property is a read/write property representing the name and path within the Outlook folder containing the Bravo Corp client records:

```
Public Shared Property ClientsFolderPath() As String
  Get
    Return m_strClientsFolderPath
  End Get
  Set(ByVal Value As String)
    m_strClientsFolderPath = Value
  End Set
End Property
```

EntryID

The EntryID property is a read/write property representing the unique ID of the folder speci-fied by ClientsFolderPath:

```
Public Shared Property EntryID() As String
  Get
    Return m_strEntryID
  End Get
  Set(ByVal Value As String)
    m_strEntryID = Value
  End Set
End Property
```

StoreID

The StoreID property is a read/write property representing the unique ID of the folder speci-fied by ClientsFolderPath:

```
Public Shared Property StoreID() As String
  Get
    Return m_strStoreID
  End Get
  Set(ByVal Value As String)
    m_strStoreID = Value
  End Set
End Property
```

Methods

The UserSettings class's two methods have each been updated to save and retrieve the three new properties.

SaveSettings

The SaveSettings method saves the specified add-in user settings to an XML file on the user's system. Three lines (shown in bold) have been added to the method to save the new proper-ties of the UserSettings class:

```
Public Shared Function SaveSettings() As Boolean
  Try
    Dim strPath As String
    strPath = strPath.Concat(UserSettings.SettingsPath, SETTINGS_XML_FILE_NAME)
    Dim xtwSettings As New XmlTextWriter(strPath.ToString, _
      System.Text.Encoding.UTF8)

    With xtwSettings
      .Formatting = Formatting.Indented
      .Indentation = 2
      .QuoteChar = """"c
```

```
         .WriteStartDocument(True)
         .WriteComment("User Settings Document Generator Add-In")
         .WriteStartElement("BravoDocGenUserSettings")
         .WriteAttributeString("UserName", UserSettings.UserName)
         .WriteAttributeString("Password", UserSettings.Password)
         .WriteAttributeString("SaveFolder", UserSettings.SaveFolder)
         .WriteAttributeString("TemplatesFolder", UserSettings.TemplatesFolder)
         .WriteAttributeString("ServerName", UserSettings.ServerName)
         .WriteAttributeString("DatabaseName", UserSettings.DatabaseName)
         .WriteAttributeString("ClientsFolderPath",UserSettings.ClientsFolderPath)
         .WriteAttributeString("EntryID", UserSettings.EntryID)
         .WriteAttributeString("StoreID", UserSettings.StoreID)
         .WriteEndElement()

         .WriteEndDocument()
         .Close()
      End With

      Return True
   Catch ex As Exception
      Return False
   End Try
End Function
```

LoadSettings

The LoadSettings method loads the specified user settings from an XML file on the user's system. Three lines (shown in bold) have been added to the method to load the new properties' values into the UserSettings class:

```
Public Shared Function LoadSettings(ByVal FilePath As String) As Boolean
   Try
      'if the settings file exists, then we know we are okay
      m_strSettingsPath = FilePath
      'create full path to settings file
      Dim strPath As String
      strPath = strPath.Concat(FilePath, SETTINGS_XML_FILE_NAME)

      'Test for the existence of the settings file
      Dim fi As New FileInfo(strPath)
      If fi.Exists Then
         'open the settings file for reading into memory
         Dim xtrSettings As New XmlTextReader(strPath.ToString)
         'move through the XML content and fill variables
         With xtrSettings
            .MoveToContent()
```

```
            m_strTemplatesFolder = .GetAttribute("TemplatesFolder")
            m_strSaveFolder = .GetAttribute("SaveFolder")
            m_strDatabaseName = .GetAttribute("DatabaseName")
            m_strServerName = .GetAttribute("ServerName")
            m_strUserName = .GetAttribute("UserName")
            m_strPassword = .GetAttribute("Password")
            m_strClientsFolderPath = .GetAttribute("ClientsFolderPath")
            m_strEntryID = .GetAttribute("EntryID")
            m_strStoreID = .GetAttribute("StoreID")
            .Close()

            Return True
        End With
      Else
        'Settings do not exist so alert the user...
        MsgBox("The Document Generator settings file does not exist." & _
        vbCrLf & vbCrLf & _
        "Please set your settings now.", MsgBoxStyle.Information, _
        "Settings Not Found")
        m_strSettingsPath = FilePath
      End If

  Catch ex As Exception
      Return False
  End Try
End Function
```

The GetUpdates Form Class

The GetUpdates form (see Figure 3-16 for the design layout) is exactly the same as the version in Chapter 2, with the exception that it downloads binaries from a different table within the database. The form demonstrates how to connect to a SQL Server database, retrieve Word document template files, and save the templates to the file system in the folder location defined in the user settings file.

For the sake of completeness, the modified DownloadTemplates method of the GetUpdates form is as follows (with the modifications shown in bold):

```
Private Function DownloadTemplates() As Boolean
  Dim cnn As New SqlConnection
  Dim da As New SqlDataAdapter("Select * From tblDocuments", cnn)
  Dim ds As New DataSet
  Dim dt As DataTable
  Dim drRecord As DataRow
  Dim btBinary() As Byte
  Dim iSize As Long
  Dim strCnn As String
```

```vbnet
    Try
        strCnn = "Server=" & UserSettings.ServerName
        strCnn = strCnn.Concat(strCnn, ";uid=" & UserSettings.UserName)
        strCnn = strCnn.Concat(strCnn, ";pwd=" & UserSettings.Password)
        strCnn = strCnn.Concat(strCnn, ";database=" & UserSettings.DatabaseName)

        cnn.ConnectionString = strCnn.ToString
        cnn.Open()
        'Fill the Dataset using the SQLDataAdapter
        da.Fill(ds, "tblDocuments")


        'Loop through all records and save to the Default Save Location
        For Each drRecord In ds.Tables("tblDocuments").Rows
            btBinary = drRecord("DocumentBinary")

            Dim strPath As String = UserSettings.TemplatesFolder
            strPath = strPath.Concat(strPath, drRecord("DocumentName").ToString)

            Dim fsFile As New FileStream(strPath, FileMode.Create)
            iSize = UBound(btBinary)
            fsFile.Write(btBinary, 0, iSize)
            fsFile.Close()
            fsFile = Nothing
            strPath = Nothing
        Next drRecord

        Return True

    Catch ex As Exception
        Return False
    Finally

        cnn.Close()
        drRecord = Nothing
        ds = Nothing
        dt = Nothing
        da = Nothing
        cnn = Nothing
    End Try
End Function
```

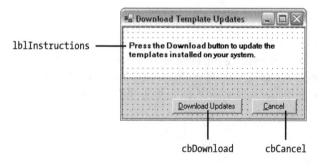

lblInstructions

cbDownload   cbCancel

Figure 3-16. *The* GetUpdates *form design layout*

The Connect Class

The Connect class for the Document Generator is a skeleton of the version discussed in Chapter 2. This version of the Connect class really only serves to provide the IDTExtensibility2 interface and initialize any classes required for the add-in to function properly at startup. Of the five methods required to implement the interface, only two have any code within them.

OnConnection

The OnConnection event looks like this:

```
Public Sub OnConnection(ByVal application As Object, _
  ByVal connectMode As Extensibility.ext_ConnectMode, _
  ByVal addInInst As Object, ByRef custom As System.Array) _
  Implements Extensibility.IDTExtensibility2.OnConnection

  applicationObject = application
  addInInstance = addInInst
  UserSettings.LoadSettings(System.Windows.Forms.Application.StartupPath)
  appOutlook.Setup(application, UserSettings.EntryID, UserSettings.StoreID)

End Sub
```

After references are set to the Outlook host application and the Document Generator add-in, the method loads the add-in's user settings and initializes the shared appOutlook class.

OnDisconnection

The OnDisconnection method shuts down the add-in as follows:

```
Public Sub OnDisconnection(ByVal RemoveMode As _
  Extensibility.ext_DisconnectMode, ByRef custom As System.Array) _
  Implements Extensibility.IDTExtensibility2.OnDisconnection

  appOutlook.ShutDown()
  UserSettings.SaveSettings()

End Sub
```

Summary

In this chapter, you learned how to automate the creation of Word documents by using Word bookmarks. In addition, you learned how to combine this strategy with the functionality of Outlook to create a familiar user interface. Lastly, you learned a strategy for saving the new generated documents to the user's system and then creating an Outlook `MailItem` containing the documents as attachments.

CHAPTER 4

■ ■ ■

Email Template Engine
Combining Outlook and Regular Expressions in a COM Add-In to Automate Frequently Used Content

Have you ever wished for a tool that could reduce the pain and frustration of having to repeat yourself? This chapter describes how to build a COM add-in for storing and retrieving email content templates for quick reuse by a user.

Outlook already includes a standard method for creating template emails based on frequently used content. The Email Template Engine in this chapter takes a similar approach but extends the idea by giving the user the ability to define, or *tag*, areas in the mail where specific kinds of text should be inserted (such as contact information, a company address, a standard footer, and so on). And by retrieving the information to be inserted from an Outlook Contact-Item, several users can create emails from the same template, and each will end up with a customized message to send out.

The Email Template Engine (ETE) is a COM add-in hosted within Microsoft Outlook. Unlike the add-ins in Chapters 2 and 3, the ETE only interacts with Outlook. No SQL Server database, no other Office applications—the add-in is the only component of the solution. The add-in is written in Visual Basic .NET, and it demonstrates the following key techniques:

- **Creating a dynamic command bar**: This chapter goes beyond creating a static menu for the add-in—the menu created here changes on the fly to reflect the templates stored in the email templates folder. The menu in this add-in basically reads the contents of the email templates folder and then builds a hierarchical menu based on the template categories in the folder. We will also look at how to use the email template folder's Change event to trigger updates to the add-in's command bar.

- **Using regular expressions**: We will use regular expressions to locate specified tags within email templates and replace them with data from an Outlook contact item. We will also look at how to create the custom tags that specify and describe areas within the email templates that will receive the contact data. First, though, we will look at how regular expressions work and how to define multiple parts to a regular expression, which allows a developer to extract only certain portions of a matched string.

- **Creating events in a class**: We will see how to create event stubs in a class by utilizing the RaiseEvent keyword inside the BravoMenu class. This technique shows how to raise events that other objects in the project can respond to as needed. Specifically, this technique shows how to create Click event stubs for each command bar button created by the BravoMenu class. This strategy allows BravoMenu to encapsulate the add-in's menu-creation code while also providing a mechanism for other classes to implement custom logic for the menu's buttons.

- **Using a single Click event for multiple dynamically created buttons**: We will use a single command bar button Click event for all of the buttons that are created for the available email templates. This technique illustrates how command bar buttons can, in effect, be used much like a VB 6 control array.

Designing the Email Template Engine

For this application, email templates will be stored in an Outlook folder, and they will be used as the basis for new emails. These templates will include text that can be used to respond to typical information requests, and they will also include tags that define data points where related text will be inserted when the add-in creates the email message. For example, the tags would define the location within the template where the user's contact information should be inserted.

Our scenario for this chapter assumes that the user has just received an email asking a fairly common question, and the user has created a template that answers this question. With Outlook open, the user creates a new template-based email by selecting an email template from a custom menu (see Figure 4-1). The Email Templates menu item consists of all available templates in the user's Outlook Email Templates folder (a folder within Outlook specified in the add-in's Settings form). This menu uses the categories assigned to each template to group related template types. For example, in Figure 4-1, the user selects a Trial Account Details template, which is one of the templates available in the Sales category.

Once the user selects the appropriate email template from the menu, the add-in creates a new email message by replacing the tagged sections of the email template with information about the user (name, job title, phone number, etc.). The resulting email message is then displayed for the user to add to or modify as necessary before sending.

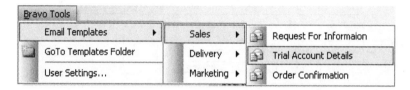

Figure 4-1. *Selecting a template to create a new email message*

Behind the scenes, several things happen when the user selects the appropriate email template from the menu:

1. The specified template is retrieved from the Email Templates folder.

2. The template is opened and scanned for any specified InfoTags. These InfoTags are simple text qualifiers that identify elements within the email that will be replaced with data from a ContactItem. The code relies on regular expressions to identify the InfoTags and replace them with the required data.

3. Each InfoTag is matched with a property from the user's ContactItem (which contains their contact information), and a new String is built containing the "usable" version of the email template.

4. A new MailItem is created that uses the String built in step 3 as its body.

5. The resulting email message is displayed so the user can make any necessary changes before sending the email to the recipient.

■**Note** Outlook allows users to create template emails (.oft files) in much the same way as this chapter's example application. This is a good feature in Outlook, but it lacks two features: text cannot be dynamically inserted at specified locations within a template-based email, and the template files are stored on the file system and require an extra level of organization. To learn more about Outlook's standard template feature, see the great article on the Microsoft web site: `http://office.microsoft.com/en-us/assistance/HA010917681033.aspx`.

The Email Template Engine (ETE) is a COM add-in hosted within Microsoft Outlook. Unlike the add-ins in Chapters 2 and 3, the ETE only interacts with Outlook. No SQL Server database, no other Office applications. The add-in is the only component of the solution (see Figure 4-2).

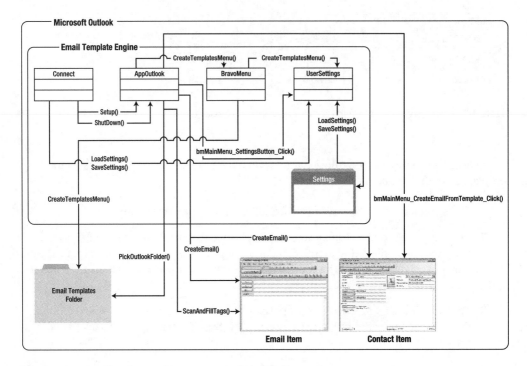

Figure 4-2. *The Email Template Engine architecture*

These are the main parts of the add-in:

- Microsoft Outlook: This is the host application for the COM add-in as well as the user interface.

- Templates folder: This is an Outlook folder that stores all email template items. Items in this folder can be MailItem and PostItem object types.

- ContactItem: A single ContactItem within the default Contacts folder stores contact information about the user.

- Connect class: This class implements the IDTExtensibility2 interface utilized by Outlook to load the add-in.

- appOutlook class: This class is the main object within the add-in. It controls the implemented logic workflow (for example, creating a new email from an email template) and it responds to the Click events of the buttons created by the BravoMenu class.

- BravoMenu class: This class encapsulates the logic required to create the add-in's menu. In addition, it raises the Click event for each command bar button created by the class.

- Settings form: This form allows the user to enter settings required by the add-in. The ETE allows the user to specify the Outlook folder that contains the email templates as well as to specify the ContactItem that contains the user's contact information.

- `UserSettings` class: This class contains the logic for writing the specified user settings to an XML file stored on the user's file system. In addition, this class includes logic for reading the values stored in the XML file and loading the values into the add-in's memory.

- Email item: The end result of the add-in's work is a newly created email based on an email template. The completed email includes contact information extracted from the `ContactItem` specified in the add-in's user settings.

The Business Scenario

Like any busy business, Bravo Corp's communications take up much valuable time. The folks at Bravo Corp are by no means antisocial, but they are always looking for ways to improve their business. After a long study and interviews with key Bravo Corp staff, an outside consultant recommended that Bravo Corp identify the most frequently repeated information, categorize each "content-bit," and build a system that allows everyone to create content templates for oft-used items.

Specifically, the consultant focused on the area of customer service, where the staff is frequently bombarded with the same questions each day. These are questions regarding

- Billing

- Product and service offerings

- Shipment status

- Support ticket status

- And so on

This chapter uses the customer service scenario as an example, but the solution could easily be modified for other situations (such as sales, operations, service delivery, internal communications, etc.).

Using Regular Expressions

Before we move on to building the template engine, it's worth taking a quick look at *regular expressions* (often abbreviated as *regex*, or *regexes* for the plural) and how they are used in this application.

Regular expressions are text patterns used to find and manipulate text. With them, you can dig through large piles of text and identify strings that match a specific pattern (such as email addresses, phone numbers, or addresses), and you can also use them to modify the text they find. The ETE uses regular expressions to locate the tags in the email template and replace them with the user's contact information.

■**Tip** A lot of tools exist for testing a regex pattern against a string. I have found the Regular Expression Evaluator by RAD Software to be invaluable when working with regular expressions. The tool is available for free at `http://www.radsoftware.com.au/web/Products/RegexDesigner/Default.aspx`.

The .NET Framework provides the System.Text.RegularExpression namespace, which provides the Regex class. The Regex class allows you to implement regular expressions in your applications for such purposes as scanning strings of text for a specified string pattern and then responding based on the scan results.

A regex pattern is typically a single line of code that looks like gibberish. Using regexes requires patience and an eye for detail, and it takes loads of testing to make them function exactly the way you want. For example, the following regex pattern is from the .NET Framework Developers Guide—it identifies a valid email address when applied to a string of text:

```
("^([\w-\.]+)@((\[[0-9]{1,3}\.[0-9]{1,3}\.[0-9]{1,3}\.)|(([\w-]+\.)+))
([a-zA-Z]{2,4}|[0-9]{1,3})(\]?)$")
```

That's 104 characters of what first may appear to be complete nonsense, but it's extremely powerful and works like a dream.

■**Note** The preceding regular expression is shown as two lines on this page because the page isn't wide enough. In actual use, regexes should be entered as one continuous line without any breaks.

I'll explain more about regexes as we go along, but a full explanation is outside the scope of this book. For more information on regexes, take a look at these web sites:

- How to Match a Pattern Using Regular Expressions and Visual Basic .NET (http://support.microsoft.com/default.aspx?scid=kb;en-us;301264)

- Regular Expressions as a Language (http://msdn.microsoft.com/library/en-us/cpguide/html/cpconregularexpressionsaslanguage.asp)

- Regular Expression HOWTO (http://www.amk.ca/python/howto/regex/)

The last link covers regexes in the context of the Python programming language, but the concepts and syntax translate well to VB and the .NET Framework.

The ETE utilizes regular expressions to identify text wrapped by specific text characters called InfoTags. Each InfoTag identifies a data-insertion point where a particular piece of text must be inserted into a template when the email is created.

Each InfoTag is composed of two parts: the *tag* and the *value*. In order to effectively fill the template with data, three steps must be accomplished:

1. All InfoTags within the template must be identified.

2. Each InfoTag value must be matched with a property value of the Outlook user's contact record in order to retrieve its value. The user's contact record is specified in the Settings form.

3. The entire InfoTag must be replaced with the value of a corresponding ContactItem property.

The following regex pattern is used in this chapter's code to complete all three steps:

```
(?<tag><!::(?<value>.*)::>
```

The pattern uses two group constructs to specify subexpressions within the pattern.

Group constructs provide a method for identifying or grouping portions of a regular expression pattern, and they are specified within a regex pattern like this:

```
?<group construct name>
```

Given this format, which is shown in Figure 4-3, it is possible to group the two matched substrings within the pattern (the tag and the value) and refer to each part by name in code. If the InfoTags use this format in a template, it's a simple matter to search for the text wrapped around the InfoTags (`<!::` & `::>`) to locate them.

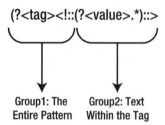

Figure 4-3. *Group constructs in a regex pattern*

Take, for example, the following InfoTag: `<!::FullName::>`. This tag identifies a data insertion point where the user's full name should be inserted. The `<!::` and `::>` characters are the tag portion of the InfoTag, while the `FullName` string identifies the value area where the intended data should be inserted at run time.

Creating the Email Template Engine

As noted earlier, the Email Template Engine (ETE) is simply a COM add-in hosted within Microsoft Outlook. Before we set about building the add-in, we need to do a bit of preparatory work in the host application, Outlook.

Creating the Email Templates Folder

The ETE relies on an Outlook folder for storing all email template files. With Outlook open, select File ➤ New ➤ Folder (or Ctrl+Shift+E). In the Create New Folder dialog box, do the following:

1. Name the folder **EmailTemplates**.

2. Select the Mail and Post Items option in the Folder Contains field.

3. Select a location for the folder in the `Bravo Corp.pst` file created in Chapter 3. Once created, the folder's location within Outlook should be `\\Bravo Corp\EmailTemplates`.

4. Click OK.

Creating the User ContactItem

We need to create a new `ContactItem` that will contain the ETE user's contact info (see Figure 4-4). Select File ➤ New ➤ Contact from Outlook's menu (or press Ctrl+Shift+C).

The information entered into this `ContactItem` will be copied into any new email created from an email template. Fill in the following fields with relevant info:

- Full Name

- Job Title

- Company

- Business Phone

- Business Fax

- Email

- Web page address

- Department (on the Details tab)

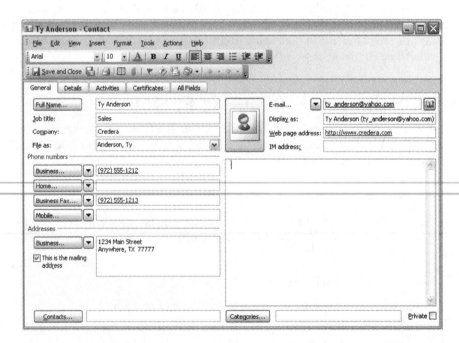

Figure 4-4. *Entering the ETE user's contact information*

Once you're done, save the contact record in the default Contacts folder.

■**Note** There is nothing magical about where you store this contact. You could save it to any folder containing `ContactItems`. The key is to remember where this record resides so that you can specify the folder in the user settings at run time.

Creating Sample Email Templates

We need to create five templates in order to provide a little content for the add-in to work with. Not only that, we need to assign at least three different Outlook categories among the five templates. Remember from the discussion in the section "The Solution" earlier that the categories help create additional submenus in the add-in's menu to group related templates (see Figure 4-1). Each of the templates must contain InfoTags that match the contact fields in the contact record (identified in the previous section).

In order to label a portion of text within the email template as an InfoTag, a string of text is used as a tag. For this add-in, the tag is `<!::`*tagname*`::>`. Table 4-1 shows how each contact field should look in the email template.

Table 4-1. *Email Template InfoTags*

ContactItem Field	InfoTag
Full Name	<!::FullName::>
Job Title	<!::JobTitle::>
Company	<!::CompanyName::>
Business Phone	<!:: BusinessTelephoneNumber::>
Business Fax	<!::BusinessFaxNumber::>
Email	<!::Email1Address::>
Web page address	<!::WebPage::>
Department	<!::Department::>

To create the first template, select File ➤ New ➤ Mail Message. Once the new mail item displays, enter **RE: Request for Information** as the subject, and enter the following as the body of the email:

```
Thank you for your request for more information regarding our services. As you
know, you can find everything you ever wanted to know about Bravo Corp at our web
site. Please feel free to visit us at:

<!::WebPage::>

If I can be of further assistance, please feel free to contact me. My information
is included below.
```

Sincerely,

```
<!::FullName::>
<!::Department::>
Bravo Corp
<!::BusinessTelephoneNumber::>
<!::BusinessFaxNumber::>
<!::Email1Address::>
```

Before saving the email template, select View ➤ Options from the email's menu (see Figure 4-5). Once the Message Options dialog box displays, enter **Sales** into the Categories field. Click Close.

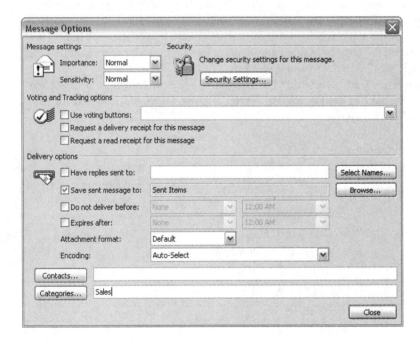

Figure 4-5. *The Message Options dialog box*

To successfully place this new email template in the Email Templates folder, you can't save it. What you need to do here is select File ➤ Move to Folder (or press Ctrl+Shift+V) and choose the Email Templates folder in the Move Item To dialog box.

Now create some more templates filled with the same InfoTags using the method just described, and give each template different categories (see Figure 4-6 for a completed example). If you like, you can use the example files provided in Chapter4.pst (which is included as part of the book's source code, available at http://www.apress.com/book/download.html). The templates are described in Table 4-2.

Table 4-2. *The Example Email Templates in* `Chapter4.pst`

Template Name	Template Category
Request for Information	Sales
Order Confirmation	Sales
Trial Account Details	Sales
Support Ticket	Support
Shipment Information	Delivery

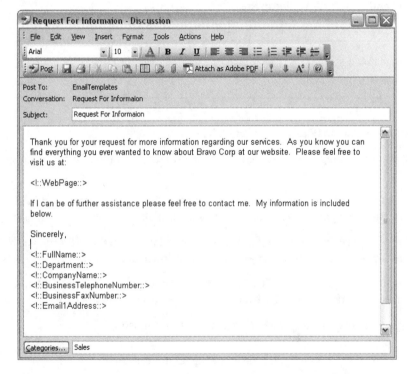

Figure 4-6. *A completed email template saved as an Outlook* `PostItem`

Building the COM Add-In

The ETE COM add-in consists of four classes and one form. Two of the classes handle the majority of the workload and will be the main focus of our discussion in this chapter. The ETE contains the following objects:

- `Connect`: This class implements the IDTExtensibility2 interface.

- `appOutlook`: This shared class acts as the main engine of the add-in. It contains the Outlook objects and events we wish to respond to. In addition, it contains a few Outlook-related utility functions that are used by other objects in the solution.

- BravoMenu: This is a utility class used to build the Outlook CommandBars required by the add-in.

- Settings: This form allows the user to change the add-in's settings. It calls the UserSettings methods that do the actual retrieving and saving of the settings.

- UserSettings: This class contains the methods for storing and retrieving the add-in's user settings.

The EmailTemplates Add-In Project

The first step is to create the ETE add-in project. With Visual Studio .NET open, create a new Shared Add-In project and name it **EmailTemplates**.

■**Note** See the "Creating the Add-In Project" section in Chapter 2 for a detailed explanation of how to create a Shared add-in project.

Complete the remaining Setup Wizard screens as follows:

1. In the Select a Programming Language window, choose Create an Add-In Using Visual Basic. Click Next.

2. The Select an Application Host window appears. You want this add-in to only load in Outlook, so uncheck all applications except Microsoft Outlook. Click Next.

3. The Enter a Name and Description window displays. Name the add-in **EmailTemplates**, and set the description to **BravoCorp Email Templates Add-in**. Click Next.

4. In the Choose Add-In Option window, select the "I would like my Add-in to load when the host application loads" option. Leave all other options unselected. Click Next.

5. The Summary screen displays all the selected options. Click Finish.

After Visual Studio creates the project, add the following references:

- Microsoft Outlook 11.0 Object Library (COM tab)

- System.Drawing.dll (.NET tab)

- System.Windows.Forms.dll (.NET tab)

The Connect Class

The Connect class's main purpose is to implement the IDTExtensibility2 interface used by the host application to call the add-in. I prefer not to put a lot of functionality here and, instead, to pass the Application object to a class that encapsulates the add-in's engine. Another purpose for the Connect class is to perform any setup or cleanup required by the objects within the add-in.

Imports Directives

The Connect class imports three assemblies, as follows:

```
Imports Microsoft.Office.Core
Imports Extensibility
Imports System.Runtime.InteropServices
```

The OnConnection Event

The OnConnection event includes the following lines of code:

```
Public Sub OnConnection(ByVal application As Object, _
  ByVal connectMode As Extensibility.ext_ConnectMode, _
  ByVal addInInst As Object, ByRef custom As System.Array) _
  Implements Extensibility.IDTExtensibility2.OnConnection

  'applicationObject = application
  'addInInstance = addInInst

  UserSettings.LoadSettings(System.Windows.Forms.Application.StartupPath)
  appOutlook.Setup(application)

End Sub
```

This gets things started by loading the user settings from the settings file stored on the user's system and then calling the Setup method of the shared appOutlook class.

■**Note** I have commented out the two lines dealing with applicationObject and addInInstance. These objects take up memory and are not used, so we can comment them out.

The OnDisconnection Event

Take a quick gander at the OnDisconnection event:

```
Public Sub OnDisconnection(ByVal RemoveMode As _
  Extensibility.ext_DisconnectMode, ByRef custom As System.Array) _
  Implements Extensibility.IDTExtensibility2.OnDisconnection

  appOutlook.ShutDown()
  UserSettings.SaveSettings()

End Sub
```

As you can see, nothing but a little bit of housekeeping is going on here. We close out any remaining Outlook references with the appOutlook class by calling its Shutdown method. In addition, we make the user happy by saving their settings for next time.

The appOutlook Class

The ETE runs as an add-in hosted within Microsoft Outlook. The appOutlook class acts as the engine for the whole solution and calls methods from all other objects in the solution.

■**Note** Although the appOutlook class has the same name as a class in Chapter 3, it is indeed different and should be created from scratch.

The appOutlook class exists, in simple terms, to respond to specific events, primarily the Click events of some very well thought out CommandBar buttons, and to control the main process of the add-in, which is creating a new email from an email template. Because the user can add, edit, or delete an email template at any time while Outlook is open, the ETE will need to respond to these changes and rebuild the menu structure as necessary. Code is needed to respond to these changes in the Email Templates folder (which is identified in the user settings).

To help control the flow of creating a new template-based email, the appOutlook class also includes code for the following tasks:

- Selecting an Outlook folder (PickOutlookFolder): This method selects a folder and stores its properties to permit access to it when needed.

- Finding a contact (LookUpContact): In this method, you'll see how to search Outlook's default contact folder for contact items matching a given name.

- Opening the templates folder (NavigateToTemplatesFolder): This method demonstrates the use of code that provides one-click access to the email templates folder in Outlook.

- Extracting an email address from a selected email message (GetCurrentSelectionEmail): This method demonstrates how to use the From email address of the currently selected email item (whether it is in the Inbox or any other folder) and insert it in the To field of a newly created email.

- Replacing InfoTags with data (ScanAndFillTags): This method identifies InfoTags inside an email template and fills them with data from the user's specified contact item. We'll look at the intricacies of identifying the InfoTag of matching the text inside the tag against a contact item property, and of replacing the entire InfoTag with the property's value.

- Creating a template-based email (CreateEmail): This method creates a new email and fills it with the strings created by ScanAndFillTags.

Imports Directives

The appOutlook class accesses the Outlook, Office.Core, and RegularExpressions namespaces.

```
Imports OL = Microsoft.Office.Interop.Outlook
Imports Microsoft.Office.Core
Imports System.Text.RegularExpressions
```

The first two lines should look familiar as they have been used in Chapters 2 and 3. The third line, however, is new. It provides quick access to the RegularExpressions namespace.

The Declarations Section

The ETE version of appOutlook contains several class-level variable declarations. Here is the full list:

```
Private Shared appOL As OL.Application
Private Shared ns As OL.NameSpace

Private Shared cbbBravoMenu As CommandBarPopup
Private Shared cbbTemplates As CommandBarPopup
Private Shared cbMenuBar As CommandBar
Private Shared fldTemplates As OL.MAPIFolder

Private Shared WithEvents itmTemplates As OL.Items
Private Shared WithEvents cbbCreateEmailFromTemplate As CommandBarButton
Private Shared WithEvents cbbSettings As CommandBarButton
Private Shared WithEvents cbbGoToTemplatesFolder As CommandBarButton
Private Shared WithEvents usData As New UserSettings

Private Shared WithEvents bmMainMenu As BravoMenu
Private Shared WithEvents bmContextMenu As BravoMenu
```

As you can see in the preceding code, we start out by declaring an Outlook Application object, as well as an Outlook NameSpace:

```
Private Shared appOL As OL.Application
Private Shared ns As OL.NameSpace
```

These variables are the topmost objects, and they will allow us to access any other Outlook objects we may need. Next is a single non-event variable:

```
Private Shared fldTemplates As OL.MAPIFolder
```

This variable will be used to hold a reference to the add-in's Email Templates folder stored within Outlook.

Next we have two event-raising variables:

```
Private Shared WithEvents usData As New UserSettings
Private Shared WithEvents bmMainMenu As BravoMenu
```

Each of these variables uses the WithEvents keyword to signify to the appOutlook class that these objects raise events. The first is the variable that will store the add-in's user settings. The other variable will store the add-in's menu.

In the previous chapters, the strategy for handling the CommandBars was to include the code in the appOutlook class. For this solution, the CommandBar-related code has its own class. This makes for cleaner, more readable code, and it also increases the chances that the class can be reused in other projects.

Methods

Once again, the appOutlook class is a shared class. It contains a mixture of methods, from utility methods to methods that implement specific business-rule logic. The strategy here is to use the appOutlook class to handle all Outlook-related tasks.

Setup

Instead of creating a New sub procedure, I have used the Setup sub procedure here. I like this way of handling a shared class because I can choose when I want the class to actually create its environment.

The New method is called whenever the class is instantiated, and since appOutlook is a Shared class, the constructor method (New) executes at the beginning of the add-in's execution. No doubt there are benefits to placing the code in this routine in the class's constructor, but for me it is an issue of control. I want to control when my shared class executes.

▓**Note** One benefit of using the constructor method is that you do not need to call the constructor. It runs at the beginning of program execution. The result would be one less method in the class.

Take a look at the Setup method:

```
Friend Shared Sub Setup(ByVal oApp As OL.Application)
  Try
    appOL = oApp
    ns = appOL.GetNamespace("MAPI")
    bmMainMenu = New BravoMenu

    fldTemplates = ns.GetFolderFromID(UserSettings.EntryID, _
      UserSettings.StoreID)

  Catch ex As Exception
    Select Case ex.Message
      Case "The operation cannot be performed because the" & _
        "object has been deleted."

        bmMainMenu = New BravoMenu
```

```
        MsgBox("You have not specified the location for your " & _
            "Bravo Corp Email Templates." & vbCrLf & vbCrLf & _
            "Please choose a location using the Settings form under the " & _
            "Bravo Tools Menu.", MsgBoxStyle.Critical, _
            "Missing Email Templates Folder")
      Case Else
    End Select
  End Try

End Sub
```

First off, this procedure uses the Friend keyword in order to make it available to the Connect class (as well as any other object in the project). The procedure also requires that an Outlook Application object be passed as an argument:

```
Friend Shared Sub Setup(ByVal oApp As OL.Application)
  Try
    appOL = oApp
```

The Application object is assigned to the class's appOL variable in order to keep a reference to the executing Outlook host alive while the add-in is loaded in memory and executing in its own right.

Continuing on, the class sets up references to the Outlook MAPI store, the Bravo Tools menu, and the Outlook folder containing the email templates:

```
ns = appOL.GetNamespace("MAPI")
bmMainMenu = New BravoMenu

fldTemplates = ns.GetFolderFromID(UserSettings.EntryID, _
  UserSettings.StoreID)
```

These are three of the main objects needed to make the ETE a workable solution. Remember, the Namespace object is the only data store object within Outlook. I am sure that Microsoft will add more at some point, but for now that's all there is. Setting up a reference to it now allows for quick access to all the Outlook data and objects the add-in will need to access later.

The bmMainMenu object is the menu of the add-in, and it will be covered in detail later in the chapter. For now, you need to know that the BravoMenu class creates the CommandBars for the add-in but does not handle any of the events related to the created CommandBars and Command-BarButtons. Instead, these events are "published" (my term) to the class that instantiated the BravoMenu. In this case, the "instantiating" class is the appOutlook class.

The Namespace object makes it possible to find the Email Templates folder and store a reference to it using the MAPI EntryID and StoreID retrieved from the UserSettings class.

The next few lines of code perform some basic error trapping:

```
Catch ex As Exception
  Select Case ex.Message
    Case "The operation cannot be performed because the" & _
      "object has been deleted."
```

```
        bmMainMenu = New BravoMenu

        MsgBox("You have not specified the location for your " & _
           "Bravo Corp Email Templates." & vbCrLf & vbCrLf & _
           "Please choose a location using the Settings form under the " & _
           "Bravo Tools Menu.", MsgBoxStyle.Critical, & _
           "Missing Email Templates Folder")
      Case Else
    End Select
  End Try
End Sub
```

These lines trap the situation where the Email Templates folder does not exist. This situation could arise in any of the following situations:

- This is the first time the add-in has executed.

- The user has deleted the folder.

- The user moved the folder to a different .pst file. (This would cause the folder to receive a new EntryID and StoreID and any previously specified settings would thus be incorrect.)

▪**Note** No problem would arise if the user were to change the name of the folder and leave it in the same location. The EntryID and StoreID would not be affected because the folder object remains the same.

If the add-in cannot find the folder, the method still creates a basic menu but it also notifies the user that the ETE cannot locate the Email Templates folder.

ShutDown

The ShutDown procedure handles the task of closing out the appOutlook class:

```
Friend Shared Sub ShutDown()
  appOL.Quit()
End Sub
```

All this method does is close the reference to Outlook. Given how much memory Outlook eats up, this is a fairly important task.

PickOutlookFolder

The ETE needs to know the location of the Email Templates folder, and the best way to give it this information is to provide the user with the means to select a folder. The following code handles this task:

```
Friend Shared Function PickOutlookFolder() As String()
  Dim fld As OL.MAPIFolder
  Dim str(2) As String
```

```
Do

  fld = ns.PickFolder

  If fld Is Nothing Then
    Exit Function

  Else
    If fld.DefaultItemType = OL.OlItemType.olMailItem _
      Or OL.OlItemType.olPostItem Then

      str(0) = fld.FolderPath
      str(1) = fld.EntryID
      str(2) = fld.StoreID
      Return str
    Else
      MsgBox("Please pick a folder containing Mail or Post items.")

    End If
  End If

  Loop While fld.DefaultItemType <> OL.OlItemType.olMailItem Or _
    OL.OlItemType.olPostItem
End Function
```

The first thing the preceding code does is create two objects to get the job done—a MAPI-Folder and a String array:

```
Dim fld As OL.MAPIFolder
Dim str(2) As String
```

The MAPIFolder object will allow us to retrieve and store the folder properties we need, and the String array will be where we store them.

Now that all objects are ready to go, the next lines implement a loop and ask the user to select an Outlook folder. Assuming a folder is selected, the method verifies that the folder uses either MailItem objects or PostItem objects as the default item type:

```
Do

  fld = ns.PickFolder

  If fld Is Nothing Then
    Exit Function

  Else
    If fld.DefaultItemType = OL.OlItemType.olMailItem _
      Or OL.OlItemType.olPostItem Then
```

If all checks out okay, the FolderPath, EntryID, and StoreID of the selected folder are stored in the method's String array:

```
str(0) = fld.FolderPath
str(1) = fld.EntryID
str(2) = fld.StoreID
Return str
```

The filled array returns as the value of PickOutlookFolder. If the user selects a folder with the wrong type of data items (TaskItem, ContactItem, etc.), the method informs the user of the correct type of folder required by the add-in, and it performs another loop to give the user another chance to select a folder:

```
      Else
        MsgBox("Please pick a folder containing Mail or Post items.")

      End If
    End If

Loop While fld.DefaultItemType <> OL.OlItemType.olMailItem Or _
  OL.OlItemType.olPostItem
```

LookupContact

The user's contact information is kept within a ContactItem stored in the default Outlook Contacts folder. When the user creates a template-based email, the information contained in the ContactItem needs to be retrieved. This is exactly where the LookupContact method comes into play.

```
Private Shared Function LookupContact(ByVal FullName As String) _
  As OL.ContactItem

  Dim ci As OL.ContactItem
  Dim fldContacts As OL.MAPIFolder

  fldContacts = ns.GetDefaultFolder _
    (OL.OlDefaultFolders.olFolderContacts)

  ci = fldContacts.Items.Find("[FullName] = '" & FullName & "'")
  If Not TypeName(ci) = "Nothing" Then
    Return ci

  Else
    MsgBox("Contact not found.")
  End If

  Return ci
End Function
```

From the top, LookupContact requires a String to represent the full name of the user. This String object is provided as a method argument:

```
Private Shared Function LookupContact(ByVal FullName As String) _
  As OL.ContactItem
```

Two objects are needed to navigate the default Contacts folder and retrieve the user's ContactItem:

```
Dim ci As OL.ContactItem
Dim fldContacts As OL.MAPIFolder
```

The next few lines search the Contacts for the desired ContactItem:

```
fldContacts = ns.GetDefaultFolder _
  (OL.OlDefaultFolders.olFolderContacts)

ci = fldContacts.Items.Find("[FullName] = '" & FullName & "'")
If Not TypeName(ci) = "Nothing" Then
  Return ci

Else
  MsgBox("Contact not found.")
End If

  Return ci
End Function
```

In these lines, LookupContact first finds the default folder and sets up a reference to it. Then the method searches the folder by calling the folder's Find method, looking for a contact record matching the passed FullName argument. If the record is found, it is returned as the value of the function. If the search fails to turn up a ContactItem, the user receives a message explaining the situation.

NavigateToTemplatesFolder

The NavigateToTemplatesFolder method provides a quick way to move the user to their selected Email Templates folder. This is done by changing the ActiveExplorer object's CurrentFolder property:

```
Private Shared Sub NavigateToTemplatesFolder()
  appOL.ActiveExplorer.CurrentFolder = fldTemplates
End Sub
```

The ActiveExplorer is simply the currently active Explorer object. Explorers are the objects that display the Outlook folder contents within the user interface. In addition, these objects provide methods for navigating Outlook's folder structure and manipulating items with code.

By assigning the CurrentFolder property of appOL.ActiveExplorer to the fldTemplates object, the method moves the user to the location in the folder hierarchy where the Email

Templates folder resides. This method executes when called by one of the `CommandBarButton` events covered later in the chapter.

Tip There is a lot of confusion about the `Explorer` and `Inspector` objects in Outlook, and I am often asked, "What's the difference?" In a nutshell, an `Explorer` object is used to access and display items in a folder, while an `Inspector` is used to access and display an individual item within an Outlook form (such as the Task form, Email form, etc.).

To learn more, read the following two articles available on MSDN: "Understanding the Explorer and Inspector Objects" (`http://msdn.microsoft.com/library/en-us/modcore/html/ deovrunderstandingexplorerinspectorobjects.asp`) and "An Introduction to Programming Outlook 2003 Using C#" (`http://www.microsoft.com/indonesia/msdn/ol03csharp.asp`).

ScanAndFillTags

We've now got the code to allow the user to select an email template, but we need a way to look inside the chosen template and scan for any existing InfoTags. Not only that, we need a method to match any InfoTags that match up with properties in the user's `ContactItem`. This is exactly what the `ScanAndFillTags` method does.

```
Private Shared Function ScanAndFillTags(ByVal TemplateBody As String, _
  ByVal UserName As String)

  'Scan the string for tags, match up to properties of a ContactItem.
  'The UserName string is used to find the CI.
  Dim strNewBody As String
  strNewBody = TemplateBody

  Dim ci As OL.ContactItem
  ci = LookupContact(UserName)

  'Create the Regex object using the ETE InfoTag pattern
  Dim re As New Regex("(?<tag><!::(?<value>.*)::>)", RegexOptions.IgnoreCase)
  Dim m As Match
  Dim gValue As Group
  Dim gTag As Group
  Dim strPropValue As String
  Try
    'Scan the email template body for matches
    For Each m In re.Matches(strNewBody)
      'For each match, extract the Value portion of the pattern
      'in order to match with ContactItem's property of the
      'same name
      gValue = m.Groups("value")
```

```
        'Retrieve corresponding value from the CI object
        strPropValue = ci.ItemProperties(gValue.Value).Value
        'Replace the entire InfoTag with the new value
        strNewBody = re.Replace(strNewBody, m.Groups("tag").Value, strPropValue)
    Next


    Return strNewBody
Catch ex As Exception
    MsgBox(ex.Message)
End Try


End Function
```

Lots of great things occur here—this is the meat of the whole add-in. In fact, everything covered so far in this chapter leads to this function.

Starting out, ScanAndFillTags requires a String object to store the text of what will become the body for the new email. In addition, the function needs to know the name of the current user, and this is also passed as a String argument:

```
Private Shared Function ScanAndFillTags(ByVal TemplateBody As String, _
    ByVal UserName As String)
```

Next, the method declares a couple of working variables and assigns the values of the passed arguments to them:

```
Dim strNewBody As String
strNewBody = TemplateBody

Dim ci As OL.ContactItem
ci = LookupContact(UserName)
```

The first variable, strNewBody, will contain the final version of the email message body. As the method executes, this variable will go through several edits—it will be filled with all the Info-Tags that exist in the template. The second variable is a ContactItem object that stores the user's contact record. It is filled by a call to the LookupContact function discussed earlier in this chapter.

In the next few lines, ScanAndFillTags creates several variables related to the ETE regular expression pattern:

```
Create the RegEx object using the ETE InfoTag pattern
Dim re As New Regex("(?<tag><!::(?<value>.*)::>)", RegexOptions.IgnoreCase)
Dim m As Match
Dim gValue As Group
Dim gTag As Group
Dim strPropValue As String
```

These variables are (in order) a regular expression (Regex) object for finding InfoTags based on the ETE pattern, a Match object for looping through re's match collection, two Group objects for easily splitting the two parts of the InfoTags, and a String object for temporary storage of data.

The remaining lines of the function apply the regex pattern to the strBody variable, loop through the Matches collection, and build a new email body String filled with data from the user's contact record:

```
Try
    'Scan the email template body for matches
    For Each m In re.Matches(strNewBody)
        'For each match, extract the Value portion of the pattern
        'in order to match with ContactItem's property of the
        'same name
        gValue = m.Groups("value")
        'Retrieve corresponding value from the CI object
        strPropValue = ci.ItemProperties(gValue.Value).Value
        'Replace the entire InfoTag with the new value
        strNewBody = re.Replace(strNewBody, m.Groups("tag").Value, strPropValue)
    Next

    Return strNewBody
Catch ex As Exception
    MsgBox(ex.Message)
End Try

End Function
```

The power here is in looping through each Match in the Matches collection. For each Match, the code does the following:

1. Retrieves the value of the InfoTag. This value should be the name of a valid Contact-Item property.

2. Uses the function's contact object (ci) to retrieve the value of the property identified in step 1.

3. Replaces the InfoTag string strNewBody with the value of the ContactItem property.

Once every match is processed, the newly built string object (strNewBody) returns as the value of the function. The strNewBody object contains the InfoTag values as well as the text that was in the template and that wasn't replaced.

CreateEmail

Once we've called and executed the ScanAndFillTags function, we have a String containing the body for an email. What is needed now is to create an email and insert this String into its Body property. This is what the CreateEmail method does.

```
Private Shared Function CreateEmail(ByVal EmailText As String, _
    ByVal Subject As String)
    Dim mi As OL.MailItem
    mi = appOL.CreateItem(OL.OlItemType.olMailItem)
    With mi
```

```
   .Body = EmailText.ToString
   .To = GetCurrentSelectionEmail()
   .Subject = Subject
   .Display()
 End With

End Function
```

The CreateEmail function requires two String objects as arguments that represent the message body and the message subject:

```
Private Shared Function CreateEmail(ByVal EmailText As String, _
   ByVal Subject As String)
```

Next, the method declares and creates an email object and assigns values to the needed properties:

```
 mi = appOL.CreateItem(OL.OlItemType.olMailItem)
 With mi

   .Body = EmailText.ToString
   .To = GetCurrentSelectionEmail()
   .Subject = Subject
   .Display()
 End With
```

Once the email object is created, the Body property receives text from the string created in ScanAndFillTags. The To field receives the email address of the currently selected MailItem and once the subject is assigned, the email is displayed to the user, and they are free to do as they please.

GetCurrentSelectionEmail

To finish the whole workflow, we need to extract the email address from the currently selected Outlook email item and insert the email address as the value for the newly created email's TO field. This strategy mimics Outlook's reply workflow where a new email is created from the currently selected email item.

```
Private Shared Function GetCurrentSelectionEmail() As String
 Dim miSelected As OL.MailItem

 Try

   miSelected = appOL.ActiveExplorer.Selection(1)
   Return miSelected.SenderEmailAddress

 Catch ex As Exception
   Return ""
 End Try

End Function
```

The method begins by defining the function's return value as a `String` and creating a `MailItem` object:

```
Private Shared Function GetCurrentSelectionEmail() As String
  Dim miSelected As OL.MailItem
```

The `MailItem` object stores the currently selected item in the `ActiveExplorer`:

```
  Try

    miSelected = appOL.ActiveExplorer.Selection(1)
    Return miSelected.SenderEmailAddress
```

All of this works as long as the `ActiveExplorer` is currently displaying the Inbox or any other folder containing `MailItems`. However, it is possible that no selection exists or that the current selection is not a `MailItem` type. The method traps this possibility (and all other possible errors) by using the `Catch` statement:

```
  Catch ex As Exception
    Return ""
  End Try

End Function
```

This is a simple way of dealing with the possible errors, but it does the job for this example. If no item is selected in the `ActiveExplorer`, or if the current selection is not a `MailItem`, the function returns an empty string. This strategy allows the user to manually select their desired recipient.

Property Procedures

Several property procedures are needed to make a few of the variables in `appOutlook` available to other classes. This could be done by declaring them all as class-level public variables, but proper object-oriented design requires the use of property procedures. It will take a little extra time, but the code will be solid.

The `appOutlook` class provides other classes with access to three key objects in the add-in: the host Outlook application object, the MAPI namespace object, and the Email Templates folder object. We don't want to allow any changes to these variables, so each will be made available through a read-only property procedure.

Since `appOutlook` is a shared class, and since we are making these objects available as properties of the class, it is possible to access them without having to create them. For example, whenever access to the Outlook `Application` object is needed, it can be accomplished with a line like this:

```
appOutlook.Application
```

Need to grab a template item? It's easy:

```
appOutlook.TemplatesFolder.Items(1)
```

Very handy stuff.

Application

The Application property returns an Outlook application object.

```
Friend Shared ReadOnly Property Application() As OL.Application
  Get
    Return appOL
  End Get

End Property
```

CurrentNamespace

The CurrentNamespace property returns an Outlook Namespace object that provides access to the underlying Outlook MAPI data store.

```
Friend Shared ReadOnly Property CurrentNamespace() As OL.NameSpace
  Get
    Return ns
  End Get
End Property
```

TemplatesFolder

The TemplatesFolder property returns a Folder object that is a reference to the Outlook folder containing the email template items. This folder is specified as part of the user settings.

```
Friend Shared Property TemplatesFolder() As OL.MAPIFolder
  Get
    Return fldTemplates
  End Get
  Set(ByVal Value As OL.MAPIFolder)
    fldTemplates = Value
  End Set
End Property
```

Tip When you declare a property (or any other object) with the Friend keyword, only objects within the project will be able to see it and reference it. No objects outside of the project will even know it exists.

Events

The appOutlook class responds to several events made available by the usData and bmMainMenu variables.

The AfterSettingsChange event takes care of the possibility that the user might make changes that affect the add-in's menu structure.

The remaining events in the class all deal with the bmMainMenu object. The first three events are thrown from the bmMainMenu's Items collection. The last three events are all thrown by the CommandBarButton objects created in the BravoMenu class. The business logic code is placed in the appOutlook class, as it is the object controlling the Outlook application and implementing the business rules.

■**Note** The code could just as easily be placed in the BravoMenu class, but in an attempt to keep the BravoMenu class business-rule agnostic, no business rules are included there, and any objects that need to throw events do so within the appOutlook class.

---

usData_AfterSettingsChange

At any time, the user could make changes that affect the menu structure of the add-in. The AfterSettingsChange event of the usData object responds to this possibility.

```
Private Shared Sub usData_AfterSettingsChange(ByVal EntryID As _
  String, ByVal StoreID As String) Handles usData.AfterSettingsChange
    Try
      If appOL.Explorers.Count > 0 Then
        bmMainMenu.CreateTemplatesMenu()
      End If
    Catch ex As Exception
      MsgBox(ex.Message)
    End Try

End Sub
```

First we check to ensure that the Explorer object count is not zero. This check is necessary because if Outlook were shutting down, the count would be zero and we would not want to respond to the change that occurs when the user settings are saved in the Connect.OnDisconnection event. If the count is greater than zero, the event recreates the add-in's menus.

bmMainMenu_TemplatesFolder_ItemAdd

This event, and the following two that deal with the items in the Email Templates folder, all respond to changes that occur within the folder. In each case, the add-in's menu is rebuilt to properly reflect the items in the Email Templates folder.

```
Private Shared Sub bmMainMenu_TemplatesFolder_ItemAdd(ByVal Item _
  As Object) Handles bmMainMenu.TemplatesFolder_ItemAdd

  bmMainMenu.CreateTemplatesMenu()
End Sub
```

bmMainMenu_TemplatesFolder_ItemChange

The ItemChange event of the bmMainMenu's TemplatesFolder object responds, calling the Create-TemplatesMenu method. By calling CreateTemplatesMenu each time a change occurs with the folder's contents, we ensure the ETE's menu is always up to date with available templates.

```
Private Shared Sub bmMainMenu_TemplatesFolder_ItemChange(ByVal Item _
  As Object) Handles bmMainMenu.TemplatesFolder_ItemChange

  bmMainMenu.CreateTemplatesMenu()
End Sub
```

bmMainMenu_TemplatesFolder_ItemRemove

The ItemRemove event of the bmMainMenu's TemplatesFolder object responds, calling the Create-TemplatesMenu method. Once again, this call to CreateTemplatesMenu ensures the ETE's menu is always up to date with available templates.

```
Private Shared Sub bmMainMenu_TemplatesFolder_ItemRemove() _
  Handles bmMainMenu.TemplatesFolder_ItemRemove

  bmMainMenu.CreateTemplatesMenu()
End Sub
```

bmMainMenu_CreateEmailFromTemplate_Click

The bmMainMenu_CreateEmailFromTemplate_Click event responds to any of the CommandBar-Buttons that represent an available template.

```
Private Shared Sub bmMainMenu_CreateEmailFromTemplate_Click(ByVal ctrl _
  As Microsoft.Office.Core.CommandBarButton, _
    ByRef CancelDefault As Boolean) _
    Handles bmMainMenu.CreateEmailFromTemplate_Click

  Dim mi As OL.MailItem
  Dim pi As OL.PostItem

  Try
    'Something funky here trying to get the Ol.OlItemType to show.
    'Have to backspace and then it appears.
    mi = ns.Application.CreateItem(OL.OlItemType.olMailItem)
    pi = fldTemplates.Items(ctrl.Parameter)

    If Not pi Is Nothing Then
      Dim str As String = ScanAndFillTags(pi.Body, UserSettings.UserName)
      CreateEmail(str, pi.Subject)

    End If
```

```
    Catch ex As Exception
      MsgBox(ex.ToString)
    End Try
  End Sub
End Sub
```

We create two objects here: a MailItem that will end up as our new email, and a PostItem that contains the content of the selected email template.

```
Dim mi As OL.MailItem
Dim pi As OL.PostItem
```

Next, we assign a newly created email object to the MailItem object:

```
mi = ns.Application.CreateItem(OL.OlItemType.olMailItem)
```

■**Tip** When I was writing the preceding line of code, I noticed a problem with IntelliSense. I couldn't get the OlItemType portion of the constant to display in the available options. However, if I pressed the Backspace key, these items would display in the usual manner.

And then we assign the selected template to the PostItem object.

```
pi = fldTemplates.Items(ctrl.Parameter)
```

The selected CommandBarControl's parameter tells us which item should be retrieved from the Email Templates folder. If the template was retrieved successfully, the method moves on and scans the template for InfoTags and fills them with data:

```
If Not pi Is Nothing Then
  Dim str As String = ScanAndFillTags(pi.Body, UserSettings.UserName)
  CreateEmail(str, pi.Subject)

End If
```

Once the InfoTags have been filled, the function calls the CreateEmail method to create the email and display it to the user.

bmMainMenu_GoToTemplatesFolder_Click

The bmMainMenu_GoToTemplatesFolder_Click event responds to the Go to Templates Folder button on the Bravo Tools menu.

```
Private Shared Sub bmMainMenu_GoToTemplatesFolder_Click(ByVal _
  ctrl As Microsoft.Office.Core.CommandBarButton, _
    ByRef CancelDefault As Boolean) Handles _
    bmMainMenu.GoToTemplatesFolder_Click

  NavigateToTemplatesFolder()
End Sub
```

The event calls the `NavigateToTemplatesFolder` function. We already covered this method, which changes the `CurrentFolder` property of the `ActiveExplorer` object to the location of the add-in's Email Templates folder. This quickly takes the user to the Email Templates folder, where they can see all the available email templates.

▓Tip You could also display the Email Templates folder by calling the `Display` method of the `fld-Templates` variable (a `MAPIFolder` object). This would display the Email Templates folder in another Outlook window, leaving the current Outlook window in its current state. The advantage of this method is that the Email Templates folder would be visible while keeping the current folder in view within the original Outlook window (thus saving the user's place). The disadvantage is that another Outlook window is displayed and could end up confusing the user.

---

bmMainMenu_SettingsButton_Click

The `bmMainMenu_SettingsButton_Click` event responds to the Settings button's `Click` event. As in previous chapters, this button instantiates and displays the `Settings` form.

```
Private Shared Sub bmMainMenu_SettingsButton_Click(ByVal ctrl _
  As Microsoft.Office.Core.CommandBarButton, _
    ByRef CancelDefault As Boolean) _
    Handles bmMainMenu.SettingsButton_Click

  Dim frmSettings As New Settings
  frmSettings.Show()
End Sub
```

The BravoMenu Class

The `BravoMenu` class's sole purpose is to create the `CommandBar` objects that make up the Bravo Tools menu. Unlike the previous two chapters where this code was part of another class within the project, the code here has been separated into a single-purpose class. This allows for easier reuse of the code in other projects, and it increases the code's maintainability.

The approach used in the previous chapters is just as acceptable. For this chapter, though, I wanted to present another way of creating the add-in's menu. Add a new class to the project and name it **BravoMenu.vb**.

Imports Directives

`BravoMenu` uses objects in the `Outlook` and `Office.Core` namespaces, so you'll need to add the following lines in the Imports section:

```
Imports OL = Microsoft.Office.Interop.Outlook
Imports Microsoft.Office.Core
```

The Declarations Section

The BravoMenu contains the following variable declarations:

```
Private cbMenuBar As CommandBar
Private cbbTemplates As CommandBarPopup
Private cbbBravoMenu As CommandBarPopup

Private WithEvents cbbCreateEmailFromTemplate As CommandBarButton
Private WithEvents cbbSettings As CommandBarButton
Private WithEvents cbbGoToTemplatesFolder As CommandBarButton
Private WithEvents itmTemplates As OL.Items


'Class Events
Public Event SettingsButton_Click(ByVal ctrl As _
  Microsoft.Office.Core.CommandBarButton, ByRef CancelDefault As Boolean)
Public Event GoToTemplatesFolder_Click(ByVal ctrl As _
  Microsoft.Office.Core.CommandBarButton, ByRef CancelDefault As Boolean)
Public Event CreateEmailFromTemplate_Click(ByVal ctrl As _
  Microsoft.Office.Core.CommandBarButton, ByRef CancelDefault As Boolean)
Public Event TemplatesFolder_ItemAdd(ByVal Item As Object)
Public Event TemplatesFolder_ItemChange(ByVal Item As Object)
Public Event TemplatesFolder_ItemRemove()
```

Notice the addition of custom-defined Events. They make it possible to notify other objects (in this case, the appOutlook class) that something important has occurred (an event).

Events are declared much like variables are—they are given a scope definition and a name. But unlike variables, they can also define arguments that will be passed to the calling object. Events can be thrown anytime using the RaiseEvent statement.

Events

The BravoMenu class contains six defined events. Each event is essentially just a wrapper for the events of objects declared in the class. Through this coding strategy, the class publishes only those events that other classes need to respond to. This simplifies the options when writing code in the calling class, because only the relevant events are available. In addition, this strategy separates the BravoMenu from the business logic written in appOutlook. Each of the six defined events is named after the object and event it handles.

cbbSettings_Click

The cbbSettings_Click event raises the SettingsButton_Click defined event.

```
Private Sub cbbSettings_Click(ByVal Ctrl As _
  Microsoft.Office.Core.CommandBarButton, ByRef _
  CancelDefault As Boolean) Handles cbbSettings.Click

  RaiseEvent SettingsButton_Click(Ctrl, CancelDefault)
End Sub
```

Notice that we pass the arguments of the cbbSettings_Click event to the Settings-Button_Click defined event. This is all we need to complete the event handler wrapper. Each of the remaining event handlers follows the same strategy.

cbbGoToTemplatesFolder_Click

The cbbGoToTemplatesFolder_Click event raises the GoToTemplatesFolder_Click defined event.

```
Private Sub cbbGoToTemplatesFolder_Click(ByVal Ctrl As _
  Microsoft.Office.Core.CommandBarButton, _
  ByRef CancelDefault As Boolean) _
  Handles cbbGoToTemplatesFolder.Click

  RaiseEvent GoToTemplatesFolder_Click(Ctrl, CancelDefault)
End Sub
```

cbbCreateEmailFromTemplate_Click

The cbbCreateEmailFromTemplate_Click event raises the CreateEmailFromTemplate_Click defined event.

```
Private Sub cbbCreateEmailFromTemplate_Click(ByVal Ctrl As _
  Microsoft.Office.Core.CommandBarButton, _
  ByRef CancelDefault As Boolean) _
  Handles cbbCreateEmailFromTemplate.Click

  RaiseEvent CreateEmailFromTemplate_Click(Ctrl, CancelDefault)
End Sub
```

itmTemplates_ItemAdd

The itmTemplates_ItemAdd event raises the TemplatesFolder_ItemAdd defined event.

```
Private Sub itmTemplates_ItemAdd(ByVal Item As Object) _
  Handles itmTemplates.ItemAdd

  RaiseEvent TemplatesFolder_ItemAdd(Item)
End Sub
```

itmTemplates_ItemChange

The itmTemplates_ItemChange event raises the TemplatesFolder_ItemChange defined event.

```
Private Sub itmTemplates_ItemChange(ByVal Item As Object) _
  Handles itmTemplates.ItemChange

  RaiseEvent TemplatesFolder_ItemChange(Item)
End Sub
```

itmTemplates_ItemRemove

The `itmTemplates_ItemRemove` event raises the `TemplatesFolder_ItemRemove` defined event.

```
Private Sub itmTemplates_ItemRemove() Handles itmTemplates.ItemRemove
  RaiseEvent TemplatesFolder_ItemRemove()
End Sub
```

Methods

The `BravoMenu` class operates under two possible scenarios:

- The menu structure does not already exist and needs to be created. This situation typically occurs when the add-in is instantiated by Microsoft Outlook.

- Changes are made to items stored within the Email Templates folder. Anytime a template is added, edited, or removed, the menu structure needs to update itself to reflect these changes.

These tasks are accomplished by the following three methods.

New

This is the class constructor method:

```
Public Sub New()
  InitializeMenu()
End Sub
```

By implementing the `New` constructor method, the class creates the Bravo Menu automatically when the `BravoMenu` is instantiated. This is done by calling the `InitializeMenu` function within the class.

InitializeMenu

The `InitializeMenu` function creates the `CommandBar` object that will become the Bravo Tools menu. This method is basically the same as the `SetupBravoMenu` method covered in previous chapters, but with one main difference. This menu does not know how many `CommandBarButtons` it will create until run time. A `CommandBarButton` will be created for every email template within the Email Templates folder, so there could be 1, or 100, or even 1,000 buttons on the menu bar. The following lines set up the base menu for the add-in.

```
Private Function InitializeMenu()
  Dim cbCommandBars As CommandBars

  cbCommandBars = appOutlook.Application.ActiveExplorer.CommandBars
  cbMenuBar = cbCommandBars.Item("Menu Bar")

  cbbBravoMenu = cbMenuBar.FindControl(tag:="Bravo Tools")
```

```
If cbbBravoMenu Is Nothing Then
  cbbBravoMenu = cbMenuBar.Controls.Add( _
    Type:=MsoControlType.msoControlPopup, _
    Before:=6, Temporary:=True)



  With cbbBravoMenu
    .Caption = "&Bravo Tools"
    .Tag = "Bravo Tools Menu"
    .OnAction = "!<EmailTemplates.Connect>"
    .Visible = True

    '=== === === === ===
    'Create Templates Button
    cbbTemplates = cbbBravoMenu.Controls.Add( _
    Type:=MsoControlType.msoControlPopup, _
     Temporary:=True)
    With cbbTemplates
      .Caption = "Email Templates"
      .Tag = "Email Templates"
      .OnAction = "!<EmailTemplates.Connect>"
      .Visible = True
    End With

    'GoToTemplastesFolder CommandBar Button Setup
    cbbGoToTemplatesFolder = .Controls.Add( _
      Type:=MsoControlType.msoControlButton, _
      Temporary:=True)
    With cbbGoToTemplatesFolder
      .Caption = "GoTo Templates Folder"
      .Style = MsoButtonStyle.msoButtonIconAndCaption
      .Tag = "Navigate to the Email Templates Folder"
      .OnAction = "!<EmailTemplates.Connect>"
      .FaceId = 1589
      .Visible = True
    End With

    'Settings Button
    cbbSettings = .Controls.Add( _
      Type:=MsoControlType.msoControlButton, _
      Temporary:=True)
    With cbbSettings
      .Caption = "User Settings..."
      .Style = MsoButtonStyle.msoButtonIconAndCaption
      .Tag = "Change the Document Generator User Settings."
      .OnAction = "!<EmailTemplates.Connect>"
```

```
        .BeginGroup = True
        .Visible = True
    End With

  End With

  CreateTemplatesMenu()

  End If
End Function
```

This function is nearly the same as the one covered in Chapter 3, with the call to Create-
TemplatesMenu (shown in bold) being the only major difference.

Note For a detailed overview of InitializeMenu, see the discussion of the SetupBravoMenu method
in the "The appOutlook Class" section of Chapter 3.

CreateTemplatesMenu

The Templates menu is a CommandBarPop button control that contains additional CommandBar-
Button controls grouped by category. Each CommandBarButton represents an email template
from the Email Templates folder (as shown earlier in Figure 4-1). The category groupings are
based on the values assigned to the individual email templates' Categories property.

Tip Did you know that any of the item types available within Outlook can have categories assigned to
them? Even MailItems? It's true, although not always obvious. For example, a MailItem type of object
does not display a field for the Categories property in the default form design. To assign a category to the
item, the easiest thing to do is open the item in its own window and select View ➤ Options. The Message
Options dialog box will open, and you can then select categories for the item.

Here's the code for the TemplatesMenu method:

```
Public Sub CreateTemplatesMenu()
  Dim itm As Object
  Dim i As Integer

  i = 1
  fldTemplates = appOutlook.CurrentNamespace.GetFolderFromID _
    (UserSettings.EntryID, UserSettings.StoreID)
```

```
  If fldTemplates.Items.Count > 0 Then
    itmTemplates = fldTemplates.Items
    If cbbTemplates.Controls.Count > 0 Then
      Dim iCount As Integer
      For iCount = 1 To cbbTemplates.Controls.Count
        'The collection reshuffles, must always delete item #1
        'or we will get an 'Invalid Index error'
        cbbTemplates.Controls(1).Delete()
      Next
    End If

    For Each itm In itmTemplates
      If TypeOf itm Is OL.PostItem Or TypeOf itm Is OL.MailItem Then
        AddTemplateCommandButton(itm.Categories, itm.Subject)
        i += 1
      End If

    Next itm
  End If
  'store reference to the folder for use later on
  appOutlook.TemplatesFolder = fldTemplates

  Catch ex As Exception
    If Err.Number = 91 Then
      MsgBox("The Email Template Engine's settings file does not exist." & _
      vbCrLf & vbCrLf & _
      "Please set your settings now.", MsgBoxStyle.Information, _
      "Settings Not Found")
    Else
      MsgBox(ex.Message, "CreateTemplatesMenu")
    End If
  End Try

End Sub
```

In this method, the first thing to do is declare the function-level variables:

```
Dim fldTemplates As OL.MAPIFolder
Dim itm As Object
Dim i As Integer
```

The method will be looping through all the items in the Email Templates folder in order to create CommandBarButtons for each. We have declared a MAPIFolder object, a generic Object (itm), and an Integer. The loop begins by initializing the counter variable and setting a reference to the Email Templates folder:

```
i = 1
fldTemplates = appOutlook.CurrentNamespace.GetFolderFromID _
  (UserSettings.EntryID, UserSettings.StoreID)
```

Next, the method checks the folder to determine whether any template items exist before it attempts to access each item:

```
If fldTemplates.Items.Count > 0 Then
  itmTemplates = fldTemplates.Items
```

If templates exist, the next step is to delete all CommandBarButton objects nested under the Templates button (cbbTemplates). This resets the stage for the regeneration of the Templates button hierarchy.

```
If cbbTemplates.Controls.Count > 0 Then
  Dim iCount As Integer
  For iCount = 1 To cbbTemplates.Controls.Count
    'The collection reshuffles, must always delete item #1
    'or we will get an 'Invalid Index error'
    cbbTemplates.Controls(1).Delete()
  Next
End If
```

After testing that child controls do indeed exist, the loop moves through each control and deletes it. A key point here is that as the loop executes and deletes buttons, it always refers to the first control in the collection. This is because, after every deletion, the collection's index is recalculated. By deleting the control in the first position each time, we ensure that this control exists, because the collection's Count upper limit is never exceeded.

The last portion of the function calls the AddCommandButton function as it loops through every item in itmTemplates:

```
  For Each itm In itmTemplates
   If TypeOf itm Is OL.PostItem or TypeOf itm Is OL.MailItem Then
      AddCommandButton(itm.Categories, itm.Subject)
      i += 1
   End If

  Next itm
End If
```

Only PostItem and MailItem objects are used to create buttons, so the method ignores any other type of Outlook objects. It would be a mistake if they existed within this folder anyway—a CalendarItem really does not translate well into an email.

Before completing, CreateTemplatesMenu stores a reference to the specified Email Templates folder in the appOutlook class:

```
'store reference to the folder for use later on
appOutlook.TemplatesFolder = fldTemplates
```

This keeps appOutlook current regarding the specified Email Templates folder, and it helps ensure that the templates will be found when the user selects them from the add-in's menu.

A Catch block exists in the method to trap the error caused when the Email Templates folder is not known (this situation causes the fldTemplates object to be Nothing). In this case, the user settings have not been specified, so the method alerts the user of the situation and exits gracefully.

```
Catch ex As Exception
  If Err.Number = 91 Then
    MsgBox("The Email Template Engine's settings file does not exist." & _
      vbCrLf & vbCrLf & _
      "Please set your settings now.", MsgBoxStyle.Information, _
      "Settings Not Found")
  Else
    MsgBox(ex.Message, "CreateTemplatesMenu")
  End If
End Try
```

AddTemplateCommandButton

This function uses the supplied argument values to attach a new button object to the cbbTemplates button.

```
Private Function AddTemplateCommandButton(ByVal _
  NewCategoryButtonName As String, ByVal NewButtonName As String) _
  As CommandBarButton
  Dim cbpRoot As CommandBarPopup

  cbpRoot = GetCategoryMenu(NewCategoryButtonName, cbbTemplates)
  cbbCreateEmailFromTemplate = cbpRoot.Controls.Add _
    (Type:=MsoControlType.msoControlButton, Temporary:=True)

  With cbbCreateEmailFromTemplate
    .Caption = NewButtonName
    .Style = MsoButtonStyle.msoButtonIconAndCaption
    'These must be the same in order to respond to the same event.
    'Assign standard tag value
    'This value must be the same for all buttons
    'to trigger the same Click event.
    .Tag = "Email Template"
    .FaceId = 1757
    .OnAction = "!<EmailTemplates.Connect>"
    .Visible = True
    .Parameter = NewButtonName

  End With

  Return cbbCreateEmailFromTemplate
End Function
```

The first thing this function does is grab a reference to the root CommanBarPop control. This control is a pop-up button residing on cbbTemplates, matching the NewCategoryButtonName argument:

```
Dim cbpRoot As CommandBarPopup
cbpRoot = GetCategoryMenu(NewCategoryButtonName, cbbTemplates)
```

With a reference to the category assigned to the template, AddTemplateCommandButton creates a new CommandBarButton and adds the button to the Controls collection that matches the button's assigned category. Then the button is prepared for action by assigning values to the most relevant properties:

```
cbbCreateEmailFromTemplate = cpbRoot.Controls.Add _
    (Type:=MsoControlType.msoControlButton, Temporary:=True)

    With cbbCreateEmailFromTemplate
      .Caption = NewButtonName
      .Style = MsoButtonStyle.msoButtonIconAndCaption
      'These must be the same in order to respond to the same event.
      .Tag = "Email Template"
      .FaceId = 1757
      .OnAction = "!<EmailTemplates.Connect>"
      .Visible = True
      .Parameter = NewButtonName

    End With

    Return cbbCreateEmailFromTemplate
End Function
```

Did you notice that the Tag property for every new CommandBarButton object receives the same value? This is a crucial point. All template-related CommandBarButton objects need to respond to the same cbbCreateEmailFromTemplate_Click event. By setting the Tag property of each button to the same value, each button triggers the Click event of the cbbCreateEmail-FromTemplate control. No matter which template the user selects, the same event will trigger.

To determine which instance of the cbbCreateEmailFromTemplate control was clicked, the Caption property (which has been set to the name of the template) is read. The button's caption corresponds directly to an available email template.

GetCategoryMenu

The purpose of GetCategoryMenu is to find and return a CommandBarPopup control that matches the supplied arguments.

```
Private Shared Function GetCategoryMenu(ByVal MenuNameToFind As String, _
    ByVal MenuControl As CommandBarPopup) As CommandBarPopup
    Looks for a menu of passed Category name.
    'If it does not exist, it is created.
    Dim ctl As CommandBarPopup
    Dim ctlSought As CommandBarPopup
    Dim fExists As Boolean

    fExists = False

    'First check that controls exist on the CommandBar.
```

```
      'If not, we know we should create one
      If MenuControl.Controls.Count > 0 Then
        'Loop through all countrols to determine if the control exists
        For Each ctl In MenuControl.Controls
          If ctl.Tag = MenuNameToFind Then
            fExists = True
            ctlSought = ctl
          End If
        Next


        'If the control exists, use it.
        If fExists Then
          Return ctlSought

        Else
          ctlSought = MenuControl.Controls.Add _
            (Type:=MsoControlType.msoControlPopup, Temporary:=True)

          With ctlSought
            .Caption = MenuNameToFind
            .Tag = MenuNameToFind
            .OnAction = "!<EmailTemplates.Connect>"
            .Visible = True
          End With

          Return ctlSought

        End If

      Else
        ctlSought = MenuControl.CommandBar.Controls.Add _
        (Type:=MsoControlType.msoControlPopup, Temporary:=True)


        With ctlSought
          .Caption = MenuNameToFind
          .Tag = MenuNameToFind
          .OnAction = "!<EmailTemplates.Connect>"
          .Visible = True
        End With

        Return ctlSought
      End If

End Function
```

The preceding function starts out by declaring the working variables:

```
Dim ctl As CommandBarPopup
Dim ctlSought As CommandBarPopup
Dim fExists As Boolean

fExists = False
```

Right away, the method tests the passed MenuControl to determine whether any child controls exist. If so, it checks the Tag of all the children until it finds the one that matches the value of MenuNameToFind. The method then sets fExists to True in order to signify that the control sought has been found. The last step of the loop sets a class-level reference to the sought control.

```
If MenuControl.Controls.Count > 0 Then
  'loop through all countrols to determine if the control exists
  For Each ctl In MenuControl.Controls
    If ctl.Tag = MenuNameToFind Then
      fExists = True
      ctlSought = ctl
    End If
  Next
```

Whether or not the control is found, the function continues processing with the following lines:

```
If fExists Then
  Return ctlSought
```

If it finds the desired button object, it returns the object as the value of the function.

However, if the control is not found, the method knows that the control does not exist and that it must be created. The following lines make this happen:

```
Else
  ctlSought = MenuControl.Controls.Add _
    (Type:=MsoControlType.msoControlPopup, Temporary:=True)

  With ctlSought
    .Caption = MenuNameToFind
    .Tag = MenuNameToFind
    .OnAction = "!<EmailTemplates.Connect>"
    .Visible = True
  End With

  Return ctlSought

End If
```

The last chunk of code deals with the situation where MenuControl does not contain any child controls. Just like the situation where the method searched the child controls and did not find one that matched, here it knows that it must create the control, since it does not currently exist.

```
ctlSought = MenuControl.CommandBar.Controls.Add _
  (Type:=MsoControlType.msoControlPopup, Temporary:=True)

  With ctlSought
    .Caption = MenuNameToFind
    .Tag = MenuNameToFind
    .OnAction = "!<EmailTemplates.Connect>"
    .Visible = True
  End With

  Return ctlSought
End If
```

This completes the BravoMenu class. In this class, we took a good look at the Office CommandBars and at how we could use them to create a menu control that is completely dynamic and adjusts to changes in the user's environment.

The Settings Form

Once again we have an elegant little Settings form to discuss (see Figure 4-7). This version of the form allows the user to specify two key pieces of data, the Outlook folder where email templates are (or will be) stored, and the user's name (used to retrieve a ContactItem containing their information). The code for this form is much like the code in previous chapters, so I will only highlight and discuss any new items.

Add a new form to the project and name it **Settings.vb**.

Designing the Form

The Settings form requires the controls listed in Table 4-3. The layout of the controls is shown in Figure 4-7.

Table 4-3. *Controls Used in the* Settings *Form*

Control	Name	Text
GroupBox	gbFolders	Templates Folder
Label	lblFolder	Folder ID
TextBox	txtTemplatesFolder	
Button	cbSelectFolder	. . .
GroupBox	gbUserInfo	Name
Label	lblItem	Name
TextBox	txtContactItem	
Button	cbOk	&OK
Button	cbCancel	&Cancel

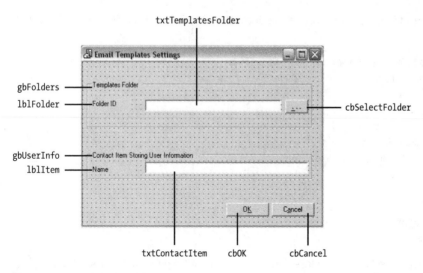

Figure 4-7. *The layout of the* Settings *form*

Variable Declarations

The Settings form maintains class-level variables as follows:

```
Private entryID As String
Private storeID As String
```

These two objects store the entryID and storeID values retrieved from the selected Email Templates folder (which is specified using the Settings form).

Methods

The SaveSettings and LoadSettings methods are once again slightly modified from the versions in previous chapters to include the new settings.

SaveSettings

This is the new SaveSettings method. The new lines of code are shown in bold.

```
Private Function SaveSettings()
  Try
    UserSettings.TemplatesFolderPath = txtTemplatesFolder.Text
    UserSettings.EntryID = entryID
    UserSettings.StoreID = storeID
    UserSettings.UserName = txtContactItem.Text
    UserSettings.SaveSettings()

  Catch ex As Exception
    MsgBox(ex.Message)
  End Try

End Function
```

LoadSettings

Here is the new SaveSettings method. Again, the new code lines are shown in bold.

```
Private Function LoadSettings()
  Try
    txtTemplatesFolder.Text = UserSettings.TemplatesFolderPath
    entryID = UserSettings.EntryID
    storeID = UserSettings.StoreID
    txtContactItem.Text = UserSettings.UserName
  Catch ex As Exception
    MsgBox(ex.Message)
  End Try
End Function
```

Events

The Settings form implements three events: cbSelectFolder_Click, cbOK_Click, and cbCancel_Click.

cbSelectFolder_Click

The cbSelectFolder_Click event calls the appOutlook.PickOutlookFolder method to prompt the user to select an Outlook folder. This is the same function as the Settings.cbPick-Folder_Click event from Chapter 3. The only difference between the two, shown in bold, is that the names of the controls have changed.

```
  Private Sub cbSelectFolder_Click(ByVal sender As System.Object, _
    ByVal e As System.EventArgs) Handles cbSelectFolder.Click
    Dim str() As String
    str = appOutlook.PickOutlookFolder()
    txtTemplatesFolder.Text = str(0)
    entryID = str(1)
    storeID = str(2)
  End Sub
```

cbOK_Click

The cbOK_Click event is used to call the SaveSettings function and close the Settings form.

```
Private Sub cbOK_Click(ByVal sender As System.Object, _
  ByVal e As System.EventArgs) Handles cbOK.Click
  Try
    SaveSettings()
  Catch ex As Exception
    MsgBox(Err.Description, MsgBoxStyle.Exclamation, "Critical Error")
  Finally
    Me.Close()
  End Try
End Sub
```

cbCancel

The cbCancel_Click event closes the Settings form without any additional method calls.

```
Private Sub cbCancel_Click(ByVal sender As System.Object, _
  ByVal e As System.EventArgs) Handles cbCancel.Click

  Me.Close()
End Sub
```

The UserSettings Class

The UserSettings class once again dutifully handles the task of storing and retrieving the user's settings. This version of UserSettings is much like the versions in the previous two chapters with one major exception—this class declares an event to allow other classes to respond to changes in the user settings.

The add-in needs this new event in order to notify and respond to changes in the Email Templates folder. This is a likely scenario, because a user could decide to change the folder where the email templates resides by adding, editing, or removing template items. If this situation were to occur and the add-in did not respond to the change, the Bravo Tools menu would not be updated and would contain valid references to the templates.

Since the UserSettings class in this add-in is similar to the versions in Chapters 2 and 3, please refer to those chapters for a full discussion of the class. This discussion will focus solely on new code (shown in bold). Slight departures from previous versions are italicized.

Variable Declarations

The UserSettings class declares the following variables:

```
Private Shared m_strTemplatesFolder As String
Private Shared m_strSettingsPath As String
Private Shared m_strEntryID As String
Private Shared m_strStoreID As String
Private Shared m_strUserName As String

Private Const SETTINGS_XML_FILE_NAME As String = "\emailtemps.xml"

Shared Shared Event AfterSettingsChange(ByVal EntryID As String, _
  ByVal StoreID As String)

'This is here only to declare and expose one instance event.
'This will allow other classes to respond to the AfterSettingsChange event.
Public Event NadaMucho()
```

In addition to the variables declared in previous versions, this class contains another class-level variable for storing the user's name. The name of the XML file used to store the user settings in the file system has also been modified to better reflect the name of this chapter's add-in.

The class is set up as a Shared class, allowing it to be referenced without having to instantiate a class instance first. Also, this class provides an event that will fire whenever a change in the user settings occurs. The AfterSettingsChange event handles the notification and is thrown by the SaveSettings method.

This works well, but there is one small problem to overcome. In order to respond to the AfterSettingsChange event, the class must be instantiated as an instance object. An *instance object* is a class object that must be dimensioned to a variable before it can be utilized (as compared to a Shared class that can be accessed without a variable assignment). The only way to expose the AfterSettingsChange event is to expose at least one instance (or non-shared) event.

The solution is to declare an additional, totally useless, Public event within the class. The public event will allow the UserSettings class to instantiate as an object in other functions and respond to the AfterSettingsChange declared event.

■**Tip** Try changing the AfterSettingsChange event to be only a Public event (remove Shared). Then comment out the NadaMucho event. The SaveSettings method will give you the following message: "Cannot refer to an instance member of a class from within a shared method or shared member initialized without an explicit instance of the class." This just means that a shared method can only refer to shared members of the class. The only way to refer to an instance member is via an instance object declared as this class's type.

Property Procedures

For the ETE, two new properties are required: UserName and TemplatesFolderPath.

UserName

The UserName property is a read/write property representing the full name of the current user of the add-in. This should correspond to a ContactItem located in the default Contacts folder in Outlook.

```
Public Shared Property UserName() As String
  Get
    Return m_strUserName
  End Get
  Set(ByVal Value As String)
    m_strUserName = Value
  End Set
End Property
```

TemplatesFolderPath

The TemplatesFolderPath property is a read/write property representing the Outlook folder that contains the email templates.

```
Public Shared Property TemplatesFolderPath() As String
  Get
    Return m_strTemplatesFolder
```

```
    End Get
    Set(ByVal Value As String)
      m_strTemplatesFolder = Value
    End Set
End Property
```

Methods

The UserSettings class contains two methods for saving and retrieving the ETE's user-specified setting values.

SaveSettings

SaveSettings handles the task of writing the current user settings to an XML file.

```
Public Shared Function SaveSettings() As Boolean
  Try
    Dim strPath As String
    strPath = strPath.Concat(UserSettings.SettingsPath, _
      SETTINGS_XML_FILE_NAME)
    Dim xtwSettings As New XmlTextWriter(strPath.ToString, _
      System.Text.Encoding.UTF8)

    With xtwSettings
      .Formatting = Formatting.Indented
      .Indentation = 2
      .QuoteChar = """"c

      .WriteStartDocument(True)
      .WriteComment("User Settings from the Bravo Email Templates Add-In")
      .WriteStartElement("BravoEmailTemplatesUserSettings")
      .WriteAttributeString("TemplatesFolderPath", _
        UserSettings.TemplatesFolderPath)
      .WriteAttributeString("EntryID", UserSettings.EntryID)
      .WriteAttributeString("StoreID", UserSettings.StoreID)
      .WriteAttributeString("UserName", UserSettings.UserName)
      .WriteEndElement()
      .WriteEndDocument()
      .Close()
    End With

    RaiseEvent AfterSettingsChange(UserSettings.EntryID, _
      UserSettings.StoreID)

    Return True
  Catch ex As Exception
    Return False
  End Try
End Function
```

Aside from a few lines that were changed to include relevant properties for the ETE (formatted in bold), this method is the same as in earlier chapters. Notice, though, that if the changes are successfully saved, the method throws the AfterSettingsChange event.

LoadSettings

LoadSettings reads the settings configuration data stored on the user's file system and stores them in the class's variables. Changes from the version in Chapter 3 are formatted in bold.

```
Public Shared Function LoadSettings(ByVal FilePath As String) As Boolean
  Try
    Dim strPath As String
    m_strSettingsPath = FilePath
    strPath = strPath.Concat(FilePath, SETTINGS_XML_FILE_NAME)
    Dim xtrSettings As New XmlTextReader(strPath.ToString)

    With xtrSettings
      .MoveToContent()
      m_strTemplatesFolder = .GetAttribute("TemplatesFolderPath")
      m_strEntryID = .GetAttribute("EntryID")
      m_strStoreID = .GetAttribute("StoreID")
      m_strUserName = .GetAttribute("UserName")
      .Close()

      Return True
    End With
  Catch ex As Exception
    Return False
  End Try
End Function
```

Summary

Although this add-in does not contain as many objects as other solutions presented in this book, it does tackle some rather fun and complex concepts. You learned how to take your Office CommandBar skills to another level by dynamically creating a menu based on items in an Outlook folder. This is a big deal, because the add-in has no idea how many categories or templates it will need to create until run time. You also learned a simple method of scanning text using regular expressions. Using this method you saw just how easy it is to scan for a pattern of text and replace it with the values you want. Finally, you learned a new method for serializing your user settings data for reuse the next time the add-in executes.

This add-in is just a starter kit for the Email Template Engine. To make it really useful, try to implement some of the following ideas:

- Alert the user when they select the wrong type of folder.

- Add a context menu that duplicates the structure of the main menu.

- Add a set of InfoTags for the client information.

- Notify the user if no `ContactItem` matching the `UserName` property exists.

- Add handling for the situation when the email address of the current selection is not in the Contacts folder.

- Highlight any tag not matched to a `ContactItem` property.

- Prevent the email from being sent if an unfilled tag still exists.

CHAPTER 5

Service-Failure Reporting Application

Creating a Custom Workflow Using InfoPath, Web Services, and Microsoft Access

This chapter demonstrates how you can use InfoPath, Microsoft Office's new tool for building forms and form-based applications, with a custom web service and Microsoft Access. We will build an application that allows you to create a service-failure report, distribute task assignments to various people, report on task completion, and provide status information at any point along the line. Variations on this application could be used in any context where assignments are handed out and progress needs to be tracked.

To develop this application, we will use InfoPath, a web service, a web page, and Microsoft Access:

- Using InfoPath, it is possible to create interactive forms that enable users to enter data and to interface with database systems and the Web. It is not much of a stretch to think of InfoPath as being like an Access or VB form—InfoPath forms similarly provide a rich interface for adding, editing, and deleting data stored in data systems. Not only that, InfoPath forms are really XML files, which means the possibilities for manipulating the data and interfacing with other systems are endless. This chapter explains how to use InfoPath to build two solid forms for data entry. In addition, the discussion explains how to connect the forms to a web service for retrieving and updating data.

- Interaction with the InfoPath form will be via an ASP .NET web service. This web service contains a layer of code between the InfoPath forms and the solution database (an Access database). This code contains the logic for creating and editing all data tracked by a service-failure report (the service failure description, task assignments, the related client, etc.). Key coding techniques here include using XML to pass data back and forth between the InfoPath forms and the web service. In addition, this discussion shows how to implement a basic workflow engine within a web service to automatically notify staff of task assignments via email.

- An ASP .NET web page will provide users with a way to track resolution progress related to the service failure. This web page retrieves data from the solution database to build a single-page report that displays the details of a service failure's status. We will look at how to create a master-detail type of web page by retrieving a service failure record and its related task records. The page relies upon a QueryString passed in the page's URL to identify and retrieve the service failure record from the solution database. We will also look at how to build a template to be used by the WebForm repeater control.

- Microsoft Access is used to store all data related to the Service-Failure Reporting application. This includes a listing of system users, service-failure records, and service-failure tasks.

InfoPath and Web Services

InfoPath is new in Office 2003, and it fills the need for a form-authoring tool within the Office family. InfoPath is the perfect tool for building and utilizing business forms that capture data. These forms allow for easier data collection and collaboration because InfoPath relies heavily on XML and thus provides a level of structure to the collected data. Each form built in InfoPath has its related XML schema attached (either provided by the form developer, or automatically built by InfoPath as the form is built), and this schema specifies what type of data is allowed. Thus, each InfoPath document is a well-formed XML document conforming to the rules of the attached XML schema.

■**Note** Microsoft decided to confuse everyone with many different bundle combinations of the Office suite. Not all bundle versions of Office include InfoPath. Be careful when attempting to purchase a copy of InfoPath.

Because each InfoPath form has an attached schema, it is easy to enforce data-validation rules without adding custom programming code. For example, the XML schema can define what data types are allowed for any given element defined in the schema. Using the rules of the XML schema, InfoPath will automatically ensure that data entered by the user is the correct type for the XML element. In addition, the resulting XML documents allow for easier data collection and reuse across all transactional data systems and business processes.

In fact, InfoPath forms could serve as the main user interface for adding and editing business data, replacing traditional Windows forms. This is the beauty of XML and InfoPath. No longer does data entered into a system's data store need to be created from inside the host application. By utilizing XML schemas, it is now possible to use all kinds of applications running on all kinds of devices to create new records in transactional systems as long as the data conforms to a published XML schema.

■Tip InfoPath Service Pack 1 adds the ability to create VB .NET and C# solutions using Visual Studio Tools for Office project templates. If you do not have SP1, InfoPath only supports VBScript or JScript code. The service pack is available for download from the Microsoft Office Update web site at http://office.microsoft.com/en-us/officeupdate/default.aspx.

As for web services, there are a lot of varying definitions for them. For the purposes of the Service-Failure Reporting application, a web service is an ASP .NET application that exposes custom methods through the use of the HTTP protocol. In addition to providing these methods, web services use XML to describe each public method so that external or cross-platform applications know how to invoke them.

■Tip There are detailed explanations of web services on the Internet. One of the best places to start is the web services section of the MSDN web site: http://msdn.microsoft.com/webservices/.

Web services can be limited for access only within a private intranet, or they can be made available to anyone with Internet access. They provide a standard way of offering existing code functions as services to any application running on any device or operating system. In short, web services can act like code libraries available to anyone with access to them.

In the Service-Failure Reporting application, web services provide a great system for centralizing code that is invoked by a remote application—InfoPath.

Designing the Service-Failure Reporting Application

The Service-Failure Reporting application provides a set of tools for tracking all service-failure data from start to finish, and it implements a basic workflow for distributing task assignments to Bravo Corp staff members (see Figure 5-1). These task assignments are created when the service-failure report is entered, and notifications are sent to task assignees as follows:

1. A staff member is informed of a service failure by a "customer" (who could be any person at the event) and completes a service-failure report form within InfoPath. As part of the reporting process, the staff member records the customer's name, company, and the problem, and creates a plan for resolving the service failure by assigning tasks to various staff members. The report is submitted by clicking a button on the InfoPath form, and it is assigned a tracking ID number.

2. When the report is submitted, the web service saves the data to the solution database and distributes emails to each task assignee. Each email contains another InfoPath form containing the task information. An email is also sent to the customer who reported the service failure and informs them of the plan to resolve it.

3. The staff member completes the task, fills in the InfoPath Task form attached to the email, and submits the data to the web service.

4. The web service updates the task record using the XML data provided by InfoPath, and the customer is again informed by email of the progress.

5. If the staff member has an additional task assigned to them in the service-failure report, they are sent another email with the details for that task.

6. Steps 3–5 are repeated until all tasks are completed. When no tasks remain, the web service marks the service-failure report complete.

7. Some time after step 2 is complete, the customer is sent an email that contains a link to the issue-tracking web page. This web page utilizes a tracking ID passed as a URL parameter, which allows the customer to retrieve the record from the solution database.

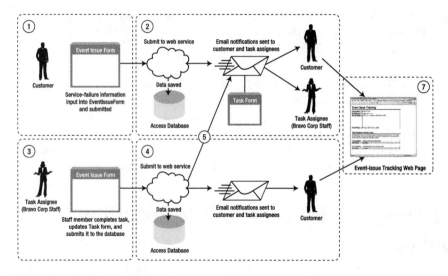

Figure 5-1. *The service-failure report workflow*

From the developer's point of view, the Service-Failure Reporting application involves the following components (see Figure 5-2):

- Solution database (EventIssues.mdb): This is the Access database, residing on a web server. It stores all data created by the InfoPath forms. The InfoPath forms do not directly access the database but instead invoke methods available from the web service to submit data for insertion into the solution database.

- Service-Failure web service (EventIssues.asmx): The web service reads and writes to the solution database. In addition to the database code, the custom workflow logic that sends new tasks via email resides here. The web service also provides web methods that accept XML data. This data is then parsed and inserted as new records inside the solution database.

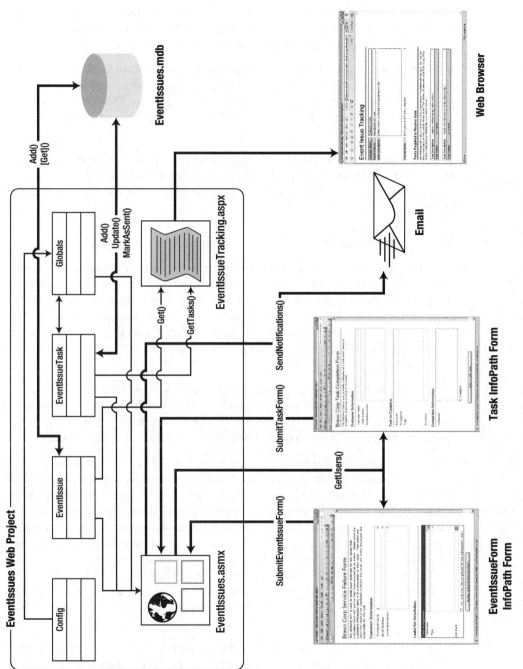

Figure 5-2. *The Service-Failure Reporting application's architecture*

- Service-failure web form (EventIssueForm.xsn): This is the InfoPath form for creating and submitting a service-failure record. The data entered into the form is submitted to the solution's web service for insertion into the solution database.

- Service-failure task form (Task.xsn): This is an additional InfoPath form for tracking task items related to a service-failure report. This form is sent, via email, to task assignees who use the form to add details related to the task's completion. The entered data is submitted to the Service-Failure web service, which updates the related task record in the solution database.

- Service-failure EventIssue-tracking web page (EventIssueTracking.aspx): This is the ASP .NET web page for tracking a service failure and its related tasks. The web page retrieves event issue and related task data from the solution database for presentation in a browser.

From a code perspective, the workflow of the overall solution works as follows:

- Using the EventIssueForm.xsn InfoPath form, a user enters the data required to create a new service-failure record. Once the form is completed, the user submits the form to the Service-Failure web service. No code is required to invoke the web method, as the form's properties are already set up to connect to the web service and call its Submit-EventIssueForm web method. Also, anytime the InfoPath form initializes, it makes a call to the web service's GetUsers web method, which is used to populate a drop-down control on the form.

- The Task InfoPath form works in the same manner as the EventIssueForm. The user completes this form and then invokes the web service's SubmitTaskForm web method to submit data that will be used to update the task record in the solution database. This form also calls the GetUsers method to populate a drop-down list on the form.

- EventIssues.asmx takes the data submitted by SubmitEventIssueForm and SubmitTask-Form and then converts it to EventIssue or EventIssueTask objects (depending on whether we are dealing with an event issue or a task). EventIssues then calls methods exposed by these objects to initiate calls to the solution database (such as Add, [Get], Update, MarkAsSent, etc.) that add and update the related database records. One last item to note is the SendNotifications method, which sends new Task InfoPath forms to task assignees. The SendNotifications method is used to distribute the tasks to be completed when a new event issue is created. This method is also invoked when a task has been completed and an additional task related to the event issue record is queued to be completed. This subsequent task is distributed inside another Task InfoPath form via email to the task assignee.

- EventIssueTracking.aspx utilizes an record ID, passed via the URL's query string, to retrieve event issue and task data from the solution database and present the information in a web page. The page utilizes the EventIssue and EventIssueTask classes and invokes their methods in order to retrieve the desired information.

- The `EventIssue` and `EventIssueTask` classes contain methods for inserting, updating, and retrieving information from the solution databases. These classes are referenced by the `EventIssues.asmx` web service class and the `EventIssueTracking.aspx` web page.

- `Config` and `Globals` provide data to all objects in the class. `Config` contains the database connection settings. `Globals`, which is a module, not a class, contains helper functions for the entire project. For example, the module contains functions for cleaning SQL apostrophes from SQL strings, as well as for returning properties provided by the `Config` class.

Bravo Corp Business Scenario

While working to prepare a quality event, things can and do go wrong, and this is especially true at the event site. The Bravo Corp event team installs all decorations, carpeting, and hardware to prepare the facility, the Bravo Corp service desk and kiosk are assembled and prepared, freight deliveries arrive and are delivered on site, and exhibits are set up and cleaned. As exhibitors arrive, they typically identify last-minute items needed for their exhibit or booth, and the Bravo Corp staff move through the event site accepting new orders and working toward order fulfillment. Huge opportunities exist for what Bravo Corp calls a service failure—failure to deliver the level and quality of service expected by Bravo Corp's clients.

The reason for the service failure is irrelevant—slow order fulfillment, a banner that will not stay hung on its rafter, a simple delivery mistake, etc. What is relevant is that the failure must be immediately identified, and a plan must be put implemented to correct the situation to the customer's satisfaction.

Bravo Corp originally used a manual system, in which a service representative, on being informed of a problem, would determine who was best suited to resolve the issue and would assign the task via their handheld radio. As events grew in size and complexity, though, the limitations of this manual process became evident, especially in tracking a task to its completion and keeping customers informed of progress.

Bravo Corp decided to build the Service-Failure Reporting application, which would allow for easier capturing of service-failure data. This solution automates several of the formerly manual processes. Instead of having to visit the service desk to create a service-failure report, staff members can use their laptops to create service-failure reports using InfoPath, assigning tasks to different people and submitting the report to the central database by email. Tasks are also handed out by email, and their completion is recorded in another InfoPath form submitted to the database. And because all the data is stored centrally, customers can be kept informed as the problem is resolved. All of this results in better customer satisfaction.

Creating the Database Tables

The code portion of the service-failure solution relies on a Microsoft Access database to serve as the solution's data repository. The database contains three tables for storing user, issue, and task-related information.

Create the database by following these steps:

1. Open Microsoft Access and create a new blank database (File ➤ New ➤ New Blank Database). Name the file **EventIssues.mdb**.

2. Create a new table called Users following the schema in Table 5-1.

Table 5-1. *The Schema for the* Users *Table*

Field Name	Data Type	Field Size	Primary Key
email	Text	255	Yes
first_name	Text	50	No
last_name	Text	50	No
occupation	Text	50	No
admin	Yes/No	n/a	No

3. Create a new table called Issue following the schema in Table 5-2.

Table 5-2. *The Schema for the* Issue *Table*

Field Name	Data Type	Field Size	Primary Key
Tracking_id	AutoNumber	Long Integer	Yes
Customer_name	Text	50	No
customer_email	Text	50	No
problem	Memo	n/a	No

4. Create a new table called Task following the schema in Table 5-3.

Table 5-3. *The Schema for the* Task *Table*

Field Name	Data Type	Field Size	Primary Key
task_id	AutoNumber	Long Integer	Yes
task_order	Number	Long Integer	No
tracking_id	Number	Long Integer	No
assignee_name	Text	50	No
comments	Memo	n/a	No
complete	Yes/No	n/a	No
task_due_date	Date/Time	n/a	No
sent	Yes/No	n/a	No

Save the database in a folder named Database residing in the same folder location that is specified as the local path for the EventIssues web service's virtual web directory.

And that's it—the environment is set up.

Creating the Service-Failure Web Service

The Service-Failure Reporting application relies on a middle-tier business-logic layer to handle all business rules and data access. A web service covers this responsibility easily and integrates well with InfoPath.

The web service consists of the following files:

- `EventIssues.asmx`: This is the class file that exposes the web methods provided by the web service. It is the main class of the application, and it calls upon the `EventIssue` and `EventIssueTask` classes to invoke database interactions for event issues and task records. The discussion of this class explains how to read and write XML data provided by the solution's InfoPath forms.

- `EventIssue.vb`: This class provides methods for adding and updating event issue records in the solution database. This is a typed class that represents a single event issue record and contains functions that encapsulate the database logic related to its record type (which, in this case, is an event issue record).

- `EventIssueTask.vb`: This class provides methods for adding and updating task records in the solution database. This is a typed class that represents a single task record and contains functions that encapsulate the database logic related to its record type (which, in this case, is a task record).

- `Globals.vb`: This module demonstrates how to provide project-level functions that are accessible to all other project objects without instantiating an object. In addition, this module provides methods that clean SQL strings and help reduce the chance of error in your SQL statements caused by the apostrophe character (').

- `Config.vb`: This is a shared class that contains the web service's configuration information.

The Web Service Project

Create the web service project by following these steps:

1. With Visual Studio open, create a new VB-based ASP .NET web service in Visual Studio.

2. In the New Project dialog box, specify **http://localhost/EventIssues** as the project's location (see Figure 5-3). Click OK.

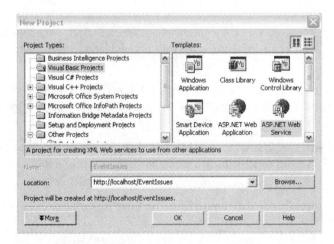

Figure 5-3. *Specifying the EventIssues web service's location*

3. Find the Solution1.asmx file in Visual Studio's Solution Explorer window and delete it.

4. After Visual Studio creates the project and loads the files inside the development environment, open the web.config file.

5. Create a new folder underneath the EventIssues web service's root folder and name it **Database**. If you followed the previous steps and created the project on your local system, the location would be C:\Inetpub\www\EventIssues\Database. Move the solution's Access database to this new folder.

The web.config File

The web.config file is used in ASP .NET applications to specify settings and to create custom properties that affect the application's behavior. The Service-Failure web service adds six custom keys in the appSettings section.

The appSettings section is not included in the web.config file by default. For this example, place the following code between the <configuration> and <system.web> tags:

```
<appSettings>
  <add key="dbFileLocation" _
    value="C:\inetpub\wwwroot\EventIssues\Database\EventIssues.mdb"/>

  <add key="dbPassword" value=""/>

  <add key="taskFormHREF" _
    value="file:///C:\Inetpub\wwwroot\EventIssues\InfoPathForms\Task.xsn"/>

  <add key="tempMailDirectory" _
    value="c:\inetpub\wwwroot\EventIssues\TempEmail"/>

  <add key="SmtpServer" value="localhost"/>
  <add key="IssueTrackingPageURL" _
    value="http://localhost/EventIssues/EventIssueTracking.aspx"/>
</appSettings>
```

Each key in the preceding code defines the location of a different Service-Failure Reporting application component, such as the InfoPath forms we will build later in the chapter. Here is a breakdown of each key and the data it defines:

- dbFileLocation: This is the fully qualified path to the solution's Access database. The value should correspond to the location where you saved the database in the "Creating the Database Tables" section earlier in the chapter.

- dbPassword: This is the administrator password for the Access database. Since we did not incorporate any lockdown security measures on the database, the password is blank.

- taskFormHREF: This is the fully qualified path of the Task InfoPath form.

- `tempMailDirectory`: This is the fully qualified path for storing temporary email files.

- `SmtpServer`: This is the host name for relaying email.

- `IssueTrackingPageURL`: This is the fully qualified path of the solution's ASP .NET page that displays issue status information (`EventIssueTracking.aspx`).

Note For the solution to work properly, make sure the server specified in the `SmtpServer` key allows relaying from the machine hosting the Service-Failure web service. The email relay settings are available within IIS.

Each of these keys comes into play throughout the remaining classes that make up the Service-Failure web service.

The EventIssues.asmx Class

The Service-Failure web service lives within the `EventIssues` class file and provides an entry point to the database services and workflow logic provided by other classes in the project. The methods included in the `EventIssues.asmx` file are intended to be accessed by the two Service-Failure InfoPath forms discussed later in this chapter—`EventIssueForm` and `Task`. In essence, the EventIssues web service is the entry point to the solution database and the basic email workflow behind the system.

The `EventIssues` class provides the main functionality of the application and includes code for the following tasks:

- Accepting a new event issue record (`SubmitEventIssueForm`): This method accepts an XML document submitted from the `EventIssueForm` InfoPath form and then processes it before inserting the data into the solution database. In this method, you will see how to read the contents of an XML file using the XML document object model, and how to convert the data in the XML document into classes built to handle the data (like the `EventIssue` and `EventIssueTask` classes). We will also see how to build and send an email that provides a link to the `EventIssueTracking.aspx` web page.

- Accepting updated task information (`SubmitTaskForm`): This method accepts an XML document submitted from the `Task` InfoPath form and then prepares the data before calling additional methods to update the record in the solution database. This method also demonstrates how to read the contents of an XML file using the XML document object model.

- Providing a listing of the application's users (`GetUsers`): This method fills a database recordset with a listing of users and then provides that data as an XML document. We will look at how quickly this can be accomplished by querying the database and then returning the query results in XML format by calling the `GetXML` method of the `DataSet` object (part of the `System.Data` namespace).

- Distributing new task assignments via email (SendNotifications): This method shows how to send to each task assignee an email that contains a newly created Task InfoPath form as an attachment. We will look at how to build a valid InfoPath file (.xsn extension) within code by utilizing the same schema of the Task InfoPath form created earlier in the chapter. Once built, this method then shows how to create a new email and attach the newly generated InfoPath form.

To create the file, add a new Web Service file to the project and name it **EventIssues.asmx**.

Imports Directives

EventIssues requires the following five namespaces:

```
Imports System.Web.Services
Imports System.Data
Imports System.Data.OleDb
Imports System.Xml
Imports Microsoft.VisualBasic.ControlChars
```

Methods

The EventIssues class defines four methods: SubmitEventIssueForm, SubmitTaskForm, GetUsers, and SendNotifications. These methods allow the two Service-Failure InfoPath forms, EventIssueForm and Task, to send and receive data to the solution database.

SubmitEventIssueForm

The SubmitEventIssueForm method submits the EventIssueForm InfoPath form from within InfoPath. The procedure accepts a String argument that contains the XML from the InfoPath form. The XML is then read node by node and is processed as needed. The end result is the creation of a new issue record in the solution database. In addition, an email is distributed to the customer containing information about how to access status information from a web page.

Take a moment to review the full code listing of SubmitEventIssueForm. A blow-by-blow explanation follows the full listing.

```
<WebMethod()> _
Public Sub SubmitEventIssueForm(ByVal XML As String)
    Dim EventIssueObj As New EventIssue
    Dim TaskCollection As New Collection
    Dim EventIssueTaskObj As EventIssueTask
    Dim TaskOrder As Long = 1
    Dim xmlReader As XmlTextReader = New XmlTextReader(XML, _
        XmlNodeType.Element, Nothing)

    Do While xmlReader.Read()
        If xmlReader.NodeType = XmlNodeType.Element Then
```

```
Select Case xmlReader.Name
  Case "my:customer_name"
    xmlReader.Read()
    EventIssueObj.CustomerName = xmlReader.Value

  Case "my:email_address"
    xmlReader.Read()
    EventIssueObj.CustomerEmail = xmlReader.Value

  Case "my:issue_description"
    xmlReader.Read()
    EventIssueObj.IssueDescription = xmlReader.Value

  Case "my:Task"

    EventIssueTaskObj = New EventIssueTask
    Do Until xmlReader.NodeType = XmlNodeType.EndElement And _
      xmlReader.Name = "my:Task"

      xmlReader.Read()

      If xmlReader.NodeType = XmlNodeType.Element Then

        Select Case xmlReader.Name

          Case "my:employee_email"
            xmlReader.Read()
            EventIssueTaskObj.AssigneeEmail = xmlReader.Value

          Case "my:task_description"
            xmlReader.Read()
            EventIssueTaskObj.Task = xmlReader.Value

          Case "my:task_due_date"
            xmlReader.Read()

            If Not xmlReader.Value = String.Empty Then
              EventIssueTaskObj.TaskDueDate = CDate(xmlReader.Value)
            End If

          Case "my:complete_before_next_task"
            xmlReader.Read()
            EventIssueTaskObj.TaskOrder = TaskOrder

            If xmlReader.Value = "true" Then
              TaskOrder += 1
            End If
```

```
              End Select

            End If

          Loop

          TaskCollection.Add(EventIssueTaskObj)

      End Select
    End If
  Loop

  If EventIssue.Add(EventIssueObj) Then
    For Each EventIssueTaskObj In TaskCollection
      EventIssueTaskObj.TrackingId = EventIssueObj.TrackingId
      If Not EventIssueTask.Add(EventIssueTaskObj) Then
        Throw New Exception("A task failed to save but did not " & _
          "explicitly throw an exception")
      End If
    Next

    Dim EmployeeFullName As String = ""
    Dim EmployeeOccupation As String = ""

    SendNotifications(EventIssueObj.TrackingId, 1, _
      EventIssueObj.CustomerName, EventIssueObj.CustomerEmail, _
      EventIssueObj.IssueDescription)

    Mail.SmtpMail.SmtpServer = Config.SmtpServer
    Mail.SmtpMail.Send("EventIssues@localhost.com", _
      EventIssueObj.CustomerEmail, "Event Issue Ticket Opened", _
      "You have recently informed us that you are having the" & _
      "following issue: " & CrLf & CrLf & EventIssueObj.IssueDescription & _
      CrLf & CrLf & CrLf & "We are committed to resolving this issue" & _
      "and have outlined a series of tasks that need to be completed" & _
      "in order to resolve your issue.  These will be completed as" & _
      "as possible.  You may review the status of this issue by " & _
      "navigating to " & Config.IssueTrackingPageURL & "?TrackingID=" & _
      EventIssueObj.TrackingId & CrLf & CrLf & "Thank You.")

  Else
    Throw New Exception("The event issue failed to save but did not" & _
      "explicitly throw an exception")
  End If

End Sub
```

■Note There is no all-encompassing error handling because InfoPath automatically recognizes errors and returns the error information to the user.

The SubmitEventIssueForm method moves through the provided XML String line by line to process the service failure and task information. The first section of the method deals with the service failure information provided by the EventIssueForm InfoPath form:

```
Do While xmlReader.Read()
  If xmlReader.NodeType = XmlNodeType.Element Then

    Select Case xmlReader.Name
      Case "my:customer_name"
        xmlReader.Read()
        EventIssueObj.CustomerName = xmlReader.Value

      Case "my:email_address"
        xmlReader.Read()
        EventIssueObj.CustomerEmail = xmlReader.Value

      Case "my:issue_description"
        xmlReader.Read()
        EventIssueObj.IssueDescription = xmlReader.Value
```

A Select...Case statement compares the value of the XML node against the value of a Case to identify and fill the appropriate property of the EventIssueObj.

If a task node is encountered, a little more work is required because the XML can contain more than one task record:

```
  Case "my:Task"

    EventIssueTaskObj = New EventIssueTask
    Do Until xmlReader.NodeType = XmlNodeType.EndElement And _
      xmlReader.Name = "my:Task"

    xmlReader.Read()

    If xmlReader.NodeType = XmlNodeType.Element Then

      Select Case xmlReader.Name

        Case "my:employee_email"
          xmlReader.Read()
          EventIssueTaskObj.AssigneeEmail = xmlReader.Value

        Case "my:task_description"
          xmlReader.Read()
          EventIssueTaskObj.Task = xmlReader.Value
```

```
            Case "my:task_due_date"
              xmlReader.Read()

              If Not xmlReader.Value = String.Empty Then
                EventIssueTaskObj.TaskDueDate = CDate(xmlReader.Value)
              End If

            Case "my:complete_before_next_task"
              xmlReader.Read()
              EventIssueTaskObj.TaskOrder = TaskOrder

              If xmlReader.Value = "true" Then
                TaskOrder += 1
              End If


        End Select
      Loop
      TaskCollection.Add(EventIssueTaskObj)
  End Select
```

Since multiple tasks can be associated with an EventIssue object, anytime the procedure comes across the my:Task element, it instantiates a new EventIssueTask object and populates it with the corresponding data. This code section is repeated until the </my:Task> element is encountered. That way, all the tasks are captured and included in the TaskCollection object.

Now that the data is retrieved from the XML String and stored in corresponding objects, the database records are created:

```
Loop

If EventIssue.Add(EventIssueObj) Then
  For Each EventIssueTaskObj In TaskCollection
    EventIssueTaskObj.TrackingId = EventIssueObj.TrackingId
    If Not EventIssueTask.Add(EventIssueTaskObj) Then
      Throw New Exception("A task failed to save but did not " & _
        "explicitly throw an exception")
    End If
  Next
```

In this section, the EventIssue must first be inserted and the record's identity value (TrackingId) retrieved. Then, utilizing the identity value of the EventIssue record, all tasks records are inserted as well.

Finally, email notifications are sent out to the task assignees to inform them of their new task assignments. In addition, an email goes out to the customer, informing them that the service-failure report was received and that a plan is in place to resolve the problem.

```
SendNotifications(EventIssueObj.TrackingId, 1, _
  EventIssueObj.CustomerName, EventIssueObj.CustomerEmail, _
  EventIssueObj.IssueDescription)
```

```
Mail.SmtpMail.SmtpServer = Config.SmtpServer
Mail.SmtpMail.Send("EventIssues@localhost.com", _
  EventIssueObj.CustomerEmail, "Event Issue Ticket Opened", _
  "You have recently informed us that you are having the" & _
  "following issue: " & CrLf & CrLf & EventIssueObj.IssueDescription & _
  CrLf & CrLf & CrLf & "We are committed to resolving this issue" & _
  "and have outlined a series of tasks that need to be completed" & _
  "in order to resolve your issue.  These will be completed as" & _
  "as possible.  You may review the status of this issue by " & _
  "navigating to " & Config.IssueTrackingPageURL & "?TrackingID=" & _
  EventIssueObj.TrackingId & CrLf & CrLf & "Thank You.")
```

Once the emails leave the email server, the Service-Failure Reporting application is done . . . at least until a Bravo Corp team member updates one of their tasks. Then there is a bit more work to do in the SubmitTaskForm method.

SubmitTaskForm

The SubmitTaskForm method submits the Task InfoPath form from within InfoPath. The procedure accepts a String argument that contains the XML from the InfoPath form. The XML is then read node by node and processed as needed. The end result is updated Issue and Task records in the solution database.

```
<WebMethod()> _
  Public Sub SubmitTaskForm(ByVal XML As String)
    'Allows for the submission of the Event Issue Resolution form from
    'InfoPath.  There is no all-encompassing error handling because
    'InfoPath will automatically recognize errors and return the error
    'information to the user.

    Dim EventIssueTaskObj As New EventIssueTask
    Dim xmlReader As XmlTextReader = New XmlTextReader(XML, _
      XmlNodeType.Element, Nothing)
    Dim CustomerName As String = ""
    Dim CustomerEmail As String = ""
    Dim IssueDescription As String = ""
    Dim EmployeeFullName As String = ""
    Dim EmployeeOccupation As String = ""

    Do While xmlReader.Read()
      If xmlReader.NodeType = XmlNodeType.Element Then
        Select Case xmlReader.Name
          Case "my:task_id"
            xmlReader.Read()
            EventIssueTaskObj.TaskId = xmlReader.Value()

          Case "my:task_order"
            xmlReader.Read()
            EventIssueTaskObj.TaskOrder = xmlReader.Value()
```

```
        Case "my:tracking_id"
          xmlReader.Read()
          EventIssueTaskObj.TrackingId = xmlReader.Value

        Case "my:task"
          xmlReader.Read()
          EventIssueTaskObj.Task = xmlReader.Value

        Case "my:assignee_email"
          xmlReader.Read()
          EventIssueTaskObj.AssigneeEmail = xmlReader.Value

        Case "my:comments"
          xmlReader.Read()
          EventIssueTaskObj.Comments = xmlReader.Value

        Case "my:complete"
          xmlReader.Read()
          EventIssueTaskObj.Complete = CBool(xmlReader.Value)

        Case "my:task_due_date"
          xmlReader.Read()
          If Not xmlReader.Value = String.Empty Then
            EventIssueTaskObj.TaskDueDate = CDate(xmlReader.Value)
          End If

        Case "my:customer_name"
          xmlReader.Read()
          CustomerName = xmlReader.Value

        Case "my:customer_email"
          xmlReader.Read()
          CustomerEmail = xmlReader.Value

        Case "my:issue_description"
          xmlReader.Read()
          IssueDescription = xmlReader.Value

        Case "my:employee_fullname"
          xmlReader.Read()
          EmployeeFullName = xmlReader.Value

        Case "my:occupation"
          xmlReader.Read()
          EmployeeOccupation = xmlReader.Value
```

```
        End Select
      End If
  Loop

  'Save the Issue and acquire the TrackingId given to the item from
  'the database.  Then set the TrackingId on all of the tasks before
  'saving them.

  If EventIssueTask.Update(EventIssueTaskObj) Then
    SendNotifications(EventIssueTaskObj.TrackingId, _
      EventIssueTaskObj.TaskOrder, CustomerName, CustomerEmail, _
      IssueDescription)
  Else
    Throw New Exception("The event issue failed to save but did not " & _
      "explicitly throw an exception")
  End If

End Sub
```

Just like the SubmitEventIssueForm method, this method moves line by line through the XML String passed as the method argument. While reading each node, a Select...Case statement determines the node value in order to correctly process the node:

```
Select Case xmlReader.Name

  Case "my:task_id"
    xmlReader.Read()
    EventIssueTaskObj.TaskId = xmlReader.Value()

  Case "my:task_order"
    xmlReader.Read()
    EventIssueTaskObj.TaskOrder = xmlReader.Value()

  Case "my:tracking_id"
    xmlReader.Read()
    EventIssueTaskObj.TrackingId = xmlReader.Value

  Case "my:task"
    xmlReader.Read()
    EventIssueTaskObj.Task = xmlReader.Value

  Case "my:assignee_email"
    xmlReader.Read()
    EventIssueTaskObj.AssigneeEmail = xmlReader.Value

  Case "my:comments"
    xmlReader.Read()
    EventIssueTaskObj.Comments = xmlReader.Value
```

```
    Case "my:complete"
      xmlReader.Read()
      EventIssueTaskObj.Complete = CBool(xmlReader.Value)

    Case "my:task_due_date"
      xmlReader.Read()
      If Not xmlReader.Value = String.Empty Then
        EventIssueTaskObj.TaskDueDate = CDate(xmlReader.Value)
      End If

    Case "my:customer_name"
      xmlReader.Read()
      CustomerName = xmlReader.Value

    Case "my:customer_email"
      xmlReader.Read()
      CustomerEmail = xmlReader.Value

    Case "my:issue_description"
      xmlReader.Read()
      IssueDescription = xmlReader.Value

    Case "my:employee_fullname"
      xmlReader.Read()
      EmployeeFullName = xmlReader.Value

    Case "my:occupation"
      xmlReader.Read()
      EmployeeOccupation = xmlReader.Value

End Select
```

Each Case statement reads the node and then stores the node's value inside a corresponding method variable declared at the beginning of the procedure.

As soon as the variables contain the data from the provided XML String, the data is saved to the database by calling the Update method of the EventIssue variable.

```
If EventIssueTask.Update(EventIssueTaskObj) Then
  SendNotifications(EventIssueTaskObj.TrackingId, _
    EventIssueTaskObj.TaskOrder, CustomerName, CustomerEmail, _
    IssueDescription)
Else
  Throw New Exception("The event issue failed to save but did not " & _
    "explicitly throw an exception")
End If
```

As long as the Update method executes successfully, the method completes its task by sending an email notification to the individual who originally identified the service failure. If the update fails, the method throws an exception and exits.

GetUsers

The GetUsers method returns an XML document containing a listing of the system users. This listing contains the names of all users allowed to use the Service-Failure Reporting application. These are the users who either fill out the EventIssueForm and Task forms or receive service-failure task assignments. The listing is supplied within an XML document, and it is meant to fill the contents of a ComboBox control.

```
<WebMethod()> _
  Public Function GetUsers() As System.Xml.XmlDocument
    Try
      Dim dbConn As OleDbConnection = GetConnection()
      Dim dbCmd As New OleDbCommand
      Dim dbAdapter As New OleDbDataAdapter
      Dim dbUserInfo As New DataSet

      dbCmd.CommandText = "SELECT *, [last_name] + ', ' + [first_name] + " & _
        "' (' + [occupation] + ')' as [name_and_occupation] FROM [Users] " & _
        "ORDER BY [last_name], [first_name]"
      dbCmd.Connection = dbConn
      dbAdapter.SelectCommand = dbCmd

      dbUserInfo.DataSetName = "UserInfo"
      dbAdapter.Fill(dbUserInfo, "[Users]")

      dbConn.Close()

      'This will create an XML Document to return to InfoPath

      Dim xmlDoc As New System.Xml.XmlDocument
      xmlDoc.LoadXml(dbUserInfo.GetXml())
      Return xmlDoc

    Catch ex As Exception
      Return Nothing
    End Try

  End Function
```

Utilizing the connection information provided by the GetConnection function, the method fills an OleDbDataAdapter object by executing a SELECT query against the solution database. The query retrieves a listing of records that includes each user's first and last name as well as their occupation. These values are used by the EventIssueForm InfoPath form to assign tasks to users as needed. All of the data from the Users table returns as the function's value as a new XML document.

The GetXML method of the dbUserInfo DataSet object makes creating the XML easy. GetXML creates a String object containing an XML representation of the data stored within the DataSet object.

SendNotifications

The SendNotifications method handles all tasks required to send task email notifications to the Bravo Corp task assignees. To distribute each email, SendNotifications queries the task information from the solution database, uses the retrieved information to build an XML document that conforms to the schema of the Task InfoPath form, and creates and sends the email along with the XML task document.

```
Public Sub SendNotifications(ByVal TrackingId As Long, _
  ByVal CurrentTaskOrderId As Long, ByVal CustomerName _
  As String, ByVal CustomerEmail As String, _
  ByVal IssueDescription As String)

  Try

    Dim SQL As String = "SELECT Task.*, Users.last_name + ', ' + " & _
      "Users.first_name as [employee_fullname], Users.occupation FROM " & _
      "Task INNER JOIN Users ON Task.assignee_email = Users.email " & _
      "WHERE [tracking_id]=" & TrackingId & " and [complete]=false " & _
      "order by [Task_Order]"
    Dim dbConn As OleDbConnection = GetConnection()
    Dim dbCmd As New OleDbCommand(SQL, dbConn)
    Dim dbReader As OleDbDataReader = dbCmd.ExecuteReader()
    Dim InitialTaskOrderId As Long = 0
    Dim HasTasks As Boolean = False
    Dim Done As Boolean = False
    Dim ns As String = "http://www.w3.org/2001/XMLSchema-instance"

    Dim XML As System.Text.StringBuilder
    Dim fileName As String
    Dim SW As System.IO.StreamWriter

    Dim Message As Mail.MailMessage
    Dim FileAttachment As Mail.MailAttachment

    If dbReader.Read Then
      HasTasks = True
      InitialTaskOrderId = dbReader.Item("task_order")

      While Not Done AndAlso dbReader.Item("task_order") = InitialTaskOrderId

        If dbReader.Item("sent") = False Then
```

```vbnet
'Create the XML to attach
'DA copied the schema from InfoPath
XML = New System.Text.StringBuilder(500)
XML.Append("<?xml version=""1.0""?><?mso-infoPathSolution" & _
  "productVersion=""11.0.6250"" PIVersion=""1.0.0.0"" href=""")
XML.Append(Config.TaskFormHREF)
XML.Append(""" name=""urn:schemas-microsoft-com:office:" & _
  "infopath:TaskForm:-myXSD-2004-07-12T03-02-23"" " & _
  "solutionVersion=""1.0.0.11"" ?><?mso-application " & _
  "progid=""InfoPath.Document""?><my:TaskData xmlns:" & _
  "my=""http://schemas.microsoft.com/office/infopath/2003/" & _
  "myXSD/2004-07-12T03:02:23"" xml:lang=""en-us"">")
XML.Append(CrLf)
XML.Append("    <my:task_id xmlns:xsi=" & ns & ">")
XML.Append(dbReader.Item("task_id"))
XML.Append("</my:task_id>")
XML.Append(CrLf)
XML.Append("    <my:task_order xmlns:xsi=" & ns & ">")
XML.Append(dbReader.Item("task_order"))
XML.Append("</my:task_order>")
XML.Append(CrLf)
XML.Append("    <my:tracking_id xmlns:xsi=" & ns & ">")
XML.Append(dbReader.Item("tracking_id"))
XML.Append("</my:tracking_id>")
XML.Append(CrLf)
XML.Append("    <my:task>")
XML.Append(dbReader.Item("task"))
XML.Append("</my:task>")
XML.Append(CrLf)
XML.Append("    <my:assignee_email>")
XML.Append(dbReader.Item("assignee_email"))
XML.Append("</my:assignee_email>")
XML.Append(CrLf)
XML.Append("    <my:comments>")
XML.Append(dbReader.Item("comments"))
XML.Append("</my:comments>")
XML.Append(CrLf)
XML.Append("    <my:complete>")
XML.Append(CBool(dbReader.Item("complete")).ToString.ToLower)
XML.Append("</my:complete>")
XML.Append(CrLf)
XML.Append("    <my:task_due_date xmlns:xsi=" & ns & ">")
XML.Append(GetDateString(dbReader.Item("task_due_date")))
XML.Append("</my:task_due_date>")
XML.Append(CrLf)
XML.Append("    <my:CustomerData>")
XML.Append(CrLf)
```

```
XML.Append("          <my:customer_name>")
XML.Append(CustomerName)
XML.Append("</my:customer_name>")
XML.Append(CrLf)
XML.Append("          <my:customer_email>")
XML.Append(CustomerEmail)
XML.Append("</my:customer_email>")
XML.Append(CrLf)
XML.Append("          <my:issue_description>")
XML.Append(IssueDescription)
XML.Append("</my:issue_description>")
XML.Append(CrLf)
XML.Append("      </my:CustomerData>")
XML.Append(CrLf)
XML.Append("      <my:EmployeeData>")
XML.Append(CrLf)
XML.Append("          <my:employee_fullname>")
XML.Append(dbReader.Item("employee_fullname"))
XML.Append("</my:employee_fullname>")
XML.Append(CrLf)
XML.Append("          <my:occupation>")
XML.Append(dbReader.Item("occupation"))
XML.Append("</my:occupation>")
XML.Append(CrLf)
XML.Append("      </my:EmployeeData>")
XML.Append(CrLf)
XML.Append("</my:TaskData>")

'Write the XML to a temporary file
fileName = Config.TempMailDirectory & "\Task" & _
   dbReader.Item("task_id") & ".xml"

SW = New System.IO.StreamWriter(fileName, False)
SW.Write(XML.ToString)
SW.Close()

'Create an email to send the XML file
Message = New Mail.MailMessage
Message.Subject = "Task to be Completed"
Message.To = dbReader.Item("assignee_email")
Message.Body = "Attached is a Task Completion Form.  Please " & _
   "complete the task as soon as possible and mark it as " & _
   "completed on the form.  You may also add any comments you" & _
   "want in the comments section.  Thank You."
Message.From = "EventIssues@localhost.com"
```

```vbnet
            'Attach XML file
            FileAttachment = New Mail.MailAttachment(fileName)
            Message.Attachments.Add(FileAttachment)
            Mail.SmtpMail.SmtpServer = Config.SmtpServer
            Mail.SmtpMail.Send(Message)

            'Mark the Item as having been sent
            EventIssueTask.MarkAsSent(dbReader.Item("task_id"))
          End If

          'Move on to the next record
          Done = Not dbReader.Read()

        End While

      Else
        Message = New Mail.MailMessage
        Message.Subject = "Notification of Issue Resolution"
        Message.To = CustomerEmail
        Message.Body = "This email was sent to notify you that your " & _
          "issue (Tracking ID: " & TrackingId & ") has been resolved.  " & _
          "If you are not satisfied with the resolution, please contact " & _
          "your customer service representative for more information."
        Message.From = "EventIssues@localhost.com"
        Mail.SmtpMail.SmtpServer = Config.SmtpServer
        Mail.SmtpMail.Send(Message)

      End If
    Catch ex As Exception
      Throw New Exception("Error sending notifications. Form data was " & _
        "successfully submitted.", ex)
    End Try

End Sub
```

There's a lot of self-explanatory code here, but there are some areas worth discussing. The first is the creation of the XML document. The method builds a String containing the XML that matches the Task form schema. The schema must match the schema of the InfoPath form exactly or the whole scheme will fail.

In addition, the following line must be present:

```vbnet
XML.Append(""" name=""urn:schemas-microsoft-com:office:" & _
  "infopath:TaskForm:-myXSD-2004-07-12T03-02-23"" " & _
  "solutionVersion=""1.0.0.11"" ?><?mso-application " & _
  "progid=""InfoPath.Document""?><my:TaskData xmlns:" & _
  "my=""http://schemas.microsoft.com/office/infopath/2003/" & _
  "myXSD/2004-07-12T03:02:23"" xml:lang=""en-us"">")
```

Notice the value of the progid attribute (shown in bold). This line tells Windows to open InfoPath any time this document is opened. In essence, the progid identifies the XML document as an InfoPath document.

Tip The XML schema of any InfoPath is simple to extract. Just open the InfoPath form inside your favorite text editor, and there you have it.

The second section to note is the creation of the email to be distributed to the task assignee. In order to attach the Task InfoPath document to an email, it must be saved to the file system.

```
fileName = Config.TempMailDirectory & "\Task" & _
dbReader.Item("task_id") & ".xml"

SW = New System.IO.StreamWriter(fileName, False)
SW.Write(XML.ToString)
SW.Close()
```

The method saves the XML document to the temporary directory defined in the project's Config class and gives the filename concatenated as "Task" plus the task_id.

The third interesting section is the email creation portion where a new email message (MailMessage) attaches the XML document and heads out to the task assignee's inbox, where it awaits even further action:

```
Message = New Mail.MailMessage
Message.Subject = "Task to be Completed"
Message.To = dbReader.Item("assignee_email")
Message.Body = "Attached is a Task Completion Form.  Please " & _
  "complete the task as soon as possible and mark it as " & _
  "completed on the form.  You may also add any comments you" & _
  "want in the comments section.  Thank You."
Message.From = "EventIssues@localhost.com"

FileAttachment = New Mail.MailAttachment(fileName)
Message.Attachments.Add(FileAttachment)
Mail.SmtpMail.SmtpServer = Config.SmtpServer
Mail.SmtpMail.Send(Message)

EventIssueTask.MarkAsSent(dbReader.Item("task_id"))
End If
```

After sending the email, then method then marks the task records as having been sent by updating the record in the solution database.

The fourth, and last, highlight of the SendNotifications method is the email sent to the customer who created the service-failure report to begin with:

```
Message = New Mail.MailMessage
Message.Subject = "Notification of Issue Resolution"
Message.To = CustomerEmail
Message.Body = "This email was sent to notify you that your " & _
  "issue (Tracking ID: " & TrackingId & ") has been resolved.  " & _
  "If you are not satisfied with the resolution, please contact " & _
  "your customer service representative for more information."
Message.From = "EventIssues@localhost.com"
Mail.SmtpMail.SmtpServer = Config.SmtpServer
Mail.SmtpMail.Send(Message)
```

The "customer" could be an actual customer or a Bravo Corp team member. Either way, if no more tasks exist for the service failure, the Service-Failure Reporting application assumes the problem is resolved and sends an email to inform the customer that the issue has been taken care of.

The Config.vb Class

The Config class provides quick access to the web service's configuration settings. The properties actually return the values specified within the <appSettings> keys added to the web.config file earlier.

Add a new class to the EventIssues web service project and name it **Config.vb**.

Imports Directives

The Config class imports two namespaces:

```
Imports System.Data.OleDb
Imports System.Configuration.ConfigurationSettings
```

Properties

The Config class contains seven properties: connectionString, dbPassword, dbFileLocation, TaskFormHREF, TempMailDirectory, SmtpServer, IssueTrackingPageURL.

connectionString

connectionString is a read-only property containing the information string for connecting with the application's Access database.

```
Public Shared ReadOnly Property connectionString()
  'Creates a connection string to the database.  The appropriate
  'connection string is used if there is a database password.
  Get
    If dbPassword = String.Empty Then
      Return "Provider=Microsoft.Jet.OLEDB.4.0;Data Source=" & dbFileLocation & _
        ";User Id=admin;Password=;"
```

```
      Else
        Return "Provider=Microsoft.Jet.OLEDB.4.0;Data Source=" & dbFileLocation & _
          ";Jet OLEDB:Database Password=" & dbPassword & ";"
      End If
    End Get
  End Property
```

The property utilizes two of the web service properties (dbFileLocation and dbPassword) contained in the web.config file. Allowance is made for the chance that the application's Access database has been secured and requires a password.

Tip If you want to use a database other than Access for this application, no worries. It is possible to use any OLE DB–compliant database systems (SQL Server, Oracle, etc.). To make the code in this chapter work, you need to change all database-related properties and settings to point to your database of choice.

---

dbPassword

The dbPassword property is read-only, and it returns the value of the password key stored in the web.config file's AppSettings section.

```
Private Shared ReadOnly Property dbPassword() As String
  'Password used to access database file (database password)
  Get
    Return AppSettings("dbPassword")
  End Get
End Property
```

dbFileLocation

The dbFileLocation property is read-only, and it returns the value of the file location key stored in the web.config file's AppSettings section.

```
Private Shared ReadOnly Property dbFileLocation() As String
  'Location of the Access database file
  Get
    Return AppSettings("dbFileLocation")
  End Get
End Property
```

TaskFormHREF

The TaskFormHREF property is read-only, and it returns the location of the application's InfoPath-based Task form. The location for the Task form is stored in the web.config file's AppSettings section.

```
Public Shared ReadOnly Property TaskFormHREF() As String
  Get
    Return AppSettings("taskFormHREF")
  End Get
End Property
```

TempMailDirectory

The TempMailDirectory property is read-only, and it returns the location in the file system for storing the application's temporary email files. This location is defined in the web.config file's AppSettings section.

```
Public Shared ReadOnly Property TempMailDirectory() As String
  'Directory in which to create attachments for email messages
  Get
    Return AppSettings("tempMailDirectory")
  End Get
End Property
```

SmtpServer

The SmtpServer property is read-only, and it returns the host name of the application's relay email server. This location is defined in the web.config file's AppSettings section.

```
Public Shared ReadOnly Property SmtpServer() As String
  'SMTP server used to send email
  Get
    Return AppSettings("SmtpServer")
  End Get
End Property
```

IssueTrackingPageURL

The IssueTrackingPageURL property is read-only, and it returns the location of the EventIssue-Tracking.aspx file. This location is defined in the web.config file's AppSettings section.

```
Public Shared ReadOnly Property IssueTrackingPageURL() As String
  'Fully qualified URL of the IssueTrackingPage
  Get
    Return AppSettings("IssueTrackingPageURL")
  End Get
End Property
```

The Globals.vb Module

The Globals module contains a set of six database-helper functions. The methods reside in this module in order to make them available, without requiring a class instance, to the two main object classes in the project: EventIssue and EventIssueTask.

Modules act just a like a Shared class in that the functions residing within the module do not require an object instance. All module methods and property functions are automatically declared as Shared by the compiler. This strategy works well when you have several global functions that need to be available throughout the project but you do not wish to create a new class object to expose them.

Add a new module to the EventIssues web service project, and name it **Globals.vb**.

Imports Directives

The Globals module imports two namespaces:

```
Imports System.Data.OleDb
Imports System.Text.RegularExpressions
```

Methods

The Globals module contains six methods: GetConnection, QuoteBooleanForSQL, QuoteDate-ForSQL, QuoteForSQL, SqlString, and GetDateString. Each of these are helper methods that either interact with the solution database directly or prepare a SQL statement for execution against the solution database.

GetConnection

The GetConnection method returns an open OleDbConnection object and is used to connect the web service to the solution database.

```
Public Function GetConnection(Optional ByVal OpenConnection As Boolean = True) _
  As OleDbConnection
  'Acquires a connection to the database

  Dim dbConn As New OleDbConnection(Config.connectionString)
  If OpenConnection Then dbConn.Open()
  Return dbConn

End Function
```

QuoteBooleanForSQL

The QuoteBooleanForSQL method accepts a Boolean value and returns it in a format acceptable for a SQL statement.

```
Public Function quoteBooleanForSQL(ByVal rawBoolean As Boolean)
  Return rawBoolean.ToString
End Function
```

By calling the ToString method of the passed Boolean object, its value is converted from a numeric value of –1 or 0 to the related text base value of True or False respectively. The text values can then be utilized in a SQL statement that executes against the solution database.

QuoteDateForSQL

The QuoteDateForSQL method accepts a Date value and an optional String that specifies how the passed Date should be formatted. The return value is the value of the passed Date object formatted in the specified manner and surrounded by quotes for use in a SQL statement. This method allows the web service to accept a date value without concern for how it is formatted and then to format it for inclusion within a SQL statement.

```
Public Function quoteDateForSQL(ByVal rawDate As Date, _
  Optional ByVal DateFormatString As String = "MM/dd/yyyy") As String

  If rawDate = Nothing Then
    Return "null"
  Else
    Return "'" & Format(rawDate, DateFormatString) & "'"
  End If

End Function
```

QuoteForSQL

In order to work properly inside a SQL statement, any String-based criteria must be wrapped in quotes. QuoteForSQL wraps a passed String with single quotes for use inside a SQL statement. The passed String object is returned unchanged and with the surrounding quotes.

```
Public Function quoteForSQL(ByVal rawString As String) As String
  'Creates a quoted string for use in a SQL statement

  Return "'" & sqlString(rawString) & "'"

End Function
```

SqlString

The sqlString function serves as a helper function to clean a passed SQL String. The method accepts a String as a parameter and, to make it compatible with SQL, looks for any single quote characters (') characters and replaces them with them with two quote characters (''). This is needed because SQL uses single quote (') characters instead of the double quote (' ') characters and keeps the SQL statement from becoming malformed when using values like (Ty's dog).

```
Public Function sqlString(ByVal rawString As String) As String
  If rawString = String.Empty Then Return ""
  Return rawString.Replace("'", "''")

End Function
```

GetDateString

GetDateString formats a passed Object and returns the object in a proper data format.

```
Public Function GetDateString(ByVal obj As Object, _
  Optional ByVal DateFormat As String = "yyyy-MM-dd") _
    As String

  If obj Is Nothing OrElse IsDBNull(obj) Then
    Return ""
  Else
    Return Format(obj, DateFormat)
  End If

End Function
```

Prior to returning a value, the method tests the object to verify that the necessary data exists and that we are not dealing with nonexistent data. The IsDBNull method returns a Boolean value indicating whether the expression has missing or nonexistent data. So long as data exists, the method returns the passed object in a date format.

■**Tip** IsDBNull is a tricky method. If it returns True, the expression was missing data or the data was nonexistent in the first place. This is different from testing against Nothing, because Nothing tests whether a variable has been initialized.

The EventIssue.vb Class

The EventIssue class is the working class related to the EventIssue InfoPath form. It provides the necessary logic for adding and retrieving service-failure records. In addition, it includes a function for reading database data and storing the data within the class.

Add another class to the project and name it **EventIssue.vb**.

Imports Directives

The EventIssue class imports a single namespace:

```
Imports System.Data.OleDb
```

Variable Declarations

The EventIssue class defines the following variables:

```
Public TrackingId As Long = 0
Public CustomerName As String = ""
Public CustomerEmail As String = ""
Public IssueDescription As String = ""
```

Methods

The EventIssue class defines three public methods: Add, [Get], and GetDataFromReader.

Add

The Add function accepts an EventIssue object, utilizes it to create a new Issue record in the solution database, and returns a Boolean object to signify the function's success or failure.

```
Public Shared Function Add(ByRef EventIssueObj As EventIssue) As Boolean
  Try
    Dim SQL As String = "INSERT INTO [Issue](customer_name, " & _
      "customer_email, problem) VALUES (" & _
      quoteForSQL(EventIssueObj.CustomerName) & "," & _
      quoteForSQL(EventIssueObj.CustomerEmail) & "," & _
      quoteForSQL(EventIssueObj.IssueDescription) & ");"
    Dim dbConn As OleDbConnection = GetConnection()
    Dim dbCmd As New OleDbCommand(SQL, dbConn)

    If dbCmd.ExecuteNonQuery() > 0 Then
      dbCmd.CommandText = "SELECT @@IDENTITY;"
      EventIssueObj.TrackingId = dbCmd.ExecuteScalar()
      Add = True
    Else
      Add = False
    End If

    dbConn.Close()

  Catch ex As Exception
    Return False
  End Try

End Function
```

This method uses the class variables to build a SQL statement for creating a new Issue database record, as you can see here:

```
Dim SQL As String = "INSERT INTO [Issue](customer_name, " & _
  "customer_email, problem) VALUES (" & _
  quoteForSQL(EventIssueObj.CustomerName) & "," & _
  quoteForSQL(EventIssueObj.CustomerEmail) & "," & _
  quoteForSQL(EventIssueObj.IssueDescription) & ");"
```

Then the function creates OleDbConnection and OleDbCommand objects to execute the SQL query:

```
Dim dbConn As OleDbConnection = GetConnection()
Dim dbCmd As New OleDbCommand(SQL, dbConn)
```

The function executes the query and tests dbCmd to ensure the query executed successfully:

```
If dbCmd.ExecuteNonQuery() > 0 Then
  dbCmd.CommandText = "SELECT @@IDENTITY;"
  EventIssueObj.TrackingId = dbCmd.ExecuteScalar()
  Add = True
Else
  Add = False
End If

dbConn.Close()
```

Assuming the query executed, the function retrieves the new Issue record's ID value using the special SQL @@IDENTITY command. This command returns the ID value generated by the last data insertion. The function then closes the database connections before terminating.

[Get]

The [Get] function accepts a Long integer object and retrieves the corresponding Issue record from the solution database. Since Get is a reserved word in the .NET Framework, the brackets are required to signify Get as the function name.

```
Public Shared Function [Get](ByVal TrackingID As Long) As EventIssue
  Try

    Dim SQL As String = "SELECT * FROM [Issue] WHERE [tracking_id]=" & TrackingID
    Dim dbConn As OleDbConnection = GetConnection()
    Dim dbCmd As New OleDbCommand(SQL, dbConn)
    Dim dbReader As OleDbDataReader = dbCmd.ExecuteReader

    If dbReader.Read Then
      [Get] = GetDataFromReader(dbReader)
    Else
      [Get] = Nothing
    End If

    dbConn.Close()

  Catch ex As Exception
    Return Nothing
  End Try

End Function
```

The method pulls data from the passed the TrackingID object to build a valid SQL statement for retrieving the desired EventIssue (service-failure) record. Then, using OleDb-Connection, OleDbCommand, and OleDbDataReader objects, the function returns an EventIssue via a pass through the GetDataFromReader function.

GetDataFromReader

The GetDataFromReader function converts data from the passed OleDbDataReader object into an EventIssue object (which is the return value of the function).

```
Private Shared Function GetDataFromReader(ByRef dbReader As _
 OleDbDataReader) As EventIssue

  Dim obj As New EventIssue
  obj.TrackingId = dbReader("tracking_id")
  obj.CustomerName = dbReader("customer_name")
  obj.CustomerEmail = dbReader("customer_email")
  obj.IssueDescription = dbReader("problem")
  Return obj

End Function
```

The function retrieves each column of the data reader and stores the value inside a corresponding EventIssue property.

The EventIssueTask.vb Class

The EventIssueTask class is the working class related to the Task InfoPath form. It provides the logic for retrieving and updating a task related to a service-failure record.

Add this class to the EventIssue web service project and name it **EventIssueTask.vb**.

Imports Directives

The EventIssueTask class imports a single namespace:

```
Imports System.Data.OleDb
```

Variable Declarations

The EventIssueTask class declares the following variables:

```
Public TaskId As Long = 0
Public TaskOrder As Long = 0
Public TrackingId As Long = 0
Public Task As String = ""
Public AssigneeEmail As String = ""
Public Comments As String = ""
Public Complete As Boolean = False
Public TaskDueDate As Date = Nothing
Public Sent As Boolean = False
```

Methods

The EventIssue class defines five public methods: Add, Update, MarkAsSent, GetTasks, and Get-DataFromReader.

Add

The Add method adds a task to the Task table residing in the solution database. In addition, the newly created task's ID number is retrieved and stored in the passed EventIssueTask object.

```
Public Shared Function Add(ByRef EventIssueTaskObj As EventIssueTask) _
  As Boolean
  Try
    Dim SQL As String = "INSERT INTO [Task](task_due_date, " & _
      "task_order, tracking_id, task, assignee_email, comments, complete, sent) " & _
      "VALUES (" & quoteDateForSQL(EventIssueTaskObj.TaskDueDate) & _
      "," & quoteForSQL(EventIssueTaskObj.TaskOrder) & "," & _
      quoteForSQL(EventIssueTaskObj.TrackingId) & "," & _
      quoteForSQL(EventIssueTaskObj.Task) & "," & _
      quoteForSQL(EventIssueTaskObj.AssigneeEmail) & "," & _
      quoteForSQL(EventIssueTaskObj.Comments) & "," & _
      quoteBooleanForSQL(EventIssueTaskObj.Complete) & ", false);"

    Dim dbConn As OleDbConnection = GetConnection()
    Dim dbCmd As New OleDbCommand(SQL, dbConn)

    If dbCmd.ExecuteNonQuery() > 0 Then
      dbCmd.CommandText = "SELECT @@IDENTITY;"
      EventIssueTaskObj.TaskId = dbCmd.ExecuteScalar()
      Add = True
    Else
      Add = False
    End If

    dbConn.Close()

  Catch ex As Exception
    Return False
  End Try

End Function
```

While building the SQL query, the method makes several calls to quoteForSQL in order to wrap the passed String object with apostrophes:

```
Dim SQL As String = "INSERT INTO [Task](task_due_date, " & _ "
  task_order, tracking_id, task, assignee_email, comments, complete, sent) " & _
  "VALUES (" & quoteDateForSQL(EventIssueTaskObj.TaskDueDate) &_
  "," & quoteForSQL(EventIssueTaskObj.TaskOrder) & "," & _
  quoteForSQL(EventIssueTaskObj.TrackingId) & "," & _
  quoteForSQL(EventIssueTaskObj.Task) & "," & _
  quoteForSQL(EventIssueTaskObj.AssigneeEmail) & "," & _
  quoteForSQL(EventIssueTaskObj.Comments) & "," & _
  quoteBooleanForSQL(EventIssueTaskObj.Complete) & ", false);"
```

Next, the code does what it was made to do. First it creates the needed OleDbConnection and OleDbCommand objects for working with the solution database:

```
Dim dbConn As OleDbConnection = GetConnection()
Dim dbCmd As New OleDbCommand(SQL, dbConn)
```

Then the query executes, and another query retrieves the new record's ID by calling the @@IDENTITY function and assigning the value to the class's TaskId property:

```
If dbCmd.ExecuteNonQuery() > 0 Then
  dbCmd.CommandText = "SELECT @@IDENTITY;"
  EventIssueTaskObj.TaskId = dbCmd.ExecuteScalar()
  Add = True
Else
  Add = False
End If
dbConn.Close()
```

Once all the queries finish their jobs, the method completes execution by closing the database connection.

Update

The Update method does what it says—it updates the database record of a given task. Anytime a user updates a task by using the InfoPath Task form, the Update method takes the provided EventIssueTask object and makes the appropriate changes to the record in the solution database. Only the Comment and Complete record fields are updated, as this is the only new information contained in the Task form. All other fields remain the same.

```
Public Shared Function Update(ByRef EventIssueTaskObj As _
  EventIssueTask)  As Boolean
  Try
    Dim SQL As String = "UPDATE [Task] SET [comments]=" & _
      quoteForSQL(EventIssueTaskObj.Comments) & ", [complete]=" & _
      quoteBooleanForSQL(EventIssueTaskObj.Complete) & _
        " WHERE [task_id]=" & EventIssueTaskObj.TaskId
    Dim dbConn As OleDbConnection = GetConnection()
    Dim dbCmd As New OleDbCommand(SQL, dbConn)

    If dbCmd.ExecuteNonQuery() > 0 Then
      Update = True
    Else
      Update = False
    End If

    dbConn.Close()

  Catch ex As Exception
    Return False
  End Try

End Function
```

The function builds the SQL UPDATE query using the information contained in the passed EventIssueTask object. The code then makes a connection to the solution database, executes the UPDATE query and returns either True or False, depending on whether the update was a success or not. Finally, the function closes the database and shuts up shop.

MarkAsSent

The MarkAsSent method updates a given Task record's Sent field to True to signify that the Bravo Corp employee assigned to the task has been sent an email notification.

```
Public Shared Function MarkAsSent(ByVal TaskId As Long) As Boolean
  'Marks a task as having had a notification sent to the assignee.

  Try
    Dim SQL As String = "UPDATE [Task] SET [sent]=true " & _
      "WHERE [task_id]=" & TaskId
    Dim dbConn As OleDbConnection = GetConnection()
    Dim dbCmd As New OleDbCommand(SQL, dbConn)

    If dbCmd.ExecuteNonQuery() > 0 Then
      MarkAsSent = True
    Else
      MarkAsSent = False
    End If

    dbConn.Close()

  Catch ex As Exception
    Return False
  End Try
End Function
```

Once again, we have the SQL statement created dynamically and the OleDbConnection and OleDbCommand objects created and ready for action. Then we have the execution of the UPDATE query to flag the record, indicating that the notification was sent to the task assignee. We even have a best practice of closing the database connection.

GetTasks

The GetTasks method does the job of retrieving all tasks associated with a given service-failure record. Using the TrackingID parameter, the functions opens the solution database, digs out all the records in the Task table, and returns them inside a Collection object where they are put to good use by the calling application.

```
Public Shared Function GetTasks(ByVal TrackingId As Long) As Collection
  'Returns a collection of tasks for a specific Tracking ID

  Dim TaskCollection As New Collection

  Try
```

```
   Dim SQL As String = "SELECT * FROM [task] WHERE "& _
            "[tracking_id]=" & TrackingId

   Dim dbConn As OleDbConnection = GetConnection()
   Dim dbCmd As New OleDbCommand(SQL, dbConn)
   Dim dbReader As OleDbDataReader = dbCmd.ExecuteReader

   While dbReader.Read
     TaskCollection.Add(GetDataFromReader(dbReader))
   End While

   dbConn.Close()

   Return TaskCollection
 Catch ex As Exception
   Return TaskCollection
 End Try

End Function
```

Let's focus on how the method fills the Collection with the desired task data. After the database is opened, the query is executed, and the OleDbDataReader is filled with data, the method loops through the query records and adds a new EventIssueTask object to the TaskCollection object.

```
While dbReader.Read
  TaskCollection.Add(GetDataFromReader(dbReader))
End While
```

The call to GetDataFromReader converts the current record to an EventIssueTask object. After dbReader finishes reading (or looping) through its records, the method returns the newly filled TaskCollection object as its value.

GetDataFromReader

The GetDataFromReader method inserts data returned from the solution database into the main object of the application, an EventIssueTask. As previously explained, the EventIssue-Task object provides all methods for manipulating task data.

```
Private Shared Function GetDataFromReader(ByRef dbReader _
  As OleDbDataReader) As EventIssueTask

  Dim obj As New EventIssueTask
  obj.TaskId = dbReader("task_id")
  obj.TaskOrder = dbReader("task_order")
  obj.TrackingId = dbReader("tracking_id")
  obj.Task = dbReader("task")
  obj.AssigneeEmail = dbReader("assignee_email")
  obj.Comments = dbReader("comments")s
```

```
obj.Complete = dbReader("complete")
obj.Sent = dbReader("sent")

If Not IsDBNull(dbReader("task_due_date")) Then _
    obj.TaskDueDate = dbReader("task_due_date")
Return obj
End Function
```

Nothing fancy here. `GetDataFromReader` just reads each column of the provided `OleDb-DataReader` object and assigns the column values to the related properties in the class's `EventIssueTask` object.

Testing the Service-Failure Web Service

At this point, all objects required by the web service are complete, and it is a good idea to test it before continuing with the development of the InfoPath forms, just to make sure it's working.

Follow these steps to test the web service:

1. Open the EventIssues project in Visual Studio, and press the F5 key to start the web service.

2. The `EventIssues.asmx` file should open in your browser and list the three available web service functions (see Figure 5-4).

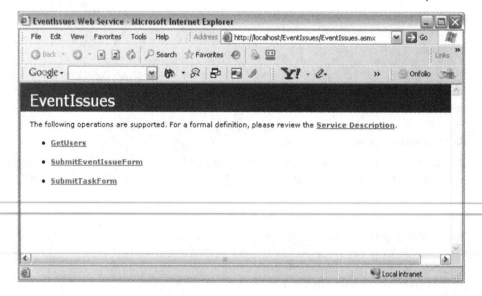

Figure 5-4. *The* `EventIssues.asmx` *file displayed in Internet Explorer*

3. Click the GetUsers link to invoke the GetUsers web service method. If a new browser window opens, displaying an XML listing of all users in the solution database (see Figure 5-5), then the web service is working as expected.

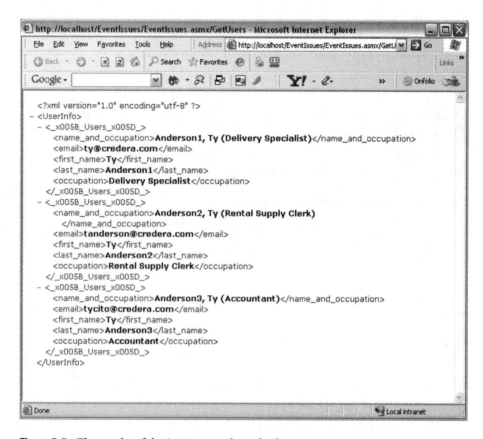

Figure 5-5. *The results of the* GetUsers *web method*

Creating the Service-Failure InfoPath Forms

Two InfoPath forms run the show and act as the primary user interfaces for the Service-Failure Reporting application. The first form is called EventIssueForm, and it kicks off the entire service-failure process (if you ignore the fact that the actual service failure itself gets things started). The second form is the Task form. This form identifies a single task that is associated with resolving a service failure, and Bravo Corp staff members use it to view information about a task assignment and to update the Task record in the database once they have completed the task.

Building InfoPath forms is a lot like building VB and Access forms. Controls are drawn on the form's "canvas," formatting is defined, and code is sprinkled in where needed. For this application, we will build two powerful InfoPath forms that interface with a web service without the need for us to write any custom code.

The EventIssueForm Form

The EventIssueForm (see Figure 5-6) is the user's tool for creating a service-failure report record.

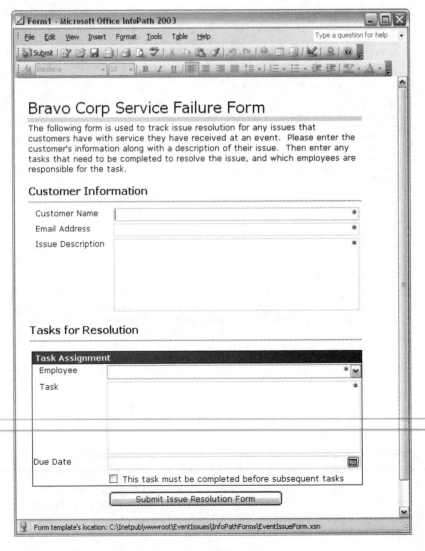

Figure 5-6. *The* EventIssueForm *InfoPath form*

Using InfoPath, the Bravo Corp staff member enters all the details of the failure in the Customer Information section of the form (customer name, email, and issue description). The Tasks for Resolution section is where the staff member lists any and all tasks that must be completed in order to resolve the identified issue. For each task, a Bravo Corp employee is assigned, the task to be completed is described, and a due date is assigned.

Designing the Form

To create the form, open up InfoPath and complete the following steps:

1. Create a new form by clicking the Design a Form option at the left side of the Fill Out a Form dialog box (see Figure 5-7).

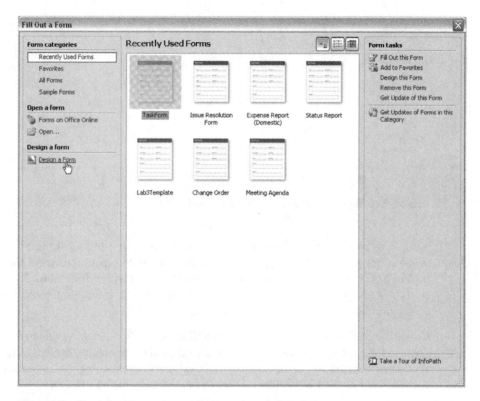

Figure 5-7. *Choosing the option to design a new InfoPath form*

2. InfoPath displays its Design a Form window and presents several more options—some similar to those in the previous window, and some not (see Figure 5-8). Click the New Blank Form option to get a blank form to work with.

Figure 5-8. *Choosing the option for a new blank form*

3. Along with loading a blank form document, InfoPath's Design Tasks task pane is now visible. Click the link for the Layout controls and drag and drop a Table with Title layout control onto the form (see Figure 5-9). Enter **Bravo Corp Service Failure Form** as the title of the form. If you feel like it, add some additional text explaining the purpose of the form in the description area of the table.

4. Create the Customer Information section by dragging a One-Column Table to the form and placing it underneath the Table with Title that was created in step 3. Type **Customer Information** in the first line of the table and format it as bold. Insert a horizontal line (Insert ➤ Horizontal Line) immediately below the new table.

5. Add a Custom Table inside the Customer Information table. The custom table needs three rows and two columns.

6. In the Design Tasks task pane, navigate to the Controls section, and add the controls listed in Table 5-4 to the custom table. Lay them out to resemble Figure 5-6.

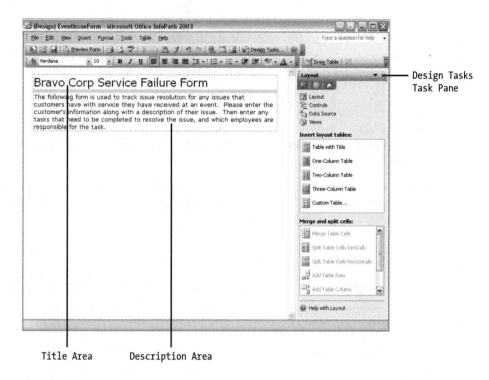

Figure 5-9. *The* EventIssueForm *in design mode with the layout controls of the Design Tasks task pane visible*

Table 5-4. *Controls for the Customer Information Section of the* EventIssueForm

Control	Field Name	Data Type	Cannot Be Blank	Height
Text box	customer_name	Text(String)	True	
Text box	email_address	Text(String)	True	
Text box	issue description	Text(String)	True	115 pixels

7. Create the Task Information section by dragging a one-column table control to the form and placing it underneath the Customer Information section. Type **Tasks for Resolution** in the first line of the table and format it as bold. Insert a horizontal line (Insert ➤ Horizontal Line) immediately below the table.

8. Add a Repeating Section inside the Task Information table. Open the control's properties and set its Field Name property to **Task**. Click OK.

■**Note** A Repeating Section is a special control that contains other controls and can be repeated. It is best used when the information to be collected inside the Repeating Section's child controls has a one-to-many relationship with the main data in the form (and with the underlying XML schema).

9. Move back to the Layout section of the Design Tasks task pane and insert a Custom Table control inside the Repeating Section added in step 8. The custom table needs four rows and two columns.

10. Switch back to the Task Pane's Controls section and add the controls listed in Table 5-5 to the table added in step 9. Once laid out, the Task Information section should look like what was shown in Figure 5-6.

Table 5-5. *Controls for the Tasks for Resolution Section of the* EventIssueForm

Control	Field Name	Data Type	Cannot Be Blank	Height	Default State
Drop-down list box	employee_email	Text(String)	True		
Text box	task description	Text(String)	True	115 pixels	
Date picker	task_due_date	Text(String)	False		
Check box	complete_before_next_task	True/False (Boolean)	Cleared		

The check box control should also have the following description property: "This task must be completed before subsequent tasks".

11. Finally, drag a button control to the bottom of the EventIssueForm. Open the Button's property window and select Submit from the Action drop-down list. Set the button's Label property to **Submit Service-Failure Report**.

■**Tip** The InfoPath button control can be used to submit data to a database or web service. In addition, a button click can initiate calls to custom InfoPath functions or custom code.

Advanced Setup of Form Controls

Drawing the controls on the form is only part of the job. To make each control truly useful, we need to go beyond the basic control properties like Field Name and Data Type. In this section, we will discuss how to call a web service to fill the form and its controls with data. In addition, we add a little validation logic to a couple of controls.

Adding Data Validation to the Email_Address Control

The key to ensuring that the service-failure workflow engine performs properly is to ensure that all email addresses are valid. A good step toward this goal is to check the data entered into the `email_address` field to make sure it is at least a well-formed email address. InfoPath provides a way to create data-validation conditions, by using a control's properties. The conditions are really tests run against data that is input into the control, and they allow the form's author to specify alerts that notify the user of invalid data.

■**Tip** To really ensure that the email address is a valid email address, you could add another function to the Service-Failure web service that checks with the solution database and returns valid and confirmed customer email addresses stored within the company's customer database. Also, if the email address does not exist in the database, the function could alert the user of the potentially invalid address.

For the `email_address` control, we want to validate the data using a regular expression pattern to test for a well-formed email address. Follow these steps:

1. Open the `email_address` control's property window. Click the Data Validation button.

2. In the Data Validation window, click the Add button to create a new validation condition.

3. We want to alert the user anytime the email address that is entered does *not* meet the standards for a well-formed email address (when it doesn't follow the pattern username@domainname.com). In the top section of the Data Validation window, set the condition to Does Not Match Pattern.

4. The third control of the top (condition) section of the Data Validation window (see Figure 5-10) is where you define the regular expression. From the drop-down, select the Select a Pattern option to open the Data Entry Pattern window.

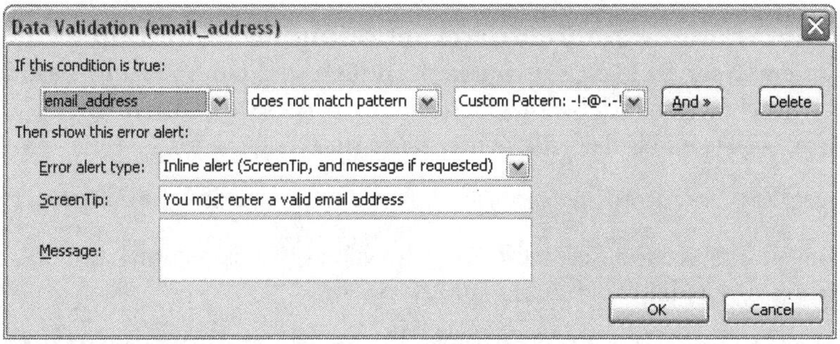

Figure 5-10. *Creating a condition that tests for a well-formed email address*

5. Select Custom Pattern from the provided pattern standards. In the Custom Pattern field, type the following regular expression:

```
[a-zA-Z0-9_\-]+(.[a-zA-Z0-9_\-]+)*@[a-zA-Z0-9_\-]+\.[a-zA-Z0-9_\-]+
    (.[a-zA-Z0-9_\-])*
```

Click OK three times to return to the InfoPath form.

■**Note** The preceding regular expression is shown as two lines on this page because the page isn't wide enough. In actual use, regexes should be entered as one continuous line without any breaks.

At run time, whenever the user enters an invalid email address, the form displays a dotted red line around the address to indicate that things aren't as they should be (see Figure 5-11). Beyond providing such useful visuals, the data-validation conditions also serve to prevent the user from submitting the form until all data is valid.

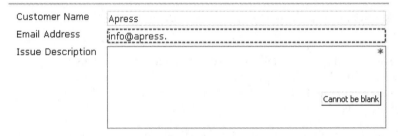

Figure 5-11. *InfoPath alerts the user of an invalid email address*

Filling the Employee_Email Drop-Down List Box Control

Currently, the employee_email control is a drop-down control without any data. Let's fix this by adding a call to the Service-Failure web service's GetUsers method. The GetUsers method returns a little XML that we can use to fill the drop-down control with data needed to fill in task information. Adding the web service call is no big deal. Just follow these steps:

1. Open the employee_email control's property window by double-clicking the control.

2. Under the List Box Entries section, select the "Look up values in a data connection to a database, Web service, or SharePoint library or list" option.

3. Create a call to the GetUsers method of the Service-Failure web service by clicking the Add button next to the Data Connection drop-down list (see Figure 5-12).

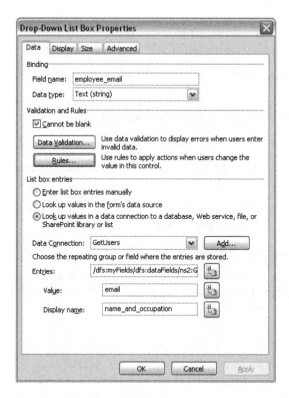

Figure 5-12. *Adding a web service call to the* employee_email *drop-down control*

4. The Data Connection Wizard opens to walk you through the data-connection process. On the first screen, select the Web Service radio button. Click Next.

5. In the Web Service details screen, enter the location for the Service-Failure web service. (For example, if you installed the web service on your local machine, the address would be http://localhost/eventissues/eventissues.asmx?WSDL.) Click Next.

6. Choose GetUsers in the Select an Operation list box. Click Next.

7. Type **GetUsers** as the name for the data connection, and click Next.

Now, whenever the EventIssueForm is opened, the employee_email drop-down list box control will automatically call the GetUsers method and fill the control with a list of Bravo Corp employee data.

Adding Logic to the Submit Button

Once the user completes the form and is ready to submit the data, the form needs to know what to do with the data. Once again, we will add a call to the Service-Failure web service. This time, we will add a call to the SubmitEventIssueForm method.

Follow these steps:

1. Open the Submit button control's property window by double-clicking the control.

2. Set the Action drop-down list to Submit. This will automatically open the Submitting Forms dialog box.

3. Select the Enable Submit Commands and Buttons radio button option.

4. In the Submit To drop-down list, select Web Service.

5. Create a call to the SubmitEventIssueForm method by clicking the Add button next to the Choose a Data Connection for Submit drop-down list.

6. In the Data Connection Wizard, enter the location for the Service-Failure web service (http://localhost/eventissues/eventissues.asmx?WSDL). Click Next.

7. Choose SubmitEventIssueForm in the Select an Operation list box. Click Next.

8. In the Data Connection Wizard window (see Figure 5-13), click the "Entire Form (XML document, including processing instructions)" radio button in the Parameter Options section. Click Next.

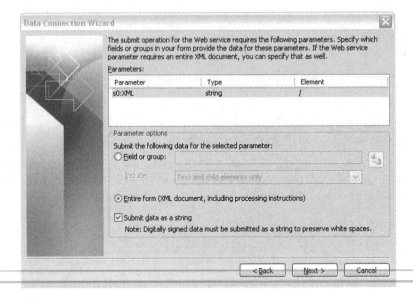

Figure 5-13. *Setting the Submit button to call the* SubmitEventIssueForm *method*

9. We'll use the default data connection name (Main submit), so just click Finish. Click OK twice to return to the form.

As you can see, the advanced properties of InfoPath allow for pain-free implementation of logic for validating code and calling web services. That's not all, either, as this chapter only covers the aspects of InfoPath needed to create the Service-Failure Reporting application. It's worth a little time and effort to investigate the full InfoPath feature set. If you do, you will find even more uses for it in your development projects.

The Task Form

Once a user creates a service-failure report by completing an EventIssueForm, a series of emails are sent to each Bravo staff member assigned a task. A one-to-one relationship exists for each task and email. If five tasks are created to resolve a service failure, and all five tasks are assigned to the same employee, that staff member will receive five emails—one for each task.

The Task form is used by a Bravo Corp staff member to update the task record residing in the solution database and add comments about the resolution. If the Task form is marked as complete, the next step in the Service-Failure Reporting application triggers.

Designing the Form

We covered the method of building an InfoPath form when we built the EventIssueForm. In this section we will only be focusing on the new things you'll need to know to build the Task form.

Figure 5-14 shows a completed version of the Task form at design time. Use it as a guide for laying out the text box controls listed in Table 5-6. In addition to those text boxes, you'll need these two controls:

- Check Box; Field Name: "complete"; Data Type: True/False(Boolean); Default State: Cleared; Description: "Complete"

- Button; Action: Submit; Label: "Update Task"

(Add layout controls as you see fit; the following discussion focuses on the data controls.)

Table 5-6. *Text Box Controls for the* Tasks *Form*

Control	Field Name	Data Type	Read-Only	Size	Default State
Text Box	customer_name	Text(String)	True		
Text Box	customer_email	Text(String)	True		
Text Box	issue_description	Text(String)	True	115 pixels	
Text Box	employee_fullname	Text(String)	True		
Text Box	occupation	Text(String)	True		
Text Box	task	Text(String)	True	115 pixels	
Text Box	task_due_date	Text(String)	True		
Text Box	comments	Text(String)	False	115 pixels	

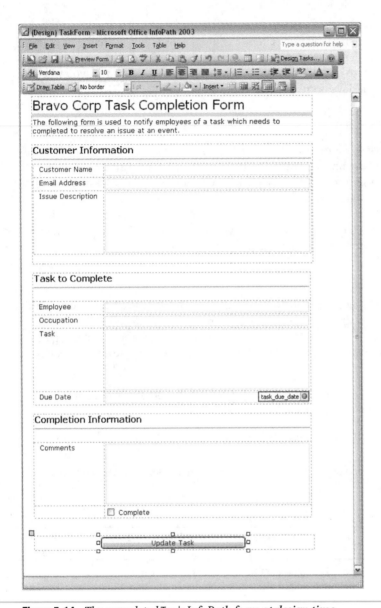

Figure 5-14. *The completed* Task *InfoPath form at design time*

Advanced Setup of Form Controls

Only one control has any advanced setup steps in the Task form.

Adding Logic to the Submit Button

After a task is completed and the user has filled out the related Task form, it must be submitted to the backend portion of the Service-Failure Reporting application. A call to the Service-Failure web service does the job once again.

Follow these steps:

1. Open the Submit button control's property window by double-clicking the control.

2. Set the Action drop-down list to Submit. This will automatically open the Submitting Forms dialog box.

3. Select the Enable Submit Commands and Buttons radio button option.

4. In the Submit To drop-down list select Web Service.

5. Create a call to the SubmitTaskForm method by clicking the Add button.

6. In the Data Connection Wizard, enter the location for the Service-Failure web service (http://localhost/eventissues/eventissues.asmx?WSDL). Click Next.

7. Choose SubmitTaskForm in the Select an Operation list box. Click Next.

8. In the Parameters wizard window, click the "Entire form (XML document, including processing instructions)" radio button in the Parameter Options section. Click Next.

9. We'll use the default data connection name (Main submit), so just click Finish. Click OK twice to return to the form.

With that, the two data-entry user-interface components are complete. There is just one additional user interface element to create—the EventIssueTracking web page.

Creating the EventIssueTracking.aspx Web Page

So far we have covered the Bravo Corp–centered portions of the Service-Failure Reporting application. Both the Service-Failure web service and the InfoPath forms are geared toward the needs of Bravo Corp and its staff because they enable an employee to create and update event issues and the associated event issue tasks.

In order to incorporate the customer-service goals of Bravo Corp, one more component is required—a web page that displays all information about an EventIssue. At this page, customers are able to view information such as the issue description, current status, task descriptions, and task status.

Once a Bravo Corp staff member creates an event issue, the customer receives an email that contains a link to the EventIssueTracking page. The page is not fancy, but it does the job.

Designing the EventIssueTracking Web Page

The EventIssueTracking web page is a simple page that makes use of standard WebForm controls (see Figure 5-15). The page is grouped into two sections, and the first contains the EventIssue parent information (customer name, email, etc.). This is the information entered in the EventIssueForm InfoPath form. The second section of the web page is the task section. Here, all the tasks required to resolve the service failure are listed, along with their current status.

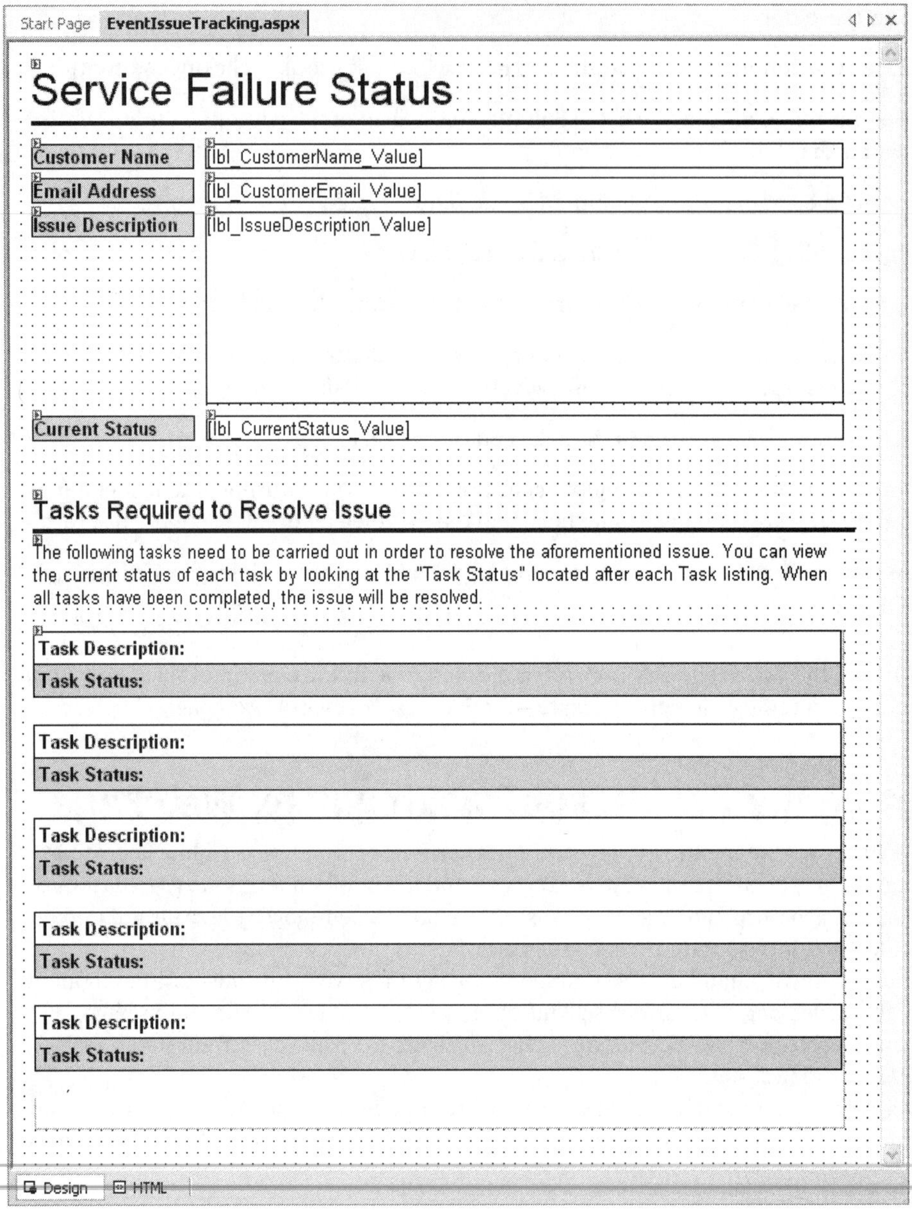

Figure 5-15. *The* EventIssueTracking *web page in design mode*

To build the EventIssueTracking web page, add a WebForm to the project and add the controls listed in Table 5-7 (we'll start at the top and work towards the bottom).

Table 5-7. *Label Controls for the* EventIssueTracking *WebForm*

Control	ID	Text
Label	lblHeading	Service-Failure Status
Label	lbl_CustomerName_Label	Customer Name
Label	lbl_CustomerEmail_Label	Email Address
Label	lbl_IssueDescription_Label	Issue Description
Label	lbl_CurrentStatus_Label	Current Status
Label	lbl_CustomerName_Value	
Label	lbl_CustomeEmail_Value	
Label	lbl_IssueDescription_Value	
Label	lbl_CurrentStatus_Value	
Label	lblTasks	Tasks Required to Resolve Issue
Label	lblDescription	The following tasks need to be carried out in order to resolve the aforementioned issue. You can view the current status of each task by looking at the "Task Status" located after each Task listing. When all tasks have been completed, the issue will be resolved.

To create the repeating Tasks Required to Resolve Issue section, follow these steps:

1. Add a panel control to the WebForm and position it underneath lblDescription. Set the control's ID property to **panel_RepHolder**.

2. Add a repeater control and place it within panel_RepHolder. Set the repeater's ID to **repTasks** and leave the other properties at their default values.

3. Change the WebForm's view to HTML, and insert the following lines with the <asp:repeater id="repTasks" runat="server"> tag:

```
<ItemTemplate>
  <table style="width: 590px; border: 1px solid black;"
      cellspacing="0" cellpadding="3">

    <tr style="font-family: arial; font-size:10pt;">
      <td style="width:125px;"><b>Task Description:</b></td>
    <TD>
      <asp:Label ID="lblTask" Runat="server"></asp:Label></TD>
    </tr>
    <tr style="font-family: arial; font-size:10pt;
        background-color: #DDDDDD;">
    <td style="border-top: 1px solid black;"><B>Task Status:</B></td>
    <td style="border-top: 1px solid black;">
```

```
        <asp:Label ID="lblTaskStatus"
              Runat="server"></asp:Label> 
    </td>
    </table>
    <br>
</ItemTemplate>
```

This HTML chunk defines the HTML that fills the repeater control's ItemTemplate property. The HTML contains two label controls wrapped inside an HTML table. It is the ItemTemplate that the repeater control wraps itself around to create a listing of given data. The repeater control, like the panel control, is a control wrapper and does not have an inherent visual design. The ItemTemplate property, in this case, provides all the formatting and visual design required via the formatted HTML table.

■**Note** A full discussion of ASP .NET, WebForms, web controls, and the like is beyond the scope of this book. For more information regarding repeater and panel controls and WebForms, refer to the extensive information available at http://msdn.microsoft.com.

Now that the page is laid out with all the required controls, let's add some code.

Events

The EventIssueTracking web page implements two event methods.

Page_Load

The Page_Load event of the web page triggers when the page is being loaded in the browser (much like a Windows form's Open event). The Load event is the place for any code needed to set up the page before it displays to the user.

In our case, the Load event accesses the solution database to retrieve the requested Event-Issue record and any related Task records. The retrieved data then fills controls on the page in a format that is easy to read.

```
Private Sub Page_Load(ByVal sender As System.Object, ByVal e As _
    System.EventArgs) Handles MyBase.Load

    Dim EventIssueObj As EventIssue = EventIssue.Get(TrackingID)
    Dim Tasks As Collection = EventIssueTask.GetTasks(TrackingID)
    Dim CompletedTasks As Integer = 0

    If EventIssueObj Is Nothing Then
      Page.RegisterStartupScript("error_script", "<SCRIPT " & _
        "language=javascript>alert('The Tracking ID provided " & _
        "could not be located. Please contact a customer service " & _
         "representative for assistance.');</SCRIPT>")
      Me.lbl_CurrentStatus_Value.Text = "Invalid Tracking ID Number"
```

```
      Exit Sub
    End If

    Me.lbl_CustomerName_Value.Text = EventIssueObj.CustomerName
    Me.lbl_CustomerEmail_Value.Text = EventIssueObj.CustomerEmail
    Me.lbl_IssueDescription_Value.Text = EventIssueObj.IssueDescription

    For Each Task As EventIssueTask In Tasks
      If Task.Complete Then CompletedTasks += 1
    Next

    'Set status text
    If Tasks.Count > 0 Then
      If CompletedTasks = Tasks.Count Then
        Me.lbl_CurrentStatus_Value.Text = _
          "Resolved (All tasks have been completed)"
      Else
        Me.lbl_CurrentStatus_Value.Text = "In Progress (" & _
        CompletedTasks & " of " & Tasks.Count & " tasks complete)"
      End If
    Else
      Me.lbl_CurrentStatus_Value.Text = _
        "Resolved (There were no tasks to complete)"
    End If

    'Databind the Tasks to the Repeater
    Me.repTasks.DataSource = Tasks
    Me.repTasks.DataBind()

End Sub
```

The Page_Load event declares three object variables that are used to store the data to be retrieved from the solution database: an EventIssue, and EventIssueTask, and an Integer:

```
Dim EventIssueObj As EventIssue = EventIssue.Get(TrackingID)
Dim Tasks As Collection = EventIssueTask.GetTasks(TrackingID)
Dim CompletedTasks As Integer = 0
```

While instantiating each variable, the method also retrieves data for the object through a call to the object's "get" method (Get or GetTasks). After these calls, it makes sense to ensure that we actually have data to display—if not, the alert shown in Figure 5-16 is displayed to the user:

```
'Ensure that we have something to show
If EventIssueObj Is Nothing Then
  Page.RegisterStartupScript("error_script", "<SCRIPT " & _
    "language=javascript>alert('The Tracking ID provided " & _
    "could not be located. Please contact a customer service " & _
    "representative for assistance.');</SCRIPT>")
```

```
  Me.lbl_CurrentStatus_Value.Text = "Invalid Tracking ID Number"
  Exit Sub
End If
```

Figure 5-16. *The alert informing the user of an invalid Tracking ID*

If no data is retrieved, the method builds HTML and JavaScript to alert the user of the situation after the page loads into the browser, and the method stops execution right here.

If data is retrieved and loaded into the method's variables, we are in good shape, and the method continues by loading the values into each page control:

```
Me.lbl_CustomerName_Value.Text = EventIssueObj.CustomerName
Me.lbl_CustomerEmail_Value.Text = EventIssueObj.CustomerEmail
Me.lbl_IssueDescription_Value.Text = EventIssueObj.IssueDescription
```

The Service-Failure Information section's controls are set to the values the EventIssueObj contains.

Continuing on, the method determines the number of completed tasks by looping through each EventIssueTask contained in the method's Tasks collection object.

```
For Each Task As EventIssueTask In Tasks
  If Task.Complete Then CompletedTasks += 1
Next
```

When the loop completes, the method will know the number of completed tasks. This is important for determining whether all tasks have been completed and what the reader of the page should be told. The following lines of code make this determination:

```
If Tasks.Count > 0 Then
  If CompletedTasks = Tasks.Count Then
    Me.lbl_CurrentStatus_Value.Text = _
      "Resolved (All tasks have been completed)"
  Else
    Me.lbl_CurrentStatus_Value.Text = "In Progress (" & _
    CompletedTasks & " of " & Tasks.Count & " tasks complete)"
  End If
Else
  Me.lbl_CurrentStatus_Value.Text = _
    "Resolved (There were no tasks to complete)"
End If
```

By comparing the Count property of the Tasks collection against the CompletedTasks integer, the method determines whether or not all tasks have been completed. If they have, the reader is told the good news. If CompletedTasks is less than Tasks.Count, the reader is told the number of task completed and the total number of tasks attached to the service-failure report.

The final step in the procedure is to bind the data that retrieved and was stored in the method's variables to the repTask repeater control:

```
Me.repTasks.DataSource = Tasks
Me.repTasks.DataBind()
```

Before binding the data, the repeater control is assigned the Tasks collection as its data source. The DataSource property represents the object containing the records to be displayed by the Repeater. Once the data source is known, it can be bound to the Repeater by calling the Repeater's DataBind method. DataBind actually loops through the data provided by the Data-Source property and creates a multi-record control that contains a listing of each record.

repTasks_ItemDataBound

The ItemDataBound event triggers immediately after data is bound to the Repeater control but before the page is rendered in the browser. Therefore, this event is the place for adding code that fills the controls in the Repeater control with data.

```
Private Sub repTasks_ItemDataBound(ByVal sender As Object, ByVal e As _
  System.Web.UI.WebControls.RepeaterItemEventArgs) _
  Handles repTasks.ItemDataBound
  'Display task information in the repeater

  If e.Item.ItemType = UI.WebControls.ListItemType.Item Or _
    e.Item.ItemType = UI.WebControls.ListItemType.AlternatingItem Then

    Dim lblTask As UI.WebControls.Label = e.Item.FindControl("lblTask")
    Dim lblTaskStatus As UI.WebControls.Label = _
        e.Item.FindControl("lblTaskStatus")
    Dim Task As EventIssueTask = CType(e.Item.DataItem, EventIssueTask)

    lblTask.Text = Task.Task
    lblTaskStatus.Text = IIf(Task.Complete, "Complete", "Incomplete")

  End If

End Sub
```

The repeater control calls the ItemDataBound event for portions of itself, including the header, footer, each item and alternating item, and so on. We only want to run our binding code if the item type is the item or the alternating item (hence the If statement enclosing the code block).

Inside the HTML for the repeater control you will see something like this:

```
<Item>
  <asp:label runat=server name=lblTask/>
  <asp:label runat=server name=lblTaskStatus/>
</Item>
```

These two labels are never declared in the codebehind page (you cannot access a lblTask variable in the page_load event handler) because they only exist within the context of a single "repeat" of the repeater control (there could be 1 or 50 of them, depending on how many times something repeats). When the ItemDataBound event fires, we have to search the item for the Label control because only then do we have the proper context for accessing the control.

We declare the variable to hold the control (lblTask) and use e.Item.FindControl("lbl-Task") to search for and return the actual control from within the item template. Once we have a reference to the Label, we can use it just like any other label control on the page. The same goes for the lblTaskStatus label.

Property Methods

The EventIssueTracking page contains one property method: TrackingID.

TrackingID

TrackingID is a read-only property that returns the numeric value of the page's TrackingID URL parameter.

```
Private ReadOnly Property TrackingID() As Long
  'Strongly Type the TrackingID querystring variable
  Get
    If Request.QueryString("TrackingID") = Nothing Then Return 0
    If Not IsNumeric(Request.QueryString("TrackingID")) Then Return 0
    Return CInt(Request.QueryString("TrackingID"))
  End Get
End Property
```

If the TrackingID URL parameter does not exist (or is Nothing), then 0 is returned as the property value, and no data will be found in the Page.Load method. If the TrackingID parameter does exist, it is first confirmed to be a numeric value, and if it, it is converted to an integer and returned as the property value.

■**Tip** Anytime a URL parameter is in play, make sure you test it to ensure that it contains the type of data you expect. If you don't, you open your code up to malicious users who like to insert SQL statements as the parameter. The result could be deleted data or worse.

Summary

InfoPath is one of the most powerful applications within the Microsoft Office System suite of applications (and it's only in its initial version). The power comes from InfoPath's simplicity—non-developers can build forms, interact with web services, and connect to databases without writing a line of code.

This chapter explained how to use InfoPath as the front-end tool in a larger solution that also utilizes a web service, a database, and custom logic controlling a basic workflow engine.

CHAPTER 6

■ ■ ■

The Budget Consolidator

Creating, Distributing, and Summarizing Budgets Using Excel Workbooks, an Excel Add-In, and VBA

Although it may be painful, budgeting is a time-honored corporate ritual that provides decision makers with a financial forecast and helps them make good decisions that benefit their companies. It really is that simple—if you listen to the folks asking for the budgets. The reality, of course, is that budgets are often created in different styles and formats. The lack of a standard makes the task of consolidating budget information from different sources too difficult for any rational person to even think about doing.

Fortunately, the Budget Consolidator simplifies this never-ending cycle of business planning—it is guaranteed to make the Accounting department smile (and that almost never happens). It allows a standard budget template to be e-mailed to various managers and for the completed and returned budgets to be incorporated into a single summary budget.

To build this solution, all you need is knowledge of the Excel object model, a basic understanding of Excel-specific add-ins (.xla files), and VBA. These are the key development points you'll learn about in this chapter:

- **How to build Excel-specific add-ins**: These add-ins are simpler and more convenient to create than COM add-ins. They are built inside a normal Excel workbook but use the .xla extension to inform Excel that the file is an add-in. XLA files are automatically hidden when opened in Excel, which means that creating an Excel add-in can be as simple as adding code to an Excel workbook and saving the file with an .xla extension. In addition, Excel automatically suppresses Excel alerts caused by code executing within the add-in.

- **How to use the registry to save the add-in's user settings**: It is simple to save the add-in's user settings to and retrieve them from the Windows registry. We'll look at how to do this.

- **How to create a menu for the add-in using VBA**: You will see how to create a custom menu for the add-in by manipulating the Office command bar objects. A key concept discussed here is how to create an Excel context menu (a right-click menu).

- **How to enforce a standard worksheet architecture**: We will look at how to lock down a budget template file to ensure that it maintains its structure and remains consistent with the standard. But although we will lock the structure, we will provide users with a method for inserting and deleting budget lines through the use of an Office UserForm that lists standard Revenue and Expense line items for completing a budget. The key coding concepts involved here include how to fill a list box with data from an Excel list, how to insert items into an Excel range, how to automate worksheet security, and how to enforce business rules that decide when a budget has been completed and is ready for submission.

- **How to consolidate completed budget templates**: We will look at how to transfer the data from a completed budget to a specified summary budget file. Key concepts include how to copy the completed budget template as worksheet in the summary budget, and how to update the summary budget worksheet to reflect the additional data.

Designing the Budget Consolidator

The users of the Budget Consolidator, in the context of Bravo Corp, will be the division vice president and the department managers. By using the Budget Consolidator, a division vice president is able to

- Distribute a standardized Budget Template to each department manager

- Consolidate budgets into a single Excel workbook

- Maintain Budget Consolidator-related settings (file locations, user email addresses, etc.)

That may not sound like much, but that's because most of the effort is pushed down to the department manager level. Each Budget Template contains VBA functions allowing the department manager to

- Insert new budget lines using standard line-item names

- Validate the budget prior to sending it to the division vice president

Figure 6-1 illustrates the application's workflow.

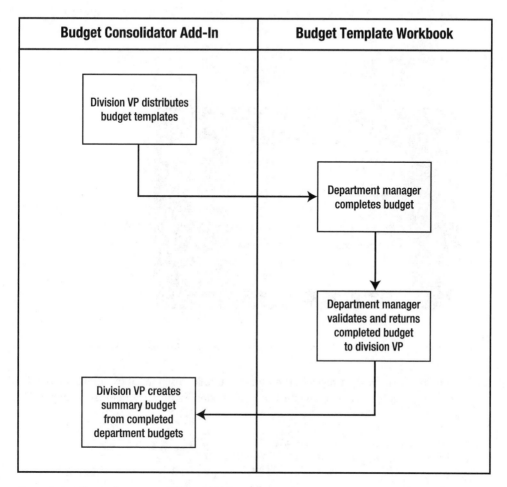

Figure 6-1. *The Budget Consolidator application workflow*

Given the purpose of the Budget Consolidator, Excel is perfectly suited for the task. Notice I didn't say it was perfect, just perfectly suited, as it handles 99 percent of the work we want to do. All Excel lacks in this case are the business rules, which is where we come in.

Let's take a brief look at the workflow of the Budget Consolidator from the user's perspective:

1. A division vice president initiates the budgeting process by opening Excel and distributing the Budget Template to each department manager by email (see Figure 6-2).

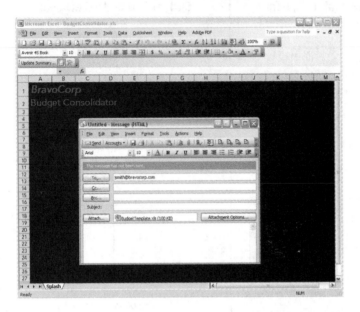

Figure 6-2. *Sending a Budget Template to a department manager*

2. The department manager receives the Budget Template in their inbox, opens the file in Excel, and fills it full of data using the tools embedded in the document (see Figure 6-3).

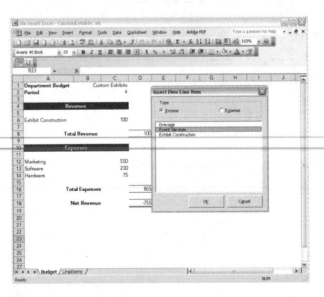

Figure 6-3. *Filling out a Budget Template*

3. The department manager, upon completing the budget, emails the file back to the division vice president. Prior to the sending the email, the document checks itself against some basic rules to verify that it is a valid budget. For example, each budget must include the department name and budget period. If the budget is invalid, the department manager will receive an alert (see Figure 6-4) and will be unable to email the budget to the division VP.

Figure 6-4. *Invalid budget alert*

4. As budgets are received by the division vice president, they are inserted into a Summary Budget. Each Budget Template is included as a separate tab within the Summary worksheet. In addition, a consolidated budget worksheet is updated to reflect the consolidated budget numbers (see Figure 6-5).

■**Note** In Excel, the terms *worksheet* and *tab* both refer to the tabbed pages (worksheets) included within an Excel file. I use these terms interchangeably.

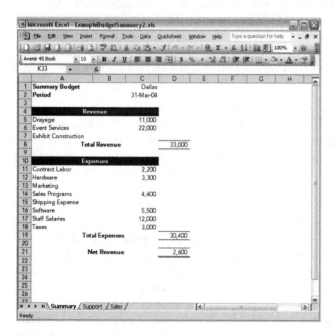

Figure 6-5. *The Budget Templates are inserted into the Summary Budget.*

As you can see, we are souping up Excel just a bit to enforce a set of rigid business rules and processes while still providing the user with the rich-client experience they enjoy in Excel.

From the user's perspective, the Budget Consolidator looks like a simple application. In fact, to most folks, the application appears to simply insert some lines into a spreadsheet, email the spreadsheet back and forth, and finally copy the spreadsheet to another Excel workbook. This impression is a reflection of the application's power. To the user, the application is simple and easy to use. To you, the solution developer, this application is a challenge and requires much more effort.

Tip The usefulness of an application can be measured by the effort required by the user to utilize the application and the developer's effort in creating the application. Since time (and money) has been allocated to the development of the application, it is only worthwhile if the effort required of the user is reduced. The user will use the application repeatedly over time, and the developer will only develop the application once, so it is often worth investing development time in reducing the user's effort.

From the developer's perspective, the Budget Consolidator has more features than the user is likely to perceive. The application is separated into three distinct pieces:

- Microsoft Excel: Excel acts as the user interface for the custom code, and it serves as the host application for the Budget Consolidator add-in and as the engine for the Budget Template files.

- BudgetTemplate.xls: The Budget Template is a normal Excel file (which has an .xls extension), and it contains two worksheets. The first is an empty budget shell named DeptName, and the second, named LineItems, is a data list of standard budget line item names (Event Services, Marketing, Contract Labor, etc.). In addition to the two worksheets, the file also includes custom VBA code and an Office UserForm. When executed, these objects walk the user through the process of inserting new line items within the budget shell.

- BudgetConsolidator.xla: The second component of the Budget Consolidator application is an Excel-specific add-in. This add-in, which is loaded only on the division vice presidents' machines, contains the logic for distributing Budget Templates to department managers and for building a consolidated budget from the completed Budget Templates. Like the Budget Template file, the add-in contains VBA algorithms in addition to Office UserForm objects.

For each of the components within this solution, we will work with several different objects provided by Excel. Excel owns the most object-rich hierarchy in the Microsoft Office System. Not only does it contain the most objects of any Office application, many of the objects are available via several different objects, which forces you to stay on your toes. A good example of this situation is the many different objects that allow you to access a specific cell.

Each file must perform a series of task in order to fulfill its purpose (see Figure 6-6). Each of these tasks will be executed through one or more subroutines that we will create this chapter.

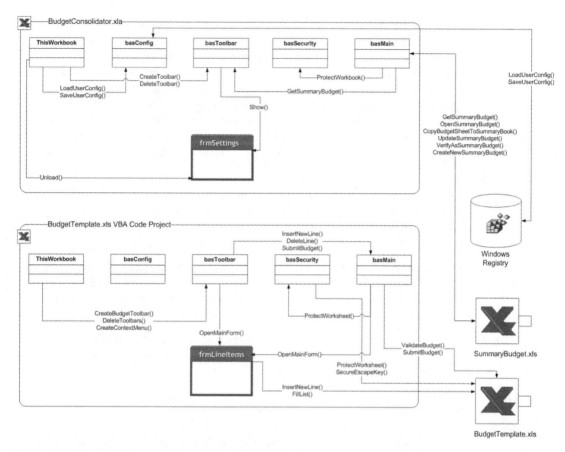

Figure 6-6. *The architecture of the Budget Consolidator*

The BudgetConsolidator.xla file completes the following tasks:

1. **Create a custom menu:** Here the add-in creates a custom Office toolbar and populates it with buttons that allow the user to invoke commands. Once the add-in opens, the add-in's ThisWorkbook_Open event triggers and invokes the CreateToolbar method within basToolbar. CreateToolbar then accesses the Office CommandBar object to create the custom toolbar. Also, when the add-in's ThisWorkbook_BeforeClose event fires (when the add-in is unloaded), the DeleteToolbar method is called to delete the custom toolbar. This helps ensure that the add-in's menu exists only when the add-in is loaded in Excel.

2. **Select the consolidated budget:** A user utilizes frmSettings to browse their file system and select a SummaryBudget.xls file to use as the summary budget for consolidating all completed budget templates. The GetBudgetFileName method (found in the frmSettings's module) handles the task of displaying the Open dialog box provided by Office and returning the path of the selected file.

3. Copy completed Budget Templates to the summary workbook: With the completed budget template opened in Excel, the code asks the user whether they would like to create a new summary budget or use an existing one. If they decide to create a new summary budget, the CreateNewSummaryBudget method is called, which creates a copy of the summary budget template specified in the user settings and makes that the new summary budget. If they decide to use an existing file, GetSummaryBudget is invoked and the code asks for the location of the existing summary budget file. Either way, the code then opens the summary budget file. Once opened, the completed budget template's budget tab is copied to the summary budget (CopyBudgetSheetToSummaryBook).

4. Update summary worksheet: Once the summary budget has had the budget template information copied into a new budget tab, the summary tab must be updated to reflect the new data. UpdateSummaryBudget completes this task by looping through the rows in the Revenue and Expense named ranges and updating the cell formulas to reference the new tab using Excel's VLOOKUP function.

5. Verify the file as a summary budget: Here the code checks an Excel property to ensure that the file is tagged as a valid summary budget file (VerifyAsSummaryBudget). This is done by checking the value of a custom document property named BudgetType and ensuring it has a value of Summary.

6. Send Budget Template file to users: SendTemplate invokes Excel's send mail dialog box to create a new Outlook email that automatically attaches a budget template file for distribution to department managers.

The BudgetTemplate.xls file completes the following tasks:

1. Create a custom menu: Once the budget template file open, its ThisWorkbook_Open method executes. This method calls CreateBudgetToolbar to create a custom toolbar for the file. In addition, the CreateContextMenu method is invoked, and it customizes the Cell command bar to create context menu buttons that allow users to insert and delete budget line items.

2. Insert a budget line item: This task opens frmSettings and calls FillList to fill its list box control with a data list on a hidden tab in the budget template. The user then selects the desired budget line item, and the code accesses either the Revenue or Expense Range object and inserts a new line (InsertNewLine) in the worksheet as the last row in the range. The last step in this process is to resize the affected range to include the new line.

3. Delete a budget line item: The DeleteLine method deletes the entire row that contains the currently active cell. The user is asked to confirm that they would like to delete the row, and once confirmed the row is deleted and other rows are shifted up.

4. Protect/unprotect a worksheet: The ProtectWorksheet method is called by the Insert-NewLine and DeleteLine methods to allow changes to the budget template file before attempting to make a change. The ProtectWorksheet method accepts a Boolean argument to specify whether the file should be protected or unprotected. Once the changes have been made to the worksheet, ProtectWorksheet is called again to protect the budget file and prevent the user from making unwanted edits.

5. Send the completed Budget Template to the division vice president: Once the user has completed their budget template, they can attempt to submit it via email to their division vice-president. The `SubmitBudget` method starts this process by first calling the `ValidateBudget` method, which enforces a simple business rule that requires a budget template to contain a department name, budget date, and at least three revenue expense lines. If these conditions are met, the budget template is deemed complete and ready for submission. Prior to submitting the file, the code changes the tab name to reflect the department name. The last step of `SubmitBudget` is to invoke Excel's send mail dialog command (`Application.Dialogs(xlDialogSendMail).Show`), which creates a new Outlook email with the completed budget template already attached.

The Business Scenario

Every quarter, each Bravo Corp division vice president must create a new financial forecast for their division. This forecast includes all of the traditional statements, such as balance sheets, income statements, cash-flow statements, etc., and it must include data from all departments within the division.

Unfortunately Bravo Corp consists of 25 different divisions spread throughout North America, and producing 25 divisional budgets that can be easily consolidated and summarized is not only a challenge, but an obstacle that has caused Bravo Corp to abandon this effort in the past.

Bravo Corp decided to create the Budget Consolidator application to ease the task of creating standardized budgets across all divisions.

Creating the Budget Template and Budget Summary Files

The Budget Template is the file sent to each department manager for them to complete and return to the division vice president. In this section, we will be creating a new Excel workbook to serve as the standard template for the budgeting process, and it will include the worksheets mentioned earlier: DeptName and LineItems.

The Budget Template includes the following objects:

-   `frmLineItems` form: This is a `UserForm` used to insert revenue and expense budget line items within the Budget Template worksheet. It contains a list box control that is filled with items from an Excel data list hidden in the budget template worksheet. We will look at how to insert new lines into the template inside various named ranges using Excel's `Range` object.

-   `basSecurity` module: This is a `Module` containing the methods for protecting and unprotecting worksheets inside the Budget Template. Here you will learn how to create helper functions that are called by other objects in the add-in (like the `frmLineItems` form) to lock and unlock the budget template when code executing within the add-in wants to edit the worksheet.

- `basToolbar` module: This is a `Module` containing the methods for creating and deleting the Budget Template's custom menu. Here you will learn how to create a custom menu for the budget template. The key concept here, however, is how to create a context menu (or a right-click menu) that is available anywhere inside the worksheet. The methods inside this module are invoked by the methods residing inside the `ThisWorkbook` module.

- `basMain` module: This is a `Module` containing the Budget Template's core business logic. In creating it, you will learn how to build a simple business rule to validate a budget as a completed budget before it can be submitted. The methods in this module are called from methods inside `basToolbar`.

- `ThisWorkbook` module: This is a `Module` containing the auto-exec code for the Budget Template's startup and shutdown routines. The code here shows how to use the `Workbook_Open` and `Workbook_BeforeClose` events to set up and clean up (respectively) the add-in's environment. The module calls methods available inside the `basToolbar` module.

This section also explains how to build the budget summary template file—the file that eventually becomes the consolidated budget as completed budget templates are received and rolled into it.

Building the BudgetTemplate.xls File

Before digging into the code, we need to create the spreadsheet file (an .xls file) that we will code against, and configure for our purposes. Follow these steps to properly set it up:

1. With Excel open, create a new blank worksheet by selecting File ➤ New ➤ Blank Workbook from the menu (or by pressing Ctrl+N).

2. Rename the first worksheet (Sheet 1) to **Budget**. This is the worksheet that will contain the blank budget.

3. Format the Budget worksheet so that it looks like the sheet shown in Figure 6-7. The formatting is not really important to our coding effort; it just helps make the worksheet more readable and keeps the users happy.

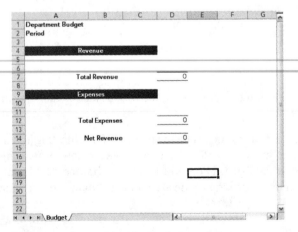

Figure 6-7. *Formatting the Budget worksheet*

4. Create a named range by selecting cells B1 and C1. With the cells selected, insert
   DeptName in the name box at the top-left corner of Excel, just above column A
   (see Figure 6-5).

5. Create three more named ranges called **Period**, **Revenue**, and **Expenses**, using
   Figure 6-8 as your guide.

Note Steps 4 and 5 are critical because we will be referring to these ranges later in our code.

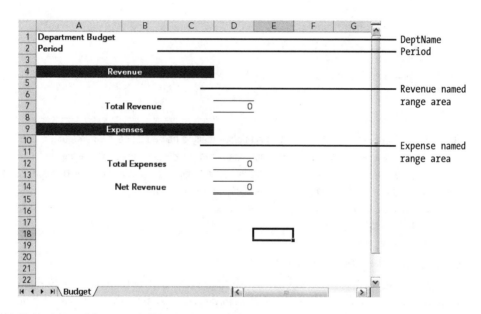

Figure 6-8. *Adding named ranges to the Budget worksheet*

6. Rename the second worksheet (Sheet 2) to **LineItems**. This worksheet will contain the
   available and allowed budget line items during the application's execution.

7. Enter **Line Item Name** in cell A1 and **Type** in cell B1.

8. Create a new data list by selecting Data ➤ List ➤ Create List (Ctrl+L). Excel will display
   the Create List dialog box, which allows you to specify a range of cells for the new list.
   Enter **=$A$2:$B$2** as the value in the Where Is the Data for Your List? field and check the
   My List Has Headers check box. Your worksheet should now look similar to Figure 6-9,
   although it will not contain the example data until you enter it.

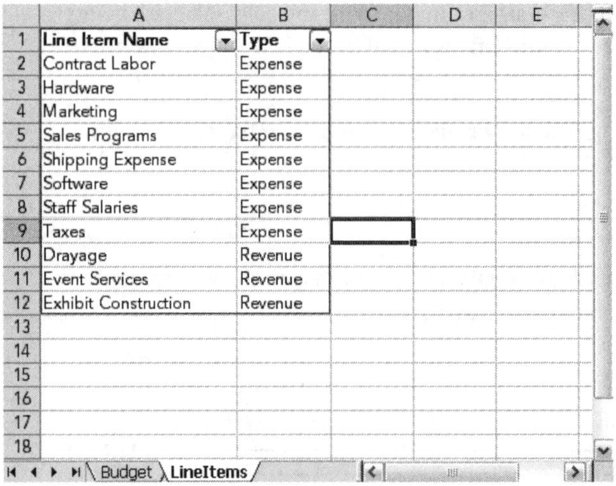

Figure 6-9. *An example data list containing budget line items*

■**Tip** Named ranges are a great tool within Excel. Essentially, a named range is a name that is applied to a cell or group of cells in a worksheet. Once named, the range of cells can then be referenced in Excel formulas and VBA code. It is much less confusing and cleaner, code-wise, to reference an area of a spreadsheet by name as opposed to searching through the cells using the R1C1 format.

Adding Worksheet Protection

One of the primary goals of the Budget Consolidator is to deliver standardized budgets to the division vice presidents for consolidation and review. To meet this objective, we need to ensure that a completed budget is delivered in a consistent format using consistent data items. To reduce the risk that a user of the application subverts the whole process by changing the format of the budget and using nonstandard line items, we need to take steps to ensure that the document maintains its current format.

A good method for locking down the structure of an Excel file is to use the workbook protection features. By properly utilizing the protection function, it is possible to prevent users from making undesired edits to data or making equally undesired and potentially catastrophic architectural changes to the layout of the worksheet. We'll look more at this later; for now, all we need to do is lock down the Budget and LineItems worksheets.

To protect the worksheets, select Tools ➤ Protection ➤ Protect Sheet. Enter **1234** as the password in the Protect Sheet dialog box's Password field. Confirm it, and you have a relatively protected document.

■**Caution** Although we're using this protection, passwords in Microsoft Office files aren't worth a hill of beans. There are numerous programs available that can crack any password embedded in an Office document. I say this so that you don't make fun of my simple little password. In my experience, a password of "wJ.8u$n>^bB" is just as easy for these programs to crack as "1234". Don't rely on a document password to provide true security for a document. However, document passwords are a good tool for preventing the curious from messing things up.

We do not want users to see the LineItems tab, as it will probably only confuse them—it is simply used to fill our custom forms with data (which we'll get to in just a bit). With the Line-Items worksheet as the active sheet, select Format ➤ Sheet ➤ Hide, and you're done.

Building the BudgetSummary.xls File

BudgetSummary.xls is the file that will be used by the Budget Consolidator to import completed Budget Templates. For our example, the summary template file is simply a renamed copy of BudgetTemplate.xls. The code for this add-in has been designed to allow for various versions of the Summary Budget that could contain different structures. For example, the Summary Budget could summarize revenue and expenses on separate tabs or in separate columns. This is why the add-in's Settings form allows the user to specify both a Budget Template file and a Summary Budget file.

To create the BudgetSummary.xls file, follow these steps:

1. Make a copy of the BudgetTemplate.xls Excel file, and rename it as **BudgetSummary.xls**.

2. Create lines for each revenue or expense line item listed in the LineItems tab of the BudgetTemplate.xls file. Figure 6-10 shows the completed BudgetSummary.xls template using the example line items from Figure 6-9. It's important that you get this step correct, as the code relies on the existence of these line items to consolidate the budget numbers.

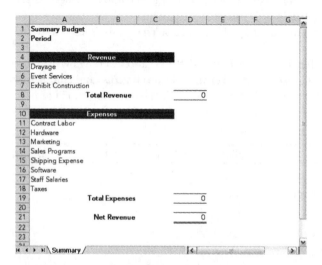

Figure 6-10. *Creating the* BudgetSummary.xls *template*

That's all we need to do with the BudgetSummary.xls file. The remainder of this section applies only to the BudgetTemplate.xls file. The summary template does not need any of the modules or forms included with the BudgetTemplate.xls file.

The frmLineItems Form

Other than the user interfaces provided by Excel, frmLineItems is the only other visual cue provided to the department manager user. This form is used to select new line items and insert them into the budget (see Figure 6-11).

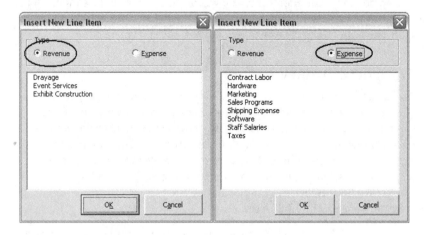

Figure 6-11. *The* frmLineItems *form showing both the revenue and expense line items*

Once the form is displayed, the user can choose between available revenue and expense line items by clicking either the Revenue or Expense radio button. The ListBox will automatically update its contents depending on which radio button is selected. The user chooses one of the available line items and clicks the Okay button to insert the line into the BudgetTemplate.xls file—revenue line items are inserted inside the Revenue named range and expense line items are inserted inside the Expense named range. Users can also change their mind and click the Cancel button.

To build this form, open the Visual Basic Editor (Alt+F11) and insert a new UserForm (from Excel's Visual Basic Editor, select Insert ➤ UserForm). Add the controls (and edit the properties) listed in Table 6-1. Lay out the form so that it looks like the one shown in Figure 6-11.

Table 6-1. *Controls Used in the* frmLineItems *Form*

Control	Name	Caption	Value	Default	Accelerator
Frame	fraType	Type			
OptionButton	optRevenue	Revenue	True		
OptionButton	optExpense	Expense			
ListBox	lstLineItems				
CommandButton	cmdOkay	OK		True	K
CommandButton	cmdCancel	Cancel			A

The ProcessLine Method

Open up the code window for the `frmLineItems` form (Alt+F11) and insert the following procedure:

```
Private Sub ProcessLine()
  If optRevenue Then
    Call InsertNewLine("Revenue", lstLineItems.Value)
  Else
    Call InsertNewLine("Expenses", lstLineItems.Value)
  End If
End Sub
```

The purpose of `ProcessLine` is to determine what type of line the user has decided to add to their budget. After a quick check of `optRevenue`'s value, the procedure calls the `InsertNewLine` procedure, telling it what type of line to insert into the spreadsheet, and providing the selected text for the line as well.

The InsertNewLine Method

The `InsertNewLine` procedure pretty much lives up to its name and handles the details of adding a new line to the currently open budget file. Here it is in all its glory.

```
Private Sub InsertNewLine(LineType As String, LineValue)
  Dim oSheet As Worksheet
  Dim oRange As Range
  Dim strLocation As String

  Set oSheet = ActiveSheet
  Call ProtectWorksheet(False, oSheet.Name)
  Application.Goto Reference:=LineType
  ActiveCell.Offset(Selection.Rows.Count, 0).Select

  Selection.EntireRow.Insert Shift:=xlDown
  Selection.Value = LineValue
  Selection.Resize(1, 3).Select
  oSheet.Names.Add "temp", "=" & ActiveCell.Address
  Set oRange = Union(Range(LineType), Range("temp"))
  oSheet.Names.Add Name:=LineType, RefersTo:="=" & oRange.Address
  Call ProtectWorksheet(True, oSheet.Name)

End Sub
```

So what are we doing here? A couple of things occur in these lines. First, we make a call to `ProtectWorksheet` and tell it to unprotect the Budget worksheet. This allows the code to make changes to the file. Next we move to the `Range` in our worksheet that matches the value of the passed `LineType` parameter:

```
Application.Goto Reference:=LineType
```

With the desired Range in hand, we move to the cell where we want to insert a new line. Using the row count of the current selection of cells, we can move to a new cell by specifying the number of rows and columns to move up or down, using the ActiveCell as a reference point:

```
ActiveCell.Offset(Selection.Rows.Count, 0).Select
```

In this implementation of the Offset method, we move to the row immediately below the last row of the current Range.

▦**Tip**   The Offset method can be used to navigate through an Excel worksheet by specifying the number of rows and columns to move. The previous example shows how to move down one row from the current position. If you want to move to the row immediately above the current row, use this code line:

```
ActiveCell.Offset(Selection.Rows.Count - 1, 0).Select
```

If you want to move over to the next column, use this code:

```
ActiveCell.Offset(0, 1).Select
```

Once we are in position, we insert a new row and effectively push the contents of the worksheet down to make room:

```
Selection.EntireRow.Insert Shift:=xlDown
Selection.Value = LineValue
Selection.Resize(1, 3).Select
```

After inserting the new row, we place the text for the new line item in the cell. Then we increase the size of the Selection object to include all three columns that comprise a line item (column C is the amount column, and the user enters data for this cell after the method inserts the line item into the worksheet). Using the new selection, we resize the named range to include the newly inserted row.

Let's assume that we are inserting a new revenue line item into the budget. At this point in the procedure's execution, we have a new line just below the Revenue named range. The trouble is that this new line is not part of the named range. This is a problem because the user may not be finished adding lines, and if the Revenue named range is not updated to include the new line, the next time the user inserts a Revenue line, it will overwrite this line and leave the user annoyed (or worse). We just can't allow that to happen. We must extend the named range (Range) to include the new line:

```
oSheet.Names.Add "temp", "=" & ActiveCell.Address
Set oRange = Union(Range(LineType), Range("temp"))
oSheet.Names.Add Name:=LineType, RefersTo:="=" & oRange.Address
```

Extending the Range is a three-step process:

1. Add a new named range to the worksheet that represents the new line.

2. Create a Union of the new line's named range and the named range (in the preceding example, this is the Revenue Range). The Union method allows us to join the two named ranges to create a new Range that includes all rows.

3. Add another Name to the worksheet using the reference to the combined Ranges.

What all this really means is that it is a bit of work to change the contents of a Range.

■Tip Ranges are funny, because once you add them, you have to live with them. The GUI of Excel doesn't provide a mechanism for deleting an existing named range. In addition, if you attempt to add to an existing range by selecting more cells and then entering the same name for the Range in the Name box, the changes will not be made, and you will be left with the original Range. In addition, the Workbooks.Names object does not have a Delete method. The only way to "delete" a Range is to replace it with a new one through code.

The last step the procedure performs is to protect the worksheet again by calling Protect-Worksheet.

The FillList Method

When frmLineItems opens, the contents of the lstLineItems list box must be filled with data prior to displaying the form. In addition, lstLineItems will need to be updated anytime the user toggles between optRevenue and optExpense.

We will accomplish this task by reading the values from the data list residing in the hidden LineItems worksheet.

```
Private Sub FillList(LineItemType As Integer)
  Dim i As Integer
  Dim r As Range

  Set r = Worksheets("LineItems").Range("LineItems")
  r.Sort key1:=Worksheets("LineItems").Columns("A"), header:=xlGuess
  lstLineItems.Clear

  If LineItemType = 1 Then
  'IncomeRevenue
    For i = 1 To r.Rows.Count
      If Worksheets("LineItems").Cells(i + 1, 2).Value = "IncomeRevenue" Then
        lstLineItems.AddItem Worksheets("LineItems").Cells(i + 1, 1).Value

    End If
  Next i
Else
```

```
'Expense
    For i = 1 To r.Rows.Count
    If Worksheets("LineItems").Cells(i + 1, 2).Value = "Expense" Then
      lstLineItems.AddItem Worksheets("LineItems").Cells(i + 1, 1).Value
    End If
  Next i
End If

End Sub
```

We get things going by referencing the LineItems named range in the LineItems worksheet:

```
Set r = Worksheets("LineItems").Range("LineItems")
r.Sort key1:=Worksheets("LineItems").Columns("A"), header:=xlGuess
```

Using the newly created reference, we sort the contents. Sorting alphabetically makes the application more user friendly, and it's a nice thing to do.

Now it's time to fill lstLineItems with data. Just to be safe, we will go ahead and clear any contents that may already exist, and then we will proceed to fill it up with the desired data:

```
If LineItemType = 1 Then
'IncomeRevenue
  For i = 1 To r.Rows.Count
    If Worksheets("LineItems").Cells(i + 1, 2).Value = "Revenue" Then
      lstLineItems.AddItem Worksheets("LineItems").Cells(i + 1, 1).Value

    End If
  Next i
Else
'Expense
    For i = 1 To r.Rows.Count
    If Worksheets("LineItems").Cells(i + 1, 2).Value = "Expense" Then
      lstLineItems.AddItem Worksheets("LineItems").Cells(i + 1, 1).Value
    End If
  Next i
End If
```

Using the LineItems Range, we loop through all the cells looking for the currently desired type (revenue or expense), adding any matches to lstLineItems.

The UserForm_Activate Method

The remaining procedures are the "glue" of the form, and they tie the relevant events to the main methods of frmLineItems.

When the form is displayed, we want to fill it with available line items and set the optRevenue as the default value.

```
Private Sub UserForm_Activate()
  FillList (1)
  optRevenue.Value = 1
End Sub
```

The optExpense_Click Method

The Click event for optExpense triggers a call to FillList, causing the form to display expense line items.

```
Private Sub optExpense_Click()
  FillList (2)
End Sub
```

The optRevenue_Click Method

The Click event for optRevenue triggers a call to FillList, causing the form to display revenue line items.

```
Private Sub optRevenue_Click()
  FillList (1)
End Sub
```

The cmdOk_Click Method

The Click event of the OK button first checks to ensure that a line item was indeed selected by the user. If a selection was made, the event invokes the ProcessLine procedure:

```
Private Sub cmdOK_Click()
  If Len(lstLineItems.Value) > 0 Then
    ProcessLine
  Else
    MsgBox "Please make a selection before continuing.", _
      vbInformation, "No Selection"
  End If

  Unload Me
End Sub
```

The cmdCancel_Click Method

The Click event of the Cancel button is boring, but I have included it for the sake of completeness. After all, users need a way to change their minds. This event closes the form and unloads it from memory.

```
Private Sub cmdCancel_Click()
  Unload Me
End Sub
```

The basSecurity Module

Our user interface for the Budget Template component is now complete, but our work is far from done. We must now add a few modules to handle the behind-the-scenes functions, and the first of these will take care of protecting the documents.

Each budget must remain in an expected, or standard, format in order to keep the work-flow streamlined and to reduce the effort required to consolidate budgets. This is where we become control freaks and lock down each worksheet, preventing users from displaying any creativity they may or may not have.

There a couple of options in Excel for protecting information. The first is to protect the entire workbook by implementing a workbook-level password. If you choose this route, all the contents in the workbook will be protected. Once it is protected in this manner, no changes can be made to any of the data in any of the individual worksheets. I do not like this option for user solutions, though it works fine when sharing a file with someone who only needs to read the information. We will only protect the entire Budget Template file just prior to submitting the budget to a division vice president.

The second option is to protect worksheets on an individual basis and to unprotect and protect them again as changes are required. This option works well, and it is very simple to employ. We can take care of it with four simple procedures: `ProtectWorksheet`, `ProtectAllWorksheets`, `ProtectWorkbook`, and `SecureEscapeKey`.

Creating the Module

To get started, open the Excel Visual Basic Editor and insert a new module into the `BudgetTemplate.xls` file. Name the module **basSecurity**.

Before we write the code for this module, we'll first add the following to the Declarations section:

```
Global Const strKey As String = "1234"
```

This `Constant` is the easy way to keep track of the protection password, and it is only for debugging purposes. It's not a best practice to store a hard-coded password in the source code where curious users could stumble upon it.

A better approach is to encrypt this information and store it on the user's file system where it can be read at run time. This strategy would reduce the risk of a curious user discovering the password.

The ProtectWorksheet Method

Protecting a worksheet isn't difficult. Here is our method for protecting individual worksheets:

```
Public Sub ProtectWorksheet(Mode As Boolean, WorkSheetName As String)
  If Mode Then
    Worksheets(WorkSheetName).Protect Password:=strKey
  Else
    Worksheets(WorkSheetName).Unprotect Password:=strKey
  End If
End Sub
```

The procedure takes the passed worksheet name and calls its `Protect` or `Unprotect` method, based on the value of `Mode`. To keep passwords consistent across the board, the procedure uses our beloved `strKey`.

The ProtectAllWorksheets Method

Sometimes, we will feel ambitious and want to protect all the worksheets at once. In the case of the Budget Consolidator, that time comes when the user invokes the `SubmitBudget` procedure (part of `basToolbar`).

Protecting all the worksheets is similar to implementing workbook-level password protection because we end up with a fully protected workbook. Unlike using the workbook password, though, we still have the ability to unprotect individual worksheets while leaving all others protected.

```
Public Sub ProtectAllWorksheets(Mode As Boolean)
  Dim oSheet As Worksheet
  Dim iLength As Integer

  Dim bMode As Boolean
  Dim sMsg As String

  On Error GoTo ProtectExpSheetsError
  SecureEscapeKey (True)
  Application.ScreenUpdating = False

  With ThisWorkbook
    For Each oSheet In .Worksheets
      Call ProtectWorksheet(Mode, oSheet.Name)
    Next oSheet
  End With

  SecureEscapeKey (False)
  Application.ScreenUpdating = True

  Exit Sub
ProtectExpSheetsError:
  Application.ScreenUpdating = True
End Sub
```

First things first: we invoke the `SecureEscapeKey` helper procedure to block the user from pressing the Ctrl+Break keyboard combination during this very important procedure. Such an action would interrupt the method's execution, and we don't want that at this point:

```
SecureEscapeKey (True)
Application.ScreenUpdating = False
```

In addition to preventing the Ctrl+Break keyboard action, we make the display appear as if nothing is happening. Doing so keeps the user from getting suspicious.

Next, the procedure rummages around the collection of worksheets in the workbook and protects each and every one by calling ProtectWorksheet.

```
With ThisWorkbook
  For Each oSheet In .Worksheet
    Call ProtectWorksheet(Mode, oSheet.Name)
  Next oSheet
End With
```

With the heavy lifting complete, we set things back to how they were before the procedure began executing. We have to do this or the user will stare at the frozen screen for at least five minutes wondering what is going on:

```
  SecureEscapeKey (False)
  Application.ScreenUpdating = True


  Exit Sub
ProtectExpSheetsError:
  Application.ScreenUpdating = True
End Sub
```

We can't take the risk here that an error will occur and cause our code to bug out. We need to make certain we return the ScreenUpdating capabilities back to the application in the case of an error.

The ProtectWorkbook Method

Just like ProtectAllWorksheets, the ProtectWorkbook method comes to life as part of the budget-submission process. Here we protect the entire workbook as one last little deterrent.

```
Public Sub ProtectWorkbook(Mode As Boolean)
  If Mode Then
    Workbooks(gCurrentBudgetName).Protect Password:=strKey
  Else
    Workbooks(gCurrentBudgetName).Unprotect Password:=strKey
  End If
End Sub
```

This is pretty much the same as ProtectWorksheet. The main difference is the use of the Workbooks collection instead of the Worksheets collection.

The SecureEscapeKey Method

Face it—some users just like to mess with the programs they use on a daily basis. Kick the tires, so to speak. They know that special things sometimes occur when they hold down the Shift or Alt keys while performing an action. These are the so-called *power users*. With a little planning and not much effort, we can keep these power users out of our stuff.

The `SecureEscapeKey` method keeps power user in their chairs and prevents them from interrupting our code while it executes.

```
Public Sub SecureEscapeKey(Mode As Boolean)
  If Mode Then
    Application.EnableCancelKey = xlDisabled
  End
    Application.EnableCancelKey = xlDisabled
  End If
End Sub
```

Luckily for us, Excel provides access to a property that specifies whether or not Excel should respond to the Ctrl+Break keyboard combination.

There are some things to keep in mind here. First, as long as the `EnableCancelKey` property is disabled, there is no way to interrupt code while it is executing. So stay away from such silly things such as infinite loops and error handlers that implement `Resume Next`. In such cases, the only way out is to open the Windows Task Manager and kill the Excel process. Not pretty.

The basToolbar Module

You simply can't build a solution for any Office application without creating a custom toolbar. It's a rule, or at least it seems to be these days. I love creating toolbars, and we will continue the habit already started in previous chapters. Add a new module to the project and name it **basToolbar**.

Variable Declarations

Only one declaration is needed for the toolbar module.

```
Const CBNAME As String = "BravoBudgetTools"
```

This declaration's only purpose is to make our calls to the custom toolbar cleaner. It also has the side benefit of easily changing the name of the toolbar, if such a change is needed—all that would be needed is a change to the value of `CBNAME`, and we would have a new toolbar name next time the template is loaded in Excel.

The CreateBudgetToolbar Method

When a Budget Template is loaded, we create a custom toolbar to provide access to the specific actions allowed by the solution.

```
Public Sub CreateBudgetToolbar()
  Dim ctl As CommandBarButton
  CommandBars.Add Name:=CBNAME, temporary:=True

  With CommandBars(CBNAME)
    'Add the Main Form button
    Set ctl = .Controls.Add(Type:=msoControlButton, temporary:=True)
      With ctl
```

```
         .OnAction = "OpenMainForm"
         .Caption = "Budget Manager"
         .TooltipText = "Open Bravo Corp Budget Manager"
         .FaceId = 3181
         .Visible = True
      End With

   ' Submit Budget button
   Set ctl = .Controls.Add(Type:=msoControlButton, temporary:=True)
     With ctl
         .OnAction = "SubmitBudget"
         .Caption = "Submit Budget"
         .TooltipText = "Send Completed Budget to Corporate Office"
         .FaceId = 5958
         .Visible = True
      End With

   .Visible = True
   .Protection = msoBarNoCustomize
   .Position = msoBarTop
  End With
End Sub
```

With the `BravoBudgetManager` toolbar in place, the method adds two new `CommandBarButton` objects to it. Note that we add a new `CommandBar` named with the value in `CBNAME`, and then we use the newly created `CommandBar` to add two buttons that call the `OpenMainForm` and `Submit-Budget` procedures (both of which are covered in the discussion of the `basMain` module shortly). `CreateBudgetToolbar` ends by positioning the `CommandBar`, protecting it from user customization, and setting its `Visible` property to True.

The CreateContextMenu Method

For the `CreateContextMenu` method, we are going to take advantage of the ability provided by the Office library to customize the right-click, or *context*, pop-up menu. A custom context menu can be created by accessing the Cell `CommandBar` object and adding all the buttons we desire.

```
Public Sub CreateContextMenu()
  Dim ctl As CommandBarControl
  'Test for existence
  Set ctl = CommandBars("Cell").FindControl(msoControlButton, , "InsertLine")

  If ctl Is Nothing Then
    With CommandBars("Cell")
      Set ctl = .Controls.Add(Type:=msoControlButton, temporary:=True)
```

```
    With ctl 'Insert Line Button
    .Tag = "InsertLine"
      .OnAction = "OpenMainForm"
      .Caption = "Insert New Budget Line"
      .FaceId = 3181
      .Visible = True
      .BeginGroup = True
    End With

    Set ctl = .Controls.Add(Type:=msoControlButton, temporary:=True)

    With ctl 'Delete Line Button
      .OnAction = "DeleteLine"
      .Caption = "Delete Budget Line"
      .Visible = True
    End With
  End With

  End If
End Sub
```

Before taking any action, we make sure that our custom buttons do not already exist. If they are nowhere to be found, we set things up in a manner eerily similar to what we did in the `CreateBudgetToolbar` procedure.

The end result of these procedures is a customized Cell command bar that looks like Figure 6-12.

Figure 6-12. *The customized Cell context menu*

DeleteToolbars

Even though we specified our custom toolbars and buttons as temporary, we still need a way to delete them ourselves when the template worksheet is closed. Implementing this strategy ensures the toolbars are removed when the add-in closes or unloads from the application space.

```
Public Sub DeleteToolbars()
  With CommandBars(CBNAME)
    .Protection = msoBarNoProtection
    .Delete
  End With

  CommandBars("Cell").Reset
End Sub
```

In addition to deleting our custom toolbar, we reset the Cell CommandBar to its original state. I guess a better name for this procedure might be DeleteAndResetToolbars, but let's leave it as is.

The basMain Module

The basMain module contains code that doesn't really belong in the other modules (it is not related to toolbar creation or security). As a result, basMain acts as a bucket for other necessary methods, such as code for initializing the add-in. In addition, basMain contains global variables accessed by objects throughout the add-in. Insert a new module in the project, and name it **basMain**.

Variable Declarations

Two variables are required while running the Budget Template file:

```
Public gCurrentBudgetName As String
Public gCurrentBudgetSheet As Boolean
```

We need to always know the name of the current budget file, because the user may click on one of the workbook's toolbar buttons when a different workbook is active. Using the value stored in gCurrentBudgetName allows us to avoid using the less reliable ThisWorkbook object. The same is true for gCurrentBudgetSheet, which stores the name of the Budget worksheet.

The ValidateBudget Function

Before allowing a department manager to submit their budget, we must make sure that a few business rules are satisfied:

- A department name must be provided.

- A valid date must be provided for the period.

- At least two revenue lines must have been inserted.

- At least two expense lines must have been inserted.

Using a series of If statements, we can check each of these rules. If they all check out, ValidateBudget returns as True to signify that the file is a valid budget. If any of the rules fail, False is returned as the value of ValidateBudget.

```
Public Function ValidateBudget() As Boolean
 ValidateBudget = False
 If Len(Range("DeptName").Value) Then
  If Len(Range("Period").Value) Then
    If IsDate(Range("Period").Value) Then
      If Range("Revenue").Rows.Count >= 3 Then
        If Range("Expenses").Rows.Count >= 3 Then
          ValidateBudget = True
        End If
      End If
    End If
  End If
 End If
End Function
```

Since the named ranges we created for Revenue and Expense already contained two lines, the code checks that the row count of each range is at least equal to three. This allows for the probability that at least one of the lines is blank.

The DeleteLine Method

DeleteLine is called by one of our custom context menu buttons, and it deletes the currently selected line.

```
Public Sub DeleteLine()
  Dim iResponse As Integer
  iResponse = MsgBox("You are about to delete the currently selected line." & _
   vbCrLf & vbCrLf & "Are you sure?", vbYesNo + vbQuestion, __
   "Delete Current Line?")

  If iResponse = 6 Then
    Call ProtectWorksheet(False, ActiveSheet.Name)
      Selection.EntireRow.Delete Shift:=xlUp
    Call ProtectWorksheet(True, ActiveSheet.Name)
  End If
End Sub
```

Since this procedure will be called via the context menu, and is therefore prone to accidental clicking, we ask the user to confirm their decision to delete the line prior to taking any action. If the user confirms, we unprotect the worksheet and delete the current selection's entire row, not just the current cell.

The ThisWorkbook Module

Older versions of Excel (and all Office applications) relied on the existence auto-macros to tell Excel to automatically run code based on certain events. Nowadays this is not necessary, because the auto-macros are now included as events in the ThisWorkbook module.

The only events we need to concern ourselves with are the Open and Close events. They are the perfect places for our code that creates and tears down our file's environment (toolbar creation, setting a reference to the currently open budget, etc.).

The ThisWorkbook module already exists as part of the BudgetSummary.xls file. There is no need to add a new module named ThisWorkbook. Just open the VB editor and add the code in the following sections.

The Workbook_Open Method

Before the user even sees the budget file, we need to create the toolbars and store the name of the workbook for later use. It's a snap, because we have already written the required procedures.

```
Private Sub Workbook_Open()
  CreateBudgetToolbar
  CreateContextMenu
  gCurrentBudgetName = ThisWorkbook.Name
End Sub
```

The Workbook_BeforeClose Method

The BeforeClose event is the best place to call the procedures that clean up after ourselves.

```
Private Sub Workbook_BeforeClose(Cancel As Boolean)
  DeleteToolbars
  gCurrentBudgetName = ""
End Sub
```

Testing the Budget Template

That's it! Why don't you take a look at our hard work and open the Budget Template in Excel (see Figure 6-13). Do you see the custom menu? Can you insert a new line item? What about the context menu—do you see the two custom buttons?

We are officially halfway through creating the Budget Consolidator application. The next task is to create the actual consolidation engine that will be used by division vice presidents to consolidate all the budgets they will be receiving.

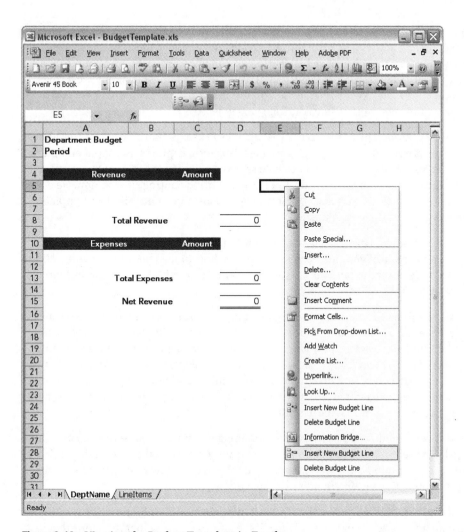

Figure 6-13. *Viewing the Budget Template in Excel*

Creating the Budget Consolidator Engine

The Budget Consolidator engine add-in piece of this solution is an Excel-specific add-in that works as a processing engine for the completed Budget Templates. As was outlined in Figure 6-1, once a VP receives a completed budget file, the Budget Consolidator performs two tasks:

1. Copies the completed Budget worksheet into the Summary worksheet (the Summary Budget is specified in the Settings form of the add-in).

2. Updates the Summary worksheet tab in the Summary Budget to include the new numbers provided by the newly received budget.

Both of these tasks are handled within the basMain module discussed in this section.

The process of writing the add-in is no different than that of creating the Budget Template piece. We will create another blank workbook (.xls file) and embed code to meet the needs of our business rules. The real difference between an add-in like the one we are about to create and the .xls file we created in the previous section is the method of deployment. We'll cover the deployment in the last (very short) section of this chapter.

The Budget Consolidator includes the following objects:

- frmSettings form: This is a UserForm that allows the user (a Bravo Corp vice president) to specify the add-in's configuration settings. This form captures user input and then calls methods in the basConfig module to save the values in the Windows registry and later retrieves the values and loads them into the form's controls. In addition, we will look at how to use the FileDialog object to ask the user to identify Budget Template and Summary Budget template files.

- basConfig module: This is a Module containing all the procedures for saving and retrieving the add-in's configuration values. You will see how to save the add-in's user settings to the Windows registry and how to retrieve them. The methods in this module are called by the ThisWorkbook module.

- basMain module: This Module contains the Budget Consolidator engine's core business logic. Here you will learn about the functions that consolidate the contents of each Budget Template into the Summary Budget file. Key concepts include how to open a completed budget file, how to verify the completed budget is indeed complete, how to copy a worksheet tab from one Excel file into another, and how to update cell formulas to reference the cells from the newly inserted tab. The only public method of this module is invoked from the basToolbar module.

- ThisWorkbook module: This is a Module containing the methods for setting up and shutting down the workbook's environment. This module calls methods from the basConfig and basToolbar modules to set up or clean up the add-in's environment (depending upon whether the add-in is loading or unloading).

- basSecurity module: This is a Module containing the methods for protecting and unprotecting budget worksheets. You will see how to create helper functions that lock and unlock the summary budget template when code executing within the Budget Consolidator add-in wants to edit the worksheet.

- basToolbar module: This is a Module containing the methods for creating and deleting the CommandBar utilized by the add-in. Here you will learn how to create a custom menu for the budget template. The methods inside this module are invoked by methods inside ThisWorkbook.

The frmSettings Form

We need a form to allow a division vice president to customize the add-in's settings. To function correctly, the add-in must know two things:

- The location of the Budget Template file. This setting lets the add-in know which file to use when distributing Budget Templates to department managers at the beginning of the budgeting process.

- The location of the Summary Budget file. This setting tells the add-in where the current Summary Budget resides on the file system. The add-in uses this setting to automatically open the Summary Budget and consolidate Budget Templates within it.

Since this is an Excel-specific add-in, we will use an Office UserForm to capture the data. The settings required for the Budget Consolidator add-in are as follows:

- **Budget Template location**: This is the folder location and the filename of the Budget Template that is distributed to department managers.

- **Summary Budget location**: This is the folder location and the filename of the Summary Budget template file. This is the file used by the division vice presidents to consolidate all Budget Templates.

The Form Layout

The frmSettings form will be the interface for setting the add-in's configuration settings.

Start by opening the Visual Basic Editor and inserting a new UserForm, naming it **frmSettings**. Add the controls listed in Table 6-2 to the form so that it resembles the one shown in Figure 6-14.

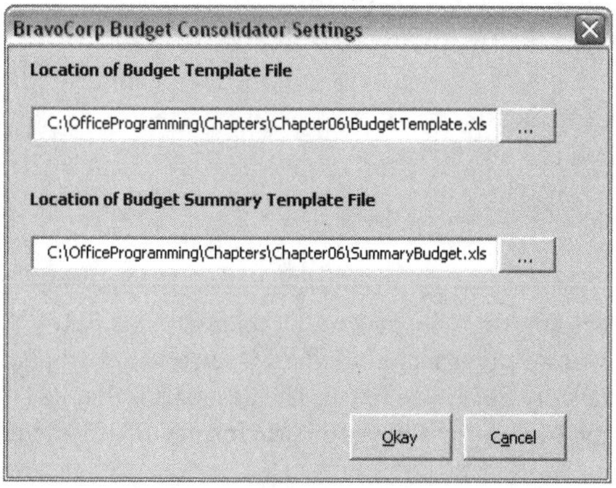

BravoCorp Budget Consolidator Settings

Location of Budget Template File

C:\OfficeProgramming\Chapters\Chapter06\BudgetTemplate.xls

Location of Budget Summary Template File

C:\OfficeProgramming\Chapters\Chapter06\SummaryBudget.xls

Okay   Cancel

Figure 6-14. *Designing the* frmSettings *form*

Table 6-2. *Controls Used in the* frmSettings *Form*

Control	Name	Caption	Text	Accelerator
Label		Location of Budget Template File		
Label		Location of Summary Budget Template File		
TextBox	txtBudgetTemplateLocation			
TextBox	txtBudgetSummaryLocation			
CommandButton	cmdBrowseBudget	. . .		
CommandButton	cmdBrowseSummary	. . .		
CommandButton	cmdOkay	Okay		O
CommandButton	cmdCancel	Cancel		a

The GetBudgetFileName Function

The Settings form performs only one task, but it performs it twice. The purpose of the form is to allow the user to specify the locations of the Budget Template and Summary Budget files. Since it's done twice, we will create one function that will be called by the two "browse" CommandButtons.

```
Public Function GetBudgetFileName() As String
    On Error Resume Next
    With Application.FileDialog(msoFileDialogOpen)
        .AllowMultiSelect = False
        .Filters.Add Description:="BravoCorp Budget Files", _
            Extensions:="*.xls", Position:=1
        .Show

        GetBudgetFileName = .SelectedItems(1)

    End With
End Function
```

Excel (like all Office applications) provides an extremely powerful, yet easy to use, File-Dialog control. This object works exactly as you would expect a standard Open and Save dialog box to function, except that this one can be customized as we see fit. The best part is that it is included as part of the Office library, so it is available across the entire Microsoft Office System.

■**Tip** There are many types for the FileDialog control. There's the Open dialog box (the one we use in the preceding code, msoFileDialogOpen), the File Picker dialog box (msoFileDialogFilePicker), the Folder Picker dialog box (msoFileDialogFolderPicker), and the Save As dialog box (msoFileDialog-SaveAs). Each has a special purpose that pretty much corresponds to its name. You can find out more in the help files.

GetBudgetFileName's job is to ask the user to select a file and then return the name of the selected file as the value of the function. We make this happen by first specifying that the dialog box should allow for only one file to be selected. In addition, we set up a filter for the dialog box so that it will only show Excel workbook files (.xls files). While adding the filter to the dialog box, we also take advantage of our ability to customize the description of the filter (making it something much more relevant to the user than "Microsoft Excel Files") and to set the filter value as the first item in the dialog box's Files of Type drop-down box.

With its properties set, the dialog box is displayed to the user and it will wait patiently for them to search through their labyrinth of folders and files and select what should be a Bravo Corp budget file of some sort. The selected file is returned as the value of GetBudgetFileName. If the user cancels the dialog box or closes it by other methods, an empty string is returned as the value.

That's really the only saucy part of frmSettings. The remaining code is a series of events used to place hooks that call other functions within the Budget Consolidator.

The cmdBrowseBudget_Click Method

The cmdBrowseBudget_Click event calls the GetBudgetFileName function and stores the folder path and filename of the selected file in txtBudgetTemplateLocation:

```
Private Sub cmdBrowseBudget_Click()
  txtBudgetTemplateLocation = GetBudgetFileName
End Sub
```

The cmdBrowseSummaryBudget_Click Method

The cmdBrowseSummaryBudget_Click event calls the GetBudgetFileName function and stores the folder path and filename of the selected file in txtBudgetSummaryLocation:

```
Private Sub cmdBrowseSummary_Click()
  txtBudgetSummaryLocation = GetBudgetFileName
End Sub
```

The cmdOkay_Click Method

The cmdOkay_Click event makes sure the user settings specified in the form are saved by calling RefreshUserConfig (part of basMain). Once this is done, the form is hidden and kept in memory.

```
Private Sub cmdOkay_Click()
  RefreshUserConfig
  Me.Hide
End Sub
```

The UserForm_Initialize Method

When the form is first loaded, the user settings are retrieved by calling GetUserConfig (part of basMain):

```
Private Sub UserForm_Initialize()
  GetUserConfig
End Sub
```

The cmdCancel_Click Method

If the user decides they don't want to make any changes after all and clicks the Cancel button, the form is hidden and any changes to the settings are ignored.

```
Private Sub cmdCancel_Click()
  Me.Hide
End Sub
```

The basConfig Module

The configuration module contains four methods that take care of storing, saving, and retrieving the settings specified by the user. The four methods perform two main functions:

- Saving the settings for the next time: SaveUserConfig and LoadUserConfig

- Storing the settings at run time: RefreshUserConfig and GetUserConfig

Insert a new module and name it **basConfig**.

Variable Declarations

When the Budget Consolidator is open, the locations of the Budget Template and Summary Budget files are stored in memory. Two module-level variables are declared here in basConfig to give us a place to store this information:

```
Public gBudgetTemplateLocation As String
Public gBudgetSummaryLocation As String
```

The GetUserConfig Method

Whenever the user opens frmSettings, the GetUserConfig method loads the form with the setting values.

```
Public Sub GetUserConfig()
  If gBudgetTemplateLocation = "" Then
    LoadUserConfig
  End If

  frmSettings.txtBudgetTemplateLocation.Value = gBudgetTemplateLocation
  frmSettings.txtBudgetSummaryLocation.Value = gBudgetSummaryLocation

End Sub
```

First off, a quick check is performed, just to see if the settings have already been loaded. If the gBudgetTemplateLocation variable is an empty string, the settings have not been loaded, and they need to be, so we call LoadUserConfig. In the end, the settings stored in memory are inserted into frmSettings's two text boxes.

The SaveUserConfig Method

Anytime the add-in's settings are set or updated, we want to make sure they are written to the registry. This saves the state of the settings for when we want to retrieve them.

```
Public Sub SaveUserConfig()
  SaveSetting appname:="Budget Consolidator", section:="UserConfig", _
    Key:="BudgetTemplateLocation", _
    Setting:=frmSettings.txtBudgetTemplateLocation.Value

  SaveSetting appname:="Budget Consolidator", section:="UserConfig", _
    Key:="BudgetSummaryLocation", _
    Setting:=frmSettings.txtBudgetSummaryLocation.Value
End Sub
```

By utilizing the SaveSettings function, we take advantage of what is arguably the easiest way to save state in an Office (or any VB or VBA) application. SaveSettings takes the information you give it and stores the values in the Windows registry. All it asks is that we supply an application name, a folder (called a section), a setting name (called a Key), and a value. No writing to an INI file, no XML to deal with. This may be an older way of dealing with application settings, but it is still the easiest to implement.

The LoadUserConfig Method

Once opened, the Budget Consolidator really needs to know where to find the template files. Luckily for us, the SaveUserConfig procedure has stored that information in the Windows registry (so long as this is not the first time the add-in is being run).

We retrieve the template locations with the GetSetting function:

```
Public Sub LoadUserConfig()
  gBudgetTemplateLocation = GetSetting(appname:="Budget Consolidator", _
    section:="UserConfig", Key:="BudgetTemplateLocation")
  gBudgetSummaryLocation = GetSetting(appname:="Budget Consolidator", _
    section:="UserConfig", Key:="BudgetSummaryLocation")

  If gBudgetTemplateLocation = "" Then
    msgbox ("No location has been specified for the template files."
      vbcrlf & vbcrlf & "Please specify the locations now." _
      ,vbCritical,"Budget Locations Unknown")

    frmSettings.Show
  End If

End Sub
```

In this code, we first perform lookups in the registry for the locations of the two template files and attempt to store them in our module-level variables:

```
gBudgetTemplateLocation = GetSetting(appname:="Budget Consolidator", _
  section:="UserConfig", Key:="BudgetTemplateLocation")
gBudgetSummaryLocation = GetSetting(appname:="Budget Consolidator", _
  section:="UserConfig", Key:="BudgetSummaryLocation")
```

If, after trying to load the settings, gBudgetTemplateLocation remains an empty String, then a good bet is that the settings have never been configured (or they just disappeared some- how). We make the user aware of this situation and then display the Settings form so the user can locate the template files:

```
If gBudgetTemplateLocation = "" Then
    msgbox ("No location has been specified for the template files." _
      vbcrlf & vbcrlf & "Please specify the locations now." _
      ,vbCritical,"Budget Locations Unknown")

    frmSettings.Show
End If
```

After all of this, either the settings will have been set and saved or they haven't. I don't believe in continually harassing the user if they just cancelled out. If they do cancel out, the location of the templates will not be known, and they will be alerted the next time they run the Budget Consolidator engine.

The RefreshUserConfig Method

When the settings are updated in the frmSettings form, the RefreshUserConfig procedure does the simple but beautiful task of updating the module-level variables in case they are needed while the add-in is running. The variables are updated using the values in frmSettings.

```
Public Sub RefreshUserConfig()
  gBudgetTemplateLocation = frmSettings.txtBudgetTemplateLocation.Value
  gBudgetSummaryLocation = frmSettings.txtBudgetSummaryLocation.Value
  SaveUserConfig
End Sub
```

The basMain Module

The core add-in "engine" code resides in basMain. This is where we will place the code that handles the budget consolidations. The assumed workflow here is somewhat simplified and only deals with the logic for adding a completed Budget Template to a Summary Budget.

We are going to assume that once a department manager completes their budget, they email it to their division vice president. Actually, this is not much of an assumption because this is exactly how we programmed the Budget Template to function in the previous section.

Upon receipt of one of these budget emails, the division vice president opens the attached budget directly from the email. With the budget open in Excel, the VP kicks things off by clicking the add-in's Update Summary button. The update process asks for the location of the file to use as the Summary Budget, inserts the existing budget into the specified file, and then updates the values contained in the Summary worksheet (see Figure 6-15).

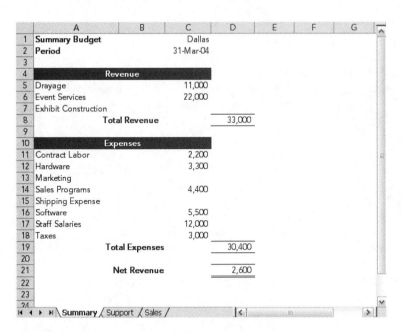

Figure 6-15. *The Summary worksheet*

Insert a new module and name it **basMain**.

Variable Declarations

To make things easier on everybody, we really should hold on to the name of the targeted Summary Budget file as well as the name of the currently open and completed Budget Template. Here are the module-level declarations for these two bits of info:

```
Public gSummaryBudget As String
Public gCurrentBudgetName As String
```

Notice that we declare both of the variables as Strings. We could declare them as Workbook objects, but doing so requires more memory than String objects, and it really isn't needed. It's easy enough just to store the name of the needed Workbook for later, and to access them later using the Workbooks collection.

The GetSummaryBudget Method

The first step in the consolidation process is to find out where the division VP's Summary Budget file is located. We will give the user the option to use an existing file if they have one, or to create a new one. This strategy allows for the fact that budgets are not received all at once and typically trickle in as the budget process moves forward. Days or weeks may pass between adding different completed Budget Templates to the Summary Budget.

```
Public Sub GetSummaryBudget()
  Dim iResponse As Integer
  gCurrentBudgetName = ActiveWorkbook.Name

  iResponse = MsgBox("Do you have an existing Summary Budget?" & _
  vbCrLf & "Click Yes to use an existing Summary Budget" & vbCrLf & vbCrLf & _
  "Click No to create a new one.", vbYesNoCancel + vbQuestion, _
  "BravoCorp Budget Compiler")
  Select Case iResponse
    Case 2 'Cancel
      'do nothing
    Case 6 'Yes
      If OpenSummaryBudget Then
        If Not VerifyAsSummaryBudget Then
          MsgBox "The workbook is not a valid Summary Budget." & _
          vbCrLf & vbCrLf & _
          "Please select a different Budget file.", _
          vbExclamation, "Invalid Summary Budget Format"
        End If
      End If
    Case 7 'No
      Call CreateNewSummaryBudget

    Case Else
  End Select
```

```
'Assumes Division budget is already open
Call CopyBudgetSheetToSummaryBook
Call UpdateSummaryBudget
End Sub
```

In this procedure, we will simply ask the user each time if they have a Summary Budget file they would like to use for this consolidation. Their answer determines what route our code will take:

```
Dim iResponse As Integer
gCurrentBudgetName = ActiveWorkbook.Name

iResponse = MsgBox("Do you have an existing Summary Budget?" & _
vbCrLf & "Click Yes to use an existing Summary Budget" & vbCrLf & vbCrLf & _
"Click No to create a new one.", vbYesNoCancel + vbQuestion, _
"BravoCorp Budget Compiler")
```

In addition to asking users for an existing Summary Budget file, we also set a reference to the current Workbook (which should be our completed Budget Template).

■Tip You can't always rely on the ActiveWorkbook object to always reference the file you intend. Use this object with the understanding that it can sometimes return very unpredictable results.

Once the user makes their decision (by clicking Yes, No, or Cancel), we read the response and branch out to take the requested action:

```
Select Case iResponse
    Case 2 'Cancel
      'do nothing
    Case 6 'Yes
      Call OpenSummaryBudget
        If Not VerifyAsSummaryBudget Then
            MsgBox "The workbook is not a valid Summary Budget." & _
            vbCrLf & vbCrLf & _
            "Please select a different Budget file.", _
            vbExclamation, "Invalid Summary Budget Format"
        End If

    Case 7 'No
      Call CreateNewSummaryBudget

      Exit Sub
    Case Else
  End Select
```

Assuming the user doesn't click the Cancel button, we execute a few tasks. First up is opening a Summary Budget file to work with. If the user clicks Yes in response to our question, then we know they have a working file somewhere, and we need to ask them where it is. The call to OpenSummaryBudget will do just that. We need to be careful that the user does not open an invalid file, so we call VerifyAsSummaryBudget to check the file for the correct property and value that signify that the file is indeed a Summary Budget file.

If the user does not have a working file, they will have clicked No, and we call CreateNew-SummaryBudget to create a new working Summary Budget file and open it within Excel.

Once we have a valid Summary Budget file, we get to the real work and insert the completed Budget Template into the Summary Budget by calling CopyBudgetSheetToSummaryBook. Then, with the new budget inserted as an additional tab, UpdateSummaryBudget updates the Summary Budget to reflect the new information:

```
  Call CopyBudgetSheetToSummaryBook
  Call UpdateSummaryBudget
End Sub
```

The CreateNewSummaryBudget Method

At some point, you just have to start from scratch. If the user needs to create a new working Summary Budget, the CreateNewSummaryBudget procedure uses the location of the Summary Budget (conveniently stored in memory in the gBudgetSummaryLocation variable) to create a copy of it and load it into Excel.

```
Private Sub CreateNewSummaryBudget()
  Dim oWB As Workbook
  Set oWB = Workbooks.Add(gBudgetSummaryLocation)
  gSummaryBudget = oWB.Name
End Sub
```

In addition, we store the name of the newly copied Workbook for later use.

The OpenSummaryBudget Function

As budgets are completed and returned to the division VP, it is more than likely that he or she will have already created a new Summary Budget file to consolidate the individually completed Budget Templates. When a newly completed Budget Template shows up in the division VP's inbox, it's time to move it into the VP's working Summary Budget file. The first thing to do is ask them where it is.

```
Private Function OpenSummaryBudget() As Boolean
  Dim strFileName As String
  strFileName = frmSettings.GetBudgetFileName

  If strFileName = "" Then
    MsgBox "You must specify a Summary Budget File to continue", _
      vbExclamation, "Please Choose a Summary Budget"
```

```
    OpenSummaryBudget = False
    Exit Function
  Else
    Workbooks.Open strFileName
    gSummaryBudget = ActiveWorkbook.Name
    OpenSummaryBudget = True
  End If

End Function
```

We already have code for selecting a budget file in the frmSettings form, so it would be silly to write similar code here. The smart thing to do is call the GetBudgetFileName function, which, as we already know, will return a string of the selected filename and path:

```
strFileName = frmSettings.GetBudgetFileName
```

To avoid looking silly, we need to make sure the user selects a file before we continue:

```
If strFileName = "" Then
  MsgBox "You must specify a Summary Budget File to continue", & _
    vbExclamation, "Please Choose a Summary Budget"

  OpenSummaryBudget = False
  Exit Function
```

If the user fails at this simple task, we tell them what we expect of them and return False as the value of the function. If they do what we expect of them, we move on:

```
  Else
    Workbooks.Open strFileName
    gSummaryBudget = ActiveWorkbook.Name
    OpenSummaryBudget = True
  End If

End Function
```

With the user's selected file in hand, we load it into Excel to make it available for the other methods that will need to execute against it. The name of the file is stored in gSummaryBudget so the other procedures will know the filename and can easily access it. The last thing we do is let the user know that everything worked out okay and that we now have a Summary Budget file containing a roll-up of each completed Budget Template.

The CopyBudgetSheetToSummaryBook Method

Once the user has told us where to find the Summary Budget, we can begin the process of updating it. CopyBudgetSheetToSummaryBook takes the budget from the completed Budget Template's Worksheet and copies it behind the last Worksheet in the Summary Budget.

```
Public Sub CopyBudgetSheetToSummaryBook()
On Error GoTo eHandler
  Dim iWSCount As Integer
```

```
    Dim strBudgetName As String
    Dim oWBSum As Workbook
    Dim oWBDept As Workbook

    Set oWBSum = Workbooks(gSummaryBudget)
    Set oWBDept = Workbooks(gCurrentBudgetName)

    iWSCount = oWBSum.Worksheets.Count
    strBudgetName = oWBDept.Sheets("Budget").Names("DeptName").RefersToRange.Value

    Application.DisplayAlerts = False
    oWBDept.Worksheets("Budget").Copy after:=oWBSum.Worksheets(iWSCount)
    oWBSum.Worksheets("Budget").Name = strBudgetName
    gCurrentBudgetName = strBudgetName
    Application.DisplayAlerts = True
    Exit Sub
eHandler:
    Application.DisplayAlerts = True
End Sub
```

To make our code a little tighter, we declare and set values for two `Workbook` objects—these provide references to the completed Budget Template and the Summary Budget.

```
Public Sub CopyBudgetSheetToSummaryBook()
On Error GoTo eHandler
    Dim iWSCount As Integer
    Dim strBudgetName As String
    Dim oWBSum As Workbook
    Dim oWBDept As Workbook

    Set oWBSum = Workbooks(gSummaryBudget)
    Set oWBDept = Workbooks(gCurrentBudgetName)
```

We could easily have forgone these declarations and accessed the two `Workbooks` in this fashion:

```
Workbooks(gSummaryBudget)
```

However, doing so would lead to code like this later in the procedure:

```
Workbooks(gCurrentBudgetName).Worksheets("Budget").Copy & _
    after:=Workbooks(gSummaryBudget).Worksheets(iWSCount)
```

You can see how our strategy will lead to code that is much easier to read.

Moving on, we count up how many `Worksheets` exists in the target Summary Budget. This number will be used shortly, when we copy the new budget. We also look inside the new completed Budget Template and grab the name of the department:

```
iWSCount = oWBSum.Worksheets.Count
strBudgetName = oWBDept.Sheets("Budget").Names("DeptName").RefersToRange.Value
```

Again, we reference a named range to go directly to the cell containing the desired information. To retrieve the value, we must call the RefersToRange property. This property returns the value of a Name object so long as the name refers to a Range; if not, an error is raised.

The next and last step for this procedure is to go ahead and copy the completed Budget Template to the selected Summary Budget. All of the completed Budget Templates contain the same set of named ranges. As a result, any time we copy a new budget, Excel will balk and inform us that the named ranges already exist, that it has no idea just what to do next, and that if we continue, all kinds of horrible things will happen.

Actually, having duplicate named-range names within a Workbook is typically less than desirable, but it is no cause for concern so long as you are aware of the situation. We can still access each range within each Worksheet, but we will have to fully qualify the ranges using a combination of *WorksheetName!NamedRangeName*:

```
Application.DisplayAlerts = False
oWBDept.Worksheets("Budget").Copy after:=oWBSum.Worksheets(iWSCount)
oWBSum.Worksheets("Budget").Name = strBudgetName
gCurrentBudgetName = strBudgetName
Application.DisplayAlerts = True
```

Before copying the new budget, we tell Excel to ignore any alerts for now. We don't want to alert the user that Excel believes a problem exists, when, in fact, one does not (at least, not while our code executes). Once the alerts are disabled, we are all set to copy the completed Budget Template to the Summary Budget, positioning it at the end of the workbook.

■**Caution** Make absolutely sure that any time you turn off the alerts, you turn them back on at the end of your code's execution. The safest thing to do is implement an error handler and re-enable the alerts there, in case anything goes wrong.

The last step (other than re-enabling the alerts) is to rename the new budget by giving it the name of the submitting department. This serves the purpose of providing better information to the division VP, as well as avoiding a situation where we may inadvertently overwrite a budget (since all completed Budget Templates have a worksheet name of "Budget").

The VerifyAsSummaryBudget Function

It would be nice to avoid a situation where the user opens up a nonstandard Summary Budget or another file that won't work for us at all. Our quick solution to this potential problem is to tag each standard Summary Budget template file with a custom property. Although this is not entirely foolproof, the strategy does provide a reasonable solution that fits the need nicely.

```
Private Function VerifyAsSummaryBudget() As Boolean
  On Error GoTo eHandler

  If Workbooks(gSummaryBudget).CustomDocumentProperties("BudgetType").Value = & _
    "Summary" Then
    VerifyAsSummaryBudget = True
```

```
   Else
      VerifyAsSummaryBudget = False
   End If

   Exit Function
eHandler:
   VerifyAsSummaryBudget = False
End Function
```

A valid Summary Budget is any file that has "Summary" as the value for its `BudgetType` custom property. The `VerifyAsSummaryBudget` function returns True if this is the situation, and False if it is not, or if the `BudgetType` custom property does not exist.

■**Tip** Custom properties are an easy way to store information about a document within the document itself. In fact, with the release of Microsoft Visual Studio Tools for Office, any Office application that supports Smart Documents uses custom properties to store the location of the attached assembly. (At the time of this writing, only Excel, Word, and InfoPath support Smart Documents.)

The UpdateSummaryBudget Method

The last step in our scenario is to update the formulas stored in the Summary Budget's Summary worksheet. Each line item needs to know about any new data that may exist in the newly inserted budget worksheet. Here's the code that makes it all come together.

```
Private Sub UpdateSummaryBudget()
   Dim oSummary As Worksheet
   Dim oNewBudget As Worksheet
   Dim r As Variant
   Dim iRow As Integer

   Set oSummary = Workbooks(gSummaryBudget).Sheets("Summary")
   Set oNewBudget = Workbooks(gSummaryBudget).Sheets(gCurrentBudgetName)
   iRow = 1

   'This is the first pass - Revenue
     For Each r In oSummary.Range("Revenue").Rows
         With oSummary.Range("Revenue")
           If Not .Cells(iRow, 3).HasFormula Then
             .Cells(iRow, 3).Formula = "=VLOOKUP(" & .Cells(iRow, 1).Address & _
               "," & oNewBudget.Name & "!Revenue,3,FALSE)"
           Else
             If .Cells(iRow, 3).Text = "#N/A" Then
               .Cells(iRow, 3).Formula = "=VLOOKUP(" & .Cells(iRow, 1).Address & _
                 "," & oNewBudget.Name & "!Revenue,3,FALSE)"
```

```
            Else
              .Cells(iRow, 3).Formula = .Cells(iRow, 3).Formula & _
                "+VLOOKUP(" & .Cells(iRow, 1).Address & "," & oNewBudget.Name & _
                "!Revenue,3,FALSE)"
            End If
          End If


          'Clear the cell in case no value
          If .Cells(iRow, 3).Text = "#N/A" Then .Cells(iRow, 3).Clear
          iRow = iRow + 1
        End With
    Next r


    iRow = 1
    'This is the second pass - Expenses
    For Each r In oSummary.Range("Expenses").Rows
        With oSummary.Range("Expenses")
          If Not .Cells(iRow, 3).HasFormula Then

            .Cells(iRow, 3).Formula = "=VLOOKUP(" & .Cells(iRow, 1).Address & _
              "," & oNewBudget.Name & "!Expenses,3,FALSE)"
          Else
            If .Cells(iRow, 3).Text = "#N/A" Then
              .Cells(iRow, 3).Formula = "=VLOOKUP(" & .Cells(iRow, 1).Address & _
                "," & oNewBudget.Name & "!Expenses,3,FALSE)"
            Else
              .Cells(iRow, 3).Formula = .Cells(iRow, 3).Formula & _
                "+VLOOKUP(" & .Cells(iRow, 1).Address & "," & oNewBudget.Name & _
                "!Expenses,3,FALSE)"
            End If
          End If
          'Clear the cell in case no value
          If .Cells(iRow, 3).Text = "#N/A" Then .Cells(iRow, 3).Clear
          iRow = iRow + 1
        End With
    Next r
End Sub
```

In this procedure, we need to move within two worksheets and rummage around each row in both the Revenue and Expenses ranges in both worksheets. We will need to know what row within these ranges is the current row. To do this, we declare a few variables and set their values to help us out:

```
Private Sub UpdateSummaryBudget()
  Dim oSummary As Worksheet
  Dim oNewBudget As Worksheet
  Dim r As Variant
  Dim iRow As Integer
```

```
Set oSummary = Workbooks(gSummaryBudget).Sheets("Summary")
Set oNewBudget = Workbooks(gSummaryBudget).Sheets(gCurrentBudgetName)
iRow = 1
```

With a few short lines, we have what we need. We have a reference to the Summary work-sheet that will receive references to the numbers contained in the other worksheet reference, the most-recently inserted Budget Template. In addition, we have a counter all set to start counting.

Now we must make the first of two passes within the worksheets. The first pass looks for Revenue line items in the new budget that match lines in the Summary worksheet. This is done by moving row by row through the Summary worksheet:

```
'This is the first pass - Revenue
    For Each r In oSummary.Range("Revenue").Rows
        With oSummary.Range("Revenue")
          If Not .Cells(iRow, 3).HasFormula Then
            .Cells(iRow, 3).Formula = "=VLOOKUP(" & .Cells(iRow, 1).Address & _
              "," & oNewBudget.Name & "!Revenue,3,FALSE)"
          Else
            If .Cells(iRow, 3).Text = "#N/A" Then
              .Cells(iRow, 3).Formula = "=VLOOKUP(" & .Cells(iRow, 1).Address & _
                "," & oNewBudget.Name & "!Revenue,3,FALSE)"
            Else
              .Cells(iRow, 3).Formula = .Cells(iRow, 3).Formula & _
                "+VLOOKUP(" & .Cells(iRow, 1).Address & "," & oNewBudget.Name & _
                "!Revenue,3,FALSE)"
            End If
          End If
```

Since the Summary worksheet contains all the standard line items, it makes sense to loop through each row on the given range and update each cell with a VLOOKUP formula. VLOOKUP is a powerful function within Excel that makes looking up values from other ranges simple. Here is the syntax:

```
VLOOKUP(lookup_value,table_array,col_index_num,range_lookup)
```

To use VLOOKUP effectively, we tell it what value we want it to find (the lookup_value), where we want to find it (table_array), which column of the row to return as the value (col_index), and whether or not we want an exact match of the lookup text (range_lookup).

For our purposes, we want to find values contained in the completed Budget Template for each standard line item contained in the Summary Budget. We know that the actual amount for each line item is stored inside column C of each line item row. We also know the range names containing line items (Revenue or Expenses) inside the completed Budget Template. All we need to do is update each line item cell in the Summary Budget to include a VLOOKUP for each worksheet's matching line item amount.

Let's get back to our code. When moving through each Summary line item, we first deter-mine whether the cell already has a formula. If it does not, we know this is the first time a completed Budget Template has included a matching line item, and we need to insert a new VLOOKUP:

```
If Not .Cells(iRow, 3).HasFormula Then
  .Cells(iRow, 3).Formula = "=VLOOKUP(" & .Cells(iRow, 1).Address & _
    "," & oNewBudget.Name & "!Revenue,3,FALSE)
```

We use the current row of the Summary worksheet's Revenue range as the lookup_value. We then use the new budget's name to create a reference to its Revenue range, and we specify column C (column number 3) as the value we want returned. Lastly, we tell VLOOKUP to find an exact match of the lookup_value.

If we do not specify False as the value for the range_lookup parameter, VLOOKUP will get a little lazy on us and return the first approximate match, which may or may not be what we are looking for. Passing a False value here forces VLOOKUP to keeping looking until it finds an exact match of the lookup_value.

If a formula already exists in the current cell, we simply update its formula with an additional VLOOKUP. The end result is a summation of all VLOOKUPs from the various completed Budget Templates contained in the workbook:

```
Else
  If .Cells(iRow, 3).Text = "#N/A" Then
    .Cells(iRow, 3).Formula = "=VLOOKUP(" & .Cells(iRow, 1).Address & _
      "," & oNewBudget.Name & "!Revenue,3,FALSE)"
  Else
    .Cells(iRow, 3).Formula = .Cells(iRow, 3).Formula & _
      "+VLOOKUP(" & .Cells(iRow, 1).Address & "," & oNewBudget.Name & _
      "!Revenue,3,FALSE)"
  End If
End If
```

If a VLOOKUP does not find a matching value for a given lookup_value, it will return "#N/A" as its value. Although we take pains to remove this value later, we should check for its existence in our cells just to be sure. If this value exists, we should replace the cell's formula with a completely new VLOOKUP and treat it as if this is the first time the cell has received a formula. On the other hand, if a valid VLOOKUP value is found in the cell, a new VLOOKUP function is tacked on to the existing cell formula.

Note A value of "#N/A", in our scenario, is the same thing as saying that none of the current worksheets contain this budget line item.

Before moving on to the next row and performing another VLOOKUP, we need to make sure a value was found by checking the Text property for a value of "#N/A". If it exists, we clear the formula of this unwanted value. We then increment our counter and move to the next row. This check is different from the check performed earlier in the procedure, which checks for the existence of "#N/A" in order to determine how to edit the cell's formula. This second check is for cosmetic purposes—if, after updating the cell's formula, the value of the cell is "#N/A", the value of the formula is cleared in order to avoid confusing the user.

```
        'Clear the cell in case no value
        If .Cells(iRow, 3).Text = "#N/A" Then .Cells(iRow, 3).Clear
        iRow = iRow + 1
    End With
Next r
```

That takes care of the first pass. The second pass uses the same logic to update the dollar amounts for the Expense line items contained in the Summary worksheet's Expenses range:

```
'This is the second pass - Expenses
    For Each r In oSummary.Range("Expenses").Rows
        With oSummary.Range("Expenses")
            If Not .Cells(iRow, 3).HasFormula Then

                .Cells(iRow, 3).Formula = "=VLOOKUP(" & .Cells(iRow, 1).Address & _
                    "," & oNewBudget.Name & "!Expenses,3,FALSE)"
            Else
                If .Cells(iRow, 3).Text = "#N/A" Then
                    .Cells(iRow, 3).Formula = "=VLOOKUP(" & .Cells(iRow, 1).Address & _
                        "," & oNewBudget.Name & "!Expenses,3,FALSE)"
                Else
                    .Cells(iRow, 3).Formula = .Cells(iRow, 3).Formula & _
                        "+VLOOKUP(" & .Cells(iRow, 1).Address & "," & oNewBudget.Name & _
                        "!Expenses,3,FALSE)"
                End If
            End If
            'Clear the cell in case no value
            If .Cells(iRow, 3).Text = "#N/A" Then .Cells(iRow, 3).Clear
            iRow = iRow + 1
        End With
    Next r
End Sub
```

The only difference between the two passes is the reference to the Revenue or Expenses range. We have now completed basMain, and I want you to see this code in action, so let's tidy everything up and create the hooks that make the add-in run.

The ThisWorkbook Module

We take advantage of the events provided by the ThisWorkbook module in order to set up and tear down the environment required by our add-in. Just like the Budget Template file, we utilize the Open and Before_Close events to take the appropriate steps. ThisWorkbook already exists by default within the BudgetConsolidator.xla file so there is no need to add it to the project.

The Open Method

Any time the Budget Consolidator add-in loads into memory, we want to create the add-in's menu and read the user-configuration settings into memory. Luckily for us, we have two procedures for these tasks already, and all we need to do here is call them.

```
Private Sub Workbook_Open()
  CreateToolbar
  LoadUserConfig
End Sub
```

The Before_Close Method

Any time Excel is closed or the Budget Consolidator add-in is unloaded, we need to clean up all the objects created by the Open event. Here we also call procedures from other modules that perform the necessary tasks.

```
Private Sub Workbook_BeforeClose(Cancel As Boolean)
  SaveUserConfig
  Unload frmSettings
  DeleteToolbar
End Sub
```

The basSecurity Module

The last two modules within the Budget Consolidator (basSecurity and basToolbar) are very similar to the two modules of the same name in the Budget Template file. To avoid boring you, I will simply highlight the differences between the two versions. Where the versions are the same, I'll just provide the code listing.

Just like in the Budget Template component, basSecurity contains the code for protecting the information contained within a budget. Insert a new module in the project and name it **basSecurity**.

The ProtectWorksheet Method

Here's the code for protecting and unprotecting a given worksheet:

```
Public Sub ProtectWorksheet(Mode As Boolean, WorkSheetName As String)
  If Mode Then
    Worksheets(WorkSheetName).Protect Password:=strKey
  Else
    Worksheets(WorkSheetName).Unprotect Password:=strKey
  End If
End Sub
```

The ProtectWorkbook Method

This is the code for protecting and unprotecting a workbook:

```
Public Sub ProtectWorkbook(Mode As Boolean)
  If Mode Then
    Workbooks(gCurrentBudgetName).Protect Password:=strKey
  Else
    Workbooks(gCurrentBudgetName).Unprotect Password:=strKey
  End If
End Sub
```

The basToolbar Module

The basToolbar module is very similar to its counterpart in the Budget Template, with a few minor differences, which are presented in bold. Insert a new module and name it **basToolbar**.

Variable Declarations

The add-in will have its own toolbar named BravoBudgetManager.

```
Const CBNAME As String = "BravoBudgetManager"
```

The CreateToolbar Method

Inside the Budget Consolidator, only a few settings for the toolbar buttons have been changed to reflect their different purposes.

```
Public Sub CreateToolbar()
  Dim ctl As CommandBarButton
  CommandBars.Add Name:=CBNAME, Temporary:=True

  With CommandBars(CBNAME)
    'Get Summary Budget Button
    Set ctl = .Controls.Add(Type:=msoControlButton, Temporary:=True)
      With ctl
        .OnAction = "GetSummaryBudget"
        .Caption = "Update Summary..."
        .TooltipText = "Send Template to Department Head"
        .Style = msoButtonCaption
        '.FaceId = 3738
        .Visible = True
      End With

    'Send Templates Button
    Set ctl = .Controls.Add(Type:=msoControlButton, Temporary:=True)
      With ctl
        .OnAction = "SendTemplate"
        .Caption = "Send Template"
```

```
          .TooltipText = "Send Template to Department Head"
          .FaceId = 3738
          .Visible = True
      End With

    'Add the Settings Form Button
    Set ctl = .Controls.Add(Type:=msoControlButton, Temporary:=True)
      With ctl
          .OnAction = "ConfigureSettings"
          .Caption = "Settings..."
          .TooltipText = "Configure Budget Compiler Settings"
          .FaceId = 548
          .Visible = True
      End With

    .Visible = True
    .Protection = msoBarNoCustomize
    .Position = msoBarTop
  End With
End Sub
```

The DeleteToolbar Method

The only change in this procedure is the lack of a line resetting the Cell CommandBar. It's not here because the add-in does not edit the Cell menu.

```
Public Sub DeleteToolbar()
On Error GoTo eHandler
  With CommandBars(CBNAME)
    .Protection = msoBarNoProtection
    .Delete
  End With

eHandler:
  Exit Sub
End Sub
```

The ConfigureSettings Method

The ConfigureSettings procedure is called by the Settings toolbar button to display the settings form.

```
Private Sub ConfigureSettings()
  frmSettings.Show
End Sub
```

The SendTemplate Method

To distribute the ActiveSheet to a department manager by email, we make a call to the Dialogs collection, specify that we want the SendMail dialog box, and tell it to show itself:

```
Private Sub SendTemplate()
 Application.Dialogs(xlDialogSendMail).Show
End Sub
```

A new email will pop up out of nowhere, and a copy of the ActiveSheet within Excel will be attached to the email.

■Tip Another method for sending an email from within Excel is to set the EnvelopeVisible property to True like this: ThisWorkbook.EnvelopeVisible = True. Instead of a separate email window appearing with the workbook attached, Excel displays a new control above the spreadsheet where you can specify the TO, CC, SUBJECT, and INTRODUCTION values.

Deploying the Solution

A more thorough explanation of add-in deployment scenarios, including security implications, is included in the Appendix. For now, you can run the add-in on your system by saving the BudgetConsolidator.xla file as a Microsoft Office Excel Add-In file. Then load the add-in using the Tools ➤ Add-Ins command inside Excel. If the add-in loads successfully, you will see the BravoBudgetManager menu bar waiting for action.

Take it for a spin by opening the BudgetTemplate.xls file and inserting some line items. Once you have a completed budget, make sure you have configured the user settings, and attempt to consolidate the new budget into a Summary Budget. The end result should be something resembling Figure 6-15.

Summary

In this chapter you learned how to automate a simplified budgeting process. This process uses two components that work together to create a Summary Budget. In building the first component, the Budget Template, you learned how to embed custom business logic within an Excel file to ensure that standard data items are used throughout. Then, when building the Budget Consolidator (the second component), you learned how to create an Excel-specific add-in that can take individual budgets and create a consolidated budget.

The example presented in this chapter could be extended to allow a user to select from a listing of available worksheet schedules that could be included in a department budget. For example, each line item on the budget could have a separate tab filled with the detailed analysis backing up that number.

CHAPTER 7

■■■

Timesheet System Using Excel
Using Visual Studio Tools for Office to Create a System for Assigning Time to Tasks

This chapter combines a familiar user interface (Microsoft Excel) with the power of Visual Basic .NET. We will build a timesheet-reporting system within Excel utilizing web services, Visual Studio Tools for Office (VSTO), and VB .NET. Using VB .NET code behind a basic Excel workbook (or Word document) is a great new option, and it exposes the full .NET experience to the typical Office developer.

This solution could just as easily be written with VBA code, but that would involve using Office's Visual Basic Editor to write the code. In addition, with VBA you cannot take advantage of the features and functions available in the .NET Framework or Visual Studio .NET.

To build this solution, we'll be making use of the following components:

- **VSTO**: Visual Studio Tools for Office is a Visual Studio add-in that allows a developer to create .NET assemblies with C# or VB .NET and attach them to Word and Excel documents. Using VSTO, it is possible to write business logic using managed code. In this chapter, we will create two VSTO projects using Excel.

- **Microsoft Excel**: Excel acts as the host for the Timesheet System's two front-end applications: Time-Manager Entry and Time-Manager Reporter. In creating these applications, you will learn how to build Excel files that utilize business logic contained in .NET managed assemblies.

- **Web services**: Like several other chapters in this book, the applications that comprise the Timesheet System utilize a web service to retrieve data from and post data to the solution's database. We will look at how to build the classes that represent database record types. These classes contain the code for interacting with the solution database in a manner that meets the needs of that data type. In addition, this section shows how to expose web service methods to be called by the two Excel workbook-based applications.

After you write .NET code, it is compiled to a DLL file (with a .dll extension) and is stored just about anywhere the developer decides it should be located. This could be on the user's machine, on a server on the company network, or at a URL available on the Internet. The decision about where to locate the code will more than likely be driven by the user base. For example, in the case of a single-user application, the proper place for the solution would be the user's machine. If the application will be used only by a company's internal staff, a network server would be appropriate. And if the user base for the application extends to users outside the organization, an Internet server would fit the bill.

Since this solution is built with managed code, the .NET Framework's no-touch deployment feature can be utilized to ensure that the users utilize the most current version. For instance, say version 1 of the Timesheet System is deployed and left alone for the first six months. Users are happy and everything goes smoothly. Then an update to one of the DLLs is deployed and we have version 1.1. Thanks to no-touch deployment, each time the user opens the targeted Excel workbook, the user's version is checked against the files on the server, and if the server contains new files, they will automatically be downloaded to the client machine by the workbook with no need to manually deploy the update on each desktop (see Figure 7-1).

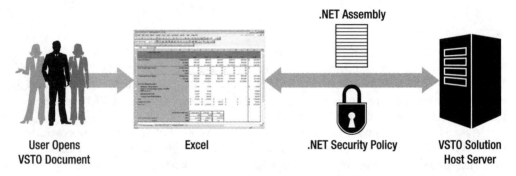

.NET Assembly

| User Opens | Excel | .NET Security Policy | VSTO Solution |
| VSTO Document | | | Host Server |

Figure 7-1. *VSTO keeps the Timesheet System current by downloading the most recent assembly version.*

■Note VSTO is not included with Office or Visual Studio, nor is it free. If you already have a subscription to MSDN, you can download VSTO from the MSDN subscriber downloads section. If you do not have a subscription to MSDN, you will have to either order an MSDN subscription or purchase a copy of VSTO in order to build this chapter's application. To find out more about how to purchase a copy of VSTO, visit `http://msdn.microsoft.com/ vstudio/howtobuy/officetools/default.aspx`.

In order to build the Timesheet System application, you will also need to make sure the Office primary interop assemblies (PIAs) are installed on your system. The PIAs are installed with a complete Office installation, but not with the default installation. If they aren't installed, you can add the PIAs to your Office installation by changing Office's installation settings and selecting .NET Programmability Support for Excel. For more information regarding the PIAs and .NET support within Office visit: `http://msdn.microsoft.com/library/ en-us/dv_wrcore/html/wrrefofficeprimaryinteropassemblies.asp`.

Designing the Timesheet System

From the user's point of view, the Timesheet System consists of two Excel worksheets: Time-Manager Entry and Time-Manager Reporter.

The Time-Manager Entry Excel worksheet implements the following workflow:

1. To initiate the time-reporting process, a staff member opens the Time-Manager Entry application using an available kiosk.

2. The Time-Manager Entry application presents a login form where the user enters their username and password. If the login is successful, the application displays the Time-Manager Entry application. If the login attempt was not successful, the user is shown a message and the login form displays again.

3. Using the Time-Manager Entry application, the user proceeds to create new time records by specifying the project, adding a description of the work performed, and specifying a length of time (see Figure 7-2). This step is repeated for as many tasks as the user wishes to report.

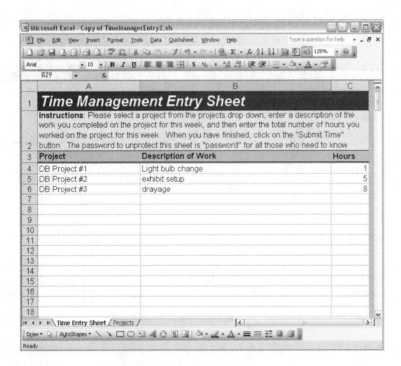

Figure 7-2. *Entering time records with the Time-Manager Entry application*

4. Once the user has completed the Time-Manager Entry application, they save the Excel file using the same Excel save process they are accustomed to using, and the application overrides Excel's save process to present the user with a custom Save dialog box allowing them to upload their time data to the solution database. If they are not ready to do so, they can still save the data to the system's hard drive like any other Excel file. In this scenario, the file could be reopened and submitted at a later time.

If a user wishes to see information that has been saved to the solution database, they would use the Time-Manager Reporter application. The workflow for that Excel worksheet is as follows:

1. The user opens the Time-Manager Reporter application on an available kiosk. The application displays a login form where the user enters their username and password. If the user is validated, the worksheet completes the loading process. Otherwise, they are alerted to the unsuccessful login attempt and allowed to try again.

2. To retrieve records from the solution database, the user selects the desired employee from a combo box and then enters the start date and end date values.

3. To initiate the record retrieval, the user clicks the Get Employee Report button. Once data has been successfully retrieved from the solution database, the Time-Manager Reporter Excel worksheet is updated to show each record in a separate line. Each line includes the date, project, hours, and description values for the record displayed on that line (see Figure 7-3).

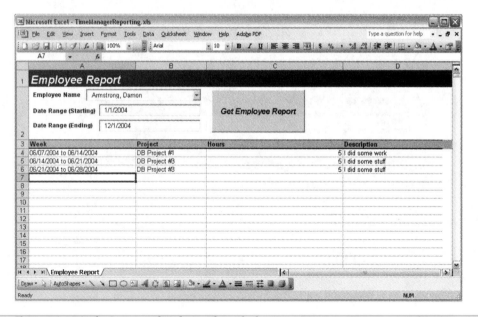

Figure 7-3. *Displaying completed records with the Time-Manager Reporter application*

From the developer's point of view, the Timesheet System application consists of three components:

- **Time Manager web service:** This web service is used by the Time-Manager Entry component to input time data, and by the Time-Manager Reporter component to summarize and report time data. This web service's primary purpose is to interface with the solution database to insert and retrieve time-entry records. In developing this web service, we will build classes that represent record types, we will encapsulate database-related code within each class, and we will use arrays to store multiple instances of the object type.

- **Time-Manager Entry application**: This is an Excel-based user interface for capturing time-entry input. This file, `TimeManagerEntry.xls`, utilizes an attached VSTO assembly that implements the necessary logic for capturing time-entry data and submitting the data to the Time Manager web service. We will see how to use VSTO to write managed code behind an Excel file. Other key concepts include how to call methods from the solution's web service, how to fill a combo box control with data provided from the web service, how to override Excel's save feature with a custom version that implements a custom save scenario, and how to read an Excel worksheet's data into an array that will be passed as an argument to a web service's method.

- **Time-Manager Reporter application:** This is an Excel-based user interface for creating time-entry reports. The `TimeManagerReporting.xls` file also utilizes an attached VSTO assembly, but the logic in this case is for retrieving records via the Time Manager web service and presenting them in a readable format inside Excel. We will look at how to use VSTO to write code behind an Excel worksheet. Key concepts here include how to call a web service method and use the returned data to populate the Excel worksheet, how to add controls to the worksheet and reference them in code, and how to populate a drop-down control with data.

In Figure 7-4, you can see that the application makes considerable use of Excel as the user interface. Both the Time-Manager Entry and Time-Manager Reporter components utilize the Time Manager web service for accessing the solution's database.

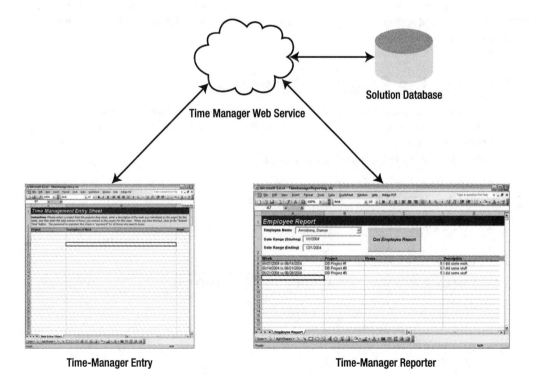

Figure 7-4. *The Timesheet System application architecture*

Each Excel-based component contains a target Excel workbook and a managed code DLL file holding the business logic to be executed against the workbook. The web service component contains all the code required to insert data into the solution's database (an Access database) as well as to retrieve and return records for reporting purposes.

The Business Scenario

During the execution of a show, orders must be taken and fulfilled, exhibits must be set up, and quality must be checked. The time required to complete each task must be captured in order to provide an accurate job cost for the event. Because Bravo Corp relies on local part-time union labor to perform most of the work for the shows, and the local union decides who to send the staff may vary from day to day. This creates a logistical nightmare for recording time against work orders.

Bravo Corp formerly had two employees enter time data manually, but this system was impractical for large events. An automated system was needed, but it had to be simple and easy to use so that regularly changing staff could quickly be trained to use it.

Bravo Corp decided to implement an Excel-based system that would allow a user to simply pick a task (or series of tasks), assign a length of time to it, and submit the time to a central database for tracking.

In addition, to alleviate the administrative bottleneck, the PIE team decided to implement the Timesheet System in such a way that it could be used in several different deployment scenarios. The Time-Manager Entry application is deployed on several PCs available throughout each event facility so that time entry can be performed on a self-service basis by the laborers. The other optional scenario would involve the use of full-time staff to enter the time when laborers returned completed work orders.

Creating the Solution Database

The code portion of the Timesheet System relies on a Microsoft Access database to serve as the solution's data repository. The database contains three tables for storing user, project, and hour-related information.

Create the database by following these steps:

1. Open Microsoft Access and create a new blank database (File ➤ New ➤ New Blank Database). Name the file **TimeManager.mdb**.

2. Create a new table called tblUser following the schema in Table 7-1.

Table 7-1. *The Schema for the* tblUser *Table*

Field Name	Data Type	Field Size	Primary Key
userID	Text	16	yes
password	Text	16	no
nameLast	Text	30	no
nameFirst	Text	30	no
admin	Yes/No	n/a	no

3. Create a new table called `tblProject` following the schema in Table 7-2.

Table 7-2. *The Schema for the* `tblProject` *Table*

Field Name	Data Type	Field Size	Primary Key
projectName_id	Text	50	yes

4. Create a new table called `tblHours` following the schema in Table 7-3.

Table 7-3. *The Schema for the* `tblHours` *Table*

Field Name	Data Type	Field Size	Primary Key
projectName	Text	50	yes
userID	Text	50	yes
startDate	Date/Time		yes
endDate	Date/Time		yes
hours	Number	Single	no
description	Text	255	no

Save the database in a folder named `Database` residing in the same folder location that is specified as the local path for the `TimeManagerWeb` web service's virtual web directory.

Once you have completed building the database, enter the same data into the `tblUser` and `tblProject` tables (such User #1, User #2, and Project #1, Project #2, etc.). This will be helpful when testing the applications.

Configuring .NET Security for VSTO

In order for the assemblies created with VSTO to execute within Excel, you will need to use the .NET Configuration tool to give proper permissions to the compiled assembly's file location. (For example, I set the location of each Timesheet System Excel component to be `C:\Projects\TimeSheet`.)

To enable execution of these two VSTO assemblies, perform the following steps:

1. Open the .NET 1.1 Configuration utility (see Figure 7-5). This tool resides in the Administrative Tools section of the Windows Control Panel.

2. Expand the Runtime Security Policy node in the tree view at the left side of the configuration utility.

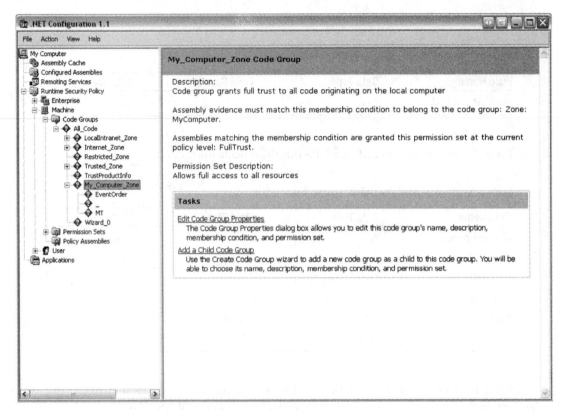

Figure 7-5. *Creating a new .NET Runtime Security Policy*

3. Navigate to the My_Computer_Zone section by expanding the tree view to display: Machine ➤ Code Groups ➤ All_Code ➤ My_Computer_Zone (see Figure 7-5).

4. Right-click the My_Computer_Zone node and select New from the pop-up menu to start up the Create Code Group Wizard.

5. Enter **TimeManager** in the Name field, and for the Description, enter **Folder location for the TimeManager VSTO assemblies** (see Figure 7-6). Click Next.

6. Select All Code from the Choose the Condition Type for This Code Group drop-down box (see Figure 7-7). Click Next.

7. Select FullTrust in the Use Existing Permission Set drop-down box. Click Next.

8. Click Finish.

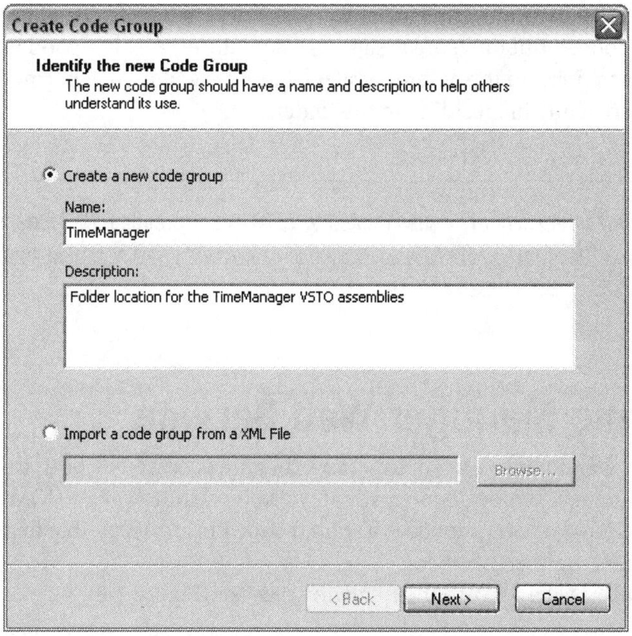

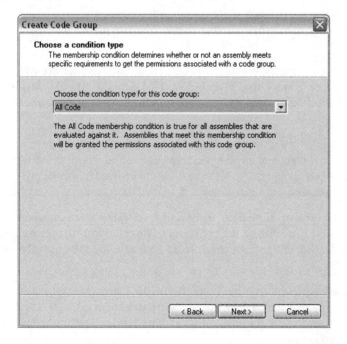

Figure 7-6. *Creating the TimeManager code group*

Figure 7-7. *Specifying a code group condition type*

The TimeManager permission group gives full trust to an entire file system folder. This is okay for development purposes, but once the assemblies actually exist, it is a good idea to modify the security settings to point to the assembly's DLL file. This will reduce permission to only the specified file instead of any file residing in the folder.

■**Note** For more information regarding security issues related to VSTO, read "Creating .NET Extensions for Office Applications" at `http://www.devsource.ziffdavis.com/article2/0%2C1759%2C1606463%2C00.asp`.

Building the Time Manager Web Service

The Time Manager web service provides a set of functions that are accessed by both the Time-Manager Entry and Time-Manager Reporter component workbooks. Much like a COM-based DLL code library, the Time Manager web service is a shared code library accessible to any application needing the functionality it provides.

The `TimeManagerWeb` web service will use the following files (see Figure 7-8):

- `TimeManagerWeb.asmx`: This file serves as the main class of the web service. It contains the web methods made available by the web service, and it is accessed by the Excel projects, which create a web reference to the web service in order to call the web service's methods. The main logic in this web service interfaces with the solution database to validate login criteria and perform database operations (add, update, and delete). This class also makes use of all other objects in the web service project (`Config`, `Globals`, `Hours`, `Project`, and `User`).

- `Config.vb`: This class contains the connection information used to interface with the solution database (connection string, password, and file location). These values are kept in property methods and accessed by methods in the `Globals` and `web.config` classes.

- `Globals.vb`: This module contains two global utility functions: one that returns an active `OleDbConnection` object and another that replaces all apostrophes (') in a given SQL statement with double quotes ("). Both methods are invoked in the `Hours`, `User`, and `TimeManagerWeb` classes.

- `Hours.vb`: This class represents time data, and it is utilized by the `TimeManagerWeb` class to store time records for a specified week in memory. The class exists to encapsulate the logic required to save, edit, and retrieve time records stored in the `tblHours` table of the solution database.

- `Project.vb`: This class represents a project record, and the `TimeManagerWeb` class uses it to store a project record retrieved from the solution database in memory. The class exists to encapsulate the logic required to retrieve time records stored in the `tblProject` table of the solution database.

- User.vb: This class represents a user account, and the TimeManagerWeb class uses it to store the current user's account information. The class exists to encapsulate the logic required to retrieve user records stored in the tblUser table of the solution database.

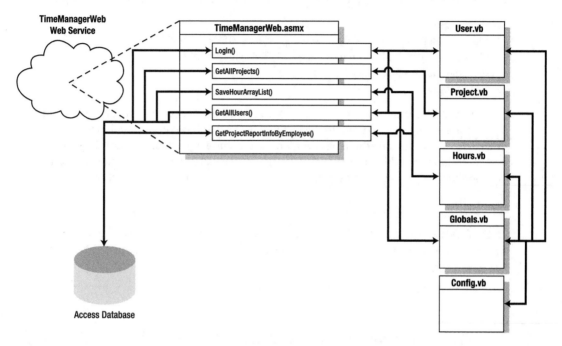

Figure 7-8. *Building the Time Manager web service*

The web service could be much more complicated, but for this chapter's application, it only provides basic data-service functions like adding, editing, and deleting records inside the solution database. To take the web service to the next level, you could add functions that go beyond these database-related tasks and institute custom business data rules. For example, the web service could easily check a user account to see whether that person is allowed overtime, or it could perform a test to ensure that a user does not enter more than 10 hours worth of time for any given day.

■**Note** Chapter 5 contains an overview of web services in the "InfoPath and Web Services" section.

The web.config File

The web.config file is used in ASP .NET applications to specify any settings required by the web service and to create custom properties that affect the application's behavior. These settings or properties can be any values used for any purpose—in this application, the setting we need to store is the location of the solution database. Visual Studio automatically creates web.config, so there is no need to create it.

The TimeManagerWeb web service utilizes two custom key/value pairs in the appSettings section of the web.config file. The appSettings section is actually a special element inside web.config used to define configuration information like database connection settings. Insert the following near the top of the web.config, between the <configuration> and <system.web> tags.

```
<appSettings>
  <add key="dbFileLocation" value="C:\projects\Office Book\" & _
    "Time Manager Application\Database\TimeManager.mdb"/>
  <add key="dbPassword" value=""/>
</appSettings>
```

The first key/value pair is the location of the solution's Access database. Be sure to edit your version of the code to point to the location of the database on your hard drive. The second key/value pair is the admin password to the database. By default, the admin password to an Access database is blank. For example purposes, we will utilize this default password, but it is a good idea to password-protect the database when it is put into a production environment.

Tip MSDN has a good article that provides a basic overview of Access security at http://msdn.microsoft.com/ library/default.asp?url=/library/en-us/dnacc2k2/html/ odc_AcSecurity.asp.

The TimeManagerWeb.asmx Class

The TimeManagerWeb class is the web service engine. It defines the core business logic and methods and exposes them as web methods that both provide data from the solution database and update the solution database (by inserting new records or editing existing records).

The main tasks handled by this class are authenticating users, saving time-entry data, and retrieving list-type data (such as projects, users, and time data) from the solution database. Most of the functions utilize the project's "object" classes (the Config, Globals, Hours, Project, and User classes), which will be created later in this section.

Here is summary of the methods included in this class:

- Login: This method accepts user login criteria (user name and password) passed by either of the two Excel applications that are part of the Timesheet System. The method performs a query against the tblUser table in the solution database to validate the passed login criteria, and it returns a User object if the login is successful.

- SaveHourArrayList: This method accepts an ArrayList object containing Hours objects and saves them to the solution database. The method also accepts a user ID and start and end date values that are used to identify the user and time period.

- GetAllProjects: This method queries the database to retrieve all records in the tblProject table. The records are returned as a Project object.

- GetAllUsers: This method queries the database to retrieve a listing of all records in the tblUser table. The records are returned as a User object.

- GetProjectReportInfoByEmployee: This method accepts a user ID and start and end dates as parameters to build a SQL statement. This SQL statement is then executed against the solution database to return a listing of all time records that meet the criteria passed as method parameters. The records are returned as an Hours object.

Custom Methods

The Time Manager web service exposes five custom methods as web methods: Login, Save-HourArrayList, GetAllProjects, GetAllUsers, and GetProjectReportInfoByEmployee.

Login

The Login method checks the passed userId and password parameters against the Timesheet System's database for a valid user account. If a valid account is discovered, the information is returned via a User object.

```
<WebMethod(Description:="Login will return a user object given a " & _
  "userId and a password. If the userId and password do not match a " & _
  "user in the database, nothing will be returned.")> _
Public Function Login(ByVal userId As String, ByVal password As _
  String) As tmUser

  Try
    Dim  tempObj As New tmUser
    Dim  dbConn As OleDbConnection = GetConnection()
    Dim  dbCmd As New OleDbCommand("SELECT * FROM [tblUser]  " & _
      WHERE  [userId]='" & sqlString(userId) & "' AND [password]='" & _
      sqlString(password) & "'", dbConn)

    Dim  dbDr  As OleDbDataReader = _
      dbCmd.ExecuteReader(CommandBehavior.SingleRow)

    If  dbDr.Read Then
      tempObj = tmUser.GetFromDR(dbDr)
    Else
      tempObj = Nothing
    End If

    dbDr.Close()
    dbConn.Close()

    Return tempObj
  Catch ex As Exception
    Return Nothing
  End Try
End Function
```

The function creates a connection to the database and issues a SQL command to create a data reader object. If the user account is found, the function creates a new User object (tmUser) and returns it as the value of the function.

SaveHourArrayList

SaveHourArrayList creates time records in the database.

```
<WebMethod(Description:="Saves all the Hour objects in an array list.")> _
Public Function SaveHourArrayList(ByVal userId As String, _
  ByVal startDate As Date, ByVal endDate As Date, _
  ByVal objCol() As Object) As Boolean

  Try
    Dim  dbConn As IDbConnection = Globals.GetConnection()
    Dim  dbTran As IDbTransaction = dbConn.BeginTransaction()
    Dim  HasError As Boolean = False

    If  Not tmHours.DeleteForGivenWeek(userId, startDate, endDate, _
      dbConn, dbTran) Then

      HasError = True
    End If

    For Each obj As tmHours In objCol
      If Not HasError Then
        If Not obj.Save(dbConn, dbTran) Then
          HasError = True
        End If
      End If
    Next

    If  Not HasError Then
      dbTran.Commit()
      dbConn.Close()
      Return True
    Else
      dbTran.Rollback()
      dbConn.Close()
      Return False
    End If

  Catch ex As Exception
    Return False
  End Try

End Function
```

Once a connection to the database is established, the first thing the method does is delete any data that may have already been entered for the user within the date range represented by startDate and endDate. Then, for each record contained in the data array (objCol), a save method executes to actually save the data to the database:

```
For Each obj As tmHours In objCol
  If Not HasError Then
    If Not obj.Save(dbConn, dbTran) Then
      HasError = True
    End If
  End If
End If
```

The Save method is provided by the Time Manager web service's Hours class, which returns a Boolean value specifying whether the record saved successfully. Utilizing the return value of Save, the code branches out to handle either possibility.

```
If  Not HasError Then
  dbTran.Commit()
  dbConn.Close()
  Return True
Else
  dbTran.Rollback()
  dbConn.Close()
  Return False
End If
```

Provided no errors were encountered, the data is committed to the database. If an error did occur, all inserted records are deleted via the Rollback method. In either case, the method wraps up by closing the connection to the database.

GetAllProjects

GetAllProjects provides a listing of all projects contained in the solution database's tbl-Project table. The project records are bundled into an ArrayList object, which is returned as the value of the function.

```
<WebMethod(Description:="Returns a string array containing a list of " & _
    "the projects.")> _
Public Function GetAllProjects() As Project()

    Dim returnArray As New ArrayList
    Dim dbConn As IDbConnection = Globals.GetConnection()
    Dim dbCmd As IDbCommand
    Dim dbDr As IDataReader
    Dim projectObj As Project

    dbCmd = dbConn.CreateCommand()
```

```
    'Insert the new items
    dbCmd.CommandText = "SELECT * FROM tblProject " & _
      "ORDER BY projectName;"
    dbDr = dbCmd.ExecuteReader(CommandBehavior.SequentialAccess)

    While dbDr.Read
      projectObj = Project.GetFromDR(dbDr)
      If Not projectObj Is Nothing Then
        returnArray.Add(projectObj)
      End If
    End While

    dbDr.Close()
    dbConn.Close()
    Return returnArray.ToArray
End Function
```

Assuming the database connection is created, the code executes a SQL command that selects all project records. The SELECT statement specifies that the returned data be sorted by project name. The user will expect to see this data sorted, so it makes sense to do it now in the SQL query.

The data returned from the SQL query is placed in a DataReader object, and it is then read sequentially from the DataReader into the returnArray object. The returnArray object is returned as the value of the function.

GetAllUsers

GetAllUsers reads the solution database and returns an ArrayList object containing a listing of all Timesheet System users.

```
<WebMethod(Description:="Returns an array containing all of the users")> _
Public Function GetAllUsers() As tmUser()

    Dim returnArray As New ArrayList
    Dim dbConn As IDbConnection = Globals.GetConnection()
    Dim dbCmd As IDbCommand
    Dim dbDr As IDataReader
    Dim userObj As tmUser

    dbCmd = dbConn.CreateCommand()

    'Insert the new items
    dbCmd.CommandText = "SELECT * FROM [tblUser] ORDER BY " & _
      "[nameLast], [nameFirst] ASC;"

    dbDr = dbCmd.ExecuteReader(CommandBehavior.SequentialAccess)
```

```
While dbDr.Read
    userObj = tmUser.GetFromDR(dbDr)
    If Not userObj Is Nothing Then
      returnArray.Add(userObj)
    End If
End While


  dbDr.Close()
  dbConn.Close()
  Return returnArray.ToArray
End Function
```

As you can see, first we create a connection to the database and declare our working variables:

```
Dim returnArray As New ArrayList
Dim dbConn As IDbConnection = Globals.GetConnection()
Dim dbCmd As IDbCommand
Dim dbDr As IDataReader
Dim userObj As tmUser
```

Next, we create an IDbCommand object, build our SQL statement, and use the two to create a DataReader.

```
dbCmd = dbConn.CreateCommand()

'Insert the new items
dbCmd.CommandText = "SELECT * FROM [tblUser] ORDER BY " & _
  "[nameLast], [nameFirst] ASC;"

dbDr = dbCmd.ExecuteReader(CommandBehavior.SequentialAccess)
```

Then, for each record, we create and insert new User objects into the returnArray object.

```
While dbDr.Read
    userObj = tmUser.GetFromDR(dbDr)
    If Not userObj Is Nothing Then
      returnArray.Add(userObj)
    End If
End While
```

Finally, the database connections close and the returnArray, filled with User objects, returns as the value of the function.

```
dbDr.Close()
dbConn.Close()
Return returnArray
```

GetProjectReportInfoByEmployee

GetProjectReportInfoByEmployee retrieves time-entry records from the solution database using the passed user ID and start and end dates as parameters for the SQL query built in the function. The SQL query returns an array of Hours objects that can then be utilized by the calling application to display the time-entry data as it sees fit.

```
<WebMethod(Description:="Returns project names and hour information.")> _
Public Function GetProjectReportInfoByEmployee(ByVal userId As String, _
  ByVal StartDate As Date, ByVal EndDate As Date) As tmHours()

  Try
    Dim returnArray As tmHours()
    Dim obj As tmHours
    Dim dbConn As IDbConnection = Globals.GetConnection()
    Dim dbCmd As IDbCommand = dbConn.CreateCommand
    Dim dbDr As IDataReader

    Dim SQL As String = "SELECT * FROM [tblHours] WHERE [userId]='" & _
      sqlString(userId) & "'"

    If Not StartDate = Nothing And Not EndDate = Nothing Then
      'Use both start date and enddate
      SQL &= " AND [startDate]>=#" & Format(StartDate, "MM/dd/yyyy") & _
        "#  AND [startDate]<=#" & Format(EndDate, "MM/dd/yyyy") & "#"

    ElseIf StartDate = Nothing And Not EndDate = Nothing Then
      'Only use startdate
      SQL &= " AND [startDate]<=#" & Format(EndDate, "MM/dd/yyyy") & "#"
    ElseIf Not StartDate = Nothing And EndDate = Nothing Then
      'Only use enddate
      SQL &= " AND [startDate]>=#" & Format(StartDate, "MM/dd/yyyy") & "#"
    End If

    SQL &= " ORDER BY [startDate], [projectName];"

    dbCmd.CommandText = SQL
    dbDr = dbCmd.ExecuteReader(CommandBehavior.SequentialAccess)
    While dbDr.Read()
      obj = tmHours.GetFromDR(dbDr)
      If Not obj Is Nothing Then
        If returnArray Is Nothing Then
          ReDim returnArray(0)
        Else
          ReDim Preserve returnArray(returnArray.Length)
        End If
        returnArray(returnArray.Length - 1) = obj
      End If
```

```
    End While
    dbDr.Close()
    dbConn.Close()
    Return returnArray

  Catch ex As Exception
    Return Nothing
  End Try
```

This method begins by creating variables required for working with the solution database. In addition to creating the variables, the method creates a connection to the database by calling the Globals.GetConnection method:

```
Dim returnArray As tmHours()
Dim obj As tmHours
Dim dbConn As IDbConnection = Globals.GetConnection()
Dim dbCmd As IDbCommand = dbConn.CreateCommand
Dim dbDr As IDataReader
```

The SQL statement is built dynamically using the start and end dates provided to the function:

```
Dim SQL As String = "SELECT * FROM [tblHours] WHERE [userId]='" & _
    sqlString(userId) & "'"

  If Not StartDate = Nothing And Not EndDate = Nothing Then
    'Use both start date and enddate
    SQL &= " AND [startDate]>=#" & Format(StartDate, "MM/dd/yyyy") & _
      "#  AND [startDate]<=#" & Format(EndDate, "MM/dd/yyyy") & "#"

  ElseIf StartDate = Nothing And Not EndDate = Nothing Then
    'Only use startdate
    SQL &= " AND [startDate]<=#" & Format(EndDate, "MM/dd/yyyy") & "#"
  ElseIf Not StartDate = Nothing And EndDate = Nothing Then
    'Only use enddate
    SQL &= " AND [startDate]>=#" & Format(StartDate, "MM/dd/yyyy") & "#"
  End If

  SQL &= " ORDER BY [startDate], [projectName];"
```

If both the start and end dates have been passed to the function, they are used to build the SQL statement. If the calling application provided only one of the dates (start or end), the provided date serves as the value for startDate.

Once the SQL statement is ready, it is executed against the database to create a DataReader object for use in a code loop. The loop reads each record in the DataReader and builds an array of Hours objects.

```
dbCmd.CommandText = SQL
dbDr = dbCmd.ExecuteReader(CommandBehavior.SequentialAccess)
While dbDr.Read()
```

```
  obj = tmHours.GetFromDR(dbDr)
  If Not obj Is Nothing Then
    If returnArray Is Nothing Then
      ReDim returnArray(0)
    Else
      ReDim Preserve returnArray(returnArray.Length)
    End If
    returnArray(returnArray.Length - 1) = obj
  End If
End While
dbDr.Close()
dbConn.Close()
Return returnArray
```

The function returns the completed returnArray filled with time-entry records meeting the criteria provided by the calling application. As we'll see later on, this array can easily be used to create a rather useful report.

The Config.vb Class

The Config class provides quick access to configuration setting values. The class does not contain any methods—just three properties related to the Timesheet System database. The provided properties are read by the GetConnection method found in the Globals class. The information is then used to create an OleDbConnection object that has a live connection to the solution database.

The connectionString Property Procedure

connectionString is a read-only property containing the information string for connecting with the solution database.

```
Public Shared ReadOnly Property connectionString()
    Get
        If dbPassword = String.Empty Then
            Return "Provider=Microsoft.Jet.OLEDB.4.0;Data Source=" & _
                dbFileLocation & ";User Id=admin;Password=;"
        Else
            Return "Provider=Microsoft.Jet.OLEDB.4.0;Data Source=" & _
                dbFileLocation & ";Jet OLEDB:Database Password=" & _
                dbPassword & ";"
        End If
    End Get
End Property
```

The property utilizes the web service properties (dbFileLocation and dbPassword) contained in the web.config file. Allowance is made for the chance that the solution's Access database requires a password.

The dbFileLocation Property Procedure

The dbFileLocation property is read-only and returns the value of the file location key stored in the web.config file's appSettings section.

```
Private Shared ReadOnly Property dbFileLocation() As String
    Get
        Return AppSettings("dbFileLocation")
    End Get
End Property
```

The dbPassword Property Procedure

The dbPassword property is read-only and returns the value of the password key stored in the web.config file's appSettings section.

```
Private Shared ReadOnly Property dbPassword() As String
    Get
        Return AppSettings("dbPassword")
    End Get
End Property
```

The Globals.vb Class

The Globals class is a database-helper class containing two methods. The methods reside in this class because they are used by the Hours, Project, User, and TimeManagerWeb classes to create a connection to the solution database (via the GetConnection method). In addition, each of these classes utilize the sqlString method to help create dynamic SQL statements.

The methods in the Globals class are GetConnection and sqlString.

The GetConnection Method

The GetConnection method returns an open OleDbConnection object.

```
Public Function GetConnection(Optional ByVal OpenConnection _
  As Boolean = True) As OleDbConnection

  Dim dbConn As New OleDbConnection(Config.connectionString)
  If OpenConnection Then dbConn.Open()
  Return dbConn
End Function
```

If the connection is not already open, the function creates an open connection to return as the value of the method.

The sqlString Method

The sqlString function serves as a helper-function to clean the passed SQL String.

```
Public Function sqlString(ByVal rawString As String) As String
  If rawString = String.Empty Then Return ""
  Return rawString.Replace("'", "''")
End Function
```

To ensure the SQL statement executes without problems, the function replaces all single quote characters (') with double quotes (").

The Hours.vb Class

The Hours class represents a time-entry record. It is utilized by the TimeManagerWeb class to retrieve time-related records from the solution database. The Hours class is utilized by the Get-ProjectReportInfoByEmployee and SaveHourArrayList methods of the TimeManagerWeb class.

Variable Declarations

The Hours class declares the following Public variables:

```
Public ProjectName As String = ""
Public userId As String = ""
Public hours As Single = 0
Public startDate As DateTime = Nothing
Public endDate As DateTime = Nothing
Public description As String = ""
```

Methods

The Hours class implements three methods for handling database tasks: GetFromDR, DeleteFor-GivenWeek, and Save.

GetFromDR

GetFromDR creates a new Hours object and fills it with the hour record data provided by the passed DataReader object (DR).

```
Public Shared Function GetFromDR(ByRef DR As IDataReader) As tmHours
  Try
    Dim obj As New tmHours
    obj.ProjectName = DR("projectName")
    obj.userId = DR("userId")
    obj.startDate = DR("startDate")
    obj.endDate = DR("endDate")
    obj.hours = DR("hours")
    obj.description = DR("description")
    Return obj
```

```
   Catch ex As Exception
     Return Nothing
   End Try
End Function
```

DeleteForGivenWeek

Just in case a user decides to update their time information after the records are posted to the database for that week, we need a way to delete the previous records to prevent data duplication and errors. The DeleteForGivenWeek method meets this requirement and deletes all time data pertaining the passed userId and date range.

```
Public Shared Function DeleteForGivenWeek(ByVal userId As String, _
  ByVal startDate As Date, ByVal endDate As Date, Optional _
  ByRef dbConn As IDbConnection = Nothing, Optional _
  ByRef dbTran As IDbTransaction = Nothing) As Boolean

  Try

    Dim dbConnOwner As Boolean = dbConn Is Nothing
    Dim dbCmd As IDbCommand

    If dbConn Is Nothing Then dbConn = Globals.GetConnection()

    dbCmd = dbConn.CreateCommand()
    dbCmd.Transaction = dbTran

    'Insert the new items
    dbCmd.CommandText = "DELETE FROM [tblHours]   " & _
      "WHERE   [userId]='sqlString(userId) & "' AND " & _
      "[startDate]=#Format(startDate, MM/dd/yyyy") & _
      "# and [endDate]=#" & Format(endDate, "MM/dd/yyyy") & "#;"
    dbCmd.ExecuteNonQuery()
    If dbConnOwner Then dbConn.Close()
    Return True

  Catch ex As Exception
    Return False
  End Try

End Function
```

Beyond the normal database-connection logic, the function utilizes the passed userId, startDate, and endDate arguments to create a SQL DELETE query for deleting the records matching the criteria specified by these values. Once completed, the updated time entry records are ready for insertion.

Save

The Save method saves the data contained in the Hours object to the database.

```
Public Function Save(Optional ByRef dbConn As IDbConnection = Nothing, _
  Optional ByRef dbTran As IDbTransaction = Nothing) As Boolean

  Try

    Dim dbConnOwner As Boolean = dbConn Is Nothing
    Dim dbCmd As IDbCommand

    If dbConn Is Nothing Then dbConn = Globals.GetConnection()

    dbCmd = dbConn.CreateCommand()
    dbCmd.Transaction = dbTran

    'Insert the new items
    dbCmd.CommandText = "INSERT INTO [tblHours](projectName, " & _
      userId,  startDate, endDate, hours, description) VALUES ('" & _
      sqlString(Me.ProjectName) & "','" & sqlString(Me.userId) & "',#" & _
      Format(startDate, "MM/dd/yyyy") & "#,#" & _
      Format(endDate, "MM/dd/yyyy") & "#,'" & Me.hours & "','" & _
      sqlString(Me.description) & "');"
    If dbCmd.ExecuteNonQuery() = 1 Then
      Save = True
      If dbConnOwner Then dbConn.Close()
    Else
      Save = False
      If dbConnOwner Then dbConn.Close()
    End If

  Catch ex As Exception
    Return False
  End Try

End Function
```

A transaction is used just in case anything goes awry and we decide the record should be rolled back. The values from the Hours object's projectName, userId, startDate, endDate, hours, and description properties are used to build the SQL INSERT statement that will insert a new time record. The SQL statement is then executed, and the database connection is closed.

The Project.vb Class

The Project class represents a single project record. It contains a single method that retrieves a project record from the solution database and returns the record inside a Project object.

This class and its only method are called from the GetAllProjects method found in the Time-ManagerWeb class.

Variable Declarations

The Project class declares the following variable:

```
Public ProjectName As String
```

The GetFromDR Method

GetFromDR returns a Project object to the calling method. Using the supplied data reader object, the method inserts the value from the projectName field contained in the data reader object. This value is stored in the Project object's ProjectName property, and the object is returned as the method's value.

```
Public Shared Function GetFromDR(ByRef dbDr As IDataReader) As Project

    Dim projectObj As New Project

    Try
        projectObj.ProjectName = dbDr("projectName")
    Catch ex As Exception
        projectObj = Nothing
    End Try

    Return projectObj

End Function
```

The User.vb Class

The User class contains data pertaining to the currently logged-in user. This class is invoked by the TimeManagerWeb class's Login method. The User class has a single method used to read column data into a User object.

Variable Declarations

The User class declares five variables that store user information:

```
Public userId As String = ""
Public password As String = ""
Public nameLast As String = ""
Public nameFirst As String = ""
Public admin As Boolean = False
```

The GetFromDR Method

The User class contains one method. GetFromDR reads the data passed in the DR parameter and creates a new User class (named tmUser) filled with user's account information read from the data reader's properties.

```
Public Shared Function GetFromDR(ByRef DR As IDataReader) As tmUser
  Try
    Dim obj As New tmUser
    obj.userId = DR("userId")
    obj.password = DR("password")
    obj.nameLast = DR("nameLast")
    obj.nameFirst = DR("nameFirst")
    obj.admin = DR("admin")
    Return obj
  Catch ex As Exception
    Return Nothing
  End Try
End Function
```

Testing the Time Manager Web Service

Before building the remaining components of the Timesheet System, let's make sure the web service functions correctly. Follow these steps:

1. With the TimeManagerWeb project open in Visual Studio, press the F5 key.

2. The TimeManagerWeb.asmx file opens inside the browser and lists its available web service functions (see Figure 7-9).

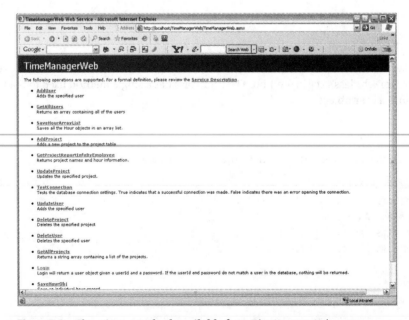

Figure 7-9. *Choosing a method available from* TimeManagerWeb.asmx

3. Click the GetAllUsers link. The browser will show the definition of the method. Click the Invoke button to test the GetAllUsers method.

If a new browser window opens showing an XML listing of all users in the solution database (see Figure 7-10), the web service is working as expected.

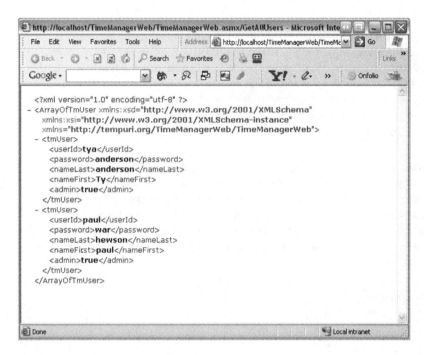

Figure 7-10. *The results of the web service test*

Building the Time-Manager Entry Application

The Time-Manager Entry application acts as the primary interface for the entire system—it is the interface for entering data, and it has the largest user base of the three Timesheet System components. The Time-Manager Entry application accepts a laborer's time data entry and posts the records to the database by calling data functions published by the solution's web service (the TimeManagerWeb web service).

Time-Manager Entry contains three classes:

- ThisWorkbook.vb: This file contains the OfficeCodeBehind class that is created automatically by Visual Studio when the project is set up. Associated with the targeted Excel workbook, it is the main class of the application and it contains the code for responding to workbook events. In building this class, we will see how to fill an Excel Range with data retrieved from the solution database, how to authenticate a user, and how to read the data entered in the Excel file and save it to the solution database by calling a web service method. This class utilizes all other classes in the application at one time or another.

- `TimeManagerLogin.vb`: This is the user login form, and it is called by the `DoLogin` method residing in the `ThisWorkbook` class. It contains only property methods and no business logic. Although it is a form, `TimeManagerLogin` is used like any other class that lacks a visual element. It presents a form to the user and captures their username and password, and these values are then accessed via the form's property methods and are ultimately passed to the `TimeManagerWeb.Login` method to authenticate the user's credentials.

- `SaveDialog.vb`: This is a custom dialog box that implements the solution's timesheet data-submission logic. The form is invoked by the `ThisWorkbook_BeforeSave` event method and thus is presented to the user when Excel's save process is initiated (either by clicking the Save icon or by selecting File ➤ Save from Excel's menu). This form allows the user to select settings related to the Time-Manager Entry application's save process. The form is used much like the `TimeManagerLogin` form, in that it is meant to collect data and make the data available via custom property methods.

These three objects work together to capture time-entry data and then submit it to the solution's web service (`TimeManagerWeb`) for insertion into the solution's database.

Figure 7-11 illustrates the interaction of the three objects that make up `TimeManagerEntry.xls`. Excel serves as user interface and captures all time data input by the user. The `OfficeCodeBehind` class contains the code for authenticating the user, accessing data within the Excel worksheet, and retrieving and saving data from and to the `TimeManagerWeb` web service.

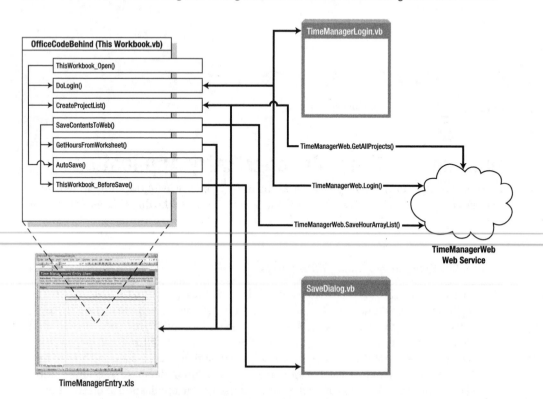

Figure 7-11. *Interactions among the objects of the Time-Manager Entry application*

Creating the Time-Manager Entry Project with Visual Studio Tools for Office

Visual Studio Tools for Office is an add-in to Visual Studio .NET that provides a set of project templates that allow a developer to create solutions behind a single Excel or Word document using either C# or VB .NET.

To create the Excel-based Time-Manager Entry application using Visual Studio Tools for Office, complete the following steps:

1. Create a new project in Visual Studio by selecting the Microsoft Office System Projects ➤ Visual Basic Project in the left pane of the New Project dialog box and selecting Excel Workbook in the Templates pane (see Figure 7-12). Click Next.

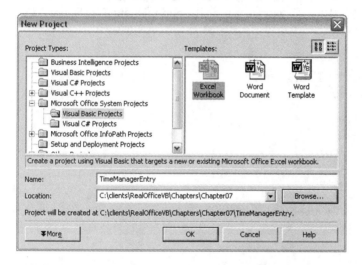

Figure 7-12. *Selecting the Excel Workbook project template*

2. In the Select a Document for Your Application window, choose Create a New Document, and name the project **TimeManagerEntry**. Specify the location for the project files, and click Finish.

3. Visual Studio builds a new VSTO project containing a single file, ThisWorkbook.vb.

By default, VSTO creates the OfficeCodeBehind class (residing inside ThisWorkbook.vb). This class implements the event handlers of the target Excel workbook file, and the Time-Manager Entry application's assembly loads the OfficeCodeBehind class when the TimeManagerEntry.xls file is opened inside Excel.

Unlike VBA, the managed code in the solution is not contained within the document but instead resides in the assembly, and custom properties in the target Excel file link it to the assembly. These custom properties are created when the VSTO project is created.

References

The TimeManagerEntry project requires the following references (beyond those initially created with the project):

- Microsoft Excel 11.0 Object Library

- System.Drawing.dll

- System.XML.dll

In addition, the project accesses the TimeManagerWeb web service, so a web reference must be added to the project. Create the web reference as follows:

1. In the Visual Studio Solution Explorer window, right-click on the TimeManagerEntry project and select Add Web Reference from the pop-up menu (see Figure 7-13).

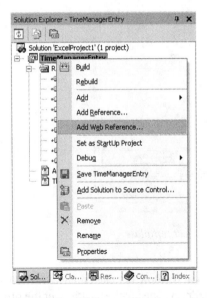

Figure 7-13. *Adding a web reference to the project*

2. The Add Web Reference dialog box displays (see Figure 7-14). Enter **http://localhost/ TimeManagerWeb/TimeManagerWeb.asmx** in the URL field, and click the Go button.

■**Tip** You could also click the "Web services on the local machine" link in the Browse To list. Doing so will cause the Add Web Reference dialog box to list all available web services on your system. From there, you would choose the TimeManagerWeb web service.

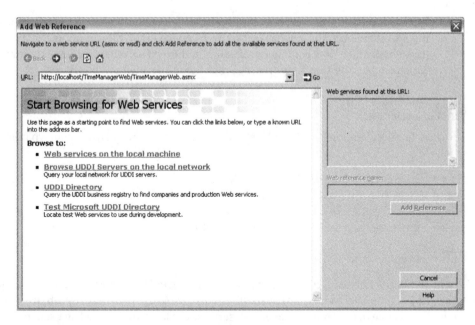

Figure 7-14. *Locating the* TimeManagerWeb *web service*

3. If the Add Web Reference dialog box locates TimeManagerWeb, it displays the methods available from the web service (see Figure 7-15). Enter **TMW** in the Web Reference Name field and click the Add Reference button.

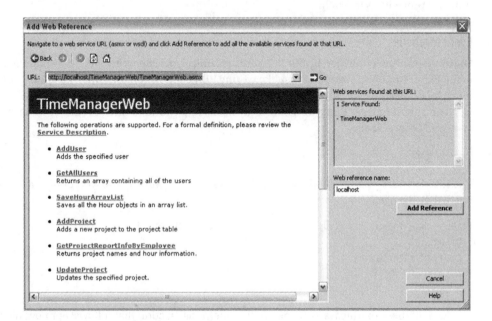

Figure 7-15. *Listing the* TimeManagerWeb *web service's public methods*

4. The Solution Explorer creates a new project folder named "Web References" containing the reference to the `TimeManagerWeb` web service (TMW). In addition, the Web References folder now contains a reference to the `System.Web.Services` assembly, which enables the `TimeManagerEntry` project to interact with web services.

Variable Declarations

The class-level declarations for the `OfficeCodeBehind` class (in the ThisWorkbook.vb file) are as follows:

```
Friend WithEvents ThisWorkbook As Excel.Workbook
Friend WithEvents ThisApplication As Excel.Application
Friend CurrentUser As TMW.tmUser = Nothing
Friend TimeManagerWeb As New TMW.TimeManagerWeb

Private InAutoSave As Boolean = False
```

In addition to the Excel references automatically created by the Visual Studio Tools for Office project template, we declare `CurrentUser` and `TimeManagerWeb` to access objects and methods available in the Time Manager web service. The last variable is a flag used to signify whether or not the solution's custom save dialog box will be used during the workbook's save routine.

The class declares all objects (except for one) using the `Friend` keyword. This strategy makes each of these objects accessible by each class within the project, while preventing access from objects external to the Time-Manager Entry application. The `Friend` keyword allows all other project classes to read and write values to these variables without creating property procedures for each.

Event Methods

Utilizing the events provided by the `ThisWorkbook` object, we can write code to respond to any of the Excel workbook events. It's just like writing VBA code within the Office VB editor, but it's much better because it's .NET code.

The Time-Manager Entry workbook only needs to respond to three events: `Open`, `BeforeSave`, and `BeforeClose`.

ThisWorkbook_Open

The `ThisWorkbook_Open` method contains the routines for setting up the workbook once it is opened by the user.

```
Private Sub ThisWorkbook_Open() Handles ThisWorkbook.Open
  DoLogin()
  CreateProjectList()
  AutoSave()
End Sub
```

Each of these routines is explained in the "Methods" section that follows. For now, all you need to know is that if all three steps are completed successfully, the user will be logged in, the workbook will be updated with data from the solution database, and it will be ready for the user to enter data. In addition, the workbook automatically saves to the file system.

ThisWorkbook_BeforeSave

We want to bypass the default Excel Save function in order to display a custom save dialog box. The BeforeSave method is the place to make this happen.

```
Private Sub ThisWorkbook_BeforeSave(ByVal SaveAsUI As Boolean, _
  ByRef Cancel As Boolean) Handles ThisWorkbook.BeforeSave

  If InAutoSave Then Return

  Dim frmSaveDialog As New SaveDialog
  Dim WS As Excel.Worksheet

  If frmSaveDialog.ShowDialog = DialogResult.OK Then
    If frmSaveDialog.SaveToWeb Then
      If SaveContentsToWeb(frmSaveDialog.StartDay) Then
        If frmSaveDialog.ClearContents Then
          WS = ThisWorkbook.Worksheets(1)
          For index As Integer = 4 To 4 + 255
            WS.Range("A" & index).Value = ""
            WS.Range("B" & index).Value = ""
            WS.Range("C" & index).Value = ""
          Next
        End If
        MsgBox("Your information was successfully saved to the " & _
          "Time Management system.", MsgBoxStyle.Information, _
          "Successfully Saved")
      Else
        MsgBox("Your information was NOT uploaded to the Time" & _
          "Management system.", MsgBoxStyle.Exclamation, _
          "Error Uploading Data")
      End If
    End If
  Else
    MsgBox("None of your changes have been saved", _
      MsgBoxStyle.Information Or MsgBoxStyle.OKOnly, "Save Cancelled")
    Cancel = True
  End If

End Sub
```

The goal of using this event is to present the user with the custom save dialog form (frm-SaveDialog, shown in Figure 7-16) and then use the settings specified by the user to take the appropriate action. If the user decides to upload, or submit, their time data to the database, the routine calls the SaveContentsToWeb function provided by the TimeManagerWeb web service.

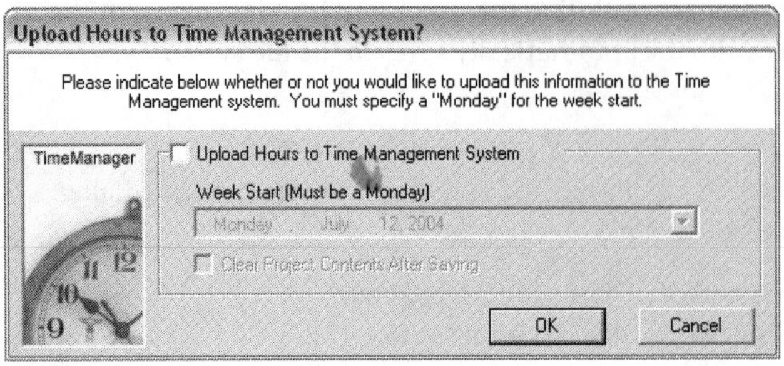

Figure 7-16. *The* frmSaveDialog *form*

If the user specified in the frmSaveDialog form that the project contents should be cleared after saving, once the time entries are posted, the code loops through rows 4 to 255 of the worksheet and deletes any values found in the cells. The code begins in row 4 because this is the first row in the Excel workbook containing time data. Row 255 is the last row in every timesheet. It is an arbitrary choice of size, but it provides a reasonable about of data-entry space.

At the end of the method, a message box is displayed to the user to notify them of the results of the save actions.

Methods

The TimeManagerEntry application's OfficeCodeBehind class does more than enable VSTO. It also contains the required methods for working with the TimeManagerEntry project's forms and for invoking the methods provided by the TimeManagerWeb web service.

The OfficeCodeBehind class contains five custom methods: AutoSave, CreateProjectList, DoLogin, SaveContentsToWeb, and GetHoursFromWorksheet.

AutoSave

When the workbook loads, it makes a call to the TimeManagerWeb web service to pull down a current listing of projects. The projects are then stored in a hidden Excel tab, and are used to populate the Project drop-down list on the data entry worksheet (see Figure 7-17).

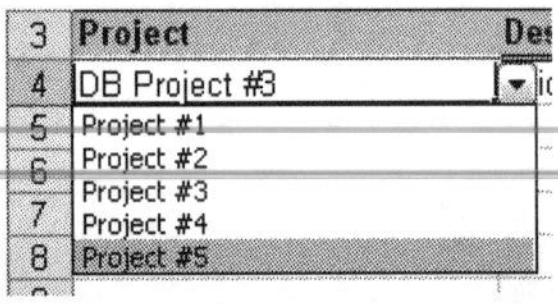

Figure 7-17. *Selecting a project from the Project drop-down list*

Updating this project list flags the workbook as "dirty" and causes Excel to prompt the user to save the file before closing, even if the user never entered a single line of time data. To avoid confusing the user, the workbook avoids this unnecessary save prompt by automatically saving the workbook file after it receives the project data from the TimeManagerWeb web service (which happens in the CreateProjectList method). Once saved, the workbook is no longer flagged as "dirty," so if the user closes the workbook without making any further changes (such as inserting time entries) they will not be prompted to save the workbook.

Here is the code for the AutoSave method, which saves the workbook when the project data is loaded:

```
Public Sub AutoSave()
  InAutoSave = True
  ThisWorkbook.Save()
  InAutoSave = False
End Sub
```

Previously, in the ThisWorkbook_BeforeSave method, the value of InAutoSave was tested—in that method, if InAutoSave's value is set to True, the ThisWorkbook_BeforeSave method exits immediately (not displaying the custom save dialog box), allowing AutoSave to save the workbook without alerting the user. This test prevents the custom frmSaveDialog form from being displayed at the wrong time.

CreateProjectList

As was mentioned in the previous section, whenever the TimeManagerEntry.xls workbook loads in Excel, it calls a method from the TimeManagerWeb web service in order to retrieve an updated listing of available projects. The CreateProjectList method uses the returned project listing to populate a hidden worksheet in the Excel file.

```
Public Sub CreateProjectList()
    Dim ProjectList As Object() = TimeManagerWeb.GetAllProjects()
    Dim WS As Excel.Worksheet = ThisWorkbook.Worksheets(2)
    Dim Index As Integer

    'Clear out the current project contents
    Try
      WS.Range("A1", "A255").Clear()
    Catch ex As Exception
      Dim x As String = ex.Message
    End Try

    If Not ProjectList Is Nothing Then
      For Index = 1 To ProjectList.Length
        WS.Range("A" & Index).Value = CStr(ProjectList(Index - 1))
      Next
      ThisWorkbook.Names.Item("ProjectList").Value = "=Projects!$A$1:$A$" & _
        ProjectList.Length
    Else
      ThisWorkbook.Names.Item("ProjectList").Value = "=Projects!$A$1:$A$1"
    End If

End Sub
```

Using a reference to the Time Manager web service (TimeManagerWeb), GetAllProjects returns a listing of current projects. Then the code clears the data in the Projects tab (worksheet 2, cells A1–A255), and so long as data exists on the next line in the ProjectList object, the code loops through the data and inserts the project names into separate rows in the Projects worksheet.

DoLogin

DoLogin creates a reference to the login form (TimeManagerLogin.vb) and uses it to capture the user's login information in order to verify it against the solution database.

```
Public Sub DoLogin()

    Dim loginForm As New TimeManagerLogin

    loginForm.ShowDialog()

    If loginForm.Cancelled = True Then
      ThisWorkbook.Close()
    Else
      CurrentUser = TimeManagerWeb.Login(loginForm.userId, _
          loginForm.password)

    If CurrentUser Is Nothing Then
        MsgBox("The credentials you supplied were invalid. Please try again.")
        loginForm = Nothing
        DoLogin()
      End If
    End If

End Sub
```

The TimeManagerWeb web service performs a credential check against the database, and, if the user exists, returns a TimeManagerWeb.User object that contains user information for use during the time-entry process.

SaveContentsToWeb

SaveContentsToWeb reads all the time entries entered into the workbook to build an array that will be submitted to the TimeManagerWeb web service. This array will be used to insert to new time records in the Time Manager database. This method is called by the ThisWorkbook_BeforeSave event method (found in the ThisWorkbook class), which also displays the custom save dialog box (see Figure 7-18).

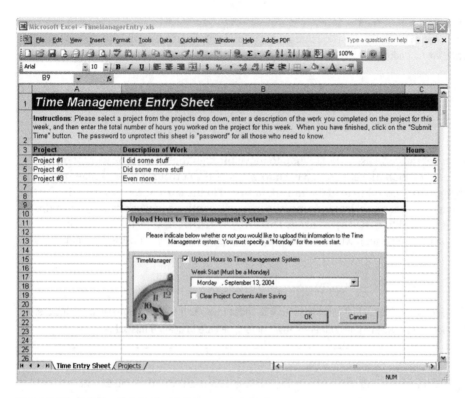

Figure 7-18. *Saving time entry data*

```
Public Function SaveContentsToWeb(ByVal StartDate As DateTime) _
  As Boolean

  Dim WS As Excel.Worksheet = ThisWorkbook.Worksheets.Item(1)
  Dim index As Integer = 4
  Dim done As Boolean
  Dim obj As TMW.tmHours
  Dim objCol As New ArrayList
  Dim ErrorFlag As Boolean
  Dim endDate As Date

  While Not done
    obj = GetHoursFromWorksheet(index, StartDate, ErrorFlag)
    If obj Is Nothing Then
      done = True
    Else
      endDate = obj.endDate
      objCol.Add(obj)
    End If
    index += 1
  End While
```

```
    If objCol.Count > 0 Then
      Return TimeManagerWeb.SaveHourArrayList(CurrentUser.userId, _
        StartDate, endDate, objCol.ToArray)
    Else
      Return Not ErrorFlag
    End If

End Function
```

The meat of the code uses a While loop to move through the rows in the workbook looking for data. As the loop moves through each row, it calls the GetHoursFromWorksheet method (shown in the next section) to read the time data stored in the current row (as specified by the index parameter). So long as data is found, the loop will continue to work its way down the workbook's rows building the objCol array. This array stores Hours objects (defined in the TimeManagerWeb web service), which contain the information that was entered in each worksheet row.

■ **Note** The index variable's initial value is set to 4 because row 4 is the first data row in our template. If your template's data rows start on a different row number, be sure to change this value accordingly.

The function passes the objCol array (assuming it contains data) to the SaveHourArrayList method provided by the TimeManagerWeb web service. The function's returned value is a Boolean signifying whether or not the data was successfully inserted into the solution database. Figure 7-19 illustrates how this data is stored in the tblHours table of the Time Manager database.

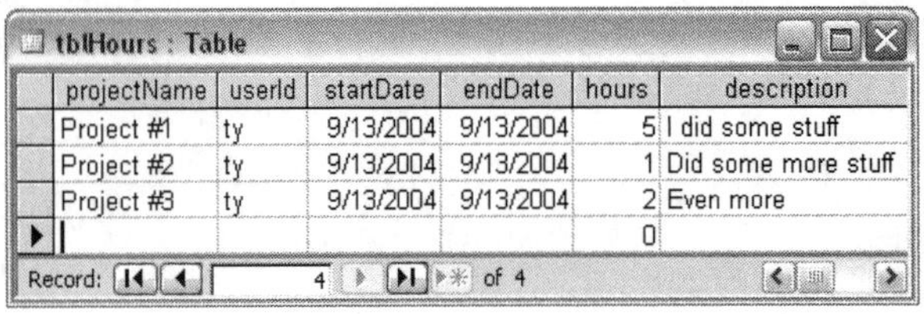

projectName	userId	startDate	endDate	hours	description
Project #1	ty	9/13/2004	9/13/2004	5	I did some stuff
Project #2	ty	9/13/2004	9/13/2004	1	Did some more stuff
Project #3	ty	9/13/2004	9/13/2004	2	Even more
				0	

Figure 7-19. *Time records saved to the solution database*

GetHoursFromWorksheet

GetHoursFromWorksheet extracts the worksheet's data and builds an Hours object, which it returns as the value of the function.

```
Public Function GetHoursFromWorksheet(ByVal index As Integer, _
  ByVal StartDate As DateTime, ByRef ErrorFlag As Boolean) _
   As TMW.tmHours
```

```
    Dim hoursObj As New TMW.tmHours
    Dim ws As Excel.Worksheet = ThisWorkbook.Worksheets.Item(1)

    hoursObj.userId = CurrentUser.userId
    hoursObj.startDate = CDate(Format(StartDate, "MM/dd/yyyy") & _
       " 12:00 AM")
    hoursObj.endDate = CDate(Format(StartDate.AddDays(7), _
       "MM/dd/yyyy") " 11:59:59 PM")

    If CStr(ws.Range("A" & index).Value) = String.Empty Then
       Return Nothing
    Else
       hoursObj.ProjectName = ws.Range("A" & index).Value
    End If

    If CStr(ws.Range("B" & index).Value) = String.Empty Then
       MsgBox("You must enter a description of the work you completed for " & _
          "the project entitled " & hoursObj.ProjectName, _
          MsgBoxStyle.Exclamation Or MsgBoxStyle.OKCancel, "Error")

       ws.Range("B" & index).Select()
       ErrorFlag = True
       Return Nothing
    Else
       hoursObj.description = ws.Range("B" & index).Value
    End If

    If CStr(ws.Range("C" & index).Value) = String.Empty Then
       MsgBox("You must enter the number of hours you worked on the " & _
        "project entitled " & hoursObj.ProjectName, MsgBoxStyle.Exclamation Or _
          MsgBoxStyle.OKCancel, "Error")
       ws.Range("C" & index).Select()
       ErrorFlag = True
       Return Nothing
    Else
       Try
          hoursObj.hours = CSng(ws.Range("C" & index).Value)
       Catch ex As Exception
          MsgBox("You must enter a numeric value for the number of hours " & _
             "you worked on the project entitled " & hoursObj.ProjectName, _
             MsgBoxStyle.Exclamation Or MsgBoxStyle.OKCancel, "Error")
          ws.Range("C" & index).Select()
          ErrorFlag = True
          Return Nothing
       End Try
    End If

    Return hoursObj

End Function
```

The first thing the function does is declare an `Hours` object and begin filling it with data provided when the user logged in (the user, and start and end dates, all captured by the `Time-ManagerLogin` form). The next step is to move through each column in the row where we expect to find time-entry data. The passed `Index` parameter is used to identify the row number of the desired data. As the row is read, each column is validated to ensure it contains data in the expected format. If it does, the value is added to the appropriate property in the `hoursObj` variable. Eventually, the function returns the `hoursObj` object filled with all the data needed to create a new time record in the solution database.

If any invalid data exists or a column lacks the required values, the function will return Nothing as its value, and processing will return to `SaveContentsToWeb`.

The TimeManagerLogin.vb Form

Whenever the Time-Manager Entry application is started, it needs to know who is going to be entering data, and it needs to verify their credentials before they use the system. Users enter their username and password in the `TimeManagerLogin.vb`.

The login form's purpose is simply to capture the user's login information. It does not actually perform any login actions but instead passes the entered username and password values to the procedure that instantiated it as an object. In this application, the calling method instantiating the login form is `ThisWorkbook.DoLogin`.

Designing the Form

Add a new Windows form to the Time-Manager Entry project and name it **TimeManager-Login.vb**. Add the controls listed in Table 7-4 so that the form's layout matches the completed form shown in Figure 7-20.

Table 7-4. *Controls in the Time-Manager Entry* `TimeManagerLogin.vb` *Form*

Control	Name	Text	BackColor
Label	lblInfo	Please enter your username and password to log in to the Timesheet System.	White
Textbox	txtUserName		
Label	lblUserName	Username	
Textbox	txtPassword		
Label	lblPassword	Password	
Button	cmdLogin	&Login	
Button	cmdCancel	&Cancel	

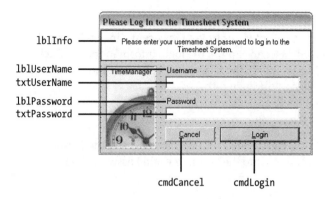

lblInfo

lblUserName
txtUserName

lblPassword
txtPassword

cmdCancel   cmdLogin

Figure 7-20. *Creating the* TimeManagerLogin *form*

Variable Declarations

With the form designed, we are ready to begin adding the code. Open the form's code window and add the following line to Declarations section:

```
Public Cancelled As Boolean = False
```

This line creates a Boolean object that will allow us to specify whether or not the login process was canceled by the user.

Property Procedures

Two read-only properties are needed to return the values of the text stored in the username and password Textbox controls: UserID and Password.

UserID

UserID is a read-only property that returns the text entered in the txtUserName text box.

```
Public ReadOnly Property userId() As String
    Get
        Return Me.txtUsername.Text
    End Get
End Property
```

password

password is a read-only property that returns the text entered in the txtPassword text box.

```
Public ReadOnly Property password() As String
    Get
        Return Me.txtPassword.Text
    End Get
End Property
```

Event Methods

The login form only needs to respond to the Button control's Click event. Since this form does not contain any business logic and is only used to capture the login information, the Click event code is very simple. All we want to do is hide the form so the calling methods can get on with what they were doing before displaying the login form.

cmdLogin_Click

When the user clicks the Login button, the form does a rudimentary check of the TextBox controls to ensure that something was entered into the Username and Password fields for the DoLogin method to process.

```
Private Sub cmdLogin_Click(ByVal sender As System.Object, _
    ByVal e As System.EventArgs) Handles cmdLogin.Click
    If Len(Me.txtUsername.Text) And Len(Me.txtPassword.Text) Then
      Me.Hide()
    Else
      MsgBox("Please enter a username and password.", MsgBoxStyle.Exclamation, _
        "Invalid Login")
    End If
  End Sub
```

With some sleight of hand, the form disappears and the user believes the login form is doing its thing (though it has really passed the information on to DoLogin).

cmdCancel_Click

If the user clicks the Cancel button, the Cancelled property is set to True to notify the calling class that the login was cancelled.

```
Private Sub cmdCancel_Click(ByVal sender As System.Object, _
  ByVal e As System.EventArgs) Handles cmdCancel.Click
  Cancelled = True
  Me.Hide()
End Sub
```

The SaveDialog.vb Form

The data-saving workflow for the Time-Manager Entry workbook is very different from the typical save routine you might expect within Office. The main difference is that we don't necessarily want to save the file to the hard drive—the data contained in the workbook should be posted to the solution's database.

The SaveDialog form bypasses the default save method provided by Excel and presents the user with a custom set of options relevant to the time-entry process.

Designing the Form

Create the SaveDialog form by adding a new Windows form to the Time-Manager Entry project and naming it **SaveDialog.vb**. Add the controls listed in Table 7-5. Figure 7-21 shows the
completed form.

Table 7-5. *Controls in the Time-Manager Entry* SaveDialog.vb *Form*

Control	Name	Text	BackColor
Label	lblInfo	Please indicate below whether or not you would like to upload this information to the Timesheet System. You must specify a "Monday" for the week start.	White
CheckBox	chkUpload	Upload Hours to Timesheet System	
Label	lblDate	Week Start (Must Be a Monday)	
DateTimePicker	dpStartDate		
CheckBox	chkClearContents	Clear Project Contents After Saving	
GroupBox	gboxSaveInfo		
Button	cmdOK	&OK	
Button	cmdCancel	&Cancel	

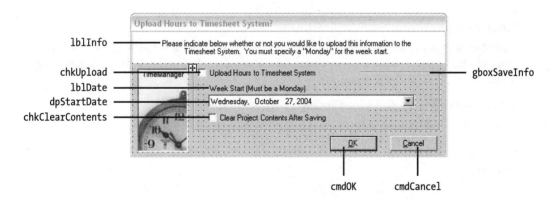

Figure 7-21. *Creating the* SaveDialog *form*

Property Procedures

Now that the interface exists, we're ready to add the code. We'll start by building the property procedures.

Like the login form, SaveDialog is controlled by the OfficeCodeBehind class contained within ThisWorkbook.vb. SaveDialog is simply a class with a visual element used to interface with the user and allow them to make some decisions.

StartDay

StartDay is a read-only property that returns the date value specified by the user in dpStart-Date. The value is used to specify the work week of the time entry items stored in the worksheet.

```
Public ReadOnly Property StartDay() As Date
  Get
    Return Me.dpStartDate.Value
  End Get
End Property
```

SaveToWeb

SaveToWeb is a read-only property that returns the value of the chkUpload check box. If enabled, the data in the workbook will be posted to the solution database.

```
Public ReadOnly Property SaveToWeb() As Boolean
  Get
    Return Me.chkUpload.Checked
  End Get
End Property
```

ClearContents

ClearContents is a read-only property specifying whether or not the user would like to clear the contents of the workbook after posting the data to the solution database. This value is read from the chkClearContents check box.

```
Public ReadOnly Property ClearContents() As Boolean
  Get
    Return Me.chkClearContents.Checked
  End Get
End Property
```

Event Methods

The SaveDialog form requires a little setup before presenting it to the user, and this is done by the SaveDialog_Load method.

In addition, once the form is completed, a bit of logic is used to make the form interactive and to ensure that the data meets the requirements of the business rules. For example, time data is accumulated on a weekly basis and is not split out according to the day an employee completed a task. All time entries must be dated using the date of the Monday to identify the work week. The dpStartDate_Validating event method ensures the specified start date is in fact a Monday. If not, it alerts the user and cancels the validating process. The chkUpload_Checked-Changed event method enables and disables the dpStartDate and chkClearContents controls depending on the value of the upload checkbox.

SaveDialog_Load

Before the SaveDialog form is displayed to the user, the enabling/disabling controls are set and the DateTimePicker value is set to the closest Monday prior to the current date (or if the current date is Monday, we just move on).

```
Private Sub SaveDialog_Load(ByVal sender As System.Object, _
  ByVal e As System.EventArgs) Handles MyBase.Load

  chkUpload_CheckedChanged(Nothing, Nothing)
  Me.dpStartDate.Value = Now()
  While dpStartDate.Value.DayOfWeek <> DayOfWeek.Monday
    dpStartDate.Value = dpStartDate.Value.AddDays(-1)
  End While
End Sub
```

To enable and disable the dpStartDate and chkClearContents controls, the chk-Upload_CheckedChanged event method sets both controls' Enabled properties to the value of the chkUpload check box's Checked property. If the check box is checked, the controls are enabled. Since dpStartDate and chkClearContents are relevant only when chkUpload is enabled, setting the value of their Enabled property to equal the value of chkUpload.Checked ensures they are only enabled when chkUpload is checked.

To set the DateTimePicker to the closest Monday, it is first set to the current date and then it is tested to see if that value is a Monday. If it is, nothing else happens. If not, we use a loop to move backwards, one day at a time, until a Monday is encountered. The first Monday found becomes the value of the DateTimePicker control.

dpStartDate_Validating

The business rules for the posting of time-entry data require that the starting date for the records be a Monday. Therefore it makes sense to use the Validating event to verify that the chosen date in dpStartDate is indeed a Monday.

```
Private Sub dpStartDate_Validating(ByVal sender As Object, _
  ByVal e As System.ComponentModel.CancelEventArgs) _
  Handles dpStartDate.Validating

  If Not Me.dpStartDate.Value.DayOfWeek = DayOfWeek.Monday Then
    MsgBox("You must specify a Monday as the start of the week.", _
      MsgBoxStyle.Exclamation, "Wrong Day of Week")
    e.Cancel = True
  End If

End Sub
```

Nothing happens so long as the chosen value is a Monday. However, if the user failed to choose a Monday, they are informed and given another chance.

chkUpload_CheckedChanged

Depending on whether or not the chkUpload check box is enabled, we need to enable or disable other controls on the form. The quick, easy, and clean way to make this happen is to base the Enabled property value of the dependant controls (dpStartDate and chkClearContents) on the value of chkUpload's Enabled property.

```
Private Sub chkUpload_CheckedChanged(ByVal sender As System.Object, _
    ByVal e As System.EventArgs) Handles chkUpload.CheckedChanged

    Me.dpStartDate.Enabled = chkUpload.Checked
    Me.chkClearContents.Enabled = chkUpload.Checked
End Sub
```

This way, anytime the chkUpload check box is enabled, the dpStartDate and chkClear-Contents check boxes are enabled as well.

Building the Time-Manager Reporter Application

The Time-Manager Reporter is management's component of the Timesheet System. It too is an Excel workbook, but instead of allowing users to input data, the Time-Manager Reporter displays time-entry data for a given user and date range so that Bravo Corp managers can manage their labor requirements.

The Time-Manager Reporter makes use of the TimeManagerWeb web service for retrieving data. It contains three classes:

- ThisWorkbook.vb: This file contains the OfficeCodeBehind class associated with the targeted Excel workbook. It is created automatically by Visual Studio when the project is set up, and it contains the code for responding to workbook events. In addition, it includes the core business logic of the application. We will see how to reference controls placed on an Excel worksheet in code and manipulate them by filling them with data and reading their properties.

- TimeManagerLogin.vb: This is the user login form. It is identical to the form discussed in the "Building the Time-Manager Entry Application" section earlier in the chapter. It is included here for completeness of this application's discussion.

These three objects work together to access submitted time-entry data and then build an Excel report that presents the data to the user—Figure 7-22 illustrates the interaction of the three objects. Just like with TimeManagerEntry.xls, Excel serves as the user interface. Once the user enters their desired report parameters (start and end dates) Time-Manager Reporter accesses the TimeManagerWeb methods and pulls in the data.

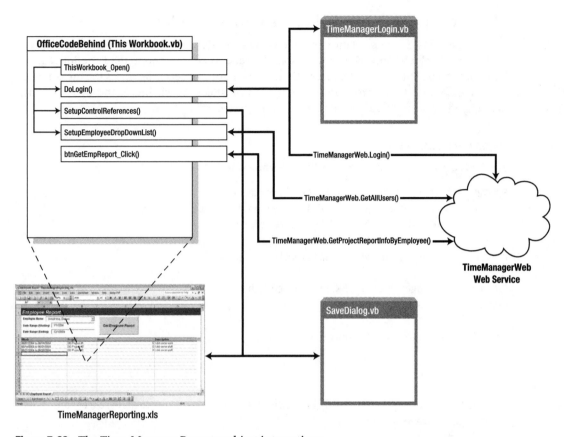

Figure 7-22. *The Time-Manager Reporter object interactions*

To get started, add a new VSTO Excel Workbook project to the current solution, name it **TimeManagerReporter**, and we are off and running.

The app.config File

The app.config file contains application settings utilized by the Time-Manager Reporter VSTO assembly. It contains a single section labeled AppSettings that contains the application keys required by the TimeManagerReporter.xls file.

```
<appSettings>
  <add key="TimeManagerReporting.localhost.TimeManagerWeb"
    value="http://localhost/TimeManagerWeb/TimeManagerWeb.asmx"/>
  <add key="TimeManagerReporting.TMW.TimeManagerWeb"
    value="http://localhost/TimeManagerWeb/TimeManagerWeb.asmx"/>
</appSettings>
```

The key settings specified in the appSettings section identify the location of the Time-ManagerWeb web service we created earlier.

The OfficeCodeBehind Class (ThisWorkbook.vb)

As usual, this class is where all the custom business logic for the targeted workbook is placed. Again, there is a lot of similarity between this class and its counterpart in the Time-Manager Entry workbook. The main difference with this version of OfficeCodeBehind is the inclusion of code that manipulates controls embedded in the worksheet. We will breeze through this code, focusing on code where the two implementations differ.

Variable Declarations

The OfficeCodeBehind class declares the following variables:

```
Friend WithEvents ThisWorkbook As Excel.Workbook
Friend WithEvents ThisApplication As Excel.Application
Private comboEmployeeNames As MSForms.ComboBox
Private txtDateRangeStart As MSForms.TextBox
Private txtDateRangeEnd As MSForms.TextBox

Private TimeManager As New TMW.TimeManagerWeb
Private UserArray() As TMW.tmUser

Private CurrentUser As TMW.tmUser
```

Methods

The ThisWorkbook class contains three methods: DoLogin, SetupControlReferences, and SetupEmployeeDropDownList.

DoLogin

This Time-Manager Reporter workbook should be accessed by administration-level users only. To ensure this level of access, the DoLogin method checks the value of the user account's admin property and closes the workbook if the user lacks the required permissions.

```
Public Sub DoLogin()
  Dim loginForm As New TimeManagerLogin

  loginForm.ShowDialog()

  If loginForm.Cancelled = True Then
    ThisWorkbook.Close()
  Else
    CurrentUser = TimeManager.Login(loginForm.userId, loginForm.password)
    If CurrentUser Is Nothing Then
      MsgBox("The credential you supplied were invalid.  Please try again")
      loginForm = Nothing
      DoLogin()
    Else
```

```
      If Not CurrentUser.admin Then
        MsgBox("You are not authorized to use this reporting tool.", _
          MsgBoxStyle.Exclamation, "Unauthorized")
        ThisWorkbook.Close()
      End If
    End If
  End If

End Sub
```

SetupControlReferences

The Time-Manager Reporter workbook contains four controls: a CommandButton, a ComboBox, and two TextBox controls. In order for VB .NET to respond to events provided by these controls (via VSTO), variables must be created to reference each one separately.

```
Public Sub SetupControlReferences()
  btnGetEmpReport = CType(Me.FindControl("btnGetEmpReport"), _
    MSForms.CommandButton)
  comboEmployeeNames = CType(Me.FindControl("comboEmployeeNames"), _
    MSForms.ComboBox)
  txtDateRangeStart = CType(Me.FindControl("txtDateRangeStart"), _
    MSForms.TextBox)
  txtDateRangeEnd = CType(Me.FindControl("txtDateRangeEnd"), _
    MSForms.TextBox)
End Sub
```

The FindControl method (one of the Excel workbook's methods) finds each control residing in the workbook using the provided name.

SetupEmployeeDropDownList

Once all the controls are properly referenced in code, we fill the Employees drop-down list (comboEmployeeNames) with data.

```
Public Sub SetupEmployeeDropDownList()
  UserArray = TimeManager.GetAllUsers()

  If Not UserArray Is Nothing Then
    comboEmployeeNames.Clear()
    For Each UserObj As TMW.tmUser In UserArray
      comboEmployeeNames.AddItem(UserObj.nameLast & ", " _
    & UserObj.nameFirst)
    Next
  End If

End Sub
```

The Time Manager web service provides a listing of all the current users. Then the procedure checks whether there is any data within the UserArray object. If data exists, the names from each user in the array are added to the Employee ComboBox.

Event Methods

The Time-Manager Reporter utilizes two workbook events: ThisWorkbook_Open and btnGetEmpReport_Click.

ThisWorkbook_Open

ThisWorkbook_Open sets up the Time-Manager Reporter workbook by calling the appropriate custom methods created earlier.

```
Private Sub ThisWorkbook_Open() Handles ThisWorkbook.Open
  DoLogin()
  CreateSettingsMenuItem()
  SetupControlReferences()
  SetupEmployeeDropDownList()
End Sub
```

btnGetEmpReport_Click

The Time-Manager Reporter workbook is a simple interface with only four controls, and only one of the four has any code behind it—the CommandButton control. When clicked by the user, this button makes a call to the Time Manager web service, gives it the data entered by the user, and then waits to receive any results from the web service's GetProjectReportInfoByEmployee method.

```
Private Sub btnGetEmpReport_Click() Handles btnGetEmpReport.Click
  Dim startDate As Date = Nothing
  Dim endDate As Date = Nothing

  If Me.txtDateRangeStart.Text <> "" Then
    If Not IsDate(Me.txtDateRangeStart.Text) Then
      MsgBox("You must specify a valid date for the starting date.")
      Exit Sub
    Else
      startDate = CDate(Me.txtDateRangeStart.Text)
    End If
  End If

  If Me.txtDateRangeEnd.Text <> "" Then
    If Not IsDate(Me.txtDateRangeEnd.Text) Then
      MsgBox("You must specify a valid date for the ending date.")
      Exit Sub
    Else
      endDate = CDate(Me.txtDateRangeEnd.Text)
    End If
```

```
   End If

   Dim HourArray() As TMW.tmHours =
     TimeManager.GetProjectReportInfoByEmployee _
     (UserArray(Me.comboEmployeeNames.ListIndex).userId, _
       startDate, endDate)

   Dim WS As Excel.Worksheet = ThisWorkbook.Worksheets(1)
   WS.Range("A4", "E2048").Clear()

   If Not HourArray Is Nothing Then
     For index As Integer = 4 To 4 + HourArray.Length - 1
       WS.Range("A" & index).Value = _
         Format(HourArray(index - 4).startDate, "MM/dd/yyyy") & _
         " to " & Format(HourArray(index - 4).endDate, "MM/dd/yyyy")
       WS.Range("B" & index).Value = HourArray(index - 4).ProjectName
       WS.Range("C" & index).Value = HourArray(index - 4).hours
       WS.Range("D" & index).Value = HourArray(index - 4).description
     Next
   End If
End Sub
```

Before the web service is called, it makes sense to check that the necessary data exists. This is exactly what goes on here:

```
If Me.txtDateRangeStart.Text <> "" Then
  If Not IsDate(Me.txtDateRangeStart.Text) Then
    MsgBox("You must specify a valid date for the starting date.")
    Exit Sub
  Else
    startDate = CDate(Me.txtDateRangeStart.Text)
  End If
End If

If Me.txtDateRangeEnd.Text <> "" Then
  If Not IsDate(Me.txtDateRangeEnd.Text) Then
    MsgBox("You must specify a valid date for the ending date.")
    Exit Sub
  Else
    endDate = CDate(Me.txtDateRangeEnd.Text)
  End If
End If
```

If the required data is present and accounted for, the web service can be called successfully:

```
Dim HourArray() As TMW.tmHours =
  TimeManager.GetProjectReportInfoByEmployee _
  (UserArray(Me.comboEmployeeNames.ListIndex).userId, _
    startDate, endDate)
```

After the report data arrives, the Time-Manager Reporter workbook must be cleared out (just in case data already exists on the worksheet) to prepare it for the new data rows:

```
Dim WS As Excel.Worksheet = ThisWorkbook.Worksheets(1)
WS.Range("A4", "E2048").Clear()
```

Now that everything is all clean, we can start inserting data into the worksheet:

```
If Not HourArray Is Nothing Then
  For index As Integer = 4 To 4 + HourArray.Length - 1
    WS.Range("A" & index).Value = _
      Format(HourArray(index - 4).startDate, "MM/dd/yyyy") & _
      " to " & Format(HourArray(index - 4).endDate, "MM/dd/yyyy")
    WS.Range("B" & index).Value = HourArray(index - 4).ProjectName
    WS.Range("C" & index).Value = HourArray(index - 4).hours
    WS.Range("D" & index).Value = HourArray(index - 4).description
  Next
End If
```

We use an index loop to move through each object stored in the array. The initial size of the array is set to 4 (the initial data row) plus the Length of the array (less one, because the array is zero-based).

To wrap everything up, we move through each column in the row and insert the appropriate data for each. Once this has run, the Time-Manager Reporter workbook should look like the one shown earlier in Figure 7-3.

The TimeManagerLogin.vb Form

This TimeManagerLogin form is an exact copy of the similarly named form in the Time-Manager Entry application. The form is used to capture a user's login credentials (username and password). The full discussion of this form can be found in the "Building the Time-Manager Entry Application" section. For the sake of completeness, a breakdown of the form's design and code is included here.

Designing the Form

Add a new Windows form to the Time-Manager Reporter project and name it **TimeManager-Login.vb**. Add the controls listed in Table 7-6 so that the form layout resembles Figure 7-21.

Table 7-6. *Controls in the Time-Manager Reporter* TimeManagerLogin.vb *Form*

Control	Name	Text	BackColor
Label	lblInfo	Please enter your username and password to login to the Time Management entry document.	White
Textbox	txtUserName		

Table 7-6. *continued*

Control	Name	Text	BackColor
Label	lblUserName	Username	
Textbox	txtPassword		
Label	lblPassword	Password	
Button	cmdLogin	&Login	
Button	cmdCancel	&Cancel	

Variable Declarations

The class declares one variable:

```
Public Cancelled As Boolean = False
```

Property Procedures

The code in this TimeManagerLogin form is an exact copy of the code in the similarly named form in the Time-Manager Entry application. For an explanation of this code see the discussion of the TimeManagerLogin.vb form in the "Building the Time-Manager Entry Application" section earlier in the chapter.

UserID

```
Public ReadOnly Property userId() As String
  Get
    Return Me.txtUsername.Text
  End Get
End Property
```

Password

```
Public ReadOnly Property password() As String
  Get
    Return Me.txtPassword.Text
  End Get
End Property
```

Event Methods

As mentioned previously, this code is explained in the discussion of the TimeManagerLogin.vb form in the "Building the Time-Manager Entry Application" section earlier in the chapter.

cmdLogin_Click

```
Private Sub cmdLogin_Click(ByVal sender As System.Object, _
  ByVal e As System.EventArgs) Handles cmdLogin.Click
  Me.Hide()
End Sub
```

cmdCancel_Click

```
Private Sub cmdCancel_Click(ByVal sender As System.Object, _
  ByVal e As System.EventArgs) Handles cmdCancel.Click

  Cancelled = True
  Me.Hide()
End Sub
```

Summary

Visual Studio Tools for Office brings the powerful capabilities of the .NET Framework and Visual Studio .NET to the Office platform. In this chapter you learned about one of the largest benefits of VSTO, which is the ability to attach VB .NET code behind an Excel or Word document and automatically deploy new versions to the user's system. Utilizing VSTO, this chapter demonstrated how to build a VSTO solution incorporating Excel and web services (not to mention an Access database).

CHAPTER 8

The Account Details Smart Tag

Putting Backend Customer Data at the User's Fingertips with Smart Tags and the Microsoft Information Bridge Framework

This chapter shows you how to build a custom smart tag that recognizes specific terms within Microsoft Office documents (Work, Excel, PowerPoint, Access, and Outlook) and permits actions related to the particular term. The Account Details smart tag we'll build in this chapter recognizes customer names and allows the user to retrieve related information from a database (address, phone, fax, contact name, etc.) and view it in the Word task pane.

Smart tags have been part of Microsoft Office since Office XP (or Office 10), and they may be the most underrated development feature on the Office platform. Smart tags execute inside Office and have been largely a desktop, or personal, productivity tool. Extending a smart tag's reach into enterprise applications used to involve writing code to interface with these systems, but with the release of the Information Bridge Framework (IBF), Microsoft has provided a set of tools developers can use to connect Office with an organization's main business applications.

Although most of the technology behind IBF is not new, the initial release of IBF (in June 2004) marked Microsoft's desire to elevate Microsoft Office applications (primarily Word and Excel) into smart client applications that increase access to, and the availability of, business application data from within Office.

This chapter shows how to build a smart tag that calls a method available from a preexisting IBF system. These are the key technologies involved:

- **Information Bridge Framework**: We will look at what the IBF is and how it can be used to build applications that connect a business's disparate data systems and present the data within Office. You will gain an understanding of how XML, web services, and user controls are used to create IBF systems.

- **Smart tags**: You will learn how to use VB .NET and XML to build a smart tag that invokes an IBF method to retrieve and display customer information inside Word.

■**Note** Smart client applications bridge the gap between feature-rich, fat-client applications, like Microsoft Outlook, and less sophisticated but highly manageable browser-based applications, like Hotmail, by incorporating the strengths of each. Some key aspects that qualify an application as a smart client are centralized deployment from a server, support for working offline, integration with web services, and utilization of local processing power and storage. Lots of information exists on this topic, and you can learn more by visiting http://msdn.microsoft.com/smartclient/understanding/.

Information Bridge Framework

This chapter utilizes a ready-made Information Bridge Framework (IBF) example system provided by Microsoft. This example system gives us a working IBF deployment without having to go through the trouble of installing and configuring IBF ourselves. This system allows us to focus on building a smart tag that invokes an available IBF web service method.

IBF combines XML, web services, smart documents, and smart tags in a framework that allows developers to build document-based solutions that place business data (stored in back-end systems) at the fingertips of business users. In addition, the information presented to the user is completely relevant to the current context within the active document. IBF does this by combining context-sensitive technologies, like smart tags and smart documents, with web services and XML.

IBF is not for the average Office developer with VBA skills and a limited knowledge of technologies extending beyond Office and the desktop. There are a lot of moving parts involved, spread across multiple logical tiers, and they work together to combine data stored in various transactional data systems. For example, an IBF solution can present customer information stored in accounting, sales, CRM, and other systems in a single view for the user. This means that a customer's complete financial history could be seen while also viewing in-process sales and customer service issues. A customer service representative can improve the quality of their responses to client complaints simply by being able to see a complete picture of the customer within Microsoft Outlook.

IBF solutions are not limited to read-only functionality. IBF relies on web services to expose data and actions stored in the organization's business applications. This includes the ability to both read data and write data to business applications. In addition, IBF can utilize web services to execute business logic within these applications. Therefore, as much or as little data and business logic stored in these systems can be exposed to IBF. It is entirely up to the developers of the solution to determine what should and should not be exposed.

From a development perspective, an IBF solution consists of four key components: web services, metadata, user interface controls, and smart tags (see Figure 8-1). These four components sit on top of a business's application layer, which provides the data and application methods that are exposed by an IBF system. This list is not exhaustive, though, as IBF is a complex development framework, and it allows for a high degree of customization. A developer can control as much or as little as they see fit in order to meet the requirements of their solution. But at a base level, a developer will need to create these four components at a minimum.

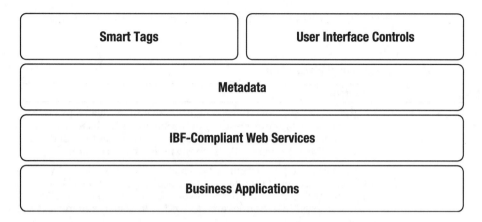

Figure 8-1. *The main IBF components requiring development*

■**Note** IBF is extremely new and involves a significant learning curve. To find out more about IBF, I recommend reading about IBF on MSDN, http://msdn.microsoft.com/office/understanding/ibframework/default.aspx, and on OfficeZealot.com, http://www.officezealot.com/ibframework/.

IBF Web Services

Web services is the layer immediately above an organization's line-of-business applications—the backend data systems used by business users to enter and retrieve transactional data (via reports or external programs). The web services are written to expose data or actions for use in the solution.

Web services intended for use within an IBF solution must conform to the following guidelines:

- The web service must return XML data that directly represents either a data object or action stored within a business application.

- The web service must expose metadata in an XML format compliant with the IBF XML metadata schema.

Other than these two requirements, an IBF-enabled web service is like any other web service, and the development process is no different.

IBF Metadata

The IBF metadata is an XML file describing the objects made available within the IBF solution. The metadata describes the types of data and methods contained within business applications and exposed by IBF. Table 8-1 summarizes the IBF objects that are included in an IBF metadata file.

Table 8-1. *IBF Objects Described by the Metadata*

Object Name	Description
Metadata scope	A grouping of defined operations, schemas, and entities related to a web service. This is the top-level grouping of the metadata file. Its function is similar to a namespace in .NET. It is used to define IBF solutions and can be used to resolve naming conflicts among multiple IBF solutions.
Entity	A conceptual data type that represents a real data object provided by a business application. Examples of an entity include an order, client, package, etc. Web services are used to expose business application data and function as entities. Entities are used by IBF to display and interact with data.
View	A subsection of data and actions related to an entity. Views define what a user can see and do, given a defined entity. Examples include order history, account balances, shipment tracking, etc.
Action	A series of sequential operations ending with a UI operation. Actions define the operations required to complete a specific task, such as updating client information or retrieving client information.
Operation	A single method for retrieving, updating, or displaying data. Client operations are used to display data, and they execute on the user's desktop. Service operations retrieve or update data using methods exposed by web services, which provide the logic for retrieving and updating information in business applications.
Reference	A link to a web service operation. IBF uses references to create Simple Object Access Protocol (SOAP) calls that invoke web services. References serve to identify entities or lists of entities.
Schema	An XML schema file that defines the shape of data within IBF operations.

The metadata file describes all objects within the IBF solution and makes those objects known to the objects on the client system. In addition, the metadata resides on the client system and receives regular updates by the server-side Metadata Service. The metadata refresh occurs at regular intervals or whenever the required metadata is missing on the client system.

IBF User Interface Controls

The IBF user interface offers a window container that can be utilized by developers to host their custom user interfaces, which are built to display and interact with IBF-exposed business application data and functions. The window container is called a *region*, and it and exposes the IRegion interface. Creating a custom IBF user control with the .NET Framework is no different than building any other user control, except for the required implementation of the IRegion interface.

User controls fit nicely inside the Document Actions portion of the host application's task pane and allow the user to view and interact with the presented data. In the case of Microsoft Outlook, which lacks a task pane, IBF presents a floating window that closely resembles the task panes found in Word and Excel (see Figure 8-2).

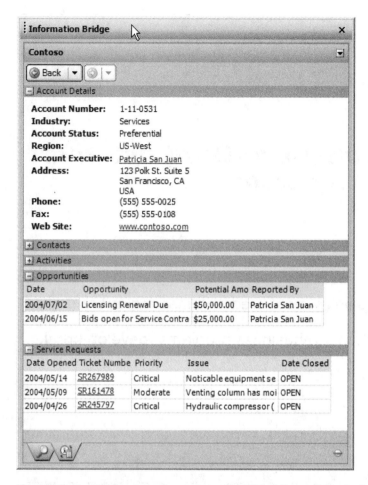

Figure 8-2. *An IBF user interface presented within Microsoft Outlook*

IBF-Enabled Smart Tags

Smart tags are one of two possible IBF entry points (the other entry point is a smart document). Smart tags link custom actions to recognized text inside Word, Excel, PowerPoint, Access, Outlook (but only if Word is set as the email editor), and Internet Explorer. Smart tags provide these actions within an open document by continually searching the document for text patterns it recognizes as having defined smart tag actions.

For example, a smart tag could be built in such a way that it recognizes stock-ticker symbols entered in a Word document. Anytime the smart tag recognizes a stock symbol, the stock symbol is underlined with a squiggly line to identify it as a recognized term. If the user desires, they can hover the cursor over the term, and a smart tag menu will display any actions available for the recognized term (see Figure 8-3). The returned data is displayed in the task pane so that users can access it without leaving the document they are working in.

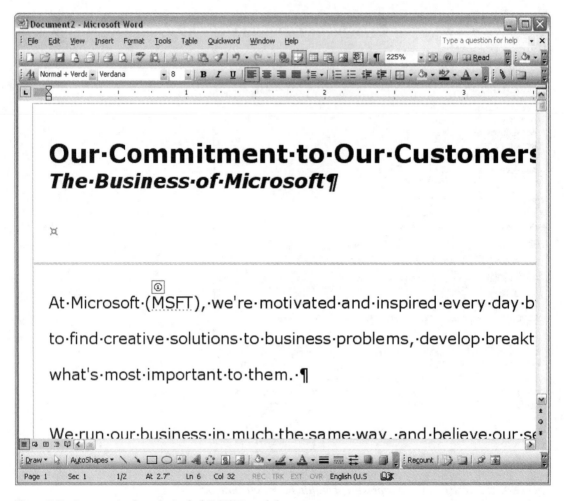

Figure 8-3. *A recognized stock symbol (MSFT) and the smart tag menu*

From a development standpoint, a smart tag is a DLL file implementing the ISmartTag-Recognizer and ISmartTagAction interfaces. The ISmartTagRecognizer interface contains the properties and methods required to create a smart tag recognizer class that recognizes smart tag data (like a stock symbol or customer name) inside a document's contents. Office 2003 introduced two additional interfaces, ISmartTagRecognizer2 and ISmartTagAction2 that include additional methods and properties to extend smart tag functionality. Both of the recognizer interfaces are documented in Table 8-2.

Table 8-2. *The* ISmartTagRecognizer *and* ISmartTagRecognizer2 *Interfaces*

Property or Method	Name	Type	Description	Interface
Property	ProgID	String	The unique identifier of the smart tag. This value is stored in the registry and is used by Word to load the smart tag.	ISmartTagRecognizer
Property	Name	String	The user-friendly name of the smart tag.	ISmartTagRecognizer
Property	Desc	String	The description of the smart tag. This is a good place to explain exactly what the smart tag does (in case it's not clear from the Name).	ISmartTagRecognizer
Property	SmartTagCount	Integer	The number of data types the smart tag recognizes. Stock-ticker symbols, customer name, and email address, are all examples of data types. These types are specified in the smart tag with XML tags.	ISmartTagRecognizer
Property	SmartTagDownload	String	The smart tag's URL where the user can download updates to the smart tag. If a URL is specified, the smart tag displays a Check for New Actions button, and when this is clicked by the user, the button will navigate to the specified URL and download any updates to the smart tag.	ISmartTagRecognizer
Property	SmartTagName	String	The unique identifier of each smart tag type included in the smart tag. Each identifier is an XML construct that conforms to the "*namespaceURI#tagname*" format. For example, the stock symbol SmartTagName looks like this: urn:schemas-microsoft-com: moneycentral#stockTickerSymbol.	ISmartTagRecognizer

continues

Table 8-2. *continued*

Property or Method	Name	Type	Description	Interface
Property	PropertyPage	Boolean	A flag that specifies whether or not the smart tag supports property pages in the Smart Tags dialog box (Tools ▶ AutoCorrect Options). Property pages provide a method for customizing what a smart tag recognizes by disabling or enabling features included with a smart tag. If this property is set to True, the Properties button will be enabled.	ISmartTagRecognizer2
Method	Recognize2		The main method of a smart tag. It uses text from the document as a passed string to check for the existence of a recognized term. In Office 2003, this is the method that should be used, instead of Recognize, as it provides more features via more method parameters. This method is where you should place the code to match the passed string with terms.	ISmartTagRecognizer2
Method	Recognize		Recognizes terms within a document. The Recognize2 method should be used instead of this method when implementing the ISmartTagRecognizer2 interface.	ISmartTagRecognizer
Method	SmartTagInitialize		Initializes the objects within the smart tag. This is a good place to configure the smart tag based on the host environment.	ISmartTagRecognizer2
Method	DisplayPropertyPage		Displays the Property dialog box for the smart tag recognizer. This method is called when a user clicks the Properties button in the smart tag's dialog box (Tools ▶ AutoCorrect Options). This is the method where you should place code that gives users a choice in the features provided by the smart tag.	ISmartTagRecognizer2

For `ISmartTagAction` and `ISmartTagAction2` interface documentation, see `http://msdn.microsoft.com/library/en-us/stagsdk/html/stobjISmartTagAction.asp` and `http://msdn.microsoft.com/library/en-us/stagsdk/html/stobjISmartTagAction2.asp`.

For more information regarding smart tag development, read the following article available on MSDN: `http://msdn.microsoft.com/library/en-us/dnsmarttag/html/odc_smarttags.asp`. In addition, Microsoft has made a Smart Tag Software Development Kit available at `http://www.microsoft.com/downloads/details.aspx?familyid=c6189658-d915-4140-908a-9a0114953721&displaylang=en`.

■**Note** The Account Details smart tag we are building in this chapter is a recognizer-only smart tag, so this chapter will focus on this aspect of smart tag development.

Designing the Account Details Smart Tag

To create the Account Details smart tag, we will deploy the Microsoft Information Bridge Framework (IBF) as the basis for a solution that will publish business data for consumption within the Microsoft Office System. By utilizing IBF, the desired data is accessible on the user's desktop via the Office task pane.

From the user's perspective, the workflow will follow these steps:

1. A manager receives an email from a customer complaint (see Figure 8-4).

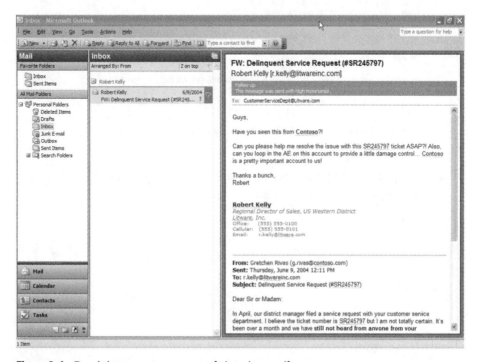

Figure 8-4. *Receiving a customer complaint via email*

2. The manager clicks on the Account Details smart tag and selects the Show Details action to display information from the Customer Relationship Management system (see Figure 8-5).

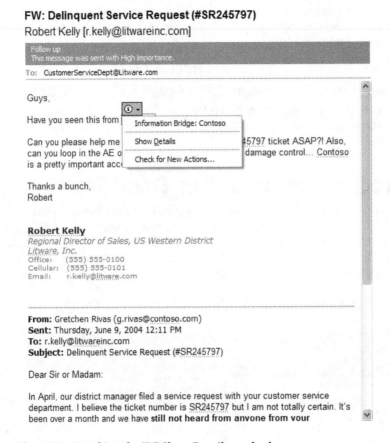

Figure 8-5. *Invoking the IBF Show Details method*

3. The information displays within Office and the manager has no need to open any additional systems (See Figure 8-6).

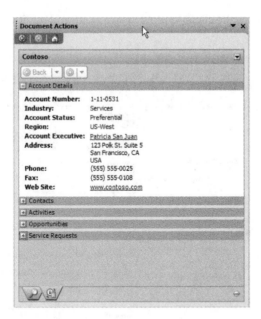

Figure 8-6. *Displaying customer data in the Office task pane*

4. After gaining an understanding of the situation, the manager reassigns the issue to a top-performing representative by executing the required forms from the Office task pane. The manager doesn't need to open the actual business application (in this case, the Customer Relationship Management system) that contains the information, because the Service Request Reassign form submits the data to a web service that updates the record (see Figure 8-7).

Figure 8-7. *Reassigning a service request*

5. Finally, the manager drafts a letter to the client to provide an update and outline the plan for resolution (see Figure 8-8).

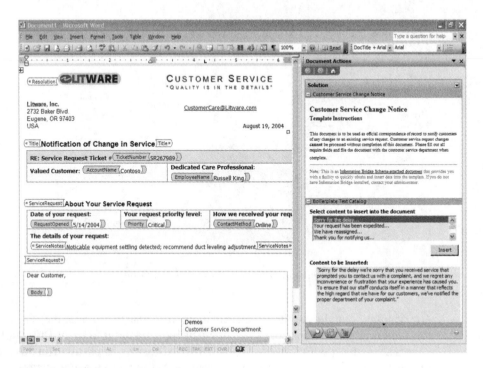

Figure 8-8. *Drafting a response letter*

Although this workflow is relatively simple, don't miss the fact that the user is able to perform all the tasks using various business applications, but they are able to complete the tasks from within an Office application, without needing to leave Office to retrieve and accumulate data from the business applications.

Many of the steps provided in the solution's workflow are taken care of by the Microsoft-provided sample IBF system. This chapter will focus on steps 2–3 of the previous workflow, which involve a smart tag that recognizes a customer name and invokes an IBF method to retrieve and display customer data inside of Word.

From the development perspective, the Account Details smart tag acts as the entry point to an already deployed IBF system (see Figure 8-9):

1. Word loads the smart tag into memory by calling the smart tag's `SmartTagInitialize` method. This method prepares the smart tag for use by loading the list of customer names that are recognized by the smart tag into memory.

2. Anytime a customer name is recognized, the smart tag's `Recognize2` method executes to display the IBF Show Details option in the smart tag menu.

3. When the user clicks the Show Details option, the Account Details smart tag sends XML data to the default smart tag action handler provided by the IBF system. The XML contains entity and view information that tells the IBF system what method to execute.

4. Using the provided entity and view information, the Information Bridge action handler invokes the `AccountDefault` view of the `Account` entity.

5. IBF calls the related web services to retrieve the data and return the requested account information back up the chain until it is displayed in Word's task pane.

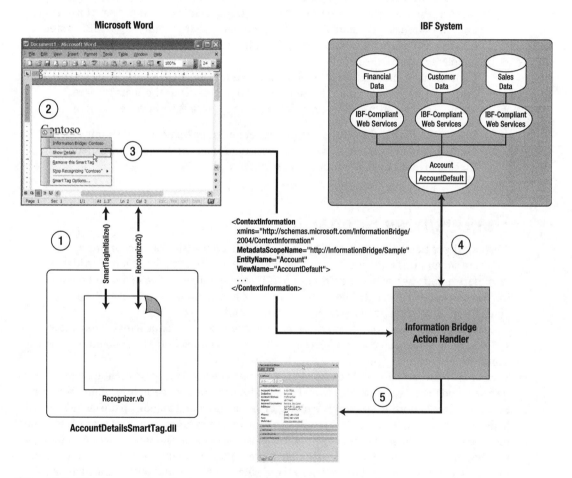

Figure 8-9. *The Account Details smart tag architecture*

The Account Details smart tag is comprised of the following components:

- `Recognizer.vb`: This class implements the `ISmartTagRecognizer` and the `ISmart-TagRecognizer2` interfaces required by an Office 2003 smart tag. We will look at how to use XML to recognize customer names in a Word document. In addition, this class demonstrates how simple it is to create an IBF-enabled smart tag.

- Word: Word acts as the host application for the smart tag. It also serves as the user interface where the smart tag menu and IBF user controls are displayed.

- Information Bridge Action Handler: The Account Details smart tag foregoes implementing the two smart tag action interfaces (`ISmartTagAction` and `ISmartTagAction2`) in favor of utilizing the default smart tag action handler provided by the IBF system. Once a term has been recognized by the smart tag, it utilizes the IBF default action handler to invoke the default IBF `AccountDefault` view. The key to connecting the smart tag recognizer class to the IBF action handler is one line of XML inside the smart tag. The smart tag must include the following XML construct as the `SmartTagName`: `http://schemas.microsoft.com/InformationBridge/2004#reference`.

- IBF System: This is the sample IBF System provided by Microsoft. It contains the IBF methods and objects (such as web services, data, user controls and XML metadata) that are invoked by the Account Details smart tag.

The Business Scenario

The majority of Bravo Corp's enterprise-capable applications (such as accounting applications) are streamlined for use by their target audience with little functionality provided to secondary or tertiary users. For example, an ERP system implements a menu and screen workflow intended to ease the data-entry process of an accounts payable clerk. These types of function-specific applications serve their target audience well.

The problem is that management users often need to access data across all business systems in order to make informed decisions. These users must hop, skip, and jump across a multitude of business applications to aggregate the desired data.

For example, a client might complain about a service failure that wasn't adequately resolved, and the service manager would need to look up the service-failure record from the Service-Failure Reporting system. The manager would also need to look up the client's record in the Accounting, Sales, and CRM systems to gain an understanding of what type of customer the client is. Then the service manager might need to access the Show-Site Service system and reassign the service failure to an appropriate representative. Finally, the manager would need to craft an email to the client to apologize for the inconvenience and outline the plan being implemented to resolve the issue as soon as possible.

The service manager already has each of these applications open on a regular basis and can navigate quickly among them. However, constant movement among applications breaks concentration—users can forget what they are looking for within an application. It also takes time to switch from one application to another, particularly if you have to switch back and forth several times to compare and collect information.

Bravo Corp decided to deploy Microsoft's IBF as the basis for a solution that makes the desired data accessible on the user's desktop via the Office task pane. To invoke the IBF system and the methods it provides, Bravo Corp built a smart tag that recognizes customer names inside Word documents. Once a customer name is recognized, the smart tag displays a menu containing IBF-related commands for displaying customer data within Office. The end result of both the IBF system and the Account Details smart tag is a streamlined process for retrieving customer information from disparate data systems. As a result, the manager has no need to open any additional systems—the data is provided inside the Word user interface.

Setting Up the IBF Sample Solution

The Account Details smart tag utilizes web services, metadata, and controls from an existing IBF solution. Each of these additional components can be built from scratch but Microsoft has made available a complete IBF sample solution, in the form of a Virtual PC image, which provides the entire foundation for this chapter's smart tag.

Note To request a copy of the IBF sample solution's Virtual PC image, send an email request to ibfinqry@microsoft.com.

A Virtual PC image requires Microsoft Virtual PC to run on your system. Virtual PC makes it possible to run other operating systems simultaneously within Windows, and it is a great tool for testing different Windows environments and configurations. If you do not already have a copy of Virtual PC, Microsoft has made a 45-day evaluation version available at http://www.microsoft.com/downloads/details.aspx?FamilyId=4A15008C-3E10-4C54-BCD5-ADC1E780715F&displaylang=en.

The sample solution provides a fully featured base IBF implementation, including a customer service scenario that provides meaningful context to the information and actions presented within the sample.

Once you receive the IBF sample solution's Virtual PC image and have installed Virtual PC, follow these steps to configure it to run on your system:

1. Copy the InfoBridge.vhd file to C:\VPC\Images (or another location of your choosing).

2. Open Virtual PC and start the Virtual Disk Wizard (File ➤ Virtual Disk Wizard). Click Next on the Welcome screen.

3. In the Disk Options window, select the Create a Virtual Disk radio button and click Next.

4. In the Virtual Disk Type window, select the radio button labeled A Virtual Hard Disk. Click Next.

5. In the Virtual Hard Disk Location window, click the Browse button and navigate to the location where you saved InfoBridge.vhd in step 1 and select it. Click Next.

6. In the Virtual Hard Disk Options window, choose the Dynamically Expanding (Recommended) option. Click Next.

7. In the Virtual Hard Disk Size window, accept the value entered in the Virtual Hard Disk Size field. Click Next and then Finish.

8. Once you have returned to the Virtual PC Console, click the Start button to load the InfoBridge.vhd image, and test that it runs correctly.

If the Virtual PC window begins to load Windows, you know you have set the image up correctly. Virtual PC literally runs a separate Windows system on your PC, so working with a virtual Windows system running in Virtual PC works exactly the same as using your real system.

There is a bit of a learning curve in that Virtual PC operates within a window. This is not a big issue, but it does cause you to click more than once in the Virtual PC window when trying to click an icon or the Windows Start button. This need for more than one click is typically caused by Virtual PC not having the focus on the first click—the first click gives Virtual PC the focus, and the second click invokes an action in the virtual Windows system running inside Virtual PC.

■**Tip** Virtual PC does not have a steep learning curve. The Virtual PC help file provides a great overview of the Virtual PC basics. I recommend spending a few minutes in the help file prior to using it if you have never used Virtual PC before.

Creating the CustomerNames XML File

The smart tag relies on the existence of an XML file named CustomerNames.xml. This file contains a short listing of customer names that the Account Details smart tag will recognize. Create a new text file named **CustomerNames.xml** in the Account Details smart tag project's bin folder, and insert the following XML into it:

```
<?xml version="1.0" encoding="UTF-8"?>
<Terms>
  <Account>Contoso</Account>
  <Account>Trey Research</Account>
  <Account>Fabrikam</Account>
</Terms>
```

Creating the Account Details Smart Tag

The Account Details smart tag recognizes client names within a Microsoft Word document and then allows the user to view the recognized client's account details by clicking a menu option provided by the smart tag's Action button (see Figure 8-10).

Figure 8-10. *The Account Details smart tag Action button menu*

The Account Details smart tag consists of a single recognizer-type class that implements all members required by the ISmartTagRecognizer and ISmartTagRecognizer2 interfaces. This class continually scans text within the open Word document looking for customer names. These customer names are loaded into memory when the Account Details smart tag initializes.

Note Although this solution is discussed in the context of a Word document, the smart tag will also work automatically in Excel without any additional effort. This is because smart tags are configured to run across Office. Once a smart tag is installed, any Office application supporting smart tags will automatically load the smart tag when opened.

This solution does not implement its own Actions class to utilize the ISmartTagAction and ISmartTagAction2 interfaces. The reason for this is that IBF provides its own smart tag loader, which attaches a smart tag property bag (a list of name/value pairs) and builds the smart tag Action button and menu.

Tip Although not implemented here, you could easily build you own Actions class by inheriting that implements the ISmartTagAction and ISmartTagAction2 interfaces. This is a desired option if you want to provide more actions than the default IBF action handler provides or if you want to provide additional actions that do not interact with IBF. To learn more about creating an actions class that extends the default action handler provided by IBF, download the IBF Development Guide at: http://www.microsoft.com/downloads/details.aspx?familyid=5ACA5705-4A5C-406B-BAD7-05EBB069B71E&displaylang=en.

Create the smart tag project within Visual Studio by starting a new Visual Basic Class Library project. Name the project **AccountDetails**. Delete the default class (Class1.vb) and add a single class named **Recognizer.vb**.

References

Three references are required for the smart tag project (see Figure 8-11):

```
Microsoft.InformationBridge.Framework.Interfaces
Microsoft.InformationBridge.Framework.UI.Interop
SmartTagLib
```

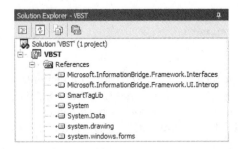

Figure 8-11. *Adding the smart tag project references*

The first two lines refer to two client components of the Information Bridge Framework—the interfaces and the interop assemblies. The last line is a reference to the smart tags 2 type library and interfaces.

Recognizer.vb

The Recognizer class implements the logic that reads text within any Word document and scans for recognized terms. As text is typed into a document, it is scanned by the code within this class to determine whether the text string is a recognized term. If it is, the text is flagged as a "type" of smart tag. The user receives a visual cue of this designation via a squiggly underline beneath the recognized term.

Our solution utilizes an XML file (CustomerNames.xml) containing a static list of recognized terms. These terms are then used to find matches within the current document. Once a match is found, a smart tag displays in the document in the form of a button next to the recognized term. The smart tag knows the relevant IBF namespace, entity, view, and corresponding data needed by IBF to determine what actions to invoke and what data to return and display inside Word's task pane.

Imports Directives

The smart tag Recognizer imports the following namespaces for ease of use within the class:

```
Imports System
Imports System.IO
Imports System.Xml
Imports System.Resources
Imports System.Threading
```

```
Imports System.Reflection
Imports System.Collections
Imports System.Globalization
Imports System.Text.RegularExpressions
Imports Microsoft.Office.Interop.SmartTag
```

Declarations

The class implements the two smart tag recognizer interfaces as follows:

```
Implements ISmartTagRecognizer
Implements ISmartTagRecognizer2
```

Tip After typing the two `Implements` lines, be sure to press the Enter key. Doing so will cause Visual Studio .NET to create stubs for the methods and properties required by each interface inside the Recognizer class. This is a great time-saver and one of my favorite features of Visual Studio .NET.

Next, the class needs a class-level `XMLDocument` variable declaration. This object will store in memory the static list of client names from the `CustomerNames.xml` file (created earlier in chapter). These customer names are the terms the smart tag looks for inside any Word document.

```
Dim _xmlDocTerms As XmlDocument
Protected Const tagNameExternal As String = _
  "http://schemas.microsoft.com/InformationBridge/2004#reference"
```

The last line declares a constant to store the required XML construct that will invoke the IBF default action handler (`tagNameExternal`). This value will be used by the `SmartTagName` property discussed next.

Properties

The Recognizer class implements the properties required by the `ISmartTagRecognizer` and `ISmartTagRecognizer2` interfaces.

Name

The `Name` property simply returns the name of the Account Details smart tag:

```
Public ReadOnly Property Name(ByVal LocaleID As Integer) As String _
  Implements Microsoft.Office.Interop.SmartTag.ISmartTagRecognizer.Name
  Get
    Return "Bravo Corp Account Details Smart Tag"
  End Get
End Property
```

ProgId

ProgId returns the unique programmatic identifier of the smart tag recognizer.

```
Public ReadOnly Property ProgId() As String _
  Implements Microsoft.Office.Interop.SmartTag.ISmartTagRecognizer.ProgId
  Get
    Return "AccountDetails.Recognizer"
  End Get
End Property
```

The value of smart tag ProgID resides in the registry and corresponds to the name of the smart tag assembly ("AccountDetails" for this project). This value is retrieved by Word to load the smart tag.

Desc

The Desc property returns the value of the smart tag's description.

```
Public ReadOnly Property Desc(ByVal LocaleID As Integer) As String _
  Implements Microsoft.Office.Interop.SmartTag.ISmartTagRecognizer.Desc
  Get
    Return "Bravo Corp Account Details Smart Tag"
  End Get
End Property
```

SmartTagCount

The SmartTagCount property specifies the number of smart tag types that are supported by the smart tag recognizer class. Smart tag types are defined by a unique URI and tag name. For example, the Account Details smart tag contains one smart tag type, which is defined by the tagNameExternal constant.

```
Public ReadOnly Property SmartTagCount() As Integer
  Get
    Return 1
  End Get
End Property
```

The smart tag interfaces use the returned value to know how many times to call the SmartTagDownload and SmartTagName properties. Each time these two properties are accessed, the number is incremented, starting with 1, until the number specified as the return value is reached.

SmartTagName

The SmartTagName property returns the name of the smart tag corresponding to the SmartTagID argument.

```
Public ReadOnly Property SmartTagName(ByVal SmartTagID As Integer) As String _
  Implements Microsoft.Office.Interop.SmartTag.ISmartTagRecognizer.SmartTagName
  Get
    If (SmartTagID = 1) Then
      SmartTagName = tagNameExternal
    End If
  End Get
End Property
```

In the case of the Account Details smart tag, a single ID (with a value of 1) is expected, and if it is passed, the function returns the string stored in the tagNameExternal object. The value stored in tagNameExternal invokes the IBF smart tag action handler, which provides the default IBF Show Details action.

SmartTagDownloadURL

The SmartTagDownloadURL property specifies the location of the smart tag actions. If the host application does not already have the actions available on the system, the value returned by this property tells the host where they may be downloaded.

```
Public ReadOnly Property SmartTagDownloadURL(ByVal SmartTagID As Integer) As _
  String Implements _
  Microsoft.Office.Interop.SmartTag.ISmartTagRecognizer.SmartTagDownloadURL
    Get
      Return "http://msdn.microsoft.com/ibframework"
    End Get
End Property
```

In this example, the property returns the URL for IBF on MSDN (http://msdn.microsoft.com/ibframework).

Methods

Although the Recognizer class implements all members required by the ISmartTagRecognizer and ISmartTagRecognizer2 interfaces, only two members require code in this solution: SmartTagInitialize and Recognize2.

SmartTagInitialize

Each time a host application loads a smart tag into its application space, the SmartTagInitialize event fires. This event allows for the placement of any code needed to create the proper environment for the smart tag. In this implementation, the SmartTagInitialize method retrieves the project's file listing the terms to be recognized (CustomerNames.xml in this case) and loads the XML into the class's XMLDocument variable.

```
Public Sub SmartTagInitialize(ByVal ApplicationName As String) _
  Implements
  Microsoft.Office.Interop.SmartTag.ISmartTagRecognizer2.SmartTagInitialize

  Dim sFolder As String = _
    Path.GetDirectoryName([Assembly].GetExecutingAssembly().CodeBase). _
    Replace("file:\", _ "")
  Dim sFile As String = sFolder & "\CustomerNames.xml"

  _xmlDocTerms = New XmlDocument

  Try
    _xmlDocTerms.Load(sFile)
  Catch ex As Exception
    System.Windows.Forms.MessageBox.Show(ex.Message, _
      "Information Bridge Framework Smart Tag")
  End Try

End Sub
```

Recognize2

The Recognize2 method is the main method of the ISmartTagRecognizer2 interface. The host application calls the method anytime it attempts to scan the active document's text for potential smart tag terms. This is the place where passed String objects are matched against values contained in the class's XMLDocument variable. If a match is found, a smart tag property bag attaches to the active document.

■**Note** A smart tag property bag is simply a list of name/value pairs.

```
Public Sub Recognize2(ByVal Text As String, _
  ByVal DataType As Microsoft.Office.Interop.SmartTag.IF_TYPE, _
  ByVal LocaleID As Integer, ByVal RecognizerSite2 As _
  Microsoft.Office.Interop.SmartTag.ISmartTagRecognizerSite2, _
  ByVal ApplicationName As _
  String, ByVal TokenList As _
  Microsoft.Office.Interop.SmartTag.ISmartTagTokenList) _
  Implements Microsoft.Office.Interop.SmartTag. _
  ISmartTagRecognizer2.Recognize2
```

```vb
Dim termItem As String = ""
Dim nd As XmlNode
For Each nd In _xmlDocTerms.SelectNodes("//Account")

  termItem = nd.InnerText
  'Implement a regular expression to determine if a term match occurred
  Dim r As Regex = New Regex(termItem, RegexOptions.IgnoreCase)
  Dim m As Match = r.Match(Text)

  'If a match is found, build a context command
  If m.Success Then

    ''IBF Sample Solution
    '==================
    Dim formatString As String = "<ContextInformation  " & _
      "xmlns=""http://schemas.microsoft.com/InformationBridge" & _
      "/2004/ContextInformation"" " & _
      " MetadataScopeName=""http://InformationBridge/Sample""" & _
      " EntityName=""Account"" ViewName=""AccountDefault""> " & _
      " <Reference> " & _
      " <AccountName xmlns=""urn-SampleSolution-Data"" " & _
      " ID=""{0}"" iwb:MetadataScopeName=" & _
      """http://InformationBridge/Sample"" " & _
      " xmlns:iwb=""http://schemas.microsoft.com/InformationBridge/2004"" " & _
      " iwb:EntityName=""Account"" iwb:ViewName=""AccountDefault"" />" & _
      "</Reference></ContextInformation>"

    'Insert the term into the context string
    Dim context As String = String.Format(formatString, m.Value)

    'Add the context to a property bag
    Dim propBag As ISmartTagProperties = _
      RecognizerSite2.GetNewPropertyBag()
    propBag.Write("data", context)

    'add the smart tag
    RecognizerSite2.CommitSmartTag(tagNameExternal, m.Index + 1, _
      m.Length, propBag)

  End If
Next
End Sub
```

The first step in the method uses a loop to navigate through each value in the Account node of the XMLDocument object:

```
Dim termItem As String = ""
Dim nd As XmlNode
For Each nd In _xmlDocTerms.SelectNodes("//Account")
```

Each node value contained in the Account node is tested against a regular expression to identify strings matching a specified smart tag term:

```
termItem = nd.InnerText
Dim r As Regex = New Regex(termItem, RegexOptions.IgnoreCase)
Dim m As Match = r.Match(Text)
```

If any matches are discovered, the method creates the smart tag menu by first building the XML string required by IBF:

```
'If a match is found, build a context command
If m.Success Then

    ''IBF Sample Solution
  '==================
  Dim formatString As String = "<ContextInformation  " & _
    "xmlns=""http://schemas.microsoft.com/InformationBridge" & _
    "/2004/ContextInformation"" " & _
    " MetadataScopeName=""http://InformationBridge/Sample""" & _
    " EntityName=""Account"" ViewName=""AccountDefault""> " & _
    " <Reference> " & _
    " <AccountName xmlns=""urn-SampleSolution-Data"" " & _
    " ID=""{0}"" iwb:MetadataScopeName=" & _
    """"http://InformationBridge/Sample"" " & _
    " xmlns:iwb=""http://schemas.microsoft.com/InformationBridge/2004"" " & _
    " iwb:EntityName=""Account"" iwb:ViewName=""AccountDefault"" />" & _
    "</Reference></ContextInformation>"
```

This XML string is known as the ContextInformation, and it is passed to the IBF via the Show Details action. It tells IBF which entity and view to invoke. The XML string built by the preceding code looks like this:

```
<ContextInformation
    xmlns="http://schemas.microsoft.com/InformationBridge/2004/ContextInformation"
    MetadataScopeName="http://InformationBridge/Sample"
    EntityName="Account"
    ViewName="AccountDefault">
    <Reference>
        <AccountName
          xmlns="urn-SampleSolution-Data"
          ID="Contoso"
```

```
        iwb:MetadataScopeName="http://InformationBridge/Sample"
        xmlns:iwb="http://schemas.microsoft.com/InformationBridge/2004"
        iwb:EntityName="Account"
        iwb:ViewName="AccountDefault" />
    </Reference>
</ContextInformation>
```

■**Note** The metadata utilized in this chapter was provided as part of the IBF sample system. A full discussion of IBF and the IBF metadata is out of this book's scope. For more information about IBF metadata,
visit http://msdn.microsoft.com/office/understanding/ibframework/training/training1/
default.aspx. Microsoft has provided several training videos that discuss all aspects of IBF, including
building the IBF metadata.

This XML block must be included as the context information of the smart tag. The information matches up with the IBF metadata and tells IBF to execute the AccountDefault view of
the Account entity.

■**Tip** If you wanted to build another smart tag that invokes different methods provided by the IBF sample
system, you would need to change the EntityName and ViewName values of the XML to call the desired
objects in the IBF system.

Once the XML is built, the recognized term is inserted into the ContextStream object, and
a smart tag property bag is attached to the recognized term within the document:

```
Dim context As String = String.Format(formatString, m.Value)

Dim propBag As ISmartTagProperties = _
  RecognizerSite2.GetNewPropertyBag()
propBag.Write("data", context)

RecognizerSite2.CommitSmartTag(tagNameExternal, m.Index + 1, _
  m.Length, propBag)
End If
```

The last statement in this code before the End If adds the smart tag type information
to the host application's active document by executing the CommitSmartTag method of the
RecognizerSite2 parameter. It's at this point that the smart tag menu becomes available to
the user.

Registering the Account Details Smart Tag

Once the smart tag classes are built and the smart tag is compiled and distributed to a user's system, a registry key must be installed to associate the smart tag with the targeted host application. To add the necessary key to the registry, create a new file named **VBST.reg** and store it in the same folder as the smart tag's Visual Studio solution file. Open the VBST.reg file and add the following text:

```
Windows Registry Editor Version 5.00

[HKEY_CURRENT_USER\Software\Microsoft\Office\Common\Smart
Tag\Recognizers\AccountDetails.Recognizer]
"Filename"="C:\\OfficeProgramming\\Chapter08\\AccountDetails\\bin\\AccountDetails.dll"
"Managed"=dword:00000001
```

Save and close the file, and then double-click it to add the key to the registry. If the key installed successfully, you will receive a message saying so.

The registry key tells Microsoft Office to load the Account Details smart tag when an application that supports smart tag is opened. The registry key contains the information required for loading the smart tag (the DLL file's location).

Configuring Security

In order for the Account Details smart tag to execute on your system, it must be given Full Trust security permission in the .NET Framework Configuration tool. Follow these steps to grant Full Trust access to the compiled AccountDetails.dll:

1. Open the Microsoft .NET Framework 1.1 Configuration utility found in the Windows Administrative Tools.

2. Navigate to the Machine ➤ Code Groups ➤ All_Code ➤ My_Computer_Zone section of the configuration utility.

3. Initiate the Create Code Group Wizard by right-clicking on My_Computer_Zone and selecting New.

4. Enter **AccountDetails** in the Name field and **Folder location for the AccountDetails smart tag** in the Description field. Click Next.

5. Select All Code from the Choose the Condition Type for This Code Group drop-down box. Click Next.

6. Select FullTrust in the Use Existing Permission Set drop-down box. Click Next and click Finish.

▪Note Chapter 7 provides a more detailed discussion of the security configuration steps. See that chapter's "Configuring .NET Security for VSTO" section.

Testing the Account Details Smart Tag

To test that the Account Details smart tag is properly configured and executes properly, follow these steps:

1. Open Word and display the AutoCorrect Options dialog box by selecting Tools ➤ AutoCorrect Options from the menu.

2. Select the smart tag tab. If everything is configured correctly, you should see "Information Bridge (Bravo Corp Account Details Smart Tag)" in the Recognizers list (see Figure 8-12). Check the box next to the Account Details smart tag to enable it, and click OK.

Figure 8-12. *Enabling the Account Details smart tag in the AutoCorrect dialog box*

3. Open a new Word document, and type **Contoso**. Press Enter.

4. The smart tag will recognize Contoso as a customer name and underline it to signify that the text has a smart tag associated with it. Move your cursor over the underline to display the smart tag button (see Figure 8-13).

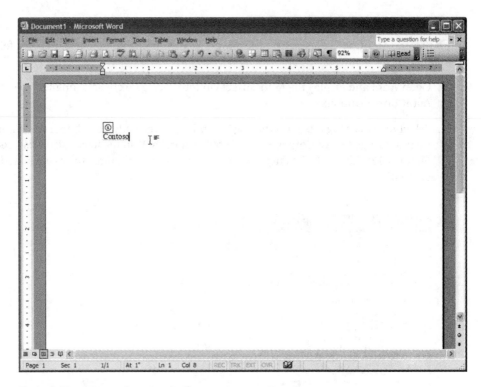

Figure 8-13. *Contoso is recognized as an Account Details smart tag term.*

5. Click the smart tag button to display the Show Details menu button (see Figure 8-14).

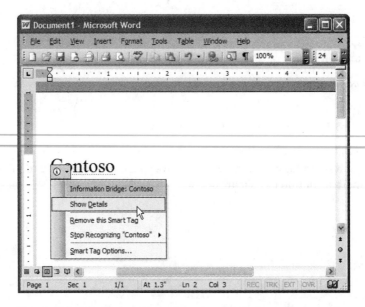

Figure 8-14. *Displaying the Account Details smart tag menu*

6. Once the Document Actions task pane displays the Contoso account information (see Figure 8-15), you know the smart tag works as expected.

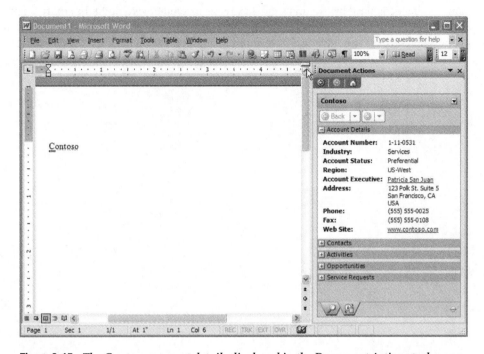

Figure 8-15. *The Contoso account details displayed in the Document Actions task pane*

If any of these steps fail, there are few things you should check:

1. Are the registry settings correct? If not, Word will not be able to locate the smart tag and load it.

2. Is security properly configured? Double check that Full Trust has been granted to the folder containing the `AccountDetails.dll` file.

3. Is the `<ContextInformation>` XML tag correct? This tag is part of the `Recognize2` method used to attach the `AccountDetails` smart tag to the recognized term. Double check to make sure this information was entered correctly. If it is incorrect, IBF will not be able to return the desired account information.

Summary

Utilizing smart tags as the entry point for initiating IBF method calls is a powerful way of presenting relevant business data to users within the applications they love most—Outlook, Excel, and Word. IBF is a great framework for consolidating necessary data and business logic within the Office system.

This chapter explained how to build a smart tag that recognizes customer names in a Word document and displays a smart tag menu that provides the user with customer-related commands. This chapter also showed how to load an XML file containing a list of customer names to be recognized by the smart tag. Lastly we covered how to build the smart tag in such a way that it utilizes the Information Bridge smart tag action handler to call an IBF system method that retrieves and displays customer information from a backend CRM system.

CHAPTER 9

■ ■ ■

The Event-Site Order System
Automating the Order-Entry Process Using Word, Smart Documents, and a Web Service

This chapter explains how to build the Event-Site Order System (ESOS), an automated order form that allows users to quickly fill out, complete, and submit an order. This solution takes advantage of the newest and most powerful XML features within Office 2003, and it will provide you with a solid foundation for working with smart documents.

Smart documents contain business-rule logic to enable the document-authoring process. These rules recognize the current position within the document and display helpful information or options in Word's (or Excel's) Document Actions task pane. For example, a legal document could include logic that recognizes the different sections of a contract and then lists relevant boilerplate text in the Document Actions task pane. A user could then simply click on the desired text to include it in the document at the appropriate place.

Office 2003 supports the first version of smart documents and the tools for building them provide only a basic framework, leaving a few labor-intensive tasks for the developer. For example, there is no visual designer that allows a developer to draw the controls on the task pane in a manner typical of Office UserForms or .NET Windows forms (Smart Documents 2005, included with the next release of Visual Studio .NET, does include this ability, through the creation of custom controls that can be invoked to display in the task pane). This makes developing smart document solutions more laborious than we might like, but they are well worth the effort.

A good indication of the current state of the smart document interface is the fact that it does not include events for each task pane control. Instead the interface relies on the developer to create a series of Case statements inside the few event methods the interface does provide to respond to changes in the document's context. That is the bad news. The good news is that smart documents provide a powerful development framework for building solutions targeted at individual documents and they are well worth the effort required to master them.

The Event-Site Order System is a smart client application hosted within a Microsoft Word document. These are the system's main components:

- **Smart documents**: This is a new technology included with Office 2003. In this chapter you will learn how to automate documents by using an XML schema to add both contextual information to a document and a .NET assembly that responds to different contexts. We will look at how to use the new Document Actions task pane to dynamically display task pane controls that help the user author a document by retrieving database data that can easily be inserted into the active document.

- **Microsoft Word**: Word acts as the host for the ESOS. Using Word, you will learn how to create an order form document, how to attach an XML schema to the document, how to define XML tags within the order form document, and how to attach a .NET assembly.

- **XML schema file**: XML is a key component of the smart document technology included in Office 2003. This chapter discusses several aspects of using XML to build a smart document. Key concepts include how to create an XML schema file, how to attach the schema to a Word document, how to define XML elements (or tags) in a Word document, and how to use XPATH queries to retrieve XML data inside an XML document.

- **Smart document .NET assembly**: The code behind a smart document solution relies on the .NET Framework. We will look at how to build a .NET assembly that implements the smart document interface, how to program the Document Actions task pane, how to use the XML schema file to respond to changes in the smart document's context, and how to attach the .NET assembly to the order form document.

- **Web services**: The ESOS relies on a web service to implement logic for interacting with the solution's database. We will look at how to implement a web service that inserts and retrieves records from the solution database. In addition, we will focus on how to use XML data based on the solution's XML schema to submit new order data and create new order records in the database. We will also look at how to parse the XML data and create the necessary SQL statements to insert the new records in the database.

The user interface is a Microsoft Word–enabled smart document that creates a customer order. The document is a typical Word document, except that it has an XML expansion pack associated with it. The expansion pack (sometimes referred to as a manifest) contains a listing of the files included in the smart document solution that should be loaded in Word whenever the smart document is opened.

The expansion pack contains two files: a DLL file and an XSD file. The DLL file is the .NET assembly containing the smart document interface and ESOS business logic. The XSD file is the XML schema file used to define data elements within the smart document. XML expansion packs are not limited to these two files. They can contain any other file needed by the smart document, but in this chapter's application, only a DLL and an XSD file are utilized.

The smart document utilizes the web service to create a new order record in the solution database.

Working with Smart Documents

From a developer's perspective, a smart document is a Word, Excel, or InfoPath file that has an XML expansion pack associated with it. The XML expansion pack describes which files (such

as a .NET assembly and an XML schema) are included in the smart document solution. The
XML schema file listed in the expansion pack describes information within the smart document and relays context information to the .NET assembly attached to the smart document
via XML elements defined in the schema. The .NET assembly then responds by invoking any
logic pertaining to the active XML element defined in the smart document.

■**Note** Smart document support for InfoPath became available with the release of Office 2003 Service
Pack 1. If you have installed SP1 for Office 2003, you can download the InfoPath Toolkit for Visual Studio
on MSDN. This toolkit installs Visual Studio projects that allow developers to automate InfoPath using
managed code. The toolkit can be downloaded from `http://www.microsoft.com/downloads/`
`details.aspx?familyid=7e9ebc57-e115-4cac-9986-a712e22879bb&displaylang=en`.

At run time, the components of the smart document work together to display controls
and data inside the Document Actions task pane (see Figure 9-1) that are directly related to
the cursor's position in the document. The general idea is to guide the user through the
process of creating the document.

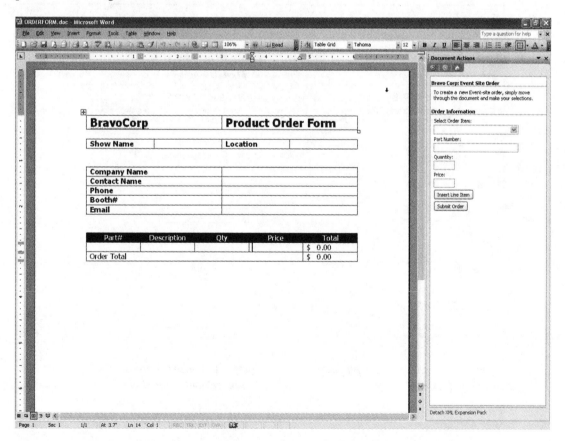

Figure 9-1. *The smart document with the Document Actions task pane*

Smart documents are an evolution of the smart tag technology but it goes beyond simply recognizing terms within a document (see the overview of smart tags in Chapter 8). Smart documents add contextual recognition to a solution and allow a developer to present relevant commands and data to the user depending upon the current focus within the document. For example, an executive completing a proposal within Word could be presented with boilerplate text describing each of the products and services provided by his company. The executive could simply click each product or service, and the text describing each would automatically be inserted into the document in the appropriate location.

At a technical level, a smart document is simply an Office document (at the time of writing, it must be a Word or Excel document) that implements the ISmartDocument interface and that includes code to respond to changes in the document's active elements. As the active element changes, the task pane is refreshed to display different data options to guide the user through creating the document. For example, Figures 9-2 and 9-3 show the task pane in the Event-Site Order System when the Customer and Show XML elements are active.

Note The full documentation for the ISmartDocument interface is available on the MSDN web site at http://msdn.microsoft.com/library/en-us/sdsdk/html/sdobjISmartDocument.asp.

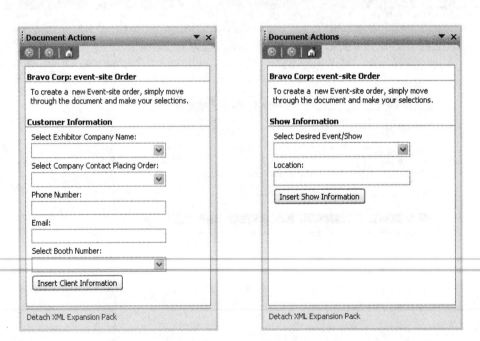

Figure 9-2. *The task pane displaying customer options*

Figure 9-3. *The task pane displaying options related to the show*

■**Note** Visual Studio Tools for Office 2005 will include the ability to use project templates for creating smart documents (currently there are no project templates for the smart document development process). This is no small change, as the full power of Visual Studio will support the entire smart document effort (not just the creation of an assembly). As a developer of smart documents, you will be able to author your own controls instead of relying on the limited features of controls provided in the Office 2003 version.

The Components of a Smart Document

Smart documents consist of the following main components:

- **Smart document**: The Word or Excel file that hosts the smart document solution.

- **XML schema**: The file that describes the data within the smart document.

- **XML expansion pack**: An XML file containing the list of files that make up the smart document solution (all files, that is, except the host document itself).

- **Action handler**: A code library (DLL) that calls the smart document APIs by implementing the ISmartDocument interface. This library monitors actions in the host document and fills the task pane with controls as necessary.

■**Note** The initial release of Office 2003 only supported smart documents in Word and Excel. Smart document support for InfoPath was added with the release of Office 2003 Service Pack 1. Since this chapter focuses on creating a smart document in Word, the rest of this chapter will refer only to Word when discussing smart documents and their capabilities. Keep in mind that comparable things can be done with Excel and InfoPath smart documents.

Each component of the smart document solution plays its part and works with the other pieces to provide the user with a powerful interface that streamlines their document-authoring process. Figure 9-4 shows how each component relates to the others. The whole solution depends on the presence of the host document in Word. Once the user opens the document, it uses the associated XML manifest file (in the expansion pack) to attach all solution documents. As the user then begins to make their way through the document, the action handler monitors their current location and runs a constant cross-check against the attached XML schema definition.

If the action handler determines that the current document location has an attached XML element, it executes to refresh the Document Actions task pane and populate it with controls targeted for the current context.

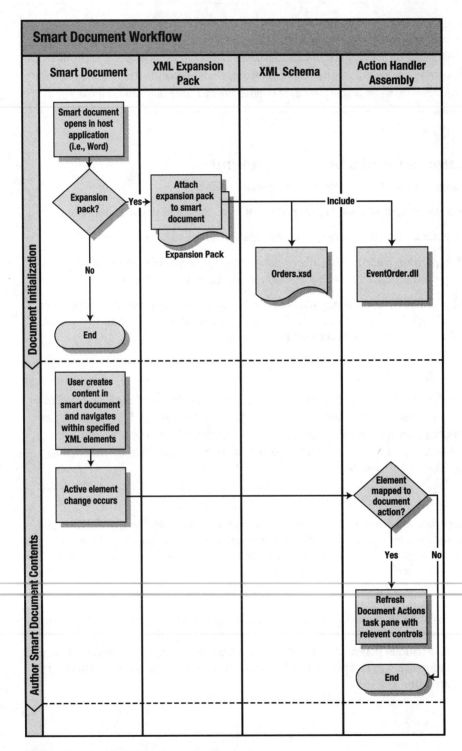

Figure 9-4. *The workflow of a smart document*

Designing the Event-Site Order System

From the user's viewpoint, a smart document is an Office document that understands what data it needs to gather. It walks the user through the creation of the document (an order, in our case). The workflow is streamlined, better documents are produced, and the time required to author a document is reduced. All of this is achieved by creating controls in the task pane that respond to items contained in the open document.

The Event-Site Order System works as follows:

1. A user (either a Bravo Corp staff member or a client) opens the Microsoft Word-based smart document OrderForm.doc file to initiate the order process.

2. The event order form contains three sections: show information, customer information, and order information. As the user moves through the document, the Document Actions task pane provides the ability to select data from a database and insert the values into the document.

3. Once the event order form has been successfully completed, the user submits the order to the solution database.

4. After the order record is created in the database, the form displays the order number in the document's header section. At this point, the user can save the event order document for their records and print a copy for the customer.

From a developer's viewpoint, the system executes according to the following workflow (see Figure 9-5):

1. As soon as the OrderForm.doc smart document is opened, Word loads the XML expansion pack associated with the smart document, which includes the XML schema file (Order.xsd) and the .NET assembly (EventOrder.dll). Once the XML expansion pack is loaded, the Document Actions task pane initializes and displays inside of Word.

2. As the user completes the order form document, the .NET assembly continually monitors the location of the cursor and uses the active XML element of the document to determine which controls should be displayed inside the task pane.

3. When the user chooses data from the task pane to insert in the document, they click a button that calls the InvokeControl method of the .NET assembly. This assembly determines which control triggered the event and responds with the logic attached to that control.

4. Once the document is completed, the order form calls the SubmitOrder method of the solution's web service. This method accepts XML data that conforms to the solution's XML schema file as a method argument. The XML data is parsed and used to create an order header record (in the tblOrders table) and the related order line-item records (in the tblOrderDetails table) in the solution database.

5. Once the order is successfully created, the SubmitOrder method returns the order ID of the new order (the OrderID field from tblOrders). The OrderForm.doc smart document inserts the order ID into the header of the document to indicate that the order was created successfully.

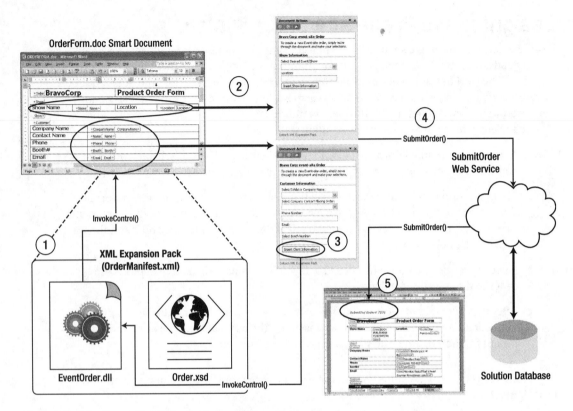

Figure 9-5. *The Event-Site Order System workflow from a developer's perspective*

The Business Scenario

The site facility of any trade show is a dynamic environment where a client's needs change on a moment-by-moment basis. The clients place orders with a Bravo Corp representative, and the urgent nature of each order calls for rapid response.

Formerly, Bravo Corp accepted orders at their service desk using a manual, paper-based system, but the form was difficult to use, and exhibitors ended up placing incorrect orders and wasting everyone's time. A friendlier, automated, and smarter process was long overdue.

The Event-Site Order System (ESOS) is a document-based solution that automates the event ordering process. Bravo Corp felt confident that providing context-sensitive data and online help would decrease their order fulfillment response time and reduce errors.

Creating the Order.xsd Schema File

In order for our smart document to populate the task pane with controls and data relevant to the document's current context, two pieces must fit together: an XML schema file named Order.xsd that defines the data elements within the document, and a DLL file that implements the ISmartDocument interface. This DLL file is known as an action handler, and we will discuss it in the "Creating the Action Handler Assembly (the DocActions Class)" section.

You can create Order.xsd in any text editor. All that matters is that it be a valid XML schema definition file. Although Visual Studio has some great XML code-formatting capabilities, I recommend you grab a copy of Altova's XMLSpy product, which you can use any time you are creating and editing XML documents. It makes working in Visual Studio look like coding in Notepad.

■Note XMLSpy can be found at http://www.altova.com.

The Order.xsd XML schema for the ESOS looks like this:

```xml
<?xml version="1.0" encoding="UTF-8"?>
<xs:schema targetNamespace="urn:schemas-bravocorp-com.namespaces.event.simple"
  elementFormDefault="qualified" attributeFormDefault="unqualified"
  xmlns="urn:schemas-bravocorp-com.namespaces.event.simple"
  xmlns:xs="http://www.w3.org/2001/XMLSchema">
  <xs:element name="Order">
    <xs:annotation>
      <xs:documentation>Event Order Schema</xs:documentation>
    </xs:annotation>
    <xs:complexType mixed="true">
      <xs:sequence>
        <xs:element name="Show">
          <xs:complexType mixed="true">
          <xs:sequence>
            <xs:element name="Name" type="xs:string"/>
            <xs:element name="Location" type="xs:string"/>
          </xs:sequence>
          </xs:complexType>
        </xs:element>
        <xs:element name="Customer">
          <xs:complexType>
            <xs:sequence>
              <xs:element name="CompanyName" type="xs:string"/>
              <xs:element name="Name" type="xs:string"/>
              <xs:element name="Phone" type="xs:string"/>
              <xs:element name="Email" type="xs:string"/>
              <xs:element name="Booth" type="xs:string"/>
            </xs:sequence>
          </xs:complexType>
        </xs:element>
        <xs:element name="OrderItems">
          <xs:complexType mixed="true">
            <xs:sequence maxOccurs="unbounded">
```

```
        <xs:element name="Item">
          <xs:complexType>
            <xs:sequence>
              <xs:element name="SKU" type="xs:string"/>
              <xs:element name="Description" type="xs:string"/>
              <xs:element name="Quantity" type="xs:string"/>
              <xs:element name="Price" type="xs:string"/>
            </xs:sequence>
          </xs:complexType>
        </xs:element>
      </xs:sequence>
    </xs:complexType>
  </xs:element>
  </xs:sequence>
  </xs:complexType>
</xs:element>
</xs:schema>
```

As you can see, this is a very basic schema outlining data elements for an order. To get a better idea of the different elements in the file, as well as their relationship to each other, take some time to review Figure 9-6. The order schema file calls for orders to include show information, customer information, and line items containing ordered products and services.

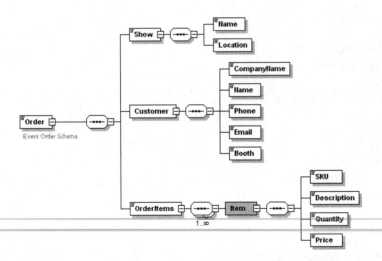

Figure 9-6. *The* Order.xsd *schema*

Creating the Target Word File (OrderForm.doc)

Now that we've created the order schema file, we need to build the target OrderForm.doc document within Microsoft Word and attach the Order.xsd file to it. This document will look and act much like a typical Word document to the user's eyes, but it will actually be taking advantage of one of the most powerful features available—the ability to describe document data through XML.

In Word 2003, extensive XML capabilities allow for full integration with the XML world. We can use these capabilities to build XML documents that not only store information about the document's formatting and layout, but also include descriptions about the data itself. This is powerful mainly because we can interface with a backend system (a web service, SQL Server database, etc.) by pulling just the XML data from a document and sending it to key systems for further action (such as creating a new order in a sales system).

A completed version of the Word template for our solution is shown in Figure 9-7.

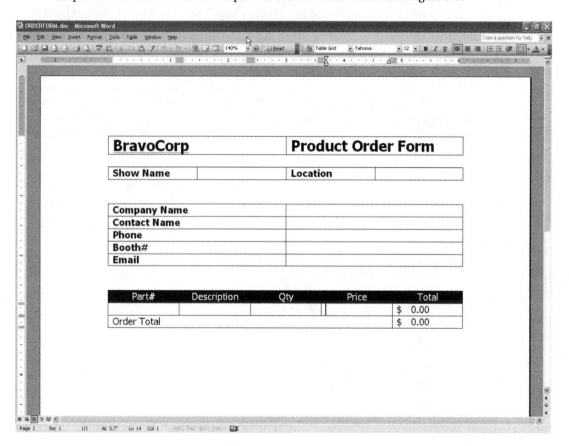

Figure 9-7. *The completed* OrderForm.doc *document*

To build this document, follow these steps:

1. Open Word and create a new document.

2. Insert a table at the top of the document by clicking Table ➤ Insert ➤ Table. Specify that the table should have 2 columns and 1 row, and click OK. In the first column of the inserted table, type **BravoCorp**. In the second column, type **Product Order Form**.

3. Insert another table, this one with 4 columns and 1 row, below the table created in step 2. Make sure there is at least one blank line separating the two tables. This line

will help when we add the XML tags later. In the first column of the table, type **Show Name**, and in the third column, type **Location**.

4. Insert another table with 5 columns and 2 rows below the table created in step 3, again leaving at least one blank line between the two tables. Insert **Company Name**, **Contact Name**, **Phone**, **Booth#**, and **Email** as the values for the first column of each row.

5. Insert one more table, this one with 5 columns and 3 rows. In the first row, label each column, in order, as **Part#**, **Description**, **Qty**, **Price**, and **Total**. In the third row, high-light the first 4 columns starting with the leftmost column (leave the last column unselected) and merge them into a single cell by clicking Table ➤ Merge Cell from the menu. In the newly merged cell, type **Order Total**.

6. To get the Total column to automatically calculate the row's total, we need to use a field formula. Set your cursor in the row under the Total column's header, and insert a field by selecting Insert ➤ Field from the menu. When the Field dialog box appears, click the Formula button. The Formula dialog box will appear, and it already includes the formula we want (see Figure 9-8). Make sure the Formula text box is set to "=PRODUCT(LEFT)" and set the Number Format text box to "$#,##0.00;($#,##0.00)". Then click OK.

■**Tip** Field codes, or *fields*, are special placeholders in a Word document. They are used to reserve the location for data that is subject to change either through code or by performing a standard Word function like a mail merge.

Figure 9-8. *Inserting the field formula in the Total column*

7. Set the cursor inside the Total column in the Order Total row. Repeat step 6 but make sure the formula is "=Sum(E:E)".

8. Associate the Order.xsd XML schema to the document by selecting Tools ➤ Templates and Add-Ins. Click on the XML Schema tab and click the Add Schema button. Navigate to your Order.xsd file, select it, and click Open.

9. In the Schema Settings dialog box, enter **Bravo Corp Event Site Order** in the Alias field. Click OK. If all goes as planned, you should be looking at a dialog box similar to the one in Figure 9-9. Go ahead and click the OK button to attach the file.

Figure 9-9. *Attaching an XML schema to a Word document*

10. Word will automatically display the XML Structure task pane. Now we need to associate XML elements to the different data sections within the OrderForm document. Use Figure 9-10 as a guide, and associate all elements from the schema to their corresponding areas in the document.

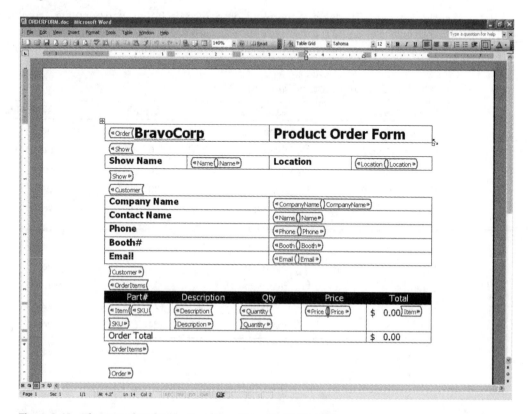

Figure 9-10. *The completed* OrderForm.doc *file with XML elements*

11. Save the document and name it `OrderForm.doc`.

It may not be apparent now, but, as you will soon discover, we have created a document that is truly three dimensional. It contains layout information, data, and descriptions of the data via an attached XML schema. By including the XML definition in the file, we can easily strip out the desired data later and do as we please with it.

Preparing the Database

As in previous chapters, we will use a SQL Server database to store information captured from the users. For this solution, we will add five tables to the BravoCorp database created in Chapter 2 (see the "Creating the Database" section in Chapter 2 for details on creating the database).

> ■**Tip** You can use any other database on the market for this solution. Just be sure to change your connection string as necessary.

Create the following tables:

- `tblCustomers`: This table contains customer records. It is used to populate a combo box with company name information, and it is used again to populate a combo box with company contact information. The data definition for this table is shown in Table 9-1.

Table 9-1. *The* `tblCustomers` *Data Definition*

Column Name	Data Type	Length	Allow Nulls
CustomerID	nchar	5	no
CompanyName	nvarchar	40	no
ContactName	nvarchar	30	yes
ContactTitle	nvarchar	30	yes
Address	nvarchar	30	yes
City	nvarchar	15	yes
Region	nvarchar	15	yes
PostalCode	nvarchar	10	yes
Country	nvarchar	15	yes
Phone	nvarchar	24	yes
Fax	nvarchar	24	yes

- `tblProducts`: This table stores product information that is used for selecting and adding items to the order. Table 9-2 shows `tblProducts`'s data definition.

Table 9-2. *The* `tblProducts` *Data Definition*

Column Name	Data Type	Length	Allow Nulls
ProductID	int	4	no
ProductName	nvarchar	40	no
CategoryID	int	4	yes
UnitPrice	money	8	yes

- `tblShows`: This table contains show and event information that is used to fill a show-data combo box. The data definition is found in Table 9-3.

Table 9-3. *The* `tblShows` *Data Definition*

Field Name	SQL Data Type
ShowID	int
Name	varchar(150)

- `tblOrders`: This table contains order header data such as the customer name and shipping address. The data definition is in Table 9-4.

Table 9-4. *The* `tblOrders` *Data Definition*

Column Name	Data Type	Length	Allow Nulls
OrderID	int	4	no
CustomerID	nchar	5	yes
OrderDate	datetime	8	yes

- `tblOrderDetails`: This table contains the order line items, and it is linked to `tblOrders` by a unique `OrderID`. The data definition is found in Table 9-5.

Table 9-5. *The* `tblOrderDetails` *Data Definition*

Column Name	Data Type	Length	Allow Nulls
OrderID	int	4	no
ProductID	int	4	no
UnitPrice	money	8	no
Quantity	smallint	2	no

Building the SubmitOrder Web Service

We have built the OrderForm.doc smart document, so we can create orders that conform to the rules of the Order.xsd schema file. Now we need to create the SubmitOrder web service, which will actually submit the new orders we create. This web service will accept a new order XML file and add the information to the order tables (tblOrders and tblOrderDetails).

The web service is fairly basic, but it does the job for our purposes. The web service accepts a valid orders XML file (valid because it conforms to the Order.xsd file) and creates a new order in the database. Once the order is in the database, the web service returns the OrderID of the newly inserted order record. Figure 9-11 illustrates this workflow.

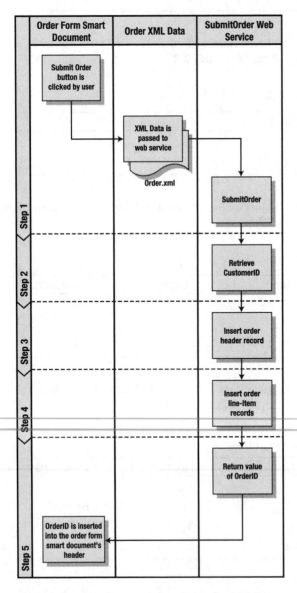

Figure 9-11. *The* SubmitOrder *web service workflow*

Let's take it one step at a time:

1. From the OrderForm.doc smart document, XML data conforming to the Order.xsd XML schema is passed to the SubmitNewOrder method. This method acts as the dispatcher and ultimately returns the OrderID of the new order records.

2. Using the CompanyName element included in the passed XML data, the SubmitOrder web service retrieves the CustomerID that matches the CompanyName. This CustomerID value is then used when creating the Order record.

3. With the CustomerID in hand, the method then inserts an order header record into the tblOrders table. The OrderID of the header record is stored for use in step 4.

4. For each order line item included within the passed XML stream (line items are specified by the Item element in the Order.xsd schema), we insert a record into the solution database's tblOrderDetails table. The OrderID from step 3 is inserted into each record to link the line items to the order header record.

5. After all the order-related data is inserted into the solution database, the submitted order's OrderID is returned as the value of the method and inserted into the header of the OrderForm.doc smart document to signify that the order was successfully submitted.

To start building our web service, open Visual Studio and create a new Visual Basic-based ASP .NET Web Service project and name it **SubmitOrderWS**. Once the project is set up within Visual Studio, delete the sample.asmx file, add a new web service file to the project, and name it **OrderWS.asmx**.

The OrderWS.asmx Class

Our web service will provide event-order web methods through a single class named OrderWS. This class accepts submitted orders from completed order form documents and inserts the submitted data into the tblOrders and tblOrderDetails tables in the solution database.

This class demonstrates how to accept a string of XML text that conforms to the Order.xsd schema and parse it in order to extract its data for insertion into the solution database. In addition, this class shows how to insert records into the solution database by creating order header and order line item records. The key to this is to use the record ID of the header record when creating the order line item records.

Imports Directives

OrderWS accesses two types of objects during its execution: SQL objects and XML objects. Edit the class's Imports statements to include the following lines:

```
Imports System.Web.Services
Imports System.Data.SqlClient
Imports System.Xml
```

These lines give us quick access to the classes within the three main namespaces relevant to our web service.

Variable Declarations

In the declarations section of the class, add the following lines of code;

```
Dim strCnn As String = "Server=coreserv;Database=BravoCorp;User " & _
    "ID=bcuser;Password=bcuser;Trusted_Connection=False"
Dim cnn As New SqlConnection
```

Here we are creating a String object and assigning to it the info needed to connect to the BravoCorp database. We also instantiate a new SqlConnection object to provide a direct connection to the SQL database anytime we need it throughout the life of the class.

The SubmitNewOrder Method

We are now ready to add some code to the web service. We'll begin with the main method, SubmitNewOrder, which looks like this:

```
<WebMethod(Description:="Submit New Event Site Order")> _
Public Function SubmitNewOrder(ByVal strXML As String) As String
Try
  Dim doc As XmlDocument = New XmlDocument
  doc.PreserveWhitespace = False
  doc.LoadXml(strXML)

  Dim xn As XmlNode = doc.SelectSingleNode("//Order/Customer/CompanyName")
  Dim strCustID As String = GetCustomerID(xn.InnerText)
  Dim strOrderID As String = InsertOrderHeader(strCustID)

  Dim xnl As XmlNodeList = doc.SelectNodes("//Order/OrderItems/Item")
  InsertOrderLineItems(xnl, strOrderID)
  Return strOrderID

Catch ex As Exception

End Try

End Function
```

The great thing about web services is that coding them is really no different than coding or creating other types of code (such as Windows forms, shared add-ins, or custom controls). All that is needed is a sub procedure or function (a method) that does something. In order to make your chosen method a web method, just add the WebMethod attribute to the beginning of the method's declaration. The one caveat is that the method must be a Public method. Private and Shared methods cannot be web methods.

The SubmitNewOrder method is the only one in the class that we want to be available as a web method, so the function's declaration looks like this:

```
<WebMethod(Description:="Submit New Event Site Order")> _
  Public Function SubmitNewOrder(ByVal strXML As String) As String
```

Notice that the function expects to receive a `String` object. The passed `String` is intended to be a valid XML string conforming to the `Order.xsd` schema created earlier.

Another detail worth noting in the preceding declaration is the use of the `WebMethod` attribute's `Description` property. This is an easy way to give the users of the web service a little more information about the function's purpose.

The next thing the function does is attempt to load the passed `String` into an `XmlDocument` object. We also tell the new `doc` variable not to worry about any white space that may or may not exist by setting the `PreserveWhiteSpace` property to False:

```
Try
  Dim doc As XmlDocument = New XmlDocument
  doc.PreserveWhitespace = False
  doc.LoadXml(strXML)
```

The `XmlDocument` object allows us to query the XML document directly, using the XML Document Object Model (DOM). There is a performance consideration here, as the XML DOM does require more memory than is required to read the text using an `XmlTextReader` object. The XML DOM provides forward and backward document-reading capabilities while the `XmlTextReader` can only read forwards.

The function then finds the name of the company stored in the order XML data. Since we know the schema of the file, we can invoke an XPath expression on the file:

```
Dim xn As XmlNode = doc.SelectSingleNode("//Order/Customer/CompanyName")
```

■**Note** You can think of XPath as being like a traditional SQL query. You create a statement that defines the data you want, and on execution, the query lists all records meeting the defined criteria. `SelectNodes` (along with an XPath expression) is the XML version of a SQL statement in a relational database. XPath uses locations and expressions to reference data contained inside an XML file or XML data stream.

This is not any different than finding files in Windows Explorer; it just requires that you know the node location within the XML structure of the data you desire. Once the name is found, we declare a new `XMLNode` and set a reference to the desired node in the XML data string.

This new node can now be used to retrieve the value of the node by calling its `Value` property:

```
Dim strCustID As String = GetCustomerID(xn.InnerText)
```

Using the node's value, we make a call to the `GetCustomerID` function to retrieve the customer's ID from the database, using the company name to look up the ID.

■**Note** The preceding code line demonstrates the power of VB .NET: we create a new `String` variable, immediately assign it a value, and at the same time call a function to retrieve that value.

With the `CustomerID` now known, we can initiate the process of creating an order record in the database by inserting a new record in the `tblOrders` table:

```
Dim strOrderID As String = InsertOrderHeader(strCustID)
```

The `InsertOrderHeader` function takes the passed `CustomerID` value, inserts a new header record, and then assigns the record's ID value to our newly created `strOrderID` object.

Now for something a little more complex. The method's passed XML string is a valid XML document conforming to the XML schema defined by `Order.xsd`. (For the ease of discussion, I will refer to this XML data as the `Order` XML data.) The passed XML data string can contain any number of order line items; therefore, we have no idea if it contains one, one hundred, or none (and is thus invalid). Since the order likely contains more than one line item, the best thing to do is grab all of the line items from the XML data file and send them off to another function where they will be parsed and individually inserted into the appropriate table within the database:

```
Dim xnl As XmlNodeList = doc.SelectNodes("//Order/OrderItems/Item")
InsertOrderLineItems(xnl, strOrderID)

Return strOrderID

Catch ex As Exception

End Try
```

In the preceding code, we create a reference to all the child nodes under the `//Order/OrderItems/Item` node by calling the `SelectNodes` method of the `doc` object. By using another XPath expression, this method retrieves a collection of node objects matching the expression.

The retrieved nodes are stored in an `XMLNodeList` object and are passed, along with the `OrderID`, to the `InsertOrderLineItems` function where the `XMLNodeList` will be used to insert each order line item into the `tblOrderDetails` table. If all the moving parts work as expected, the new `OrderID` (stored within `strOrderID`) is returned as the value of the function.

The GetCustomerID Method

The submitted `Order` XML data, while containing all the information needed to fulfill an order, does not contain all of the information needed to insert the new order details into the database. What's missing is the `CustomerID`, which will serve as the foreign key in the `tblOrders` table. `GetCustomerID` uses a given customer name (passed as a `String` parameter) to look up the customer record and return the `CustomerID`.

```
Private Function GetCustomerID(ByVal CustomerName As String) As String
  Try
    cnn.Open()
    Dim strSQL As String = "Select CustomerID from tblCustomers where " & _
      "CompanyName ='" & CustomerName & "'"
    Dim cmm As SqlCommand
```

```
cmm = New SqlCommand(strSQL, cnn)
Dim drID As SqlDataReader = cmm.ExecuteReader()
drID.Read()
Dim strId As String = drID.Item("CustomerID")

'Clean up, clean up, everybody everywhere
drID.Close()
cnn.Close()
Return strId

Catch ex As Exception

End Try

End Function
```

Since this function will access the database, we open up the cnn object, which prepares for the query we are about to execute. Using the SQL statement we conveniently stored in the strSQL object, we then create a new SQLCommand object to execute our query against the SQL database. We then execute the query and use the resulting SQLDataReader object to retrieve the record's CustomerID, which is returned as the value of the function. We also close the new data reader and the connection.

The InsertOrderHeader Method

We now have an order submitted to our web service with valid XML data based on the Order.xsd schema file. Provided our code executed correctly and the order contained a valid customer name, we also now have a valid CustomerID value. The next step is to create a new order record.

A good normalized database will contain at least two tables that store the order records. In our case we have an order header table (tblOrders) and an order details table (tblOrder-Details). Creating a new order involves coordinating inserts into both tables. The first step is to create the order header record and retrieve the OrderID of the newly inserted record, all of which is done by the InsertOrderHeader function. Here is the code:

```
Private Function InsertOrderHeader(ByVal strCustomerID As String) As Long
Try
  cnn.Open()

  Dim cmd As New SqlCommand("sp_InsertNewOrder", cnn)
  cmd.CommandType = CommandType.StoredProcedure

  Dim prmCustomerID As SqlParameter
  Dim prmOrderDate As SqlParameter
  Dim id As Object
```

```
prmCustomerID = cmd.Parameters.Add("@CustomerID", SqlDbType.NChar, 20)
prmCustomerID.Direction = ParameterDirection.Input
prmCustomerID.Value = strCustomerID.ToString

prmOrderDate = cmd.Parameters.Add("@OrderDate", SqlDbType.DateTime)
prmOrderDate.Direction = ParameterDirection.Input
prmOrderDate.Value = Now().ToShortDateString

id = cmd.ExecuteScalar()

cnn.Close()
Return id

Catch ex As Exception
   If cnn.State = ConnectionState.Open Then cnn.Close()
   MsgBox(ex.Message)
End Try

End Function
```

This function calls a stored procedure named sp_InsertNewOrder, which works much like a typical VB function does—it accepts a couple of parameters, does its thing, and then returns a value. In this case, the two parameters are CustomerID (a type representing the customer number) and OrderDate (a date value representing the date of the new order). The function takes these values and inserts a new order header record. If the record was inserted correctly, the OrderID is returned, and if not, zero is returned.

The function starts by opening the class-level connection object. The subsequent lines set up the objects needed to execute the stored procedure:

```
Try
   cnn.Open()

   Dim cmd As New SqlCommand("sp_InsertNewOrder", cnn)
   cmd.CommandType = CommandType.StoredProcedure

   Dim prmCustomerID As SqlParameter
   Dim prmOrderDate As SqlParameter
   Dim id As Object
```

Just as in the GetCustomerID function, we implement a SqlCommand object for executing commands against the SQL Server database. This time, however, we set the command object's type to StoredProcedure to let it know that we will be calling a stored procedure in the database instead of passing along a SQL statement. Since we are dealing with stored procedures, we also need to declare SqlParameter objects to represent the two parameters expected by the sp_InsertNewOrder stored procedure. The last object created is a generic Object variable that we will use to store the returned value of the stored procedure.

Before we can make a successful call to the sp_InsertNewOrder stored procedure, we need to set a reference to each SqlParameter variable declared earlier by calling the Add method of the command object's parameters collection. Once the new parameter is added to the parameters collection, its properties are set to indicate its direction and value. This process is repeated for each stored procedure parameter:

```
prmCustomerID = cmd.Parameters.Add("@CustomerID", SqlDbType.NChar, 20)
prmCustomerID.Direction = ParameterDirection.Input
prmCustomerID.Value = strCustomerID.ToString

prmOrderDate = cmd.Parameters.Add("@OrderDate", SqlDbType.DateTime)
prmOrderDate.Direction = ParameterDirection.Input
prmOrderDate.Value = Now().ToShortDateString
```

As you can see, we add each parameter to the SQLCommand object's parameters collection and, by setting the Direction property, specify it as an input parameter. With that all set, the parameter receives the value to be used when the stored procedure executes.

All that's left is to execute the stored procedure and return the OrderID of the new order header record.

```
id = cmd.ExecuteScalar()

cnn.Close()
Return id
```

Since we only want to return a single value (the new OrderID) we execute the stored procedure using the ExecuteScalar method of the SQLCommand object. ExecuteScalar is the best execute method for situations like this where all that is desired is the first column of the first row of the resulting data set—it is significantly faster than the other execute methods, such as Execute-Reader. Once the stored procedure executes, we close the database connection and return the new order's OrderID.

The InsertOrderLineItems Method

We now know the CustomerID, and we have a new order all queued up. Next we need to insert each order line item into the line-items table in the order form Word document. We'll accomplish this task with two functions: InsertOrderLineItems and InsertOrderLineItem.

The only purpose of InsertOrderLineItems is to prepare the way for its sister function, InsertOrderLineItem. The former function loops through each node in the passed XMLNodeList, retrieves our desired values, and calls the latter function (passing the retrieved values as parameters).

```
Private Function InsertOrderLineItems(ByVal NodeList As XmlNodeList, _
  ByVal OrderID As String)
  Dim xNode As XmlNode

  For Each xNode In NodeList
    Dim xEl As XmlElement = DirectCast(xNode, XmlElement)

    Dim strSKU As String = xEl.GetElementsByTagName("SKU")(0).Value()
    Dim strQty As String = xEl.GetElementsByTagName("Quantity")(0).Value()
    Dim strPrice As String = xEl.GetElementsByTagName("Price")(0).Value()

    InsertOrderLineItem(OrderID, strSKU, strQty, strPrice)
  Next
End Function
```

Here, we simply use the GetElementsByTagName method of the current XML node to retrieve an element value. It's really not any different than looping through a database recordset and accessing a row's column by name. The retrieved values are then sent to InsertOrderLineItem.

The InsertOrderLineItem Method

In the case of inserting single records into the order details table (tblOrderDetails), it makes perfect sense to create a helper function to do the work. We have no way of knowing at design time just how many line items will be included in any given Order XML file, so the best thing to do is implement a strategy that allows for an infinite number of line items.

The helper function doesn't care how many line items exist. It simply does one thing—insert an order line item into the file. The job of discovering how many line items exist is left to the InsertOrderLineItems method (described previously).

```
Private Function InsertOrderLineItem(ByVal OrderID As String, ByVal SKU As String, _
  ByVal QTY As String, ByVal Price As String) As Boolean
  Try
    Dim cmd As New SqlCommand("sp_InsertNewOrderLineItem", cnn)
    Dim prmOrderID As SqlParameter
    Dim prmSKU As SqlParameter
    Dim prmQTY As SqlParameter
    Dim prmPrice As SqlParameter
```

```
        cmd.CommandType = CommandType.StoredProcedure
        prmOrderID = cmd.Parameters.Add("@OrderID", SqlDbType.Int)
        prmOrderID.Direction = ParameterDirection.Input
        prmOrderID.Value = CInt(OrderID.ToString)

        prmSKU = cmd.Parameters.Add("@SKU", SqlDbType.Int)
        prmSKU.Direction = ParameterDirection.Input
        prmSKU.Value = CInt(SKU.ToString)

        prmQTY = cmd.Parameters.Add("@QTY", SqlDbType.Int)
        prmQTY.Direction = ParameterDirection.Input
        prmQTY.Value = CInt(QTY.ToString)

        prmPrice = cmd.Parameters.Add("@Price", SqlDbType.Money)
        prmPrice.Direction = ParameterDirection.Input
        prmPrice.Value = CInt(Price.ToString)

    cnn.Open()
    cmd.ExecuteNonQuery()
    cnn.Close()

    Return True

    Catch ex As Exception
      cnn.Close()
      Return False
    End Try
End Function
```

We will look through this code quickly, as it is similar to code already covered in this chapter. First, we declare a few SQLParameter objects so we can pass information to the sp InsertNewOrderLineItem stored procedures. Next, we create the parameters, set their direction, and give them each a value. And finally we open the database connection, execute the stored procedure, and close the database connection.

One thing you should take note of here is that we are using the ExecuteNonQuery method to run the stored procedure. The best time to utilize ExecuteNonQuery is in situations where all you want to do is execute a command without returning any data rows. This is exactly our scenario, as all we want to do is insert a new row.

Testing the Web Service

We now have a fully functional SubmitOrder web service that accepts an XML file in the form of the Order.xsd schema. Using the data in the XML file, the service looks up the customer record and inserts rows into the order header and order details tables. The end result is a completely new order record (see Figure 9-12).

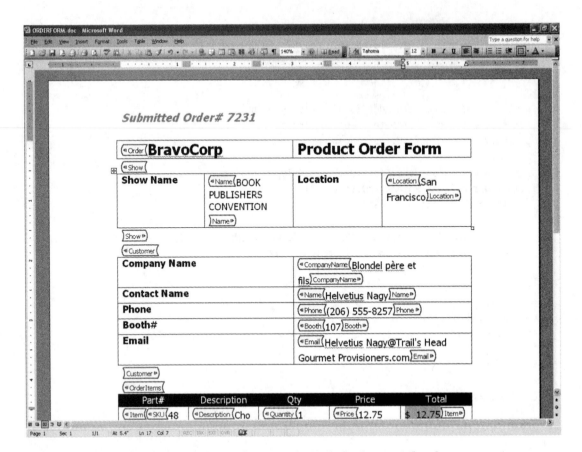

Figure 9-12. *A submitted order displaying the new* OrderID *in the document header*

Now that the code is complete, let's test the web service to be sure it is working correctly. Follow these steps:

1. With the SubmitOrder project open in Visual Studio, press the F5 key.

2. The OrderWS.asmx file opens inside the browser and lists its available web service functions.

3. Enter **http://localhost/SubmitOrderWS/OrderWS.asmx?wsdl** as the URL for the browser to view. This is the URL for the Web Service Description Language (WSDL) file that describes the web service and its available methods (see Figure 9-13). The WSDL file is used by other projects (like the OrderForm.doc smart document created in this chapter) to create a web reference and invoke the web service's available methods.

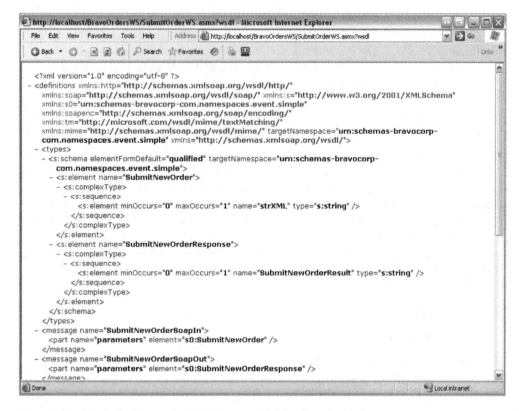

Figure 9-13. *The* OrderWS.asmx *WSDL file*

Building the Smart Document Front-End

The ESOS implements a rich client interface using Microsoft Word as the front-end tool for capturing data and interfacing with the end user. This strategy combines a familiar tool with extended functions for automating the process of creating an order. The best part of the smart-document strategy is that it enables developers to build complex tools, which normally might intimidate users, inside Word where they appear friendly and inviting.

We have already created the XML schema and the target document, which are the first two steps in creating a smart document. These are the final steps:

1. Create the action handler DLL assembly file, which implements the ISmartDocument interface for accessing the smart document API.

2. Configure .NET security. We will create a code group using the .NET Framework Configuration utility that grants Full Trust privileges to the action handler assembly.

3. Create the manifest (XML expansion pack). We will look at how to create the expansion pack, which lists the files that comprise the smart document application.

4. Attach the manifest (XML expansion pack). We will tell the `OrderForm.doc` document that it is a smart document by attaching the manifest file (created in step 3) to the document. This final step provides the document with the information needed to invoke the action handler assembly and match the logic with XML elements defined in the `Order.xsd` XML schema file.

Creating the Action Handler Assembly (the DocActions Class)

The action handler is a .NET assembly containing a single class named `DocActions.vb`, which implements the `ISmartDocument` interface. This class demonstrates how code can monitor the XML elements contained in the `OrderForm.doc` smart document and display controls in the Document Actions task pane depending on which XML element in the order form is active.

Controls in a smart document are standard control types (such as list boxes, check boxes, text boxes, etc.) that reside in a special Office task pane called the Document Actions task pane.

To create the action handler, open Visual Studio and create a new Visual Basic Class Library project, and name it **EventOrder**. Once the project has been created, add the following references (Project ➤ Add Reference):

- ADODB (.NET)

- System.Web.Services.dll (.NET)

- System.Windows.Forms.dll (.NET)

- Microsoft Forms 2.0 Object Library (COM)

- Microsoft Word 11.0 Object Library (COM)

- Microsoft Smart Tags 2.0 Object Library (COM)

■**Note** The smart documents interface, `ISmartDocument`, resides within the Smart Tags 2.0 object library.

We also need a reference to the `SubmitOrder` web service. To add the reference, follow these steps:

1. Select Project ➤ Add Web Reference from the Visual Studio menu.

2. In the Add Web Reference dialog box, enter **http://localhost/SumbitOrderWS/ OrderWS.asmx** and click Go.

3. Once the Add Web Reference dialog box discovers the web service and displays its methods, enter **BravoOrders** as the Web Reference Name and click the Add Reference button to create the reference.

The smart document interface requires the implementation of 17 procedures and 8 properties. In order to better explain how these work in the `DocActions` class, it is easiest to break the required properties and methods down into groups that help explain their purpose. We'll consider them under the following headings:

- **Creating the Controls**: The properties and procedures in this group are the first to be accessed or executed and are used to create the required number of controls and associate them to elements in the schema file.

- **Populating the Controls**: The properties and procedures in this group are the second to be accessed or executed, and they act to fill the created controls with data.

- **Responding to User Action**: The procedures in this group are triggered by the user's actions and are the last to be accessed or executed. These properties are where we will store the business logic of the solution.

The smart document API executes each property and procedure in a particular order. We'll look at the imports and declarations next, and then at the three groups of properties and methods in the order they are called in the life cycle of the document.

Imports and Declarations

This class makes use of Microsoft Word and Office's smart tag objects (the smart tag namespace is the location for the smart document interface).

```
Imports ST = Microsoft.Office.Interop.SmartTag
Imports W = Microsoft.Office.Interop.Word
```

Make sure the namespaces are imported and given an alias to keep the typing to a minimum and to avoid conflicts among objects with the same name in each namespace.

Next we need to declare that this class must implement the smart document interface, ISmartDocument. Insert the following line directly underneath the DocAction class declaration (I have included the class declaration to show context, but there is no need to add the first line):

```
Public Class DocActions
    Implements Microsoft.Office.Interop.SmartTag.ISmartDocument
```

■**Tip** After inserting the preceding Implements statement, be sure to press the Enter key. Doing so will cause Visual Studio to create blanket methods for each of the methods required by ISmartDocument. This is an incredible time-saver and helps ensure that the rules of the interface are met.

We must fully implement all methods specified by the interface, and we will begin by declaring a global variable to store the namespace of the XML schema file we created earlier (Order.xsd). When each task pane control is created, the control's ID number is appended, along with a pound sign (#), to the namespace, and this notation must be used when referencing a control. The full control name for a control in this solution looks like this:

```
urn:schemas-bravocorp-com.namespaces.event.simple#101
```

As you can imagine, this quickly leads to long lines of code, so we will store the main portion of the namespace in a string for use throughout the class:

```
Const cNAMESPACE As String = "urn:schemas-bravocorp-com.namespaces.event.simple"
Const cXNS As String = _
  "xmlns:ns='urn:schemas-bravocorp-com.namespaces.event.simple'"
```

These two variables both store the Uniform Resource Identifier (URI) of the schema file. The first variable will be used to create the name for each control we attach to an element. The second variable stores the schema's namespace alias. The alias will allow us to quickly query an XML document that is based on the Order.xsd schema, using XPath queries.

■**Note** The value for the schema's namespace element is completely arbitrary and could be anything you want it to be. The example here is like a real-world solution, indicative of the type of data involved. However, you could just as easily use a namespace value of "bonoandtheedgerock". What matters is that the namespace value is unique; you want to avoid namespace conflicts, and the simplest way to do that is to use a namespace that reflects an organization's domain name. No matter what value you give the namespace, be careful to keep the cNAMESPACE constant synchronized with the namespace specified in the Order.xsd schema file. If they do not match, the code will not execute.

Next, we will use several constants to define regions that will have the smart document controls associated with them:

```
Const cORDER As String = cNAMESPACE & "#Order"
Const cSHOW As String = cNAMESPACE & "#Show"
Const cCONTACT As String = cNAMESPACE & "#Customer"
Const cITEMS As String = cNAMESPACE & "#Item"
Public Const cTYPES As Integer = 4
```

The first four constants contain the schema elements with which we want to associate controls. For example the cCONTACT constant identifies the Customer element of the XML schema (Order.xsd):

```
<xs:element name="Customer">
  <xs:complexType>
    <xs:sequence>
      <xs:element name="CompanyName" type="xs:string"/>
      <xs:element name="Name" type="xs:string"/>
      <xs:element name="Phone" type="xs:string"/>
      <xs:element name="Email" type="xs:string"/>
      <xs:element name="Booth" type="xs:string"/>
    </xs:sequence>
  </xs:complexType>
</xs:element>
```

Anytime the `Customer` element has the focus inside the `OrderForm.doc` document, the smart document code responds by repainting the Document Actions task pane to display the controls associated with the `Customer` element. Each of the constants created previously will be used to link our code logic to actions in the document (the linking process is described in the "Populating the Controls" and the "Responding to User Interaction" sections). The last constant, `cTYPES`, specifies how many controls will be created by the smart document API at run time (in this case, the number is four).

As discussed earlier, this solution makes use of a SQL Server database to populate certain controls with data. We store the connection string to the database in a `String` for easy access:

```
Dim ConnectString As String = "Server=BCServ;Database=BravoCorp;User" & _
  "ID=bravo;Password=bravocorp;Trusted_Connection=False"
```

Users of the application will likely move back and forth throughout the document, causing different schema elements to move in and out of the current context, so the task pane will need to refresh and display the controls relevant to the current position in the document. That's not a problem, except that a smart document does not automatically save its state between different contexts. If a user moves backward in the document, and the task pane refreshes, the default behavior is for the document to act as if this were the first time the user visited this portion of the document. The task pane will not "remember" their previous selections and will show controls with no values.

It is up to the developer to add code to store selections and retrieve them as necessary. For this solution, we need four variables to handle the job:

```
Dim mlSelectedShow As Long
Dim mlSelectedCompany As Long
Dim mlSelectedContact As Long
Dim mlSelectedBooth As Long
```

The final class variable is a Word document object:

```
Dim oDoc as W.Document
```

This variable will help us to manipulate the Word file throughout the order-completion process.

Each of these variables will make further sense in the next section as we look at each of the properties and procedures in the smart document portion of the ESOS.

Creating the Controls

Several steps must be completed before the smart document can be displayed to the user. A lot goes on here, but it's all simple stuff—each property or procedure performs a single task for all elements.

The SmartDocInitialize Event

Anytime the smart document is opened or an XML expansion is attached, the `SmartDoc-Initialize` procedure executes. Since it is always the first method to run, it is the proper place for setting up the environment.

```
Public Sub SmartDocInitialize(ByVal ApplicationName As String, ByVal Document _
   As Object, ByVal SolutionPath As String, ByVal SolutionRegKeyRoot As String) _
   Implements Microsoft.Office.Interop.SmartTag.ISmartDocument.SmartDocInitialize
   mlSelectedShow = -1
   mlSelectedCompany = -1
   mlSelectedContact = -1
   mlSelectedBooth = -1
End Sub
```

Here the state variables are initialized with values to indicate that no controls have had any values selected.

The SmartDocXmlTypeCount Property

To specify the number of controls we want to associate with schema elements, the Smart-DocXmlTypeCount property returns the value of cTYPES, telling the smart document API to create four controls.

```
Public ReadOnly Property SmartDocXmlTypeCount() As Integer _
   Implements Microsoft.Office.Interop.SmartTag.ISmartDocument.SmartDocXmlTypeCount
   Get
      Return cTYPES
      End Get
   End Property
```

Keep in mind that the Order.xsd XML schema file contains more than four elements. We could easily add actions to each element within the file, but that is not always necessary. The ability to choose and attach actions only to desired elements is a powerful feature of smart documents.

At the end of this property procedure, four controls are created in numerical order (1, 2, 3, and 4). These numbers represent the ControlIDs of the controls in the Document Actions task pane. Then we associate each ControlID with a type name in the SmartDocXMLTypeName property to match the created control with an element from the document's attached Order.xsd schema.

The SmartDocXmlTypeName Property

SmartDocXMLTypeName matches up the ControlIDs created in SmartDocXMLTypeCount with the element names from the schema.

```
Public ReadOnly Property SmartDocXmlTypeName(ByVal XMLTypeID As _
   Integer) As String Implements _
   Microsoft.Office.Interop.SmartTag.ISmartDocument.SmartDocXmlTypeName

   Get
      Select Case XMLTypeID
      Case 1
         Return cORDER
      Case 2
         Return cSHOW
```

```
      Case 3
        Return cCONTACT
      Case 4
        Return cITEMS
        Case Else
      End Select
   End Get
End Property
```

This property procedure is called once for each control to be created. In the ESOS application, that means SmartDocXmlTypeName is called four times. The only way to determine which control has been passed to the property procedure is through a Select...Case statement that reads the value of the XMLTypeID variable.

■**Note** The majority of the procedures that comprise the ISmartDocument interface require the use of the Select...Case statement to determine which control is currently being worked with.

The assignment of XML elements to the XMLTypeID variables is up to the developer. We could just as easily change the order of the values returned by the Case statements and the solution would work the same. All that matters here is that ControlIDs are matched with element names contained within our schema. Table 9-6 shows how the ControlIDs and element names look in memory once SmartDocXMLTypeName completes executing.

Table 9-6. Order.xsd *Element Names Stored in Memory*

ControlID	Element Name
1	urn:schemas-bravocorp-com.namespaces.event.simple#Order
2	urn:schemas-bravocorp-com.namespaces.event.simple#Show
3	urn:schemas-bravocorp-com.namespaces.event.simple#Customer
4	urn:schemas-bravocorp-com.namespaces.event.simple#Item

The SmartDocXmlTypeCaption Property

The SmartDocXmlTypeCaption property procedure is used to set the captions for each XML element that will have controls displayed in the task pane (see Figure 9-14). This property does not return the captions for controls displayed in the task pane (that would be the Control-CaptionFromID property).

```
Public ReadOnly Property SmartDocXmlTypeCaption(ByVal XMLTypeID _
   As Integer, ByVal LocaleID As Integer) As String Implements _
   Microsoft.Office.Interop.SmartTag.ISmartDocument.SmartDocXmlTypeCaption

Get
```

```
    Select Case XMLTypeID
      Case 1
        Return "Bravo Corp: Event Site Order"
      Case 2
        Return "Show Information"
      Case 3
        Return "Customer Information"
      Case 4
        Return "Order Information"
      Case Else
    End Select
  End Get
End Property
```

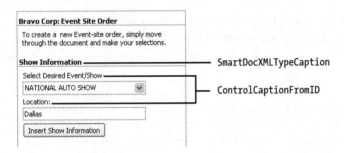

Figure 9-14. *Creating captions for the smart document controls*

The ControlCount Property

The ControlCount property specifies how many controls the smart document API should expect to create for each target XML element. All that it does is return the number of controls for each XMLTypeName. Once each type ControlCount is accessed, the numbering starts over again beginning with 1.

```
Public ReadOnly Property ControlCount(ByVal XMLTypeName As String) _
  As Integer Implements _
  Microsoft.Office.Interop.SmartTag.ISmartDocument.ControlCount
```

```
  Get
    Select Case XMLTypeName
      Case cORDER
        ControlCount = 1
      Case cSHOW
        ControlCount = 3
      Case cCONTACT
        ControlCount = 6
      Case cITEMS
```

```
            ControlCount = 6
        Case Else
    End Select
  End Get
End Property
```

Tip It's probably a good idea to keep a notepad close by when creating these functions, to keep track of which control is which. Otherwise, you may spend all of your time flipping back and forth through your code trying to figure out what `ControlID` 304 is supposed to be.

The ControlID Property

Each control must have a unique identifier, or number, which is used by the smart document API to distinguish and manipulate each control in code. The `ControlID` property provides the ability to create our own control identification scheme.

The `ControlIndex` is an integer that signifies the control's position in the current XML element's collection of controls, and in this code we use the passed `ControlIndex` property of each control to increment the returned property value according to the value assigned to the control's `XMLTypeName` (also a passed parameter).

For example, consider the element represented by the `cOrder` constant—the first time the `ControlID` property procedure executes for that XML element, the `ControlIndex` would be 1, the second time 2, and so on.

```
Public Read Only Property ControlID(ByVal XMLTypeName As String, _
  ByVal ControlIndex As Integer) As Integer _
  Implements Microsoft.Office.Interop.SmartTag.ISmartDocument.ControlID
    Get
      Select Case XMLTypeName
        Case cORDER
          ControlID = ControlIndex
        Case cSHOW
          ControlID = ControlIndex + 100
        Case cCONTACT
          ControlID = ControlIndex + 200
        Case cITEMS
          ControlID = ControlIndex + 300
      End Select
    End Get
End Property
```

Each control within the `cNamespace#Show` element (`Case cSHOW`) is grouped in the 100s by incrementing each `ControlIndex` by 100. Likewise the controls within the `cNamespace#Contact` element are part of the 200s, and the `cNamespace#Items` element's controls comprise the 300s group. Table 9-7 shows how the resulting control set looks in memory.

Table 9-7. `ControlID` *Values for Each Targeted Element*

XMLTypeName	Number of Controls	ControlIDs
urn:schemas-bravocorp-com.namespaces.event.simple#Order	1	1
urn:schemas-bravocorp-com.namespaces.event.simple#Show	3	201,202,203
urn:schemas-bravocorp-com.namespaces.event.simple#Customer	6	301,302,303,304,305,306
urn:schemas-bravocorp-com.namespaces.event.simple#Item	6	401,402,403,404,405,406

The ControlNameFromID Property

The `ControlNameFromID` property can be used to set up a unique name for each control in the smart document. This name can then be accessed within VBA using the `SmartTagActions` collection. Here, `ControlNameFromID` is implemented only to satisfy the requirements of the smart document interface.

```
Public ReadOnly Property ControlNameFromID(ByVal ControlID As Integer) _
  As String Implements _
  Microsoft.Office.Interop.SmartTag.ISmartDocument.ControlNameFromID

  Get
    Return ControlID.ToString
  End Get
End Property
```

We only return the `ControlID`'s string value as the unique name for the control. The `ControlNameFromID` property is not utilized in the ESOS, so the value returned is of no consequence expect to fulfill the requirements of the `ISmartDocument` interface.

Tip If you needed to access the smart document controls in the Document Actions task pane using VBA, you could use a `Select...Case` statement to identify the referenced control and provide a control name that conformed to the Hungarian naming convention. Although this approach would not improve performance, it would help the make the VBA code more readable than simply using the `ControlID` values.

The ControlCaptionFromID Property

Each task pane control should have a caption—a good caption informs the user of the purpose of the control (or at least provides a good hint). The `ControlCaptionFromID` property allows us to grab the passed `ControlID` and assign a caption to the referenced task pane control. The `ControlCaptionFromID` property's returned value is the text that will be displayed next to the control in the task pane (see Figure 9-14).

```vb
Public ReadOnly Property ControlCaptionFromID(ByVal ControlID As Integer, _
  ByVal ApplicationName As String, ByVal LocaleID As Integer, _
  ByVal Text As String, ByVal Xml As String, ByVal Target As Object) _
  As String Implements _
  Microsoft.Office.Interop.SmartTag.ISmartDocument.ControlCaptionFromID

  Get
    Select Case ControlID
      Case 1
        Return "To create a new Event-site order, simply move through the document " & _
          "and make your selections."
      Case 101
        Return "Select Desired Event/Show"
      Case 102
        Return "Location:"
      Case 103
        Return "Insert Show Information"
      Case 201
        Return "Select Exhibitor Company Name:"
      Case 202
        Return "Select Company Contact Placing Order:"
      Case 203
        Return "Phone Number:"
      Case 204
        Return "Email:"
      Case 205
        Return "Select Booth Number:"
      Case 206
        Return "Insert Client Information"
      Case 301
        Return "Select Order Item:"
      Case 302
        Return "Part Number:"
      Case 303
        Return "Quantity:"
      Case 304
        Return "Price:"
      Case 305
        Return "Insert Line Item"
      Case 306
        Return "Submit Order"
      Case Else
    End Select
  End Get
End Property
```

As you can see, we use a Select...Case statement to branch out and return a different caption for each control.

> **Tip** Depending on the state or context of the document, you may want to hide certain controls that are not currently relevant. To hide a control, just set the caption's value to a blank string.

The ControlTypeFromID Property

The last step when creating the controls is to assign a control type for each control. Since we can't draw the controls on the task pane at design-time, as is possible when creating a Windows form, we will do it with code. To specify the type of control to display in the task pane, a C_Type constant is assigned to a control. There are C_Type constants for all the usual controls expected by a developer (label, combo box, text box, button, etc.).

The ControlTypeFromID property determines which control has been passed to the property procedure by checking the value of the ControlID parameter with a Select...Case statement and assigning a C_Type constant to signify the type of control it is.

```
Public ReadOnly Property ControlTypeFromID(ByVal ControlID As Integer, _
  ByVal ApplicationName As String, ByVal LocaleID As Integer) _
  As Microsoft.Office.Interop.SmartTag.C_TYPE Implements _
  Microsoft.Office.Interop.SmartTag.ISmartDocument.ControlTypeFromID

  Get
    Select Case ControlID
      Case 1
        Return ST.C_TYPE.C_TYPE_LABEL
      Case 101    'select show
        Return ST.C_TYPE.C_TYPE_COMBO
      Case 102    'location
        Return ST.C_TYPE.C_TYPE_TEXTBOX
      Case 103    'insert button
        Return ST.C_TYPE.C_TYPE_BUTTON
      Case 201    'company
        Return ST.C_TYPE.C_TYPE_COMBO
      Case 202    'customer contact
        Return ST.C_TYPE.C_TYPE_COMBO
      Case 203    'phone#
        Return ST.C_TYPE.C_TYPE_TEXTBOX
      Case 204    'email
        Return ST.C_TYPE.C_TYPE_TEXTBOX
      Case 205    'select booth
        Return ST.C_TYPE.C_TYPE_COMBO
      Case 206    'insert button
        Return ST.C_TYPE.C_TYPE_BUTTON
      Case 301    'select Part desc
        Return ST.C_TYPE.C_TYPE_COMBO
```

```
      Case 302    'part#
        Return ST.C_TYPE.C_TYPE_TEXTBOX
      Case 303    'qty
        Return ST.C_TYPE.C_TYPE_TEXTBOX
      Case 304    'price
        Return ST.C_TYPE.C_TYPE_TEXTBOX
      Case 305    'insert button
        Return ST.C_TYPE.C_TYPE_BUTTON
      Case 306    'submit button
        Return ST.C_TYPE.C_TYPE_BUTTON
      Case Else
  End Select
End Get
```

Most of the controls you'd expect are available for use. Table 9-8 provides a full listing of them.

Table 9-8. *Smart Document Control Types—the C_Type Constant*

Control Type	C_Type Constant	Description
ActiveX control	C_TYPE_ACTIVEX	Adds any ActiveX control. This is a good method for inserting a custom control with functionality not available from other control types.
Button	C_TYPE_BUTTON	Adds a normal command button.
CheckBox	C_TYPE_CHECKBOX	Adds a check box.
ComboBox	C_TYPE_COMBO	Adds a combo box.
Document fragment	C_TYPE_DOCUMENTFRAGMENT	This is a new type of control used to provide a link that inserts hard-coded text into the document.
Document fragment URL	C_TYPE_DOCUMENTFRAGMENTURL	This is another new control type used to specify the location of a file that contains text to insert into the document.
Help	C_TYPE_HELP	Creates a help link control filled with hard-coded text.
Help URL	C_TYPE_URL	Creates a help link control whose content is contained in an external file.
Image	C_TYPE_IMAGE	Specifies the location of an image to insert inside the task pane.
Label	C_TYPE_LABEL	Adds a label to the task pane.
Link	C_TYPE_LINK	Places a URL in the task pane.
ListBox	C_TYPE_LISTBOX	Creates a list-box control.
Radio buttons	C_TYPE_RADIOGROUP	Creates a group of radio buttons.
Separator	C_TYPE_SEPARATOR	Creates a line-separator control.
TextBox	C_TYPE_TEXTBOX	Creates a text-box control.

We now have all the code that sets up the smart document by creating all the controls and matching them up with the targeted elements within the attached Order.xsd XML schema file. It's not quite like drawing a form, but it's not bad once you get used to it.

Populating the Controls

In the previous section, we created the controls for our solution. In this section, we will take these newly created controls a step further and fill them with data that will be useful when a user completed an OrderForm.doc smart document. The smart document API provides nine different "populate" methods for populating controls. Each method is named to match the type of control it populates—for example, PopulateTextboxContent inserts values into a Textbox control.

The "populate" methods are actually good for more than filling controls with data. They are also the place where we set the display properties of the controls, such as the Width and Height.

For the ESOS, we only need to implement two of the nine available "populate" event methods: PopulateListOrComboContent and PopulateTextboxContent.

■Note Full documentation of the ISmartDocument interface, including each event method, is available on MSDN at http://msdn.microsoft.com/library/en-us/sdsdk/html/sdobjISmartDocument.asp.

The PopulateListOrComboContent Event Method

PopulateListOrComboContent applies to both ListBox and ComboBox controls. Our solution implements five ComboBox controls, which means that the PopulateListOrComboContent method will be called five times—once for each control. The code looks like this:

```
Public Sub PopulateListOrComboContent(ByVal ControlID As Integer, _
  ByVal ApplicationName As String, ByVal LocaleID As Integer, ByVal _
  Text As String, ByVal Xml As String, ByVal Target As Object, ByVal _
  Props As Microsoft.Office.Interop.SmartTag.ISmartDocProperties, ByRef _
  List As System.Array, ByRef Count As Integer, ByRef InitialSelected As Integer) _
  Implements _
  Microsoft.Office.Interop.SmartTag.ISmartDocument.PopulateListOrComboContent

  Dim rs As New ADODB.Recordset
  Select Case ControlID
    Case 101
      FillListOrComboControlWithDBData("Select * from qryShows", _
        ConnectString, Count, List)

      InitialSelected = mlSelectedShow
      Props.Write("w", 200)
```

```
Case 201
   FillListOrComboControlWithDBData("Select * from qryCompanies", _
     ConnectString, Count, List)
   InitialSelected = mlSelectedCompany
   Props.Write("w", 200)
Case 202
   FillListOrComboControlWithDBData("Select * from qryContacts", _
     ConnectString, Count, List)
   InitialSelected = mlSelectedContact
   Props.Write("w", 200)
Case 205
  FillListOrComboControlWithDBData("Select * from qryBooths", _
     ConnectString, Count, List)
   InitialSelected = mlSelectedBooth
   Props.Write("w", 200)
Case 301
   FillListOrComboControlWithDBData("Select * from qryProducts", _
     ConnectString, Count, List)
   InitialSelected = -1
   Props.Write("w", 200)
Case Else

End Select
End Sub
```

Our goal within this procedure is threefold: to discover the current control (thankfully, the method provides the ControlID), to fill the current control with data, and to set the control's display properties:

```
Select Case ControlID
   Case 101
      FillListOrComboControlWithDBData("Select * from qryShows",_
        ConnectString, Count, List)

      InitialSelected = mlSelectedShow
      Props.Write("w", 200)
```

The Select...Case statement branches out based on the value of the ControlID and allows different logic for each ComboBox, if needed. In this case, each of the five controls does pretty much the same thing. The only difference is the SQL statement provided to the FillListOr-ComboControlWithDBData helper function. This function requires that we pass a SQL statement, a connection string, the total number of rows in the control (the Count parameter), and a reference to the control's List array object.

Once the FillListOrComboControlWithDBData method fills the List array with data, we complete the control's related "state" variable (in this case mlSelectedShow) and then set the width of the control to 200 pixels.

▓**Tip** If we do not set the control's width, it will expand to the entire width of the task pane, leaving only what appears to be a 1-pixel space between the control and the edge of the task pane. Setting the control's width makes for a cleaner GUI.

The PopulateTextboxContent Event Method

We will not add any code to maintain the state of the Textbox controls in the ESOS. However, we do want to add some formatting instructions to bring these controls in line with the Combo-Box controls. PopulateTextboxContent is the place for this code.

```
Public Sub PopulateTextboxContent(ByVal ControlID As Integer, _
  ByVal ApplicationName As String, ByVal LocaleID As Integer, _
  ByVal Text As String, ByVal Xml As String, ByVal Target As Object, _
  ByVal Props As Microsoft.Office.Interop.SmartTag.ISmartDocProperties, _
  ByRef Value As String) _
  Implements Microsoft.Office.Interop.SmartTag.ISmartDocument.PopulateTextboxContent

  Select Case ControlID
    Case 102  'location
      Props.Write("w", 200)
    Case 203  'phone#
      Props.Write("w", 200)
    Case 204  'email
      Props.Write("w", 200)
    Case 302  'part desc
      Props.Write("w", 200)
    Case 303  'qty
      Props.Write("w", 50)
    Case 304  'price
      Props.Write("w", 50)
    Case Else

  End Select
End Sub
```

In every case, we use the Write method of the property collection to create a new property in the smart document's property bag. Properties are written into the property bag using a key/value format as specified in the following syntax:

```
Props.Write(key,value)
```

Width and height are just a couple of the properties available for use. Table 9-9 provides a listing of properties available to all controls, plus an additional three that pertain only to Textbox controls.

Table 9-9. *Properties Available for Controls*

Property Name	Description	Pertains To
X	Sets the left position of the control relative to the task pane's left edge; must be a positive integer	All controls
Y	Specifies the top position of the control relative to the bottom of the control directly above it (or the bottom of the task pane if this is the first control); must be a positive integer	All controls
H	Sets the height of the control; must be a positive integer	All controls
W	Sets the width of the control; must be a positive integer	All controls
Align	Sets the horizontal alignment of the control; must be one of the following strings: "Center", "Left", "Right"	All controls
Layout	Specifies the direction of the text flow of the control; must be a string specifying either "LTR" (left-to-right) or "RTL" (right-to-left)	All controls
SectionCaptionDirection	Specifies the control's caption text-flow direction; must be a string specifying either "LTR" (left-to-right) or "RTL" (right-to-left)	All controls
NumberOfLines	Specifies the number of lines to be visible without requiring scrolling; must be a positive integer	Textbox control only
IsEditable	Specifies whether or not the control is editable; must be a Boolean value	Textbox control only
ControlOnSameLine	Specifies whether or not the control is displayed on the same line as its caption; must be a Boolean value	Textbox control only

Responding to User Interaction

The smart document API provides seven methods that fire in response to user actions. The majority of these execute as the result of a change made to a control. For example, the On-CheckboxChange event method triggers as a result of the user checking or unchecking a CheckBox control. Like the "populate" methods, these "onchange" event methods correspond directly to the various types of available controls.

For the ESOS application, we will only add code to one of the "onchange" methods, the OnListOrComboSelectChange method.

The OnListOrComboSelectChange Event Method

As the user makes their way through creating a new order, the task pane will continually refresh to display controls relevant to the user's current position in the document. In each case, a ComboBox control filled with order choices is made available to the user.

When a selection is made in a ComboBox, we want to update other controls in the task pane with additional data from the selection. Doing so provides a simple review capability so the user can edit the selected data prior to inserting the values into the document.

```
Public Sub OnListOrComboSelectChange(ByVal ControlID As Integer, _
  ByVal Target As Object, ByVal Selected As Integer, ByVal Value As String) _
  Implements _
  Microsoft.Office.Interop.SmartTag.ISmartDocument.OnListOrComboSelectChange

  Dim xNode As W.XMLNode
  xNode = Target.XMLNodes(1)
  Try
  Select Case ControlID
    Case 101
      mlSelectedShow = Selected
      Dim rs As New ADODB.Recordset
      rs.Open("Select * from tblShows Where Name = '" & Value & "'", _
        ConnectString, ADODB.CursorTypeEnum.adOpenStatic)

        xNode.SmartTag.SmartTagActions("102").TextboxText = rs.Fields("Location").Value
        rs.Close()
        rs = Nothing
    Case 201
      mlSelectedCompany = Selected
    Case 202
      mlSelectedContact = Selected
      Dim rs As New ADODB.Recordset
      rs.Open("Select * From tblCustomers Where ContactName='" & Value & "'", _
        ConnectString, ADODB.CursorTypeEnum.adOpenStatic)
        xNode.SmartTag.SmartTagActions("203").TextboxText = rs.Fields("Phone").Value
        xNode.SmartTag.SmartTagActions("204").TextboxText = rs.Fields("Email").Value

        rs.Close()
        rs = Nothing

    Case 205
      mlSelectedBooth = Selected
    Case 301
      Dim rs As New ADODB.Recordset
      rs.Open("Select * From tblProducts Where ProductName='" & Value & "'", _
        connectString, ADODB.CursorTypeEnum.adOpenStatic)
      xNode.SmartTag.SmartTagActions("302").TextboxText = rs.Fields("ProductID").Value
      xNode.SmartTag.SmartTagActions("303").TextboxText = "1"
      xNode.SmartTag.SmartTagActions("304").TextboxText = _
      Format(rs.Fields("UnitPrice").Value, "C")
```

```
      rs.Close()
      rs = Nothing
    Case Else

  End Select
  Catch ex As Exception

  End Try

End Sub
```

OnListOrComboSelectChange is actually five different methods rolled into one, but this is not a big deal, as we can use the value of ControlID to determine which control is referenced and branch accordingly to execute the code relevant for that control. In this case, no matter what control caused this event to trigger, the goal is always to retrieve additional data from the database and insert the values into the other controls displayed in the task pane.

Since the code is very similar for each Case, let's limit our discussion to Case 202—the code for the ComboBox filled with contact records retrieved from the solution database. Here's the code again:

```
Case 202
  mlSelectedContact = Selected
  Dim rs As New ADODB.Recordset
  rs.Open("Select * From tblCustomers Where ContactName='" & Value & "'", _
  ConnectString, ADODB.CursorTypeEnum.adOpenStatic)
  xNode.SmartTag.SmartTagActions("203").TextboxText = rs.Fields("Phone").Value
  xNode.SmartTag.SmartTagActions("204").TextboxText = rs.Fields("Email").Value

  rs.Close()
  rs = Nothing
```

In this code, the Selected value (provided by the OnListOrComboSelectChange method) is stored in the global variable for the currently selected contact. Then we create a new recordset to retrieve the selected contact's additional data. The data is easily retrieved with a SQL statement that uses the Contact control's Value. With the data in hand, all that is left to do is fill the additional controls in the task pane with the retrieved data.

Controls within the task pane are accessed and referenced through the SmartTagActions collection. This collection contains all the controls we created in the previous section (the smart document controls we associated with various XML elements contained within the attached XML schema file—Order.xsd).

Notice that not all the cases in the function retrieve data from the solution's database. In some instances, all that is needed is to store the selected value for state-maintenance purposes. In each of these cases, there are no other fields to be populated at present, and the value stored is the actual user-friendly "description" field and not the computer-friendly "ID" field.

The InvokeControl Event Method

The InvokeControl method is the important method—the one that ties everything together. It performs the actions initiated by the button, hyperlink, and document fragment control types (see Table 9-8 for the relevant C_Type constant values). Like every other method provided by the smart document API, InvokeControl is a single method pretending to be several different methods. What happens depends upon which control triggers the method.

The only control that will trigger InvokeControl in the ESOS application is the Button control, and it is used (with one exception) to insert data into the OrderForm.doc smart document.

```vb
Public Sub InvokeControl(ByVal ControlID As Integer, ByVal ApplicationName _
  As String, ByVal Target As Object, ByVal Text As String, ByVal Xml As _
  String, ByVal LocaleID As Integer) _
  Implements Microsoft.Office.Interop.SmartTag.ISmartDocument.InvokeControl

  Dim xNode As W.XMLNode
  Dim rng As W.Range
  rng = Target
  xNode = rng.XMLNodes(1)

  Try
    Select Case ControlID
      Case 103 'Insert Show Information
        xNode.SelectSingleNode("//ns:Show/ns:Name", cXNS).Range.Text = _
          xNode.SmartTag.SmartTagActions("101").TextboxText
        xNode.SelectSingleNode("//ns:Show/ns:Location", cXNS).Range.Text = _
          xNode.SmartTag.SmartTagActions("102").TextboxText
      Case 206 'Insert Client Information
        xNode.SelectSingleNode("//ns:Customer/ns:CompanyName", cXNS).Range.Text = _
          xNode.SmartTag.SmartTagActions("201").TextboxText
        xNode.SelectSingleNode("//ns:Customer/ns:Name", cXNS).Range.Text = _
          xNode.SmartTag.SmartTagActions("202").TextboxText
        xNode.SelectSingleNode("//ns:Customer/ns:Phone", cXNS).Range.Text = _
          xNode.SmartTag.SmartTagActions("203").TextboxText
        xNode.SelectSingleNode("//ns:Customer/ns:Email", cXNS).Range.Text = _
          xNode.SmartTag.SmartTagActions("204").TextboxText
        xNode.SelectSingleNode("//ns:Customer/ns:Booth", cXNS).Range.Text = _
          xNode.SmartTag.SmartTagActions("205").TextboxText()
      Case 305 'Insert Line Item
        IF xNode.SmartTag.SmartTagActions("301").ListSelection = -1 Then
          MsgBox("Please select a Product item before attempting an insert, bro!", _
            MsgBoxStyle.Exclamation, "Pick Something Jack! What's up with that?")
        Else
          Dim strSku As String = xNode.SmartTag.SmartTagActions("302").TextboxText
          Dim strDesc As String = xNode.SmartTag.SmartTagActions("301").TextboxText
          Dim strQty As String = xNode.SmartTag.SmartTagActions("303").TextboxText
          Dim strPrice As String = xNode.SmartTag.SmartTagActions("304").TextboxText
```

```
    With rng.Application.Selection
      .Tables(1).Rows(.Tables(1).Rows.Count - 2).Select()

      If .Tables(1).Rows(.Tables(1).Rows.Count - 2). _
        Range.Fields(1).Result.Text <> "$   0.00" Then
        .InsertRowsBelow(1)
        .Cells(5).Formula("=Product(Left)", "$#,##0.00;($#,##0.00)")
      End If

      xNode = .Rows.Last.Range.XMLNodes(1)
    End With
    With xNode.ChildNodes
      .Item(1).Range.Text = strSku
      .Item(2).Range.Text = strDesc
      .Item(3).Range.Text = strQty
      .Item(4).Range.Text = strPrice
    End With
  End If

  rng.Application.Selection.Tables(1).Range.Fields.Update()


Case 306 'Submit Order
    If oDoc.CustomDocumentProperties("OrderID").value = "0" Then
  'Invoke the Submit Order Web Service
  'Send the Target docs XML data file
  Dim boPO As New BravoOrders.ProcessOrders
  Dim strOrderID As String
  Dim strXML As String = oDoc.XMLNodes(1).XML(True)
  strXML = Replace(strXML, "xmlns", "xmlns:ns")
  strOrderID = boPO.SubmitNewOrder(oDoc.XMLNodes(1).XML(True))

  With oDoc
    .CustomDocumentProperties("OrderID") = strOrderID
    With .Application
      .ActiveWindow.ActivePane.View.SeekView = _
      W.WdSeekView.wdSeekCurrentPageHeader
      .Selection.HeaderFooter.Range.Text = "Submitted Order# " & strOrderID
      .Selection.Font.Name = "Tunga"
      .Selection.Font.Bold = True
      .Selection.Font.Size = 20
      .ActiveWindow.ActivePane.View.SeekView = _
        W.WdSeekView.wdSeekMainDocument
    End With
  End With
  MsgBox("This order has been submitted. The Order Number is " & _
    strOrderID & ".", MsgBoxStyle.Information, "Order Submitted")
  Else
```

```
            MsgBox("This order has already been submitted.", MsgBoxStyle.Information, _
               "Submitted Order")
         End If

      Case Else

   End Select

   Catch ex As Exception
      MsgBox(Err.Description)
   End Try
End Sub
```

Let's work our way through this method in a few sections, as it actually handles four different cases and can be a little complex. The method opens by declaring a few variables that will allow us to manipulate the XML within the target document:

```
Dim xNode As W.XMLNode
Dim rng As W.Range
Dim xElement As W.XMLNode
rng = Target
xNode = rng.XMLNodes(1)
```

The required objects for executing the function are a Word XMLNode and a Range object. The XMLNode will be used to maintain a reference to the Target document's XML data, while the Range object will be used for inserting values into the Target.

The first Case handles the Insert Show Information button's event (ControlID 103). This button is available anytime the Show element is the current context.

```
Case 103 'Insert Show Information
   xNode.SelectSingleNode("//ns:Show/ns:Name", cXNS).Range.Text = _
   xNode.SmartTag.SmartTagActions("101").TextboxText
   xNode.SelectSingleNode("//ns:Show/ns:Location", cXNS).Range.Text = _
   xNode.SmartTag.SmartTagActions("102").TextboxText
```

Retrieving the value of the controls in the task pane works just like setting the control's values. Once again, we access the control via the SmartTagActions collection and retrieve the value stored in the TextboxText property. The values are inserted into the OrderForm.doc smart document by first finding the control's associated XML element within the document and then assigning the retrieved control's value to the element's Range.

To find the control's associated XML element, we pass an XPath query to the Select-SingleNode method, which recursively searches the XML contained within the xNode object and returns the first node matching the passed XPath query. This could be a problem if the XML contains multiple references to the same element, but that's not the case here. Just keep it in mind when dealing with more complex XML documents and schemas.

The second case executes the code for the Insert New Client button, which displays as the user places the cursor anywhere inside the areas of the document mapped to the Customer element:

```
xNode.SelectSingleNode("//ns:Customer/ns:CompanyName", cXNS).Range.Text = _
  xNode.SmartTag.SmartTagActions("201").TextboxText
xNode.SelectSingleNode("//ns:Customer/ns:Name", cXNS).Range.Text = _
  xNode.SmartTag.SmartTagActions("202").TextboxText
xNode.SelectSingleNode("//ns:Customer/ns:Phone", cXNS).Range.Text = _
  xNode.SmartTag.SmartTagActions("203").TextboxText
xNode.SelectSingleNode("//ns:Customer/ns:Email", cXNS).Range.Text = _
  xNode.SmartTag.SmartTagActions("204").TextboxText
xNode.SelectSingleNode("//ns:Customer/ns:Booth", cXNS).Range.Text = _
  xNode.SmartTag.SmartTagActions("205").TextboxText()
```

This is not any different from the previous case so let's move on.

The third case (Case 305) contains the code for the Insert Line Item button, which is displayed anytime the OrderItems element is in play. Once this button is clicked, a new line item is inserted into the line item table of the OrderForm.doc smart document.

```
Case 305 'Insert Line Item
    IF xNode.SmartTag.SmartTagActions("301").ListSelection = -1 Then
      MsgBox("Please select a Product item before attempting an insert.", _
        MsgBoxStyle.Exclamation, "Select Something, Anything")
      Exit Sub
    Else
      Dim strSku As String = xNode.SmartTag.SmartTagActions("302").TextboxText
      Dim strDesc As String = xNode.SmartTag.SmartTagActions("301").TextboxText
      Dim strQty As String = xNode.SmartTag.SmartTagActions("303").TextboxText
      Dim strPrice As String = xNode.SmartTag.SmartTagActions("304").TextboxText

      With rng.Application.Selection
        .Tables(1).Rows(.Tables(1).Rows.Count - 2).Select()
        If .Tables(1).Rows(.Tables(1).Rows.Count - 2). _
        Range.Fields(1).Result.Text <> "$   0.00" Then
          .InsertRowsBelow(1)
          .Cells(5).Formula("=Product(Left)", "$#,##0.00;($#,##0.00)")
        End If

        xNode = .Rows.Last.Range.XMLNodes(1)
      End With
      With xNode.ChildNodes
        .Item(1).Range.Text = strSku
        .Item(2).Range.Text = strDesc
        .Item(3).Range.Text = strQty
        .Item(4).Range.Text = strPrice
      End With
    End If

    rng.Application.Selection.Tables(1).Range.Fields.Update()
```

This is a lot of code to insert a single line item, and it may look somewhat intimidating. However, four actions occur in this code. First, we ensure that a product has indeed been selected before continuing. If no selection has been made, we notify the user and exit the procedure:

```
IF xNode.SmartTag.SmartTagActions("301").ListSelection = -1 Then
  MsgBox("Please select a Product item before attempting an insert.", _
    MsgBoxStyle.Exclamation, "Select Something, Anything")
  Exit Sub
Else
  Dim strSku As String = xNode.SmartTag.SmartTagActions("302").TextboxText
  Dim strDesc As String = xNode.SmartTag.SmartTagActions("301").TextboxText
  Dim strQty As String = xNode.SmartTag.SmartTagActions("303").TextboxText
  Dim strPrice As String = xNode.SmartTag.SmartTagActions("304").TextboxText
```

If the user made a selection, we store the values of the selected items (which should be available as values in the task pane controls) in four variables for use at the end of the case. Once the values are safely stored in memory, we need to put them in a new line in the order line items table (in the OrderForm.doc smart document):

```
With rng.Application.Selection
  .Tables(1).Rows(.Tables(1).Rows.Count - 2).Select()

  If .Tables(1).Rows(.Tables(1).Rows.Count - 2). _
    Range.Fields(1).Result.Text <> "$    0.00" Then
    .InsertRowsBelow(1)
    .Cells(5).Formula("=Product(Left)", "$#,##0.00;($#,##0.00)")
  End If

  xNode = .Rows.Last.Range.XMLNodes(1)
End With
```

Using the entire document as the Selection, we manipulate the first table in the document and immediately select the row second from the bottom (see Figure 9-15). This should be the last row containing an order item. (The last row is the order total row and the next to last row is blank.) Before inserting a new row, we check the Text property of the row's one and only field to ensure it equals "$ 0.00". This is the field that auto-multiplies the values of the Price and Units columns to fill the row's Total column.

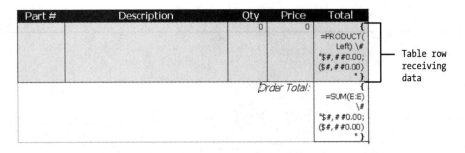

Figure 9-15. *Selecting a table row to insert a new order line*

If we are in the correct location, we insert a new row below the current row and insert the same formula we created manually when we initially built the OrderForm.doc document. Inserting a formula into the Total column (the fifth column in the row), creates a new field code in the row and sets up the row for the next time this code executes to insert an additional row. Before moving to the next step, the newly inserted row is set up as the current Node.

Next, each column in the new row receives the order values stored in memory:

```
With xNode.ChildNodes
  .Item(1).Range.Text = strSku
  .Item(2).Range.Text = strDesc
  .Item(3).Range.Text = strQty
  .Item(4).Range.Text = strPrice
End With
```

Instead of assigning the values to the row columns, it is easier to use the ChildNodes collection and assign the values to each element. The result is the same as inserting text into the row columns.

The fourth and last step is to update the OrderTotal row to include the value of the new row's Total column.

```
rng.Application.Selection.Tables(1).Range.Fields.Update()
```

The fourth Case executes the code for the Submit Order button, which is available anytime the user is inside the OrderItems section of the document. The purpose of this Case is to submit the document's XML data to the SubmitOrder web service we will create shortly.

```
Case 306 'Submit Order
  If oDoc.CustomDocumentProperties("OrderID").value = "0" Then
    Dim boPO As New BravoOrders.ProcessOrders
    Dim strOrderID As String
    Dim strXML As String = oDoc.XMLNodes(1).XML(True)
    strXML = Replace(strXML, "xmlns", "xmlns:ns")
    strOrderID = boPO.SubmitNewOrder(oDoc.XMLNodes(1).XML(True))

    With oDoc
      ".CustomDocumentProperties("OrderID") = strOrderID
      With .Application
        .ActiveWindow.ActivePane.View.SeekView = _
          W.WdSeekView.wdSeekCurrentPageHeader
        .Selection.HeaderFooter.Range.Text = "Submitted Order# " & strOrderID
        .Selection.Font.Name = "Tunga"
        .Selection.Font.Bold = True
        .Selection.Font.Size = 20
        .ActiveWindow.ActivePane.View.SeekView = _
          W.WdSeekView.wdSeekMainDocument
      End With
    End With
    MsgBox("This order has been submitted. The Order Number is " & _
      strOrderID & ".", MsgBoxStyle.Information, "Order Submitted")
```

```
Else
  MsgBox("This order has already been submitted.", MsgBoxStyle.Information, _
    "Submitted Order")
End If
```

Next, we want to prevent an already submitted order from being submitted again. A submitted order will contain an order number in the document's custom properties. Therefore, the way to determine if the order is a new one is to check the value of the custom OrderID document property. If the value equals 0, then we can submit the order.

```
If oDoc.CustomDocumentProperties("OrderID").value = "0" Then
  Dim boPO As New BravoOrders.ProcessOrders
  Dim strOrderID As String
  Dim strXML As String = oDoc.XMLNodes(1).XML(True)
  strXML = Replace(strXML, "xmlns", "xmlns:ns")
  strOrderID = boPO.SubmitNewOrder(oDoc.XMLNodes(1).XML(True))
```

Next, submitting the order is as simple as creating a reference to the web service's wrapper class and passing the document's XML data to the web service's ProcessOrders class. Before doing so, though, a little cleanup work is required of the completed OrderForm.doc smart document's underlying XML data: when accessing just the data of the XML, the namespace assigned to the XML data will not match the namespace defined by the order schema definition (Order.xsd). A simple search and replace easily corrects this problem and gives the submitted data the namespace name expected by the web service.

Assuming the order is successfully created, and the web service returns a new OrderID, the next thing to do is to tag the OrderForm.doc smart document as a submitted order. As mentioned earlier, a submitted order is one that contains an order number in the OrderID custom document property.

```
With oDoc
  .CustomDocumentProperties("OrderID") = strOrderID
  With .Application
    .ActiveWindow.ActivePane.View.SeekView = _
      W.WdSeekView.wdSeekCurrentPageHeader
    .Selection.HeaderFooter.Range.Text = "Submitted Order# " & strOrderID
    .Selection.Font.Name = "Tunga"
    .Selection.Font.Bold = True
    .Selection.Font.Size = 20
    .ActiveWindow.ActivePane.View.SeekView = _
      W.WdSeekView.wdSeekMainDocument
  End With
End With
MsgBox("This order has been submitted. The Order Number is " & _
  strOrderID & ".", MsgBoxStyle.Information, "Order Submitted")
```

The OrderID value provided by the web service is inserted into the custom document properties. In addition, to provide a visual clue that the order has been submitted, we insert the

OrderID in the Header section of the document and format the text. Assuming everything went according to plan, we let the user know the order number.

The InvokeControl event is the event method for all button, hyperlink, document-fragment, and document-fragment URL controls (the C_Type constants for these controls are C_TYPE_BUTTON, C_TYPE_LINK, C_TYPE_DOCUMENTFRAGMENT, C_TYPEDOCUMENTFRAGMENTURL, respectively). There is only one InvokeControl event method in the class which means it must act as "virtual dispatcher" for these types of controls and include code to identify the control and provide the desired event logic pertaining to it. InvokeControl is triggered by a user clicking on these controls in the task pane.

The ideal situation would be a method that created a single procedure for each control (like a typical Windows form), but this is a version 1 implementation of smart documents, so a "virtual dispatcher" scenario is what we have to deal with. Just think of InvokeControl as several, often unrelated, event methods rolled into a single, larger event method, and separated from each other by a long Select...Case statement. If you can handle that, you're fine.

The FillListOrComboControlWithDBData Event Method

FillListOrComboControlWithDBData is a helper function used to populate ListBox or ComboBox controls. Like the PopulateListOrComboContent method, this one is called once for each of the ComboBox controls in the solution. This function's single purpose is to populate a ComboBox or ListBox control with data from the solution's database. It only needs to know what data is required (as defined by a SQL statement) and where the data is located (as identified by a connection string).

The key point to FillListOrComboControlWithDBData is that the last two defined parameters, iCount and List, are passed ByRef, allowing the calling method to see any edits made during execution.

Tip ByVal and ByRef are sometimes confusing. If you find yourself uncertain about their meaning, try thinking of them this way: When you want to pass only the value of a variable and not the variable itself, use ByVal. When you want to pass the both the variable and its value, use ByRef.

Here's the code for the method:

```
Public Function FillListOrComboControlWithDBData(ByVal strSQL As String, _
  ByVal strConnect As String, ByRef iCount As Long, ByRef List As Array)

  Try
    Dim rs As New ADODB.Recordset
    rs.Open(strSQL, strConnect, ADODB.CursorTypeEnum.adOpenStatic)

    If Not rs.EOF Then
      rs.MoveLast()
      rs.MoveFirst()
```

```
      iCount = rs.RecordCount
      Do Until rs.EOF
        List(rs.AbsolutePosition) = rs(1).Value
        rs.MoveNext()
      Loop

    End If

    rs.Close()

  Catch ex As Exception
    MsgBox(Err.Description)
  End Try

End Function
```

The function begins by creating a `Recordset` object and filling it with records using the SQL statement and connection string provided by `strSQL` and `strConnect` respectively:

```
Dim rs As New ADODB.Recordset
rs.Open(strSQL, strConnect, ADODB.CursorTypeEnum.adOpenStatic)
```

Next, the total number of records is determined by moving to the end of the recordset (provided records exist). This record count is stored in `iCount`, which lets the calling function know how many rows to create for the `ListBox` or `ComboBox` control:

```
If Not rs.EOF Then
  rs.MoveLast()
  rs.MoveFirst()
  iCount = rs.RecordCount
```

Finally, the function wraps up by looping through the recordset and filling the `List` array with values from the recordset's first column.

```
  Do Until rs.EOF
    List(rs.AbsolutePosition) = rs(1).Value
    rs.MoveNext()
  Loop

End If

rs.Close()
```

Once again, keep in mind that the `List` array object was passed to the function `ByRef`. All the changes made to `List` will automatically be visible to the calling function, and we do not need to return these values. Once the array is successfully filled with the recordset data, we close the recordset (which closes the database connection).

We have finished writing the code for the smart document, so it makes sense to kick the tires and see if it really works. Go ahead and compile the EventOrder.dll file, and then follow the remaining sections, which describe the additional steps required to successfully run the smart document.

Configuring Security

In order for the EventOrder.dll assembly to execute on your system, it must be given Full Trust security permission in the .NET Framework Configuration tool. Follow these steps to do so:

1. Open the Microsoft .NET Framework 1.1 Configuration utility found in the Windows Administrative Tools.

2. Navigate to the Machine ➤ Code Groups ➤ All_Code ➤ My_Computer_Zone section of the configuration utility.

3. Initiate the Create Code Group Wizard by right-clicking on My_Computer_Zone and selecting "New".

4. Enter **EventOrder** in the Name field and **Folder location for the EventOrder smart document assemblies** as the Description. Click Next.

5. Select All Code from the Choose the Condition Type for This Code Group drop-down box. Click Next.

6. Select FullTrust in the Use Existing Permission Set drop-down box. Click Next and click Finish.

▓**Note** Chapter 7 provides a more detailed discussion of the security configuration steps. See that chapter's "Configuring .NET Security for VSTO" section.

Creating the Manifest and Expansion Pack

The XML expansion pack is the group of files that, when working together, turn a regular document into a smart document. The key component of the expansion pack is what's called the manifest file. The manifest is an XML document that conforms to the XML Expansion Pack Manifest schema and contains a listing of the files included with the smart document solution.

This means that the manifest file conforms to a standard structure and tells the target document what files to include in the solution, along with their locations. At the very minimum, the manifest XML file should include the name and location of the smart document's action handler DLL file and the solution's XML schema.

Our solution takes this bare-minimum approach, although we could just as easily include any additional files of any format (images, sound, video, additional Office documents, etc.).

> **Note** To learn all there is to know about the XML expansion packs and their expansion pack schema, including creating and using your own XML expansion pack, read the following articles available on MSDN:
>
> • Using XML Expansion Pack Collections: `http://msdn.microsoft.com/library/en-us/sdsdk/html/ sdcondeployingusingxepcollections.asp`
>
> • How Office Installs XML Expansion Packs: `http://msdn.microsoft.com/library/en-us/sdsdk/ html/sdconDeploymentHowXEPInstalled.asp`
>
> • XML Expansion Pack Manifest Schema Overview: `http://msdn.microsoft.com/library/en-us/ sdsdk/html/xsconOverview.asp`

Open Notepad (or any text editor) and type the following XML:

```
<SD:manifest xmlns:SD="http://schemas.microsoft.com/office/xmlexpansionpacks/2003">
  <SD:version>1.1</SD:version>
  <SD:updateFrequency>20160</SD:updateFrequency>
  <SD:uri>urn:schemas-bravocorp-com.namespaces.event.simple</SD:uri>
  <SD:solution>
    <SD:solutionID>EventOrder.DocActions</SD:solutionID>
    <SD:type>smartDocument</SD:type>
    <SD:alias lcid="*">BravoCorp Event Order - VB .NET</SD:alias>
    <SD:file>
      <SD:type>solutionActionHandler</SD:type>
      <SD:version>1.0</SD:version>
      <SD:filePath>EventOrder.dll</SD:filePath>
      <SD:CLSNAME>EventOrder.DocActions</SD:CLSNAME>
      <runFromServer>True</runFromServer>
      <SD:managed/>
    </SD:file>
  </SD:solution>
  <SD:solution>
    <SD:solutionID>schema</SD:solutionID>
    <SD:type>schema</SD:type>
    <SD:alias lcid="*">BravoCorp Event Order Schema</SD:alias>
    <SD:file>
      <SD:type>schema</SD:type>
      <SD:version>1.0</SD:version>
      <SD:filePath>simple.xsd</SD:filePath>
    </SD:file>
  </SD:solution>
</SD:manifest>
```

Once you're done entering the code, name the file **OrderManifest.xml** and place it in the solution's folder. See Table 9-10 for a rundown of the tags defined in the XML Expansion Pack Manifest schema.

Table 9-10. *The XML Expansion Pack Manifest Scheme Tags*

Tag	Purpose/Description
manifest	The root element of any XML expansion pack manifest file.
version	The version number of the expansion pack and any included files. This number helps specify whether any updates to the solution and the solution's files are required.
updateFrequency	How often the solution should check for a new version on the host server.
uri	The expansion pack's URI.
solution	The root tag signifying a smart document solution.
type	The type of solution or type of file (depending on whether the root element is a solution or file).
alias	The friendly name of the smart document solution.
file	The root tag defining a file to be included in the smart document solution.
filePath	The file's path on the smart document solution's host server.
CLSNAME	The class name of the file (VB .NET only).
runFromServer	If this is set to True, the solution will run from the server without downloading to the client machine.
Managed	Specifies that the included file contains .NET managed code.

Attaching the Manifest and Expansion Pack

Before the smart document can execute the code, the XML expansion pack must be added to Microsoft Word using the Templates and Add-Ins dialog box. To attach the expansion pack, complete these steps:

1. Open the `OrderForm.doc` smart document in Word.

2. From the Word menu, open the Templates and Add-Ins dialog box by selecting Tools ➤ Templates and Add-Ins from the menu.

3. Navigate to the XML Expansion Packs tab in the Templates and Add-Ins dialog box (see Figure 9-16). Click the Add button to browse and select the `OrderManifest.xml` file created earlier in the chapter. Once the file is selected, click Open. If the manifest loads successfully, it will be displayed in the dialog box. Click OK to close the dialog box.

■Tip If you receive an error in step 3, it could be due to any number of reasons, and the error messages provided are extremely vague and unhelpful. Fortunately, a great article is available on MSDN that can help you isolate the problem: http://msdn.microsoft.com/library/en-us/dno2k3ta/html/ odc_oftrsmartdocerrors.asp.

Figure 9-16. *Attaching the XML expansion pack to the* OrderForm.doc *smart document*

As soon as the Templates and Add-Ins dialog box closes, the Document Actions task pane should become visible and display the controls relevant to the current context of the document. Figure 9-17 shows the OrderForm.doc with the customer XML element controls in the task pane.

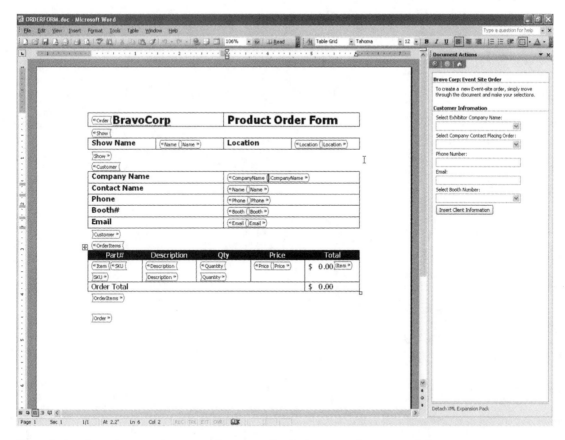

Figure 9-17. *The* OrderForm.doc *smart document displaying XML elements and the Document Actions task pane*

Summary

Smart documents deliver the goods in terms of powerful and easy access to key corporate data. As you learned in this chapter, smart documents provide a framework for incorporating backend business data within a Word document. In addition, by adding code to the various methods exposed by the smart document API, custom workflows centered on unique business rules and processes are now possible and can be targeted at the document level.

In addition to learning how to create the smart documents, we saw just how simple accessing a web service form a smart document can be. We covered several topics including how to create a smart documents, how to create an XML schema file and attach it to a Word document, how to map XML elements from the attached schema to locations in a Word document, and how to build a .NET assembly that responds to changes in the smart document's context, as defined by changes in the active XML element. In addition, we looked at how to pass XML data to a web service and then parse the data for insertion in the solution database. The end result is a workable order-entry solution that can easily be extended to suit any additional business rules.

■ ■ ■

How to Deploy a Managed Add-In Utilizing a Shim to Bridge the Gap Between the COM and Managed Code

Security is an important aspect of any application, and solutions built upon the Microsoft Office System platform are no exception. It is important to provide appropriate levels of application security and to ensure that any add-in code will execute at the highest security settings by conforming to the standards of Office security.

This appendix discusses the execution of managed code within the Component Object Model (COM) world of Microsoft Office. We'll look at the problem with managed code, review Office 2003 security, and see a method for solving the security issues of running managed code within Office.

The topics presented in this discussion are too large to properly cover here, but this discussion should provide enough information to guide you through the tasks required to securely deploy COM add-in code.

The Problem with Managed Code

As demonstrated in several chapters in this book, managed code and the Common Language Runtime (CLR) are powerful tools in the hands of a knowledgeable developer. The power of .NET can be utilized to create managed add-ins, smart documents, smart tags, and much more. But while managed code offers tremendous benefits to authoring Office-based solutions, deployment security is a problem.

Before Office 2003 and .NET, deploying an Office solution was relatively simple. The solution was built, the code protected from prying eyes, and the executables were installed on the user's machine. The main security concern with these versions of Office was to secure the developer's source code from tampering.

With Office 2003, the focus of security has switched from protecting the developer's code to protecting the user from potentially malicious code. As a result, the security mechanism within Office 2003 is more restrictive than in previous Office versions. And when you create

.NET solutions that utilize the Office platform, the .NET Framework's security policy also comes into play.

These security changes mean that deploying an Office-based solution is not as simple as it once was. Office has its own security system, and any Office application based on managed code also involves the .NET Framework's security policies. When developing managed code for Office applications, it is important to understand how these two security systems—Office security and .NET Framework security—work together. Dealing with the restrictions of these two systems requires more development time than in the past.

Office 2003 Security

By default, the security settings in Office 2003 are set to Trust All Installed Add-Ins and Templates. This means that any unsigned COM add-in deployed on the user's machine will automatically be trusted and considered safe. That might be okay for us developers who write and run our own code. However, it is not such a good idea where a high degree of security is needed.

The safest (and most professional) strategy for deploying a COM add-in is to digitally sign the code and set the Office security settings to the highest state for add-in code. This means disabling the Trust All Installed Add-Ins and Templates option as well as setting the macro security settings to High. These changes require any installed add-ins to have been both digitally signed and recognized as originating from a trusted source (the user can choose to define any digital certificate author as a trusted source).

▪Note The Office security settings are accessed by clicking Tools ➤ Macros ➤ Security from the main menu of any Office application.

Office 2003 provides several levels of macro security, and the various combinations of macro security and add-in security can be a bit confusing. For example, if the macro security settings are set to Very High, but the Trust All Installed Add-Ins and Templates option is checked, then all installed COM add-ins will be allowed to execute, regardless of whether or not they have been digitally signed and regardless of whether they originate from a trusted source or not. It does not take long to realize that the best solution is to protect the user by implementing the highest possible security measures. Table A-1 lists all the security combinations and their effects.

Table A-1. *The Office 2003 Security Matrix*

Macro Security Level	Digitally Signed?	Trusted Source?	Trust All Installed Add-Ins and Templates?	Result
Very High	Yes	Yes	No	Add-in will load without displaying a security warning
Very High	Yes	No	No	Add-in will not load

Table A-1. *continued*

Macro Security Level	Digitally Signed?	Trusted Source?	Trust All Installed Add-Ins and Templates?	Result
Very High	No	No	No	Add-in will not load
High	Yes	Yes	No	Add-in will load without displaying a security warning
High	Yes	No	No	Security warning will display; add-in will load if user decides to trust the source
High	No	No	No	Add-in will not load
Medium	Yes	Yes	No	Add-in will load without displaying a security warning
Medium	Yes	No	No	Security warning will display; add-in will load if user decides to trust the source
Medium	No	No	No	Security warning will display; add-in will not load if user decides to load the add-in
Low	Yes/No	Yes/No	No	Add-in will load without displaying a security warning
High	**Yes/No**	**Yes/No**	**Yes**	**Add-in will load without displaying a security warning**
Medium	**Yes/No**	**Yes/No**	**Yes**	**Add-in will load without displaying a security warning**
Low	**Yes/No**	**Yes/No**	**Yes**	**Add-in will load without displaying a security warning**

For the purposes of this discussion, let's assume that the targeted deployment environment is an Office 2003 desktop system with macro security set to High and with Trust All Installed Add-Ins and Templates disabled.

The Shim Solution

With the highest Office security setting enabled, a COM add-in will fail to load in the host application if it is not both digitally signed and trusted. For the host application to trust and accept the COM add-in, the add-in must be signed with an Authenticode digital signature. This signature will meet the requirements of Office 2003 security, and the targeted application will load the add-in without any warning or notice to the user, even at the highest security levels.

A managed COM add-in, on the other hand, can be signed with a digital signature, but this will not meet Office 2003 security requirements. When a managed COM add-in is registered on a system, the actual file specified to load within the host Office application is the CLR engine (mscoree.dll), which is not digitally signed. If this file were signed, any managed COM add-in, whether signed and trusted or not, would run without the user ever knowing about it. No method exists for signing a managed COM add-in DLL file that will meet the COM requirements of Office 2003, so the .NET approach to creating and securing managed COM add-in's does not apply in the COM-based world of Microsoft Office—signing a managed assembly is a waste of time.

The solution to this security problem is to implement a proxy known as a *shim*. The shim acts a broker between Office and the managed assembly. It can be signed and loaded into the Office application space in Windows, making it secure. In addition, it can invoke methods residing in the managed add-in, making it appear to the user that the managed add-in is loaded and working like any other COM-based add-in. This shim must be authored in VB 6 and conform to the rules of COM. The shim can then be digitally signed and registered to load within the host Office application instead of mscoree.dll.

The shim is a VB 6 solution containing a single class named Connect, which implements the IDTExtensibility2 interface required to implement a COM add-in. However, instead of implementing any custom logic of its own, the Connect class only serves as a link to the managed COM add-in. Each of the methods required by the IDTExtensibility2 interface access a corresponding method within the managed COM add-in's Connect class, redirecting the application execution to the custom business code included in that class (see Chapter 2 for a full discussion of the Presentation Generator's Connect class).

To create an unmanaged COM add-in shim (assuming the managed COM add-in already exists), you just need to follow these steps:

1. Create a VB 6–based shim to act as a proxy and load the managed code COM add-in.

2. Test the shim solution to verify that it functions under the Medium security setting.

3. Sign the shim DLL file.

4. Test the signed shim DLL file.

5. Deploy the shim and managed COM add-in solutions together on the user's machine.

These steps are discussed in the following sections.

Creating the VB 6 Unmanaged COM Add-In Shim

For the purposes of this discussion, let's create a shim that will allow the proper installation of the PowerPoint Presentation Generator created in Chapter 2.

To create the VB 6 shim solution, follow these steps:

1. Create a new add-in project within VB 6.

2. Implement each method required by the IDTExtensibility2 interface. Here is the code for the entire Connect.dsr class file:

```
Dim managedAddIn As IDTExtensibility2

Private Sub AddinInstance_Initialize()
    Set managedAddIn = CreateObject("PresentationGenerator.Connect")
End Sub

Private Sub AddinInstance_OnAddInsUpdate(custom() As Variant)
    managedAddIn.OnAddInsUpdate custom
End Sub

Private Sub AddinInstance_OnBeginShutdown(custom() As Variant)
    managedAddIn.OnBeginShutdown custom
End Sub

Private Sub AddinInstance_OnConnection(ByVal Application As Object, _
  ByVal ConnectMode As AddInDesignerObjects.ext_ConnectMode, ByVal _
  AddInInst As Object, custom() As Variant)

    managedAddIn.OnConnection Application, ConnectMode, AddInInst, custom
End Sub

Private Sub AddinInstance_OnDisconnection(ByVal RemoveMode As _
  AddInDesignerObjects.ext_DisconnectMode, custom() As Variant)

    managedAddIn.OnDisconnection RemoveMode, custom
 End Sub

Private Sub AddinInstance_OnStartupComplete(custom() As Variant)
    managedAddIn.OnStartupComplete custom
End Sub
```

The first line of the code creates a new object of type IDTExtensibility2. Then within the Initialize method, the code sets the managedAddIn object with a reference to the managed COM add-in's Connect class. This reference is what enables us to link each of the IDTExtensibility2 methods in the two COM add-ins together.

In each of the IDTExtensibility2 methods, the shim calls the corresponding method within the referenced managed COM add-in and passes to it the same objects passed by the method. The result is a clean handoff from the unmanaged COM add-in shim to the managed COM add-in containing the business logic.

Once you complete the Connect class in the VB 6 project, compile the add-in and name it **PPTGENSHIM.dll**.

Testing the Shim

Before signing the shim, we should verify that it loads inside of PowerPoint and triggers the security warning dialog box. Follow these steps:

1. Open PowerPoint.

2. From the main menu, select Tools ➤ Macro ➤ Security.

3. On the Security Level tab of the Security dialog box, set the macro security setting to Medium.

4. On the Trusted Publishers tab, disable the Trust All Installed Add-Ins and Templates setting.

5. Close and then re-open PowerPoint to trigger the shim add-in within the new security context. Once you are presented with the security warning dialog box shown in Figure A-1, click the Enable Macro button.

6. Ensure that the add-in functions correctly by selecting Bravo Tools ➤ Settings from the main PowerPoint menu.

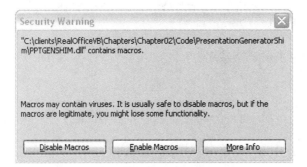

Figure A-1. *Triggering the macro Security Warning dialog box*

Signing the Shim

Once the shim add-in is confirmed and working properly, we can sign it. Properly following the Office 2003 security guidelines requires the shim to be signed with an Authenticode digital signature.

Creating a Test Digital Certificate

Microsoft provides the Makecert tool for creating test certificates, so you don't need to purchase one just to build the solutions in this book. The Makecert tool creates an unverified, self-signed certificate, meaning that the identity embedded in the certificate has not been verified by a third-party certifying authority such as thawte or VeriSign.

Note The topic of digital certificates is huge and it is beyond the scope of this book. If you want to learn more about it, you can start here: http://msdn.microsoft.com/library/default.asp?url=/library/en-us/dnsmarttag/html/odc_dcss.asp.

To create a test certificate for signing the shim, we will use the Makecert tool. Open the Visual Studio .NET 2003 command prompt and type the following statement (as shown in Figure A-2):

```
Makecert -sk DevTestKey -r -n "CN=Ty Anderson, OU=Certification,O=Bravo Corp", -ss _
   my Appendix.cer
```

The syntax for the command is as follows:

```
Makecert [basic options | extended options] outputFile
```

Table A-2 explains the Makecert options used in this example.

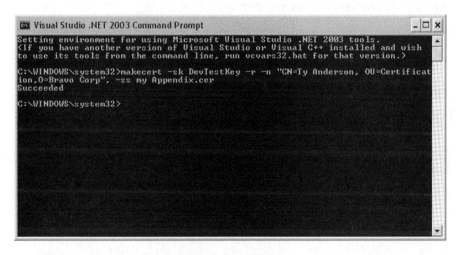

Figure A-2. *Creating a test certificate with* Makecert

Table A-2. *Some* Makecert *Command Options*

Option	Description
–sk	This is the subject key, which is used to specify the location of the subject key's private key. This parameter is optional. If it is not provided, the default container will be created and used.
–r	This option specifies the certificate as self-signed.
–n	This option is used to specify the name for the certificate. The name must conform to the X.500 certificate standards. At a minimum, the name must include "CN=*Name*".
–ss	This option is used to specify the filename that will store the output of the certificate.

Once executed successfully, the Makecert utility creates a test certificate based on the X.509 standard. The certificate holds the provided name (in this example, Ty Anderson) as part of the public key.

Tip Full documentation of `Makecert.exe`, with all its command-line options, can be found at: http://msdn.microsoft.com/library/en-us/cptools/html/cpgrfcertificatecreationtoolmakecertexe.asp.

Signing the Shim Using the Test Certificate

Now that we have a test certificate, the shim file (`PPTGENSHIM.dll`) can be tagged as your creation by signing it with the `Appendix.cer` certificate file. Follow these steps:

1. Open the Visual Studio .NET 2003 command prompt.

2. Initialize the Digital Signature Wizard by typing **signcode** at the command prompt. Click Next when the Welcome screen is displayed.

3. In the wizard's File Selection window (see Figure A-3), browse to the location of the `PPTGENSHIM.dll` file and click Next.

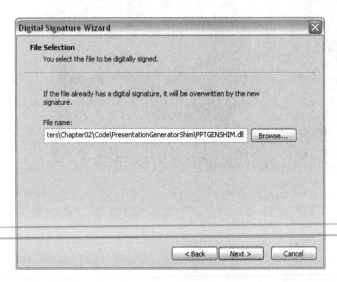

Figure A-3. *Selecting the shim file in the Digital Signature Wizard*

4. In the wizard's Signing Options window, choose Custom and click Next.

5. In the wizard's Signature Certificate window, click the Select from Store button to view a listing of available certificates on the machine (see Figure A-4).

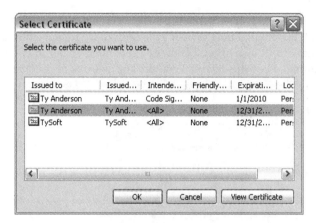

Figure A-4. *Choosing a digital certificate to sign the shim file*

6. Select the desired certificate and click OK to return to the wizard. Data from the certificate will display in the wizard (see Figure A-5). Click Next.

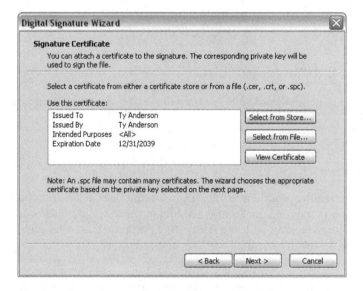

Figure A-5. *The selected certificate in the wizard's Signature Certificate window*

■Tip Sometimes it is difficult to determine which certificate is the desired one. You can always view the details of the certificates on your system by clicking the View Certificate button in the Select Certificate dialog box (see Figure A-4). Doing so will open the Certificate dialog box and will show additional certificate properties, such as the certificate issuer.

---

7. In the wizard's Private Key window, ensure that the Private Key in a CSP option is selected (see Figure A-6). Ensure that the Provider Type drop-down list specifies RSA Full. In the Key Container drop-down list, select the key generated earlier (named DevTestKey in this example). Keep the default Signature key type and click Next.

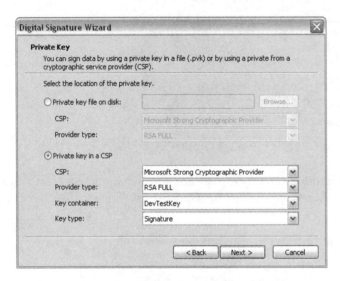

Figure A-6. *Setting the Private Key options*

8. Click Next in the rest of the wizard windows until the Digital Signature Wizard completes its work.

Testing the Signed Shim

The last step in the shim-creation process is to once again test the shim in the host application. This time the purpose of the test is make sure the shim meets the requirements of Office security settings at the highest level for add-in security (High, with the Trust All Installed Add-Ins and Templates setting disabled) and that it executes in that context.

Test the shim by following these steps:

1. Open PowerPoint, select Tools ➤ Macro ➤ Security from the menus. Set the Office security settings to High, and disable the Trust All Installed Add-Ins and Templates option. Close PowerPoint.

2. Open PowerPoint to initialize the Presentation Generator add-in shim created and signed in this appendix.

3. At this point, the shim is not registered as a trusted source, and the Security Warning dialog box will be triggered (see Figure A-7). The dialog box lists the name of the code

author (which will correspond to the name used in the Makecert command earlier). If you like, you can click the Details button to verify that the correct certificate is attached. Click the Always Trust Macros From This Publisher check box, and click the Enable Macros button.

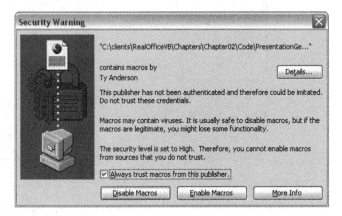

Figure A-7. *Choosing to trust macros from this publisher*

4. Once PowerPoint fully loads, test the add-in and ensure that it functions correctly.

5. Close PowerPoint.

6. Open PowerPoint yet again. The security warning should not display and the add-in should function normally. This means the code complies fully with Office security requirements and is ready for deployment on user systems.

Note Before actually deploying the solution in a real-world scenario, you will need to re-sign the shim file with an Authenticode certificate issued by a certification authority.

Deploying the Shim and the Managed COM Add-In

Deploying the complete solution (both the managed COM add-in and the unmanaged shim COM add-in) requires building a setup deployment project within Visual Studio, which is easy to do. Follow these steps:

1. Open the Presentation Generator project from Chapter 2.

2. In the Solution Explorer, right-click on the PresentationGeneratorSetup project and select View ➤ Registry from the pop-up menu. The project's registry key settings will be displayed as a tab within Visual Studio (see Figure A-8).

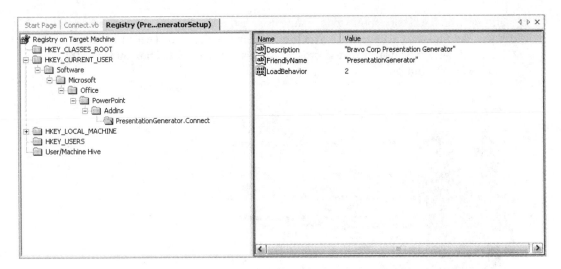

Figure A-8. *Viewing the setup project's registry settings*

3. Delete the key for `PresentationGenerator.Connect`.

4. Add the `PPTGENSHIM.dll` file to the project.

5. Rebuild the PresentationGeneratorSetup program.

The rebuilt setup program can now be used to deploy both the managed COM add-in and the COM-based shim add-in. The setup program will auto-register both add-ins, and the next time PowerPoint loads in the operating system, the user will be asked to enable and trust the add-in.

Summary

Managed code is definitely the easiest and most powerful code yet. It could even be argued that managed code is also the easiest to create and deploy, unless you are dealing with Microsoft Office. Office still lives in the COM world and will remain there for several more years (and versions). In the meantime, developers can still build powerful add-ins with the advanced tools of the .NET platform. As long as you are willing to perform a few extra steps to ensure proper deployment and security, there is no reason not to create as much Office-targeted code within .NET as you like. You might as well start now, because Office will swim deeper and deeper into the .NET end of the pool as more and more tools are released that enable .NET development on the Office platform.

Index

forums.apress.com

FOR PROFESSIONALS BY PROFESSIONALS™

JOIN THE APRESS FORUMS AND BE PART OF OUR COMMUNITY. You'll find discussions that cover topics of interest to IT professionals, programmers, and enthusiasts just like you. If you post a query to one of our forums, you can expect that some of the best minds in the business—especially Apress authors, who all write with *The Expert's Voice*™—will chime in to help you. Why not aim to become one of our most valuable participants (MVPs) and win cool stuff? Here's a sampling of what you'll find:

DATABASES

Data drives everything.

Share information, exchange ideas, and discuss any database programming or administration issues.

INTERNET TECHNOLOGIES AND NETWORKING

Try living without plumbing (and eventually IPv6).

Talk about networking topics including protocols, design, administration, wireless, wired, storage, backup, certifications, trends, and new technologies.

JAVA

We've come a long way from the old Oak tree.

Hang out and discuss Java in whatever flavor you choose: J2SE, J2EE, J2ME, Jakarta, and so on.

MAC OS X

All about the Zen of OS X.

OS X is both the present and the future for Mac apps. Make suggestions, offer up ideas, or boast about your new hardware.

OPEN SOURCE

Source code is good; understanding (open) source is better.

Discuss open source technologies and related topics such as PHP, MySQL, Linux, Perl, Apache, Python, and more.

PROGRAMMING/BUSINESS

Unfortunately, it is.

Talk about the Apress line of books that cover software methodology, best practices, and how programmers interact with the "suits."

WEB DEVELOPMENT/DESIGN

Ugly doesn't cut it anymore, and CGI is absurd.

Help is in sight for your site. Find design solutions for your projects and get ideas for building an interactive Web site.

SECURITY

Lots of bad guys out there—the good guys need help.

Discuss computer and network security issues here. Just don't let anyone else know the answers!

TECHNOLOGY IN ACTION

Cool things. Fun things.

It's after hours. It's time to play. Whether you're into LEGO® MINDSTORMS™ or turning an old PC into a DVR, this is where technology turns into fun.

WINDOWS

No defenestration here.

Ask questions about all aspects of Windows programming, get help on Microsoft technologies covered in Apress books, or provide feedback on any Apress Windows book.

HOW TO PARTICIPATE:

Go to the Apress Forums site at **http://forums.apress.com/**.

Click the New User link.